ORESAMA TEACHER

Vol. 24

Story & Art by

Izumi Tsubaki

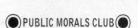

ORESAMA TEACHER

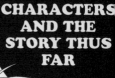

CHARACTERS AND THE STORY THUS FAR

Mafuyu Kurosaki

● PUBLIC MORALS CLUB ●

THE FORMER BANCHO OF SAITAMA EAST HIGH. SHE TRANSFERRED TO MIDORIGAOKA ACADEMY AND JOINED THE PUBLIC MORALS CLUB. SHE ALSO PLAYS THE PARTS OF NATSUO AND SUPER BUN. SHE IS CONCERNED BY THE FACT THAT SHE HAS NO FEMALE FRIENDS.

NATSUO

Same Person

SUPER BUN

Takaomi Saeki

THE ONE WHO CRUELLY TRAINED MAFUYU. HE WAS MAFUYU'S HOMEROOM TEACHER AND THE PUBLIC MORALS CLUB ADVISER, BUT IN THE FIRST SEMESTER OF MAFUYU'S FINAL YEAR, HE RESIGNED AND DISAPPEARED.

Mr. Maki	Aki Shibuya	Shinobu Yui	Hayasaka
A NEW TEACHER. HE REPLACED TAKAOMI AS THE PUBLIC MORALS CLUB ADVISER.	A TALKATIVE AND WOMANIZING UNDERCLASS-MAN. HIS NICKNAME IS AKKI. HE'S NOT GOOD AT FIGHTING.	HE WORSHIPS MIYABI, THE FORMER STUDENT COUNCIL PRESIDENT, BUT REJOINED THE PUBLIC MORALS CLUB. HE IS A SELF-PROCLAIMED NINJA.	MAFUYU'S CLASSMATE. HE APPEARS TO BE A PLAIN AND SIMPLE DELINQUENT, BUT HE'S ACTUALLY QUITE DILIGENT.

PUBLIC MORALS CLUB

NEW

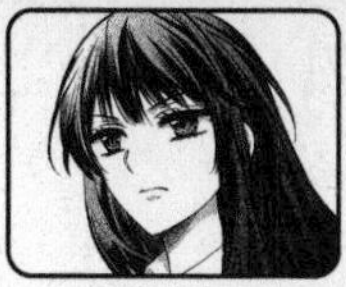

Toko Hanabusa

NEWLY ENROLLED AT MIDORIGAOKA THIS PAST SPRING. MIYABI HANABUSA'S YOUNGER SISTER, BUT MIYABI WAS RAISED BY THEIR MOTHER AND TOKO WAS RAISED BY THEIR FATHER. RESERVED, YET A PERSON OF ACTION. INDIFFERENT, BUT CUTTHROAT.

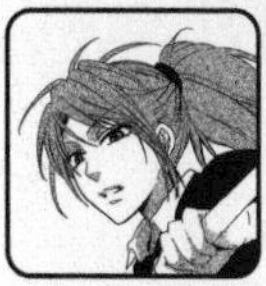

Wakana Hojo

SHE HAS A STOIC ATTITUDE AND WATCHES OVER HANABUSA, AND SHE HAS FEELINGS FOR YUI. SHE'S THE NEW STUDENT COUNCIL PRESIDENT.

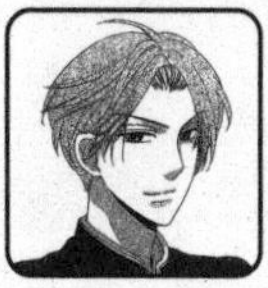

Shuntaro Kosaka

HE'S OBSESSED WITH DOING THINGS BY THE BOOK. HE DOES NOT HANDLE UNEXPECTED EVENTS WELL.

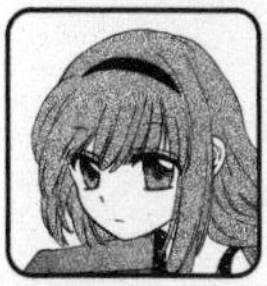

Komari Yukioka

USING HER CUTE LOOKS, SHE CONTROLS THOSE AROUND HER WITHOUT SAYING A WORD. INSIDE, SHE'S LIKE A DIRTY OLD MAN.

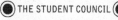

THE STUDENT COUNCIL

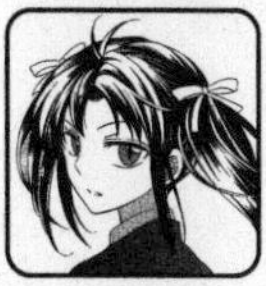

Kanon Nonoguchi

SHE HATES MEN. HER FAMILY RUNS A DOJO, SO SHE'S STRONG. SHE PLANNED TO DESTROY THE PUBLIC MORALS CLUB OUT OF GRATITUDE TOWARD MIYABI.

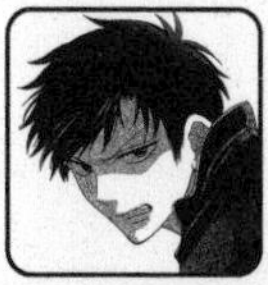

Reito Ayabe

HE LOVES CLEANING. HE GETS STRONGER IN DIRTY PLACES. HE IS A STUDENT COUNCIL OFFICER, BUT HE'S FRIENDS WITH MAFUYU.

THE GRADUATES

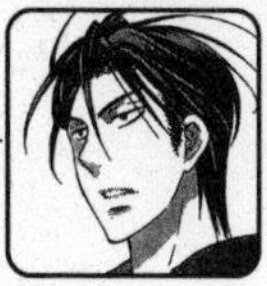

Kyotaro Okegawa

THE FORMER BANCHO OF EAST HIGH. HE IS ATTENDING A LOCAL COLLEGE. HE AND MAFUYU ARE ANONYMOUS PEN PALS.

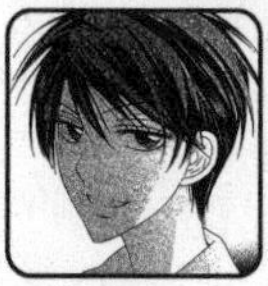

Miyabi Hanabusa

THE SCHOOL DIRECTOR'S SON AND THE FORMER PRESIDENT OF THE STUDENT COUNCIL. HE CAN CHARM OTHERS WITH HIS GAZE. HE IS ATTENDING COLLEGE IN TOKYO.

STORY

★ MAFUYU KUROSAKI WAS A BANCHO FROM EAST HIGH WHO CONTROLLED ALL OF SAITAMA, BUT ONCE SHE TRANSFERRED TO MIDORIGAOKA ACADEMY, SHE COMPLETELY CHANGED AND BECAME A SPIRITED HIGH SCHOOL GIRL...OR AT LEAST SHE WAS SUPPOSED TO. TAKAOMI SAEKI, HER CHILDHOOD FRIEND AND HOMEROOM TEACHER, FORCED HER TO JOIN THE PUBLIC MORALS CLUB AND SHE HAS TO CONTINUE TO LIVE A LIFE THAT IS FAR FROM AVERAGE.

★ THE PUBLIC MORALS CLUB AND THE STUDENT COUNCIL ARE FIGHTING FOR OWNERSHIP OF THE SCHOOL. THE PUBLIC MORALS CLUB HAS THWARTED STUDENT COUNCIL OFFICERS LIKE KOSAKA, AYABE, NONOGUCHI AND KOMARI, AND ARE JOINED BY BANCHO OKEGAWA AND A FIRST-YEAR STUDENT BY THE NAME OF SHIBUYA. DESPITE THE CHAOS THAT YUI CAUSES WITH THE ART OF THE ECHO AND MOMOCHI'S USE OF HYPNOSIS TO GET HAYASAKA SUSPENDED, THE PUBLIC MORALS CLUB IS MORE UNITED THAN EVER. MEANWHILE, A FAKE SUPER BUN HAS SHOWN UP AT SCHOOL AND THE MEMBERS OF THE STUDENT COUNCIL HAVE BECOME THE TARGETS OF VERY PERSONAL PRANKS. MAFUYU AND HER FRIENDS CHASE DOWN THE FAKE SUPER BUN, AND WHEN THEY FINALLY CATCH IT, THEY DISCOVER THAT IT'S MIYABI HANABUSA. MIYABI IS GRADUATING SOON AND HAS BEEN USING SUPER BUN AS A MEANS TO SEE HOW WELL THE MEMBERS OF THE STUDENT COUNCIL HAVE OVERCOME THEIR ISSUES.

★ SPRING IS HERE, AND MAFUYU AND HER FRIENDS ARE FINALLY THIRD-YEAR STUDENTS! MIYABI HANABUSA'S YOUNGER SISTER, TOKO, ENROLLS AS A FIRST-YEAR STUDENT. WILL SHE BE A NEW ENEMY FOR THE PUBLIC MORALS CLUB?! THEN, AS SOON AS THE NEW SEMESTER STARTS, TAKAOMI RESIGNS AND DISAPPEARS. MEANWHILE, MIDORIGAOKA STUDENTS HAVE BEEN ATTACKING KIYAMA HIGH SCHOOL AND THERE ARE RUMORS THAT NOGAMI IS KEEPING A HUGE BEAST AS A PET. MAFUYU AND OKEGAWA HEAD OVER TO FIND OUT WHAT'S GOING ON!

ORESAMA TEACHER

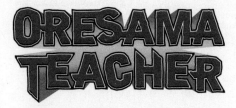

Volume 24
CONTENTS

Chapter 135

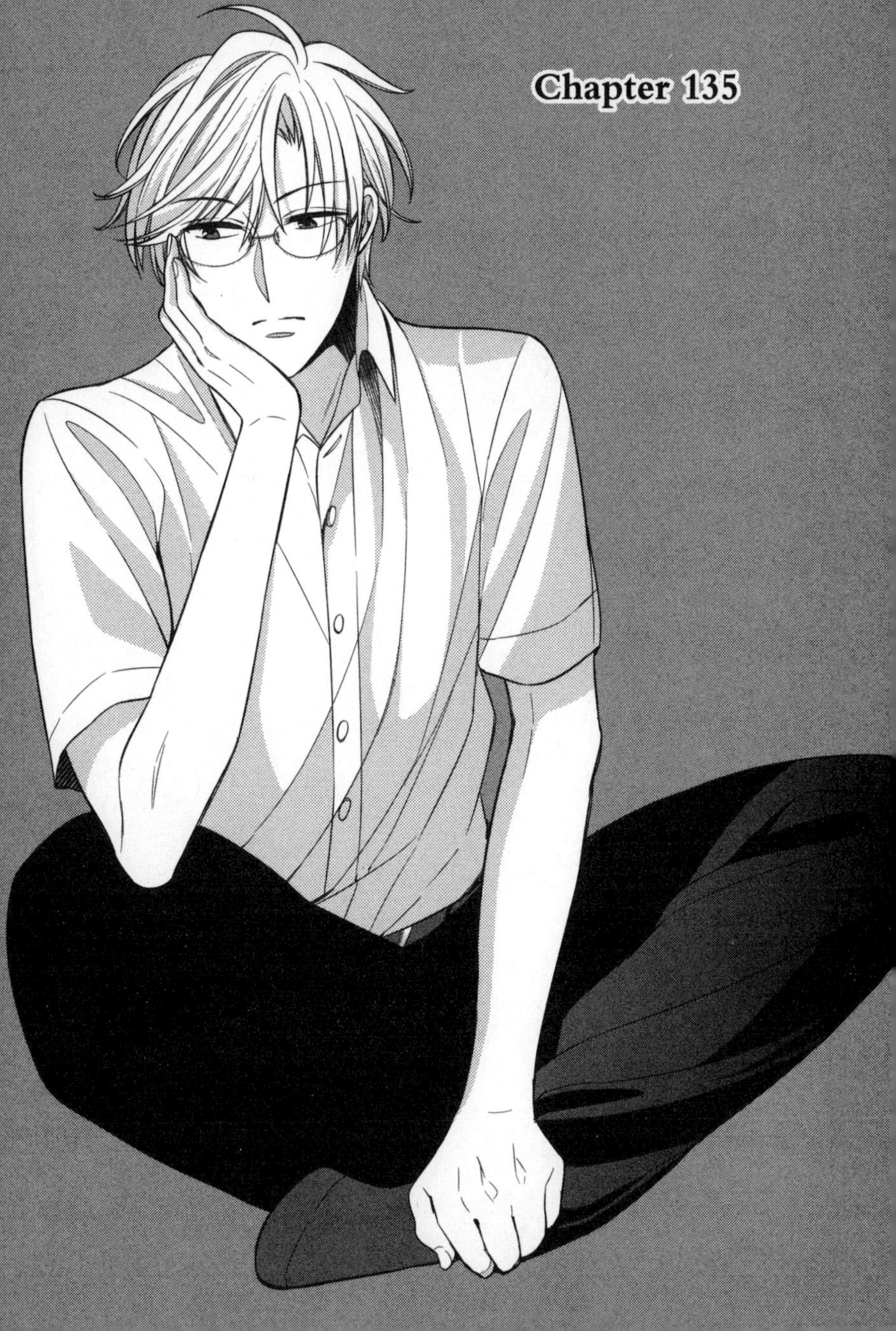

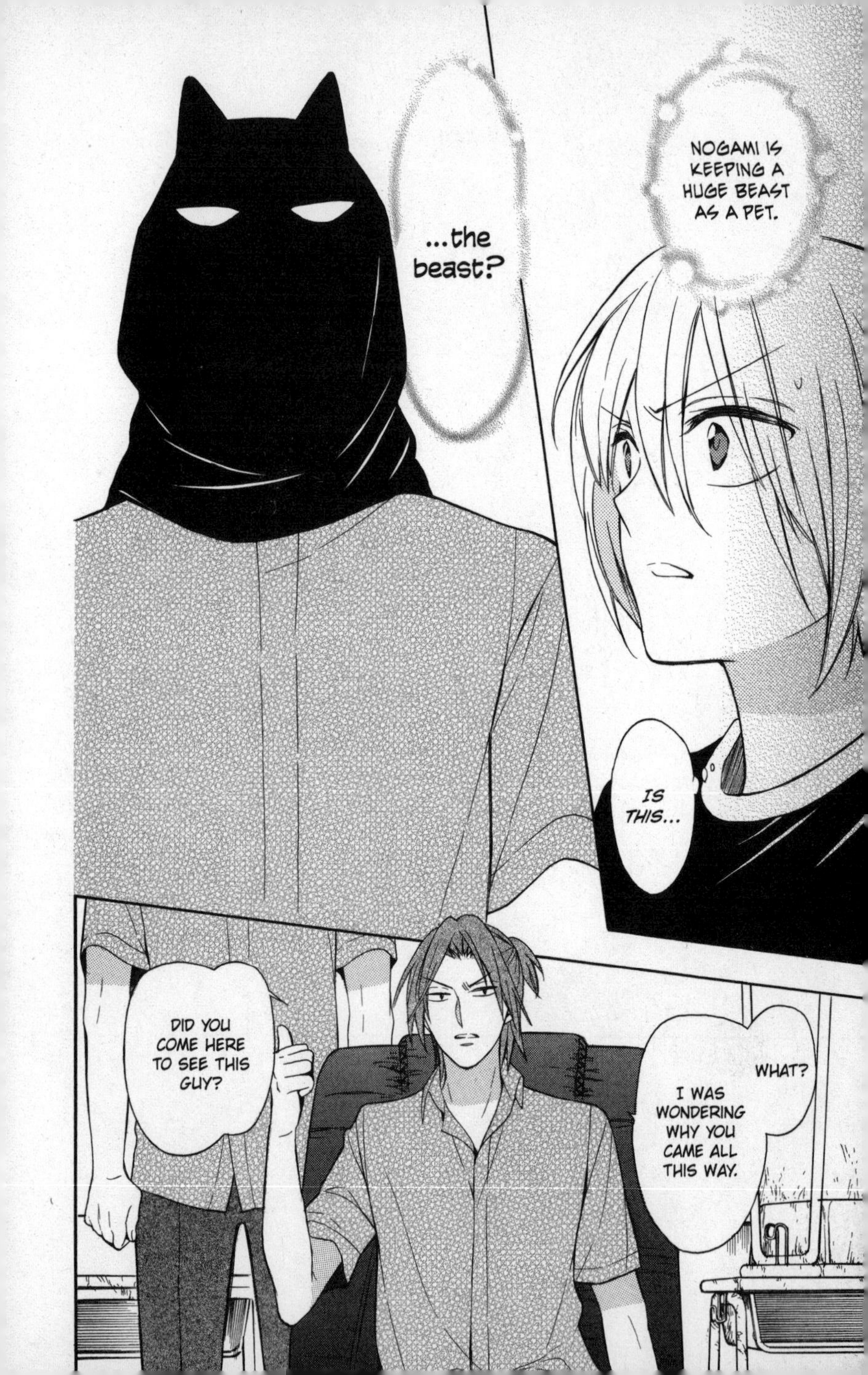
NOGAMI IS KEEPING A HUGE BEAST AS A PET.
IS THIS...
...the beast?
WHAT? I WAS WONDERING WHY YOU CAME ALL THIS WAY.
DID YOU COME HERE TO SEE THIS GUY?

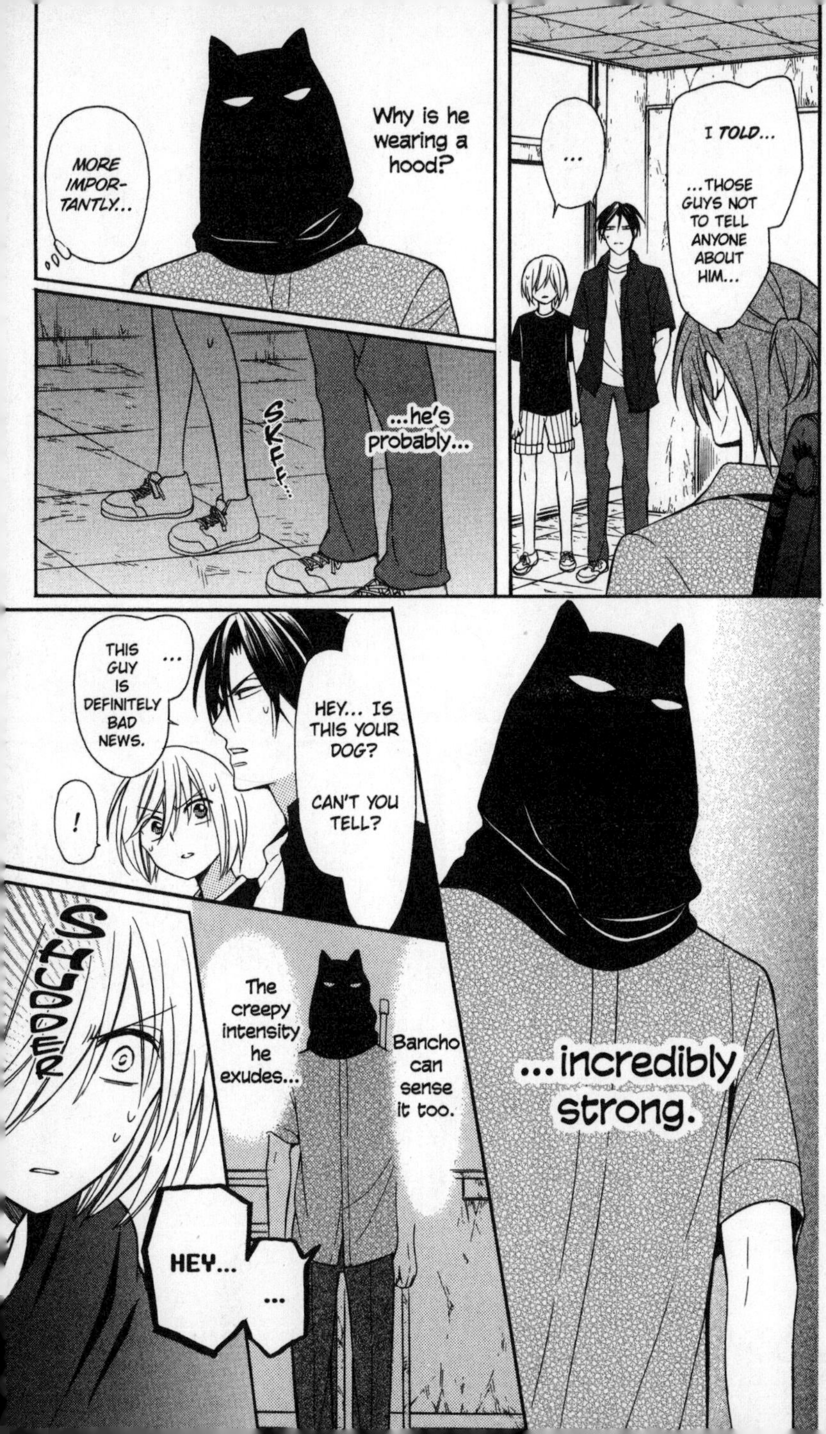
I TOLD...
...THOSE GUYS NOT TO TELL ANYONE ABOUT HIM...
...
Why is he wearing a hood?
MORE IMPORTANTLY...
...he's probably...
SKFF...
...incredibly strong.
HEY... IS THIS YOUR DOG?
CAN'T YOU TELL?
THIS GUY IS DEFINITELY BAD NEWS.
...
!
Bancho can sense it too.
The creepy intensity he exudes...
SHUDDER
HEY...
...

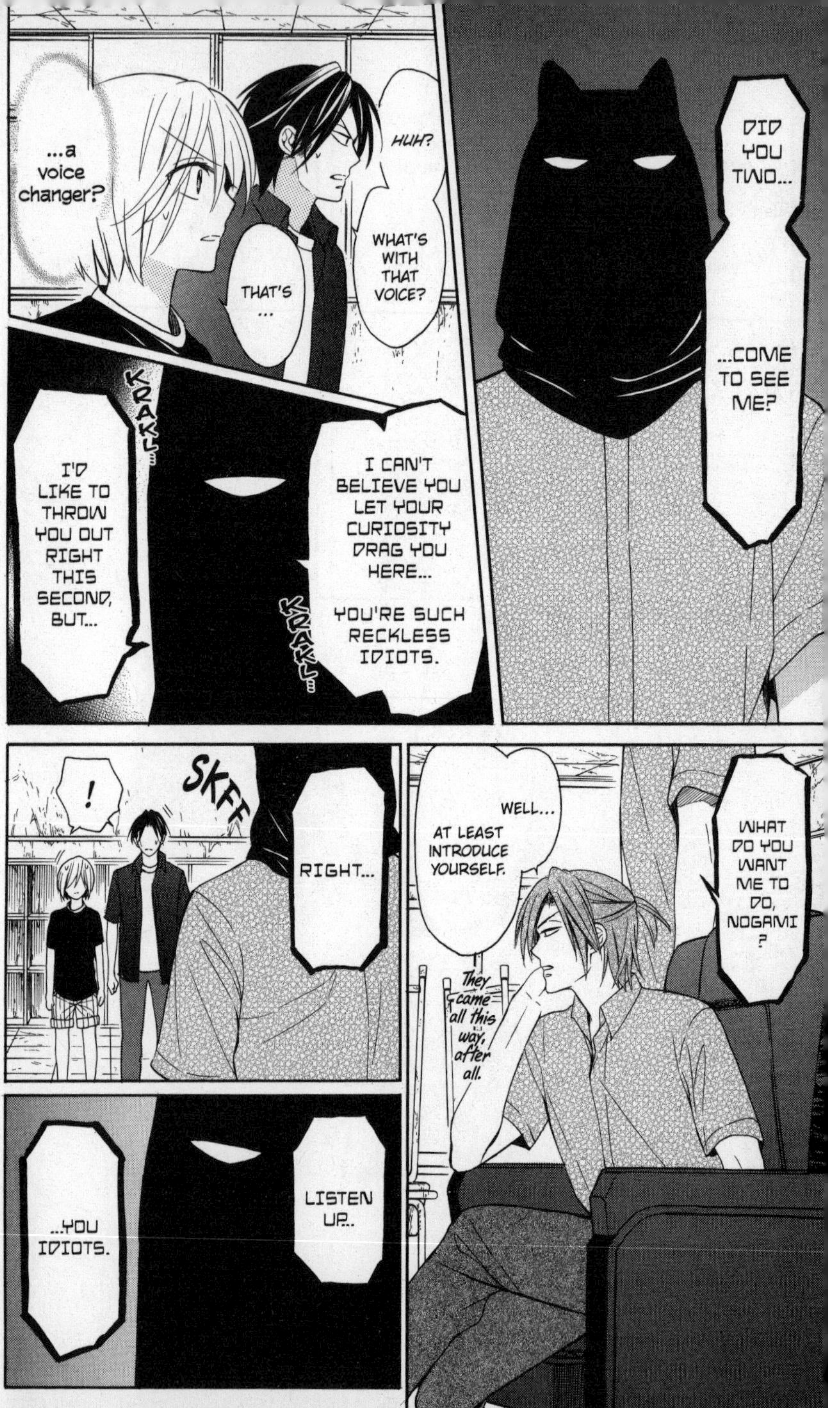
DID YOU TWO...
...COME TO SEE ME?
HUH?
WHAT'S WITH THAT VOICE?
THAT'S...
...a voice changer?
KRAKL...
I CAN'T BELIEVE YOU LET YOUR CURIOSITY DRAG YOU HERE...
YOU'RE SUCH RECKLESS IDIOTS.
KRAKL...
I'D LIKE TO THROW YOU OUT RIGHT THIS SECOND, BUT...
WHAT DO YOU WANT ME TO DO, NOGAMI?
WELL...
AT LEAST INTRODUCE YOURSELF.
They came all this way, after all.
SKFF
RIGHT...
!
LISTEN UP..
...YOU IDIOTS.

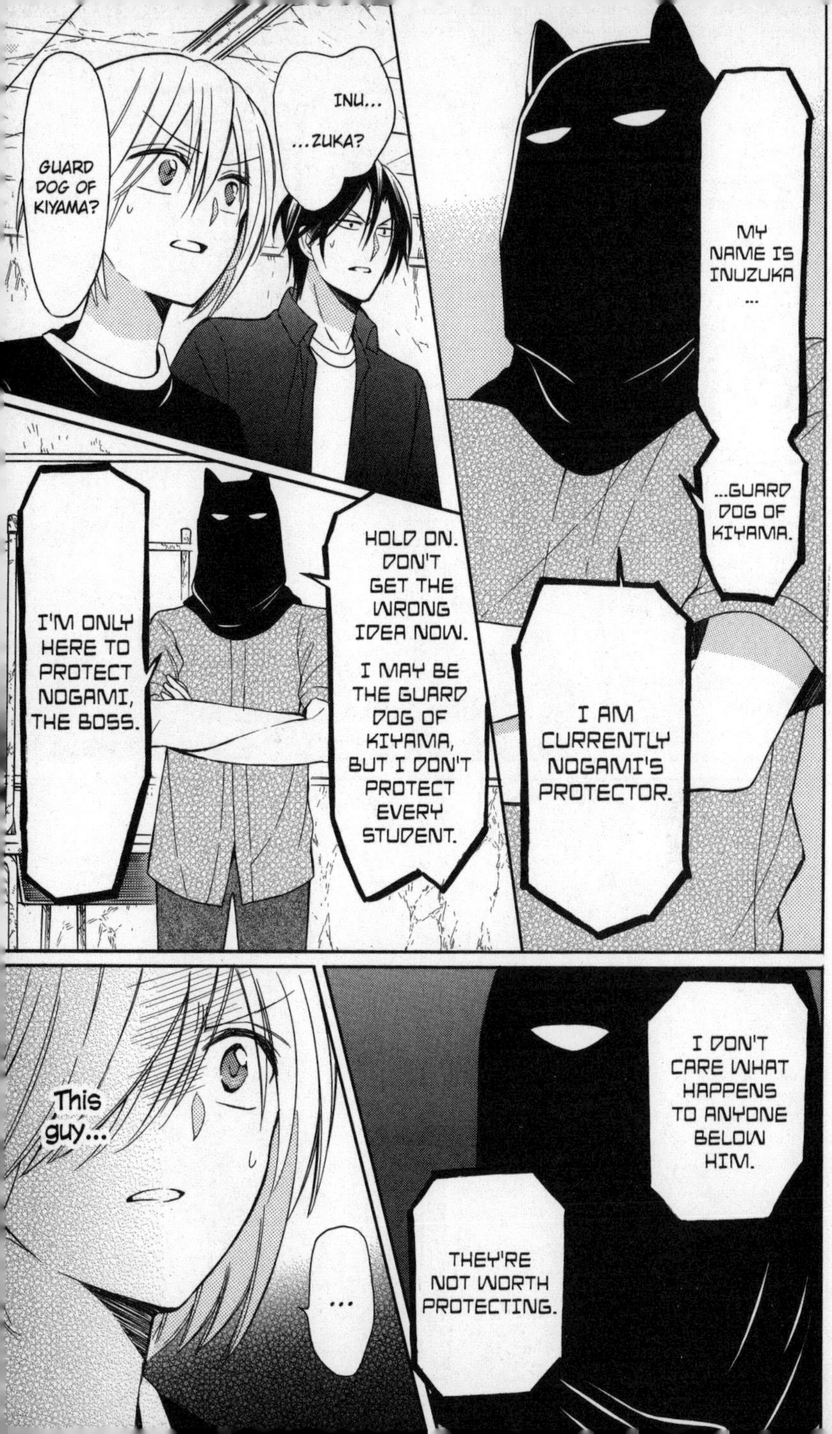
MY NAME IS INUZUKA ...
...GUARD DOG OF KIYAMA.
I AM CURRENTLY NOGAMI'S PROTECTOR.
INU...
...ZUKA?
GUARD DOG OF KIYAMA?
HOLD ON. DON'T GET THE WRONG IDEA NOW.
I MAY BE THE GUARD DOG OF KIYAMA, BUT I DON'T PROTECT EVERY STUDENT.
I'M ONLY HERE TO PROTECT NOGAMI, THE BOSS.
I DON'T CARE WHAT HAPPENS TO ANYONE BELOW HIM.
THEY'RE NOT WORTH PROTECTING.
...
This guy...

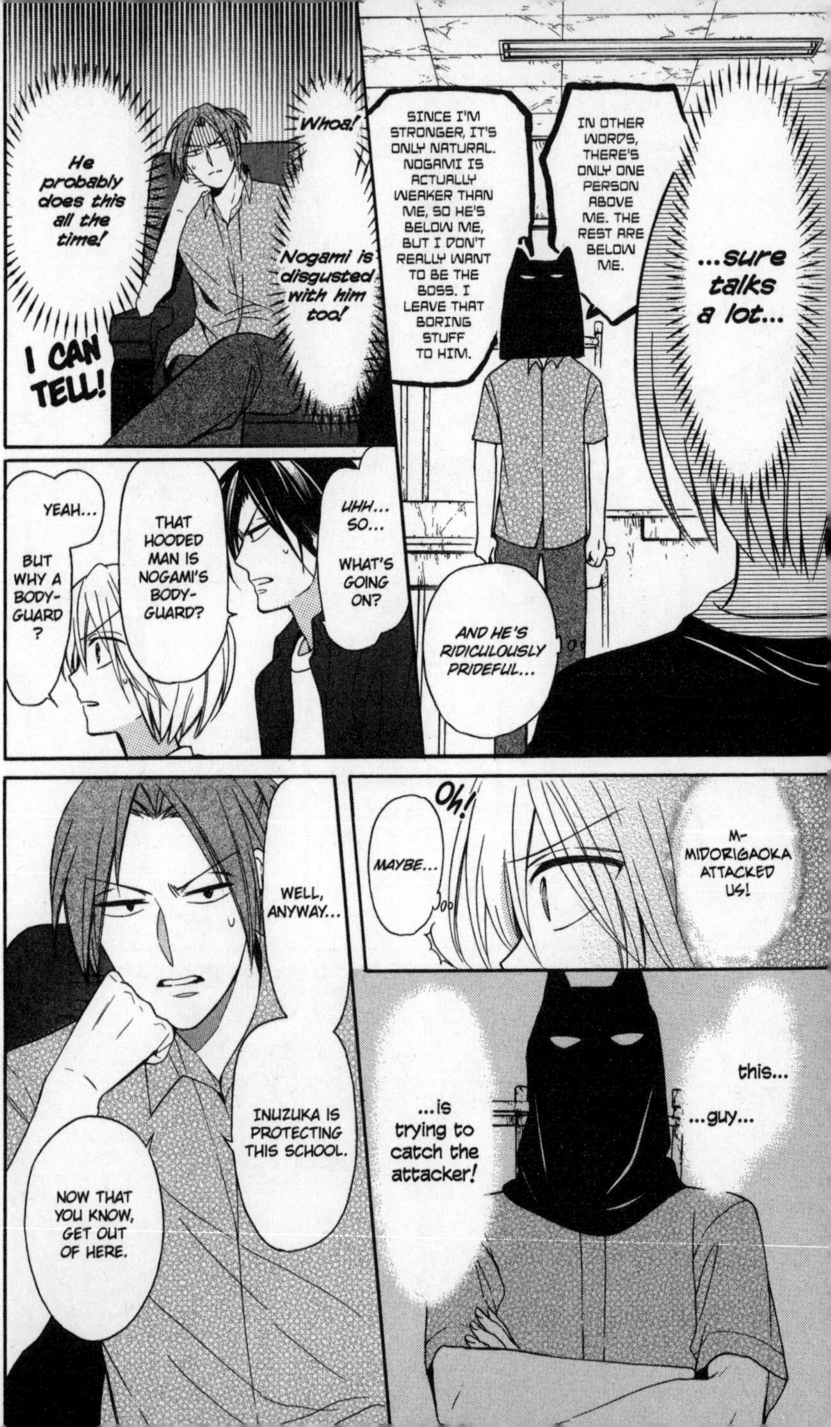
...sure talks a lot...
IN OTHER WORDS, THERE'S ONLY ONE PERSON ABOVE ME. THE REST ARE BELOW ME.
SINCE I'M STRONGER, IT'S ONLY NATURAL. NOGAMI IS ACTUALLY WEAKER THAN ME, SO HE'S BELOW ME, BUT I DON'T REALLY WANT TO BE THE BOSS. I LEAVE THAT BORING STUFF TO HIM.
AND HE'S RIDICULOUSLY PRIDEFUL...
Whoa!
Nogami is disgusted with him too!
He probably does this all the time!
I CAN TELL!
UHH... SO...
WHAT'S GOING ON?
THAT HOODED MAN IS NOGAMI'S BODYGUARD?
YEAH...
BUT WHY A BODYGUARD?
M-MIDORIGAOKA ATTACKED US!
Oh!
MAYBE...
this...
...guy...
...is trying to catch the attacker!
WELL, ANYWAY...
INUZUKA IS PROTECTING THIS SCHOOL.
NOW THAT YOU KNOW, GET OUT OF HERE.

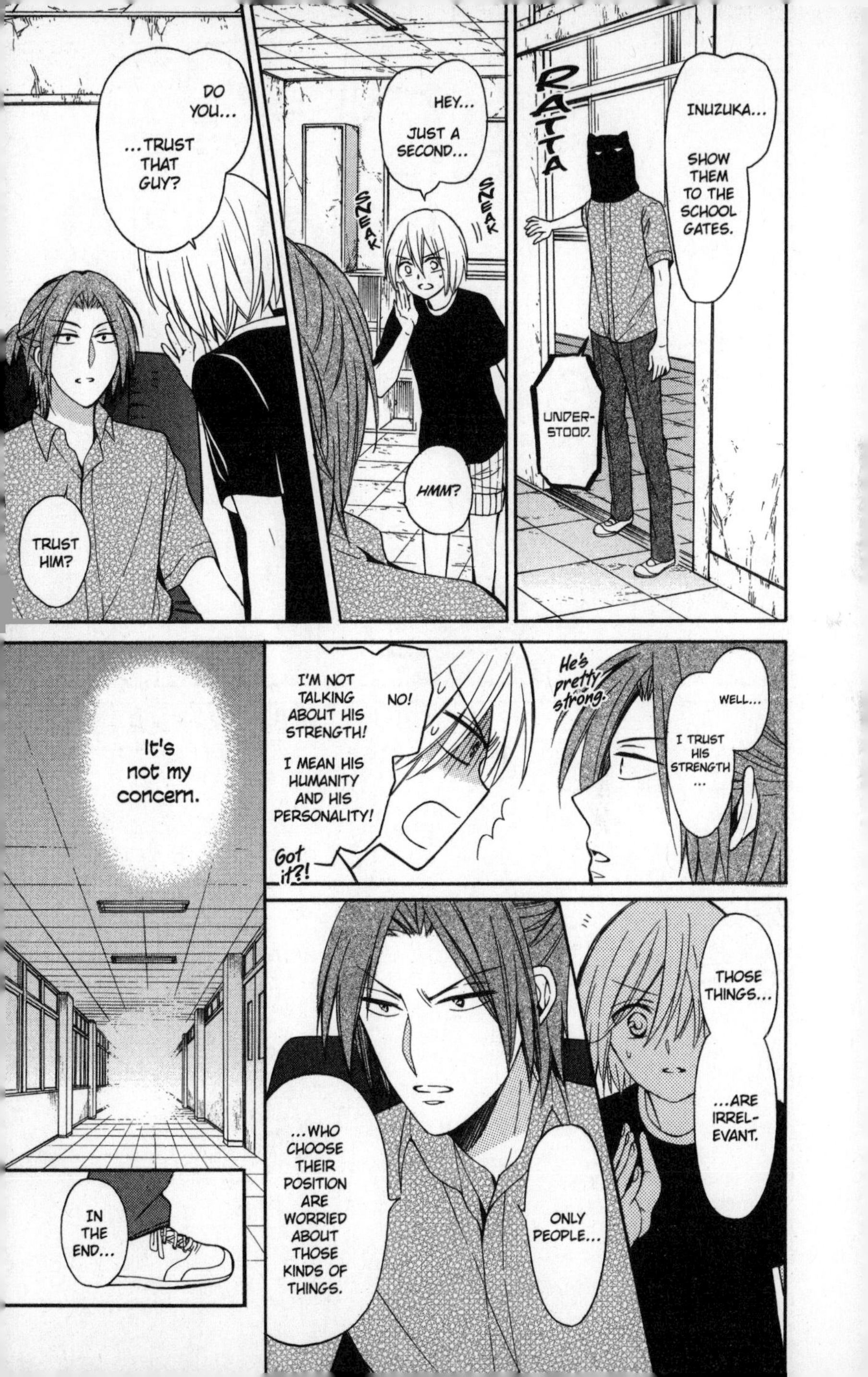
INUZUKA... SHOW THEM TO THE SCHOOL GATES.
RATTA
UNDER-STOOD.
HEY... JUST A SECOND...
SNEAK
SNEAK
HMM?
DO YOU... ...TRUST THAT GUY?
TRUST HIM?
WELL... I TRUST HIS STRENGTH...
He's pretty strong.
NO!
I'M NOT TALKING ABOUT HIS STRENGTH! I MEAN HIS HUMANITY AND HIS PERSONALITY!
Got it?!
THOSE THINGS... ...ARE IRREL-EVANT.
ONLY PEOPLE...
...WHO CHOOSE THEIR POSITION ARE WORRIED ABOUT THOSE KINDS OF THINGS.
It's not my concern.
IN THE END...

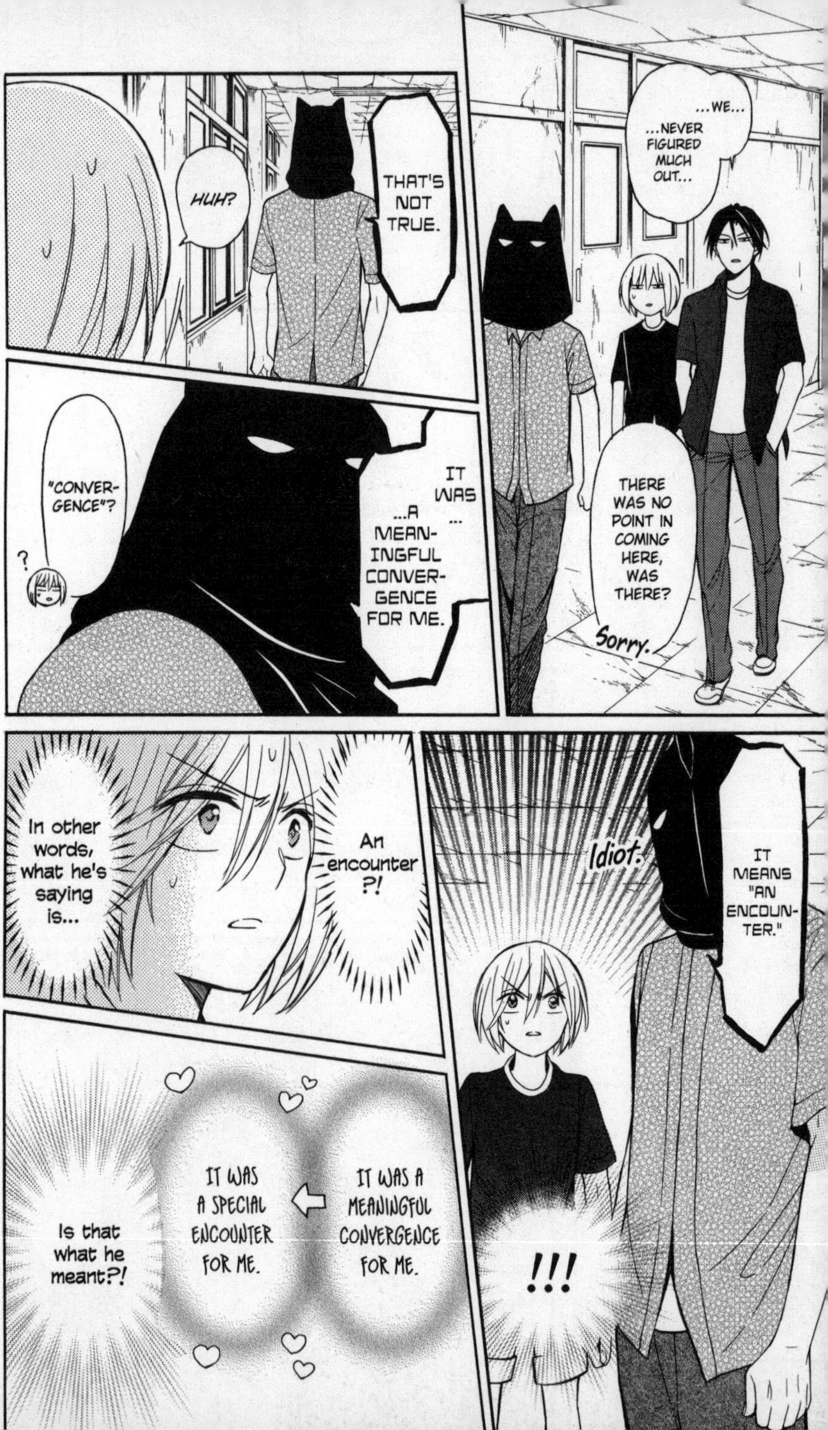
...WE...
...NEVER FIGURED MUCH OUT...
THERE WAS NO POINT IN COMING HERE, WAS THERE?
Sorry.
THAT'S NOT TRUE.
HUH?
IT WAS ...
...A MEANINGFUL CONVERGENCE FOR ME.
"CONVERGENCE"?
?
IT MEANS "AN ENCOUNTER."
Idiot.
!!!
An encounter?!
In other words, what he's saying is...
IT WAS A MEANINGFUL CONVERGENCE FOR ME.
IT WAS A SPECIAL ENCOUNTER FOR ME.
Is that what he meant?!

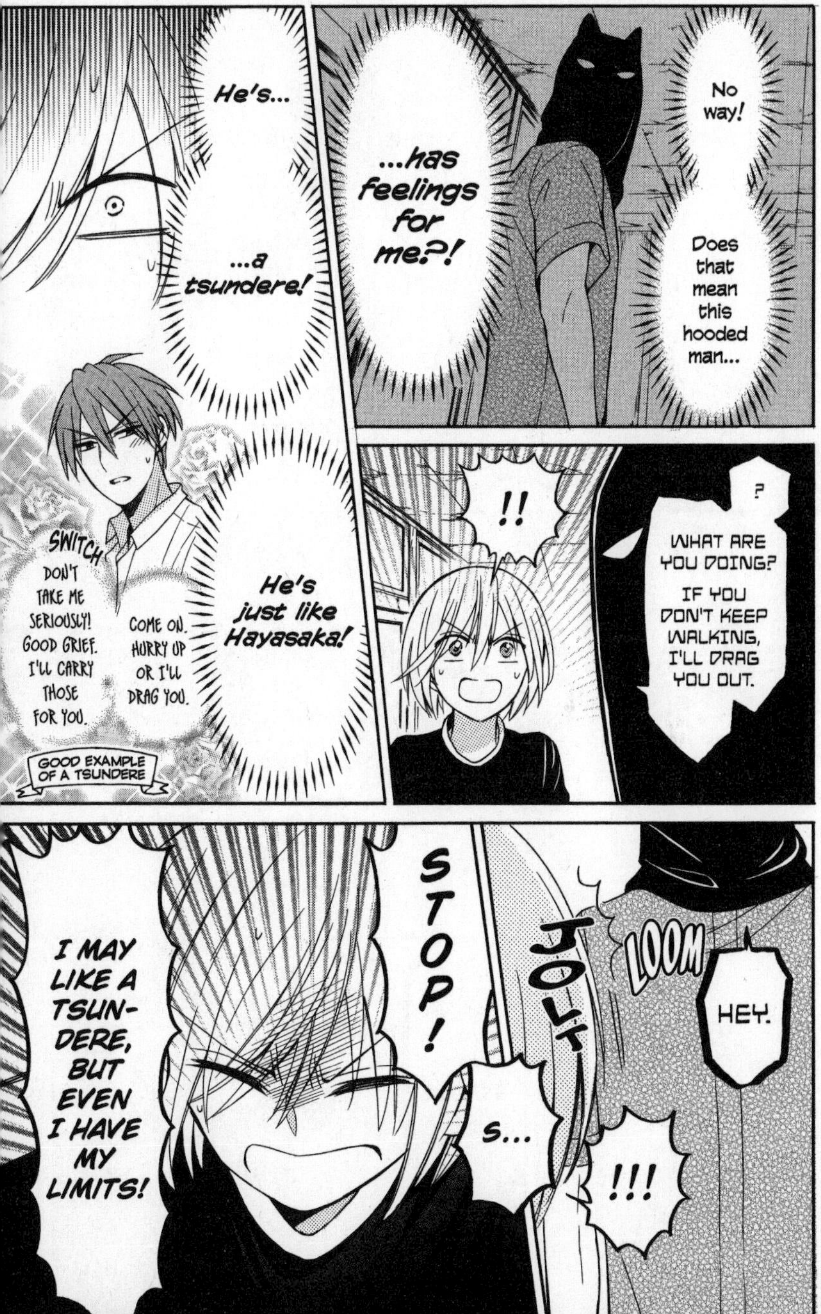
No way!
Does that mean this hooded man...
...has feelings for me?!
?
WHAT ARE YOU DOING?
IF YOU DON'T KEEP WALKING, I'LL DRAG YOU OUT.
!!
He's...
...a tsundere!
He's just like Hayasaka!
COME ON. HURRY UP OR I'LL DRAG YOU.
SWITCH
DON'T TAKE ME SERIOUSLY! GOOD GRIEF. I'LL CARRY THOSE FOR YOU.
GOOD EXAMPLE OF A TSUNDERE
LOOM
HEY.
JOLT
!!!
STOP!
S...
I MAY LIKE A TSUNDERE, BUT EVEN I HAVE MY LIMITS!

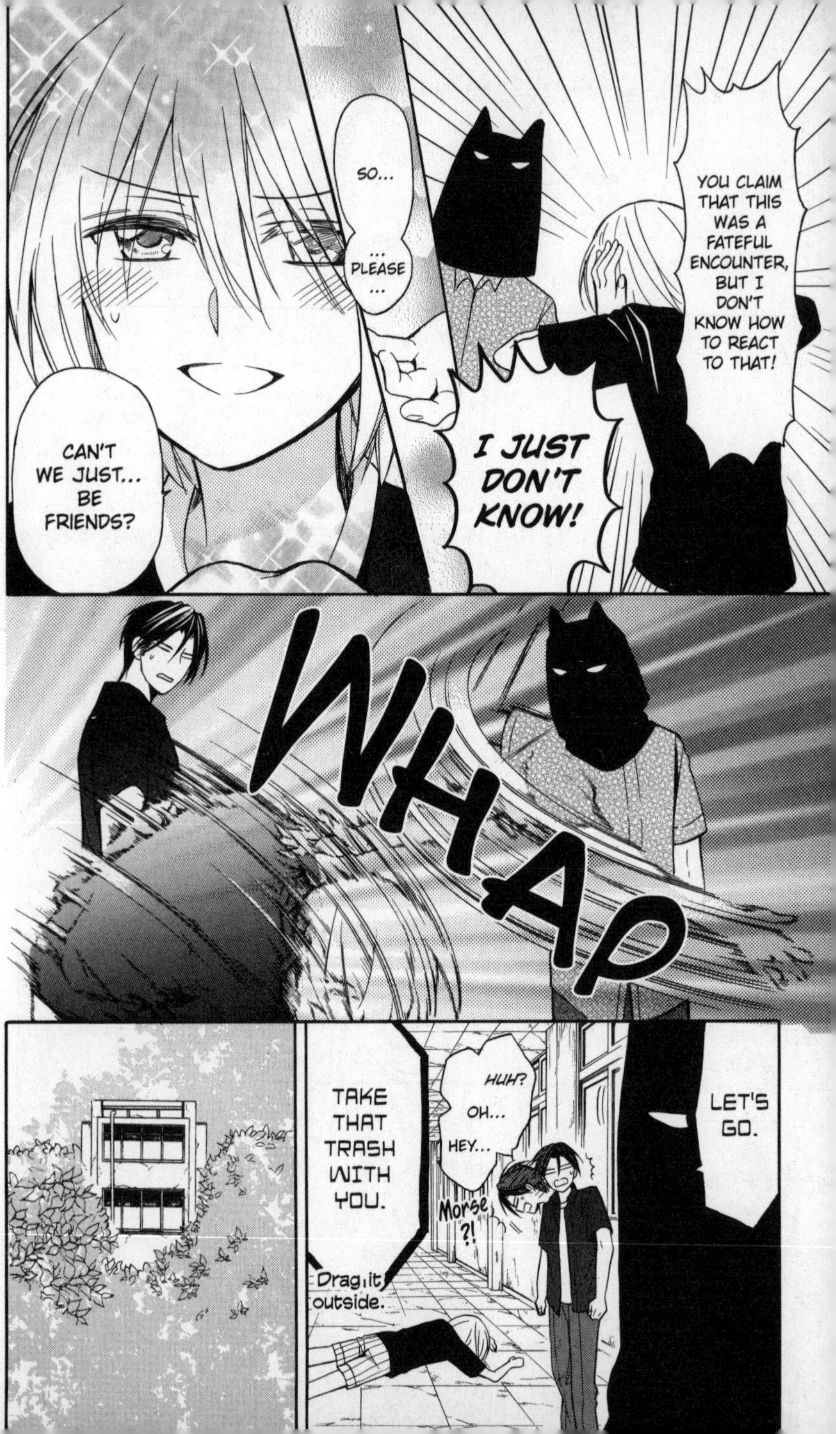
YOU CLAIM THAT THIS WAS A FATEFUL ENCOUNTER, BUT I DON'T KNOW HOW TO REACT TO THAT!
I JUST DON'T KNOW!
SO...
...PLEASE...
CAN'T WE JUST... BE FRIENDS?
WHAP
LET'S GO.
HUH?
OH...
HEY...
Morse ?!
TAKE THAT TRASH WITH YOU.
Drag it outside.

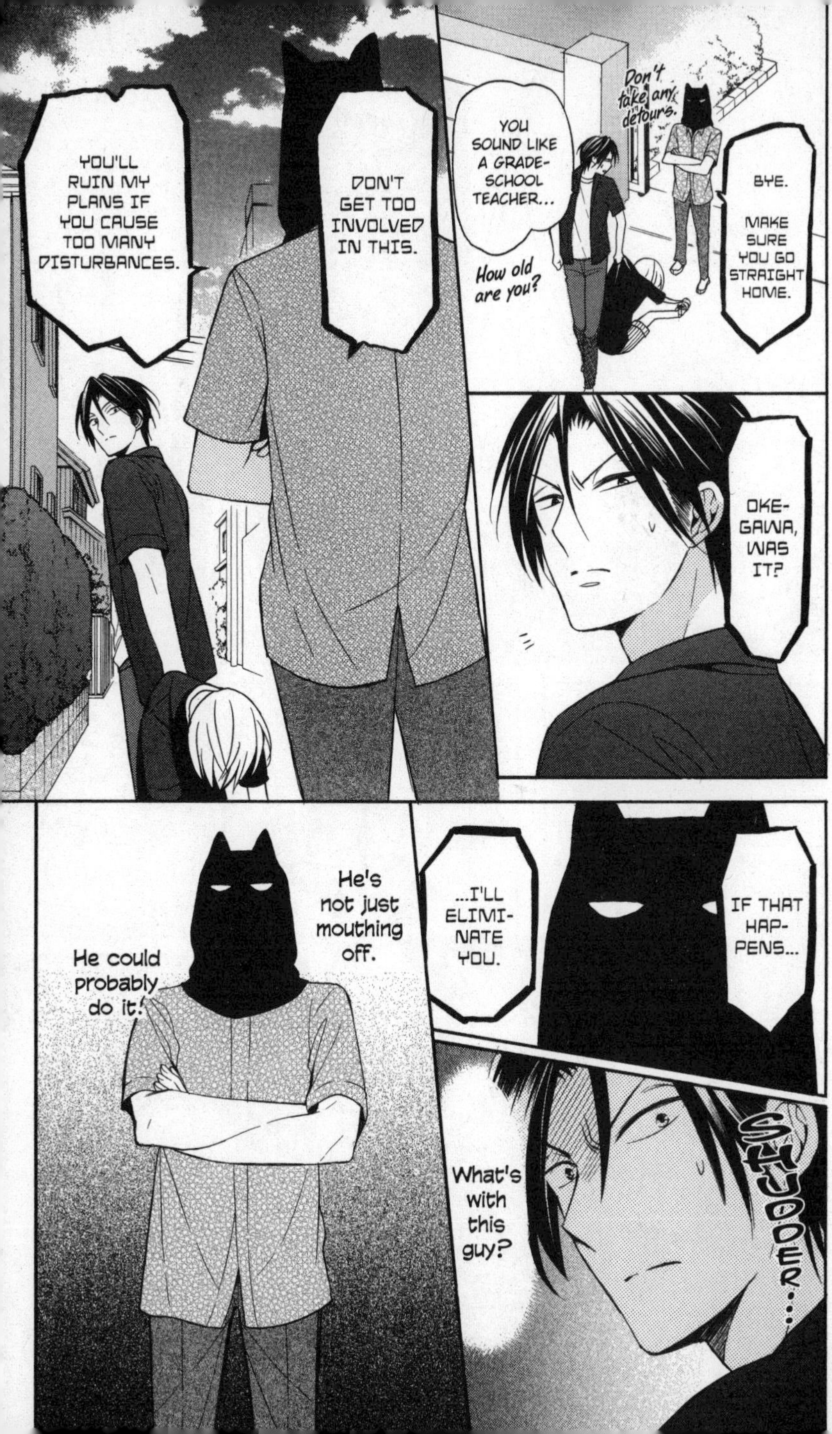
BYE.
MAKE SURE YOU GO STRAIGHT HOME.
Don't take any detours.
YOU SOUND LIKE A GRADE-SCHOOL TEACHER...
How old are you?
OKE-GAWA, WAS IT?
DON'T GET TOO INVOLVED IN THIS.
YOU'LL RUIN MY PLANS IF YOU CAUSE TOO MANY DISTURBANCES.
IF THAT HAP-PENS...
...I'LL ELIMI-NATE YOU.
SHUDDER...
What's with this guy?
He's not just mouthing off.
He could probably do it.

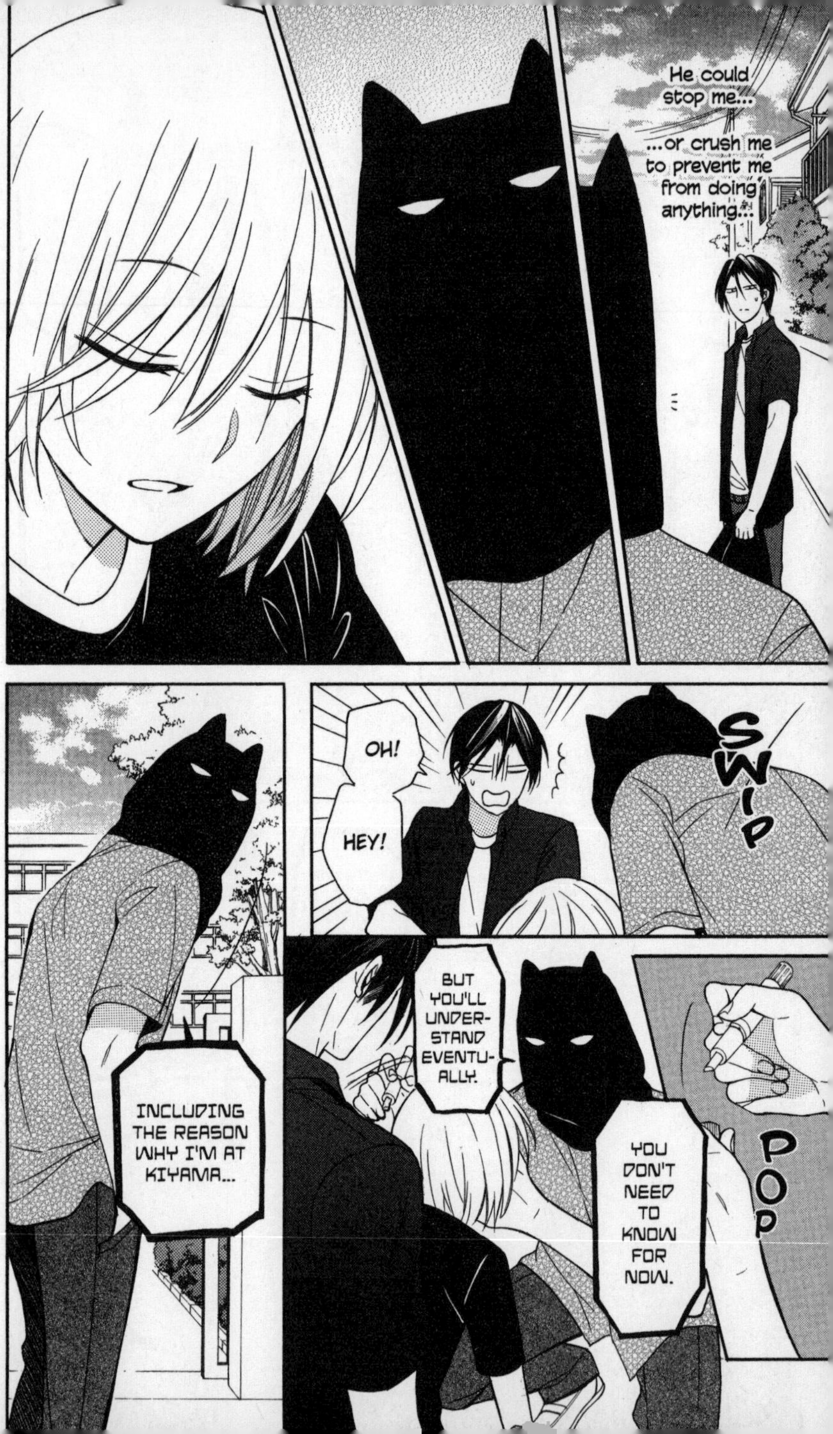
He could stop me...
...or crush me to prevent me from doing anything...
SWIP
OH!
HEY!
POP
YOU DON'T NEED TO KNOW FOR NOW.
BUT YOU'LL UNDER-STAND EVENTU-ALLY.
INCLUDING THE REASON WHY I'M AT KIYAMA...

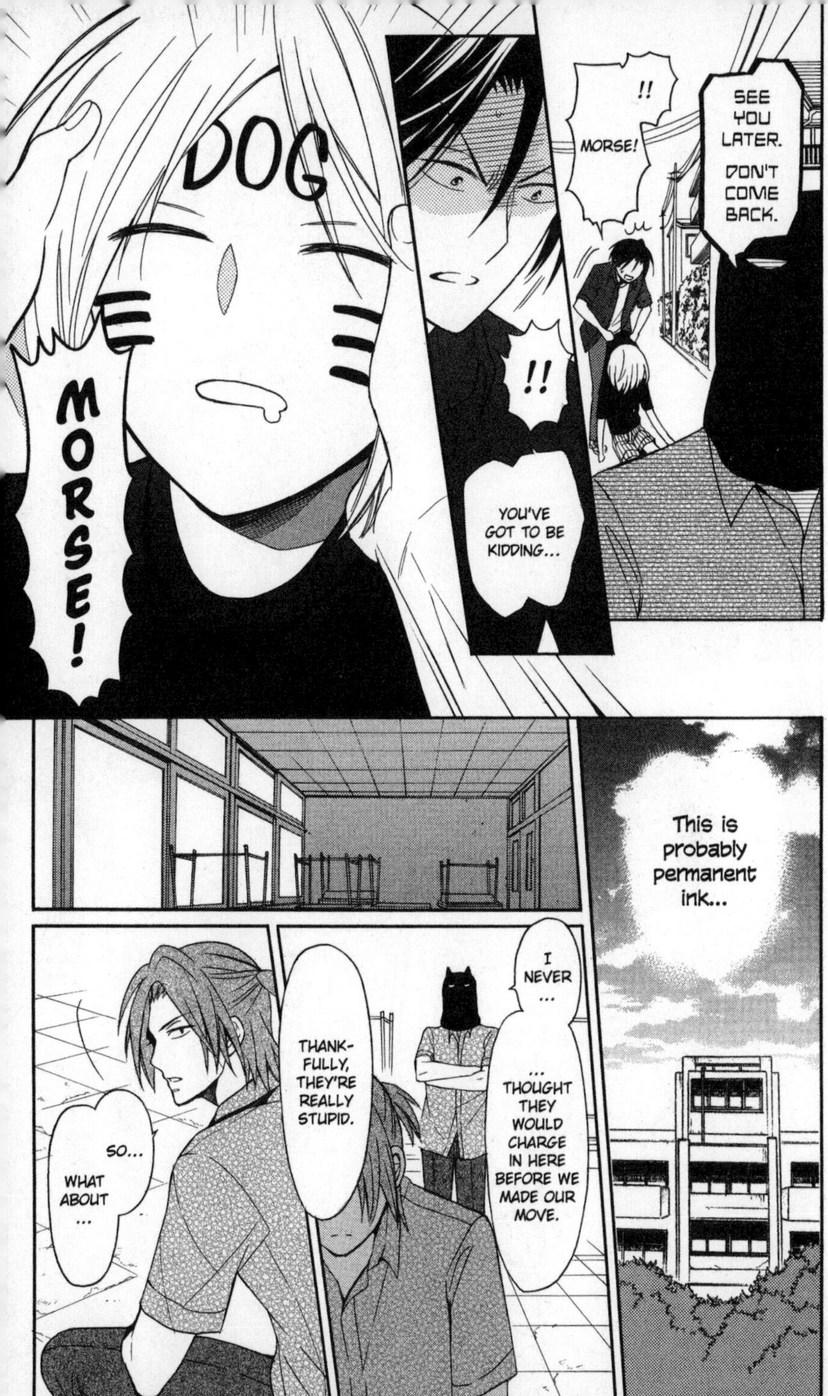
SEE YOU LATER.
DON'T COME BACK.
!!
MORSE!
!!
YOU'VE GOT TO BE KIDDING...
DOG
MORSE!
This is probably permanent ink...
I NEVER ...
... THOUGHT THEY WOULD CHARGE IN HERE BEFORE WE MADE OUR MOVE.
THANK-FULLY, THEY'RE REALLY STUPID.
SO... WHAT ABOUT ...

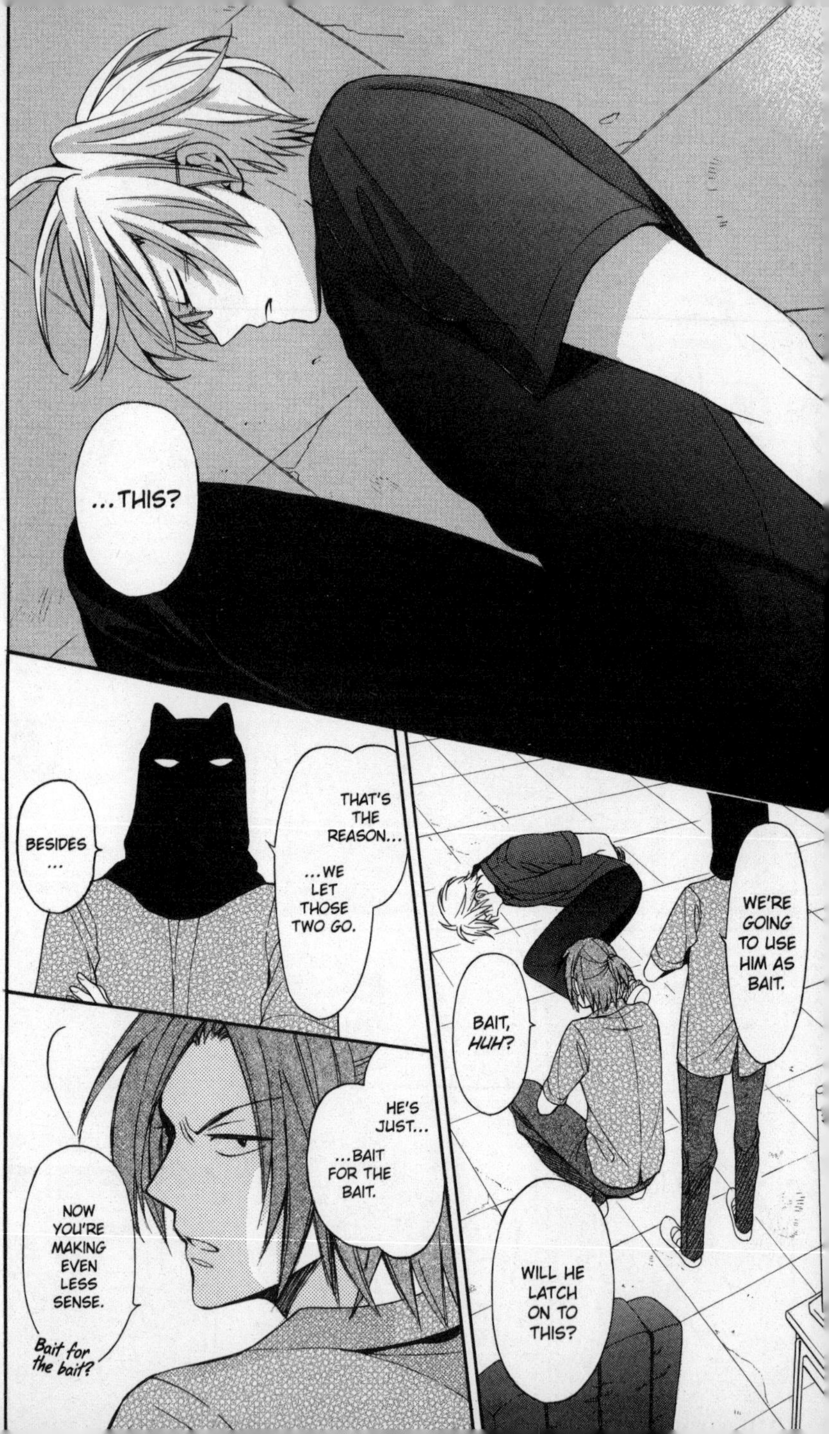
...THIS?
WE'RE GOING TO USE HIM AS BAIT.
BAIT, HUH?
WILL HE LATCH ON TO THIS?
THAT'S THE REASON...
...WE LET THOSE TWO GO.
BESIDES...
HE'S JUST...
...BAIT FOR THE BAIT.
NOW YOU'RE MAKING EVEN LESS SENSE.
Bait for the bait?

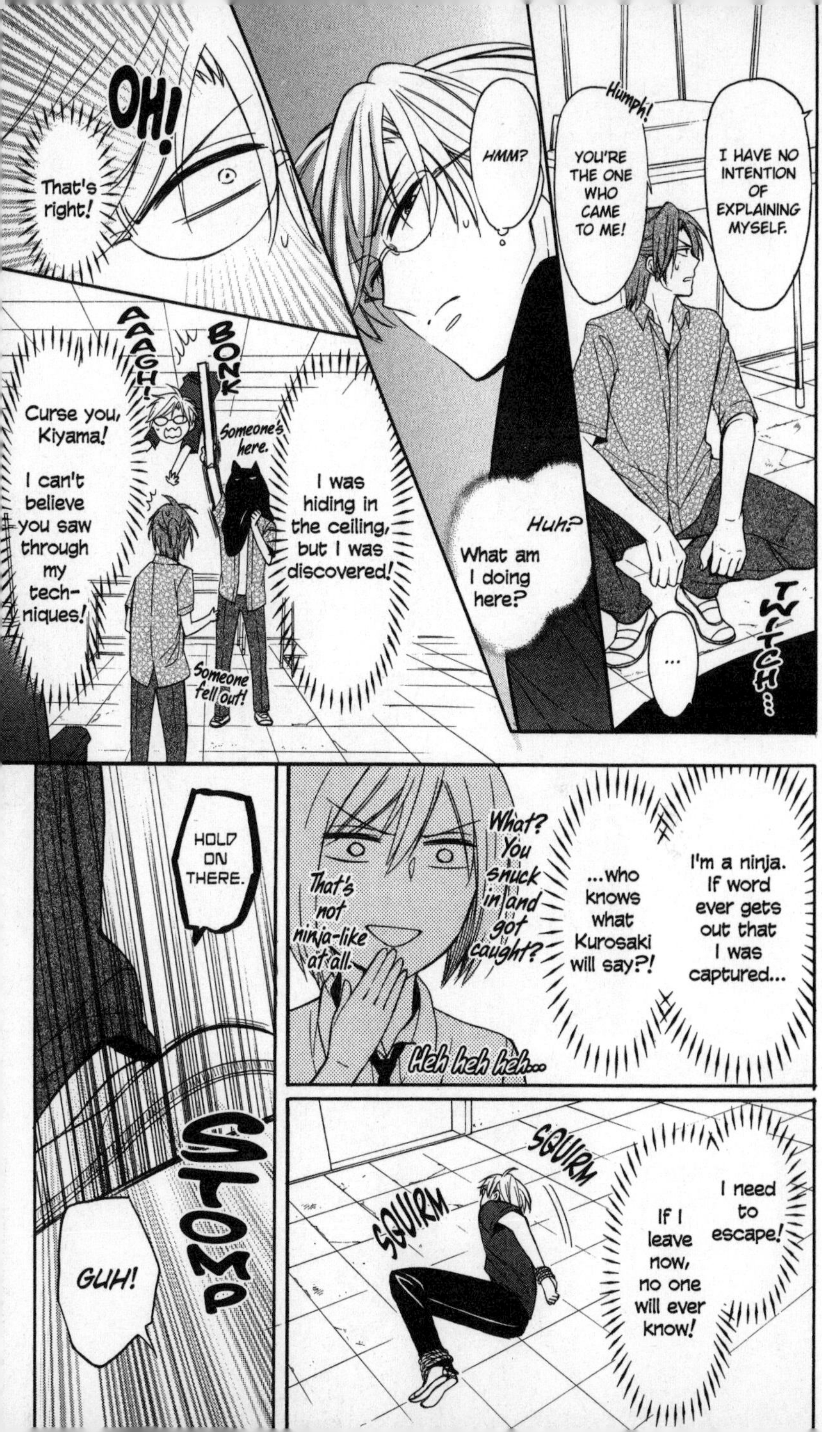
I HAVE NO INTENTION OF EXPLAINING MYSELF.
Humph!
YOU'RE THE ONE WHO CAME TO ME!
...
TWITCH...
HMM?
Huh?
What am I doing here?
OH!
That's right!
I was hiding in the ceiling, but I was discovered!
Someone's here.
BONK
AAAGH!
Curse you, Kiyama!
I can't believe you saw through my techniques!
Someone fell out!
I'm a ninja. If word ever gets out that I was captured...
...who knows what Kurosaki will say?!
What? You snuck in and got caught?
That's not ninja-like at all.
Heh heh heh...
I need to escape!
If I leave now, no one will ever know!
SQUIRM
SQUIRM
HOLD ON THERE.
STOMP
GUH!

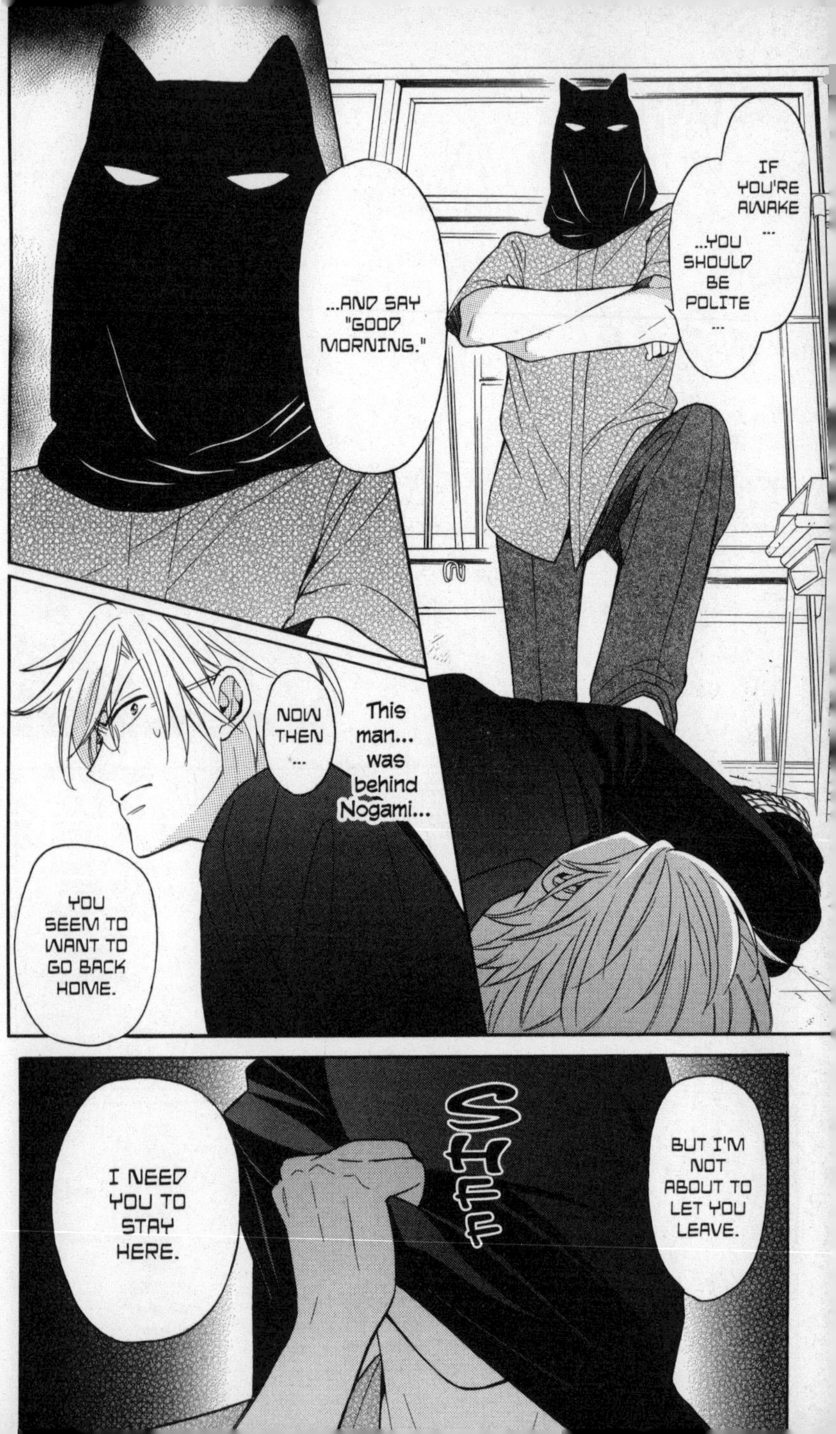
IF YOU'RE AWAKE ... ...YOU SHOULD BE POLITE ...
...AND SAY "GOOD MORNING."
This man... was behind Nogami...
NOW THEN ...
YOU SEEM TO WANT TO GO BACK HOME.
BUT I'M NOT ABOUT TO LET YOU LEAVE.
SHFF
I NEED YOU TO STAY HERE.

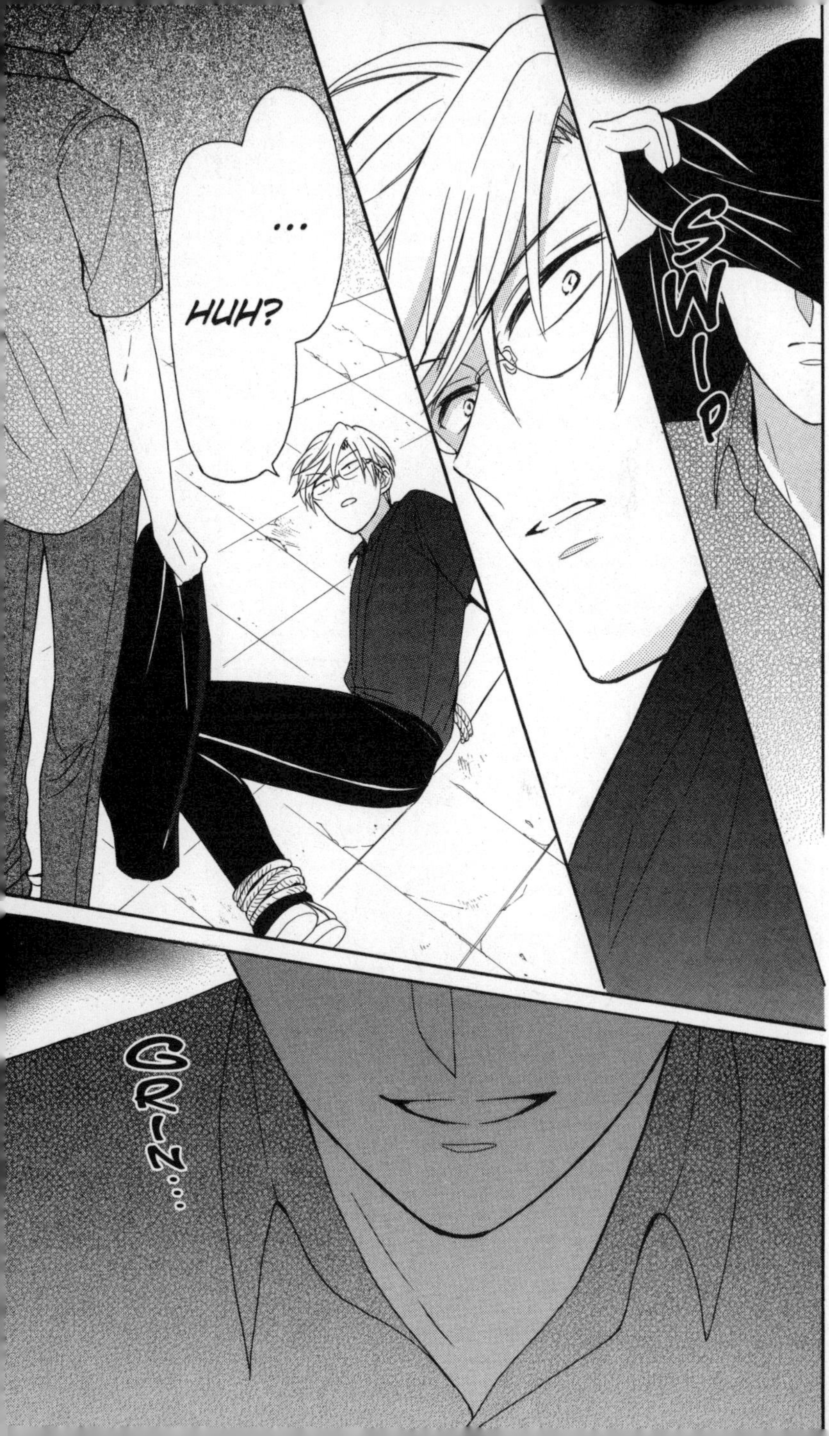
SWIP
...
HUH?
GRIN...

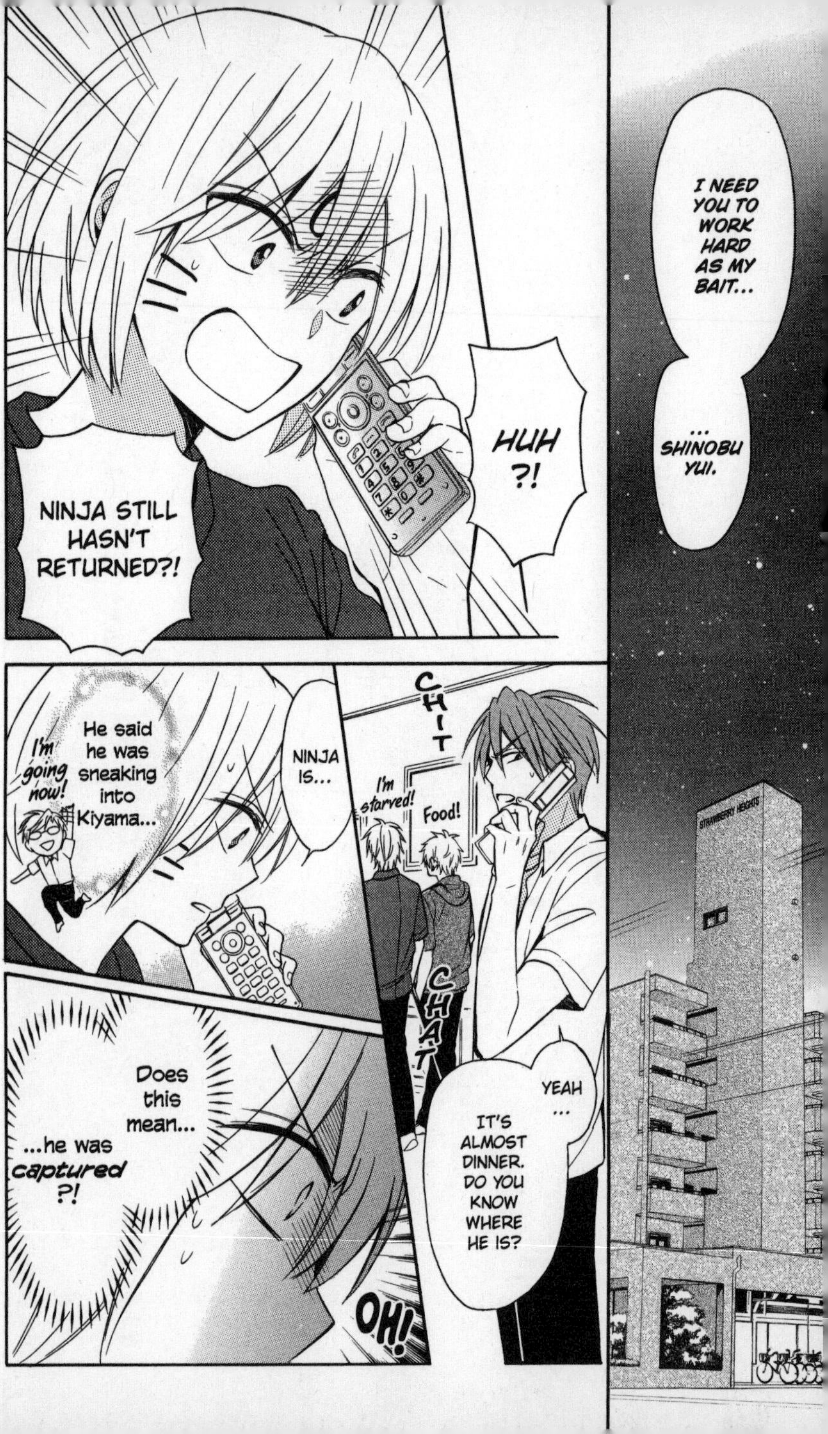
I NEED YOU TO WORK HARD AS MY BAIT...
...SHINOBU YUI.
HUH?!
NINJA STILL HASN'T RETURNED?!
CHIT
I'm starved!
Food!
CHAT
YEAH...
IT'S ALMOST DINNER. DO YOU KNOW WHERE HE IS?
NINJA IS...
He said he was sneaking into Kiyama...
I'm going now!
OH!
Does this mean...
...he was *captured*?!

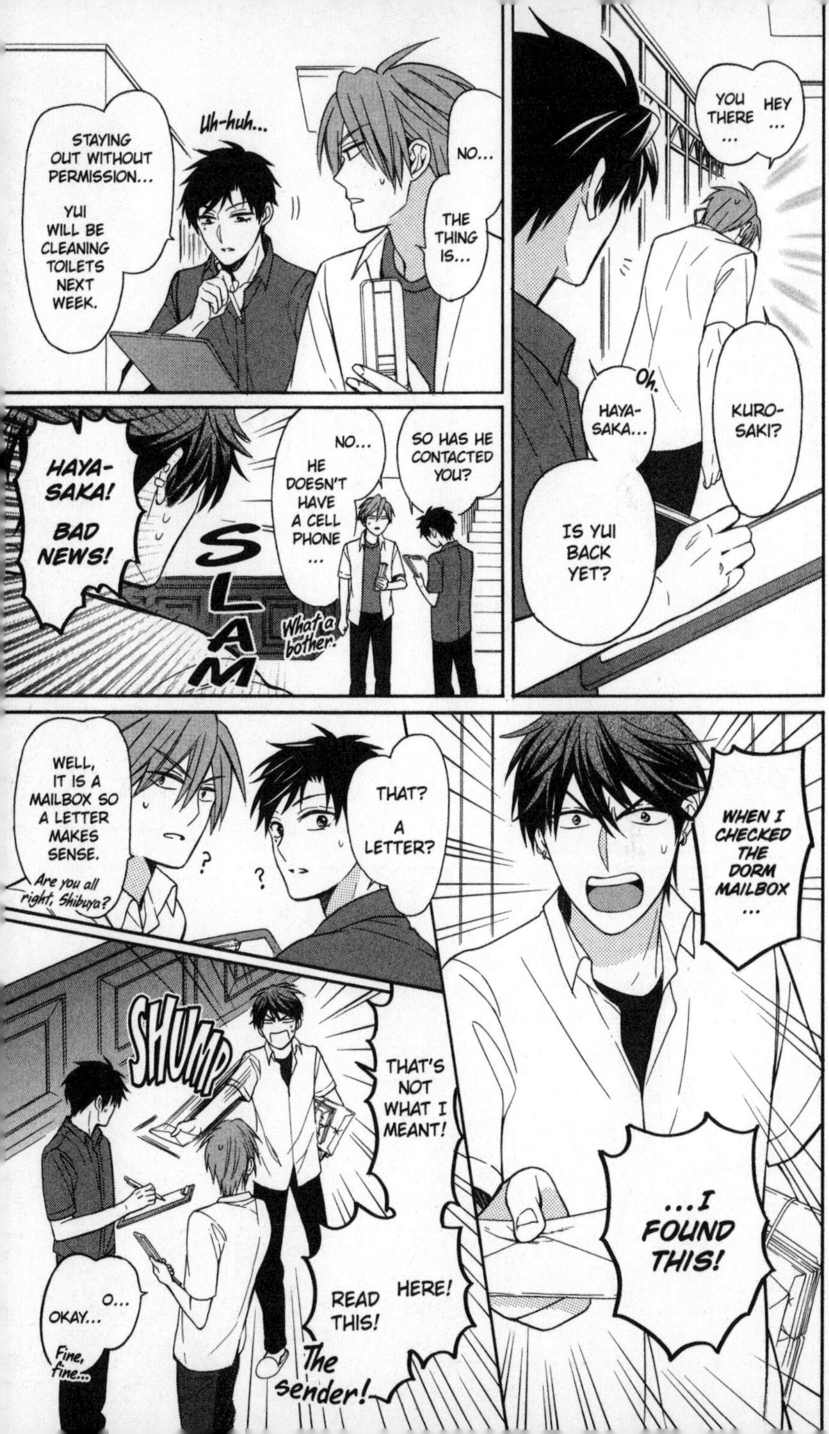

HEY... YOU THERE...
KURO-SAKI?
Oh. HAYA-SAKA...
IS YUI BACK YET?
NO... THE THING IS...
Uh-huh...
STAYING OUT WITHOUT PERMISSION... YUI WILL BE CLEANING TOILETS NEXT WEEK.
SO HAS HE CONTACTED YOU?
NO... HE DOESN'T HAVE A CELL PHONE...
What a bother.
SLAM
HAYA-SAKA! BAD NEWS!
WHEN I CHECKED THE DORM MAILBOX...
...I FOUND THIS!
THAT? A LETTER?
WELL, IT IS A MAILBOX SO A LETTER MAKES SENSE.
Are you all right, Shibuya?
THAT'S NOT WHAT I MEANT!
HERE! READ THIS!
The sender!
SHUMP
O... OKAY...
Fine, fine...

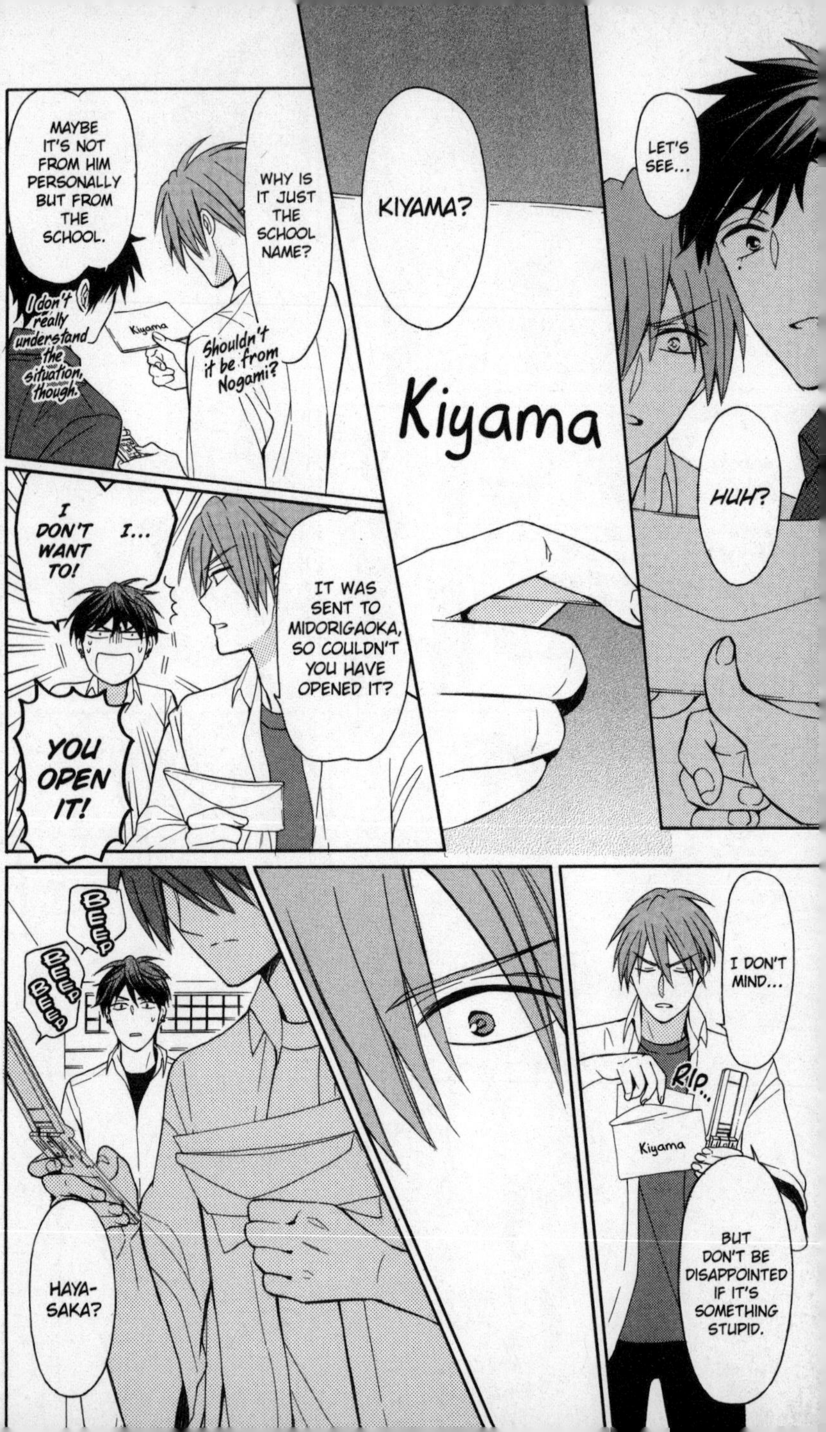
LET'S SEE...
HUH?
KIYAMA?
Kiyama
WHY IS IT JUST THE SCHOOL NAME?
Shouldn't it be from Nogami?
MAYBE IT'S NOT FROM HIM PERSONALLY BUT FROM THE SCHOOL.
I don't really understand the situation, though.
Kiyama
IT WAS SENT TO MIDORIGAOKA, SO COULDN'T YOU HAVE OPENED IT?
I... I DON'T WANT TO!
YOU OPEN IT!
I DON'T MIND...
RIP...
Kiyama
BUT DON'T BE DISAPPOINTED IF IT'S SOMETHING STUPID.
BEEP
BEEP
BEEP
HAYA-SAKA?

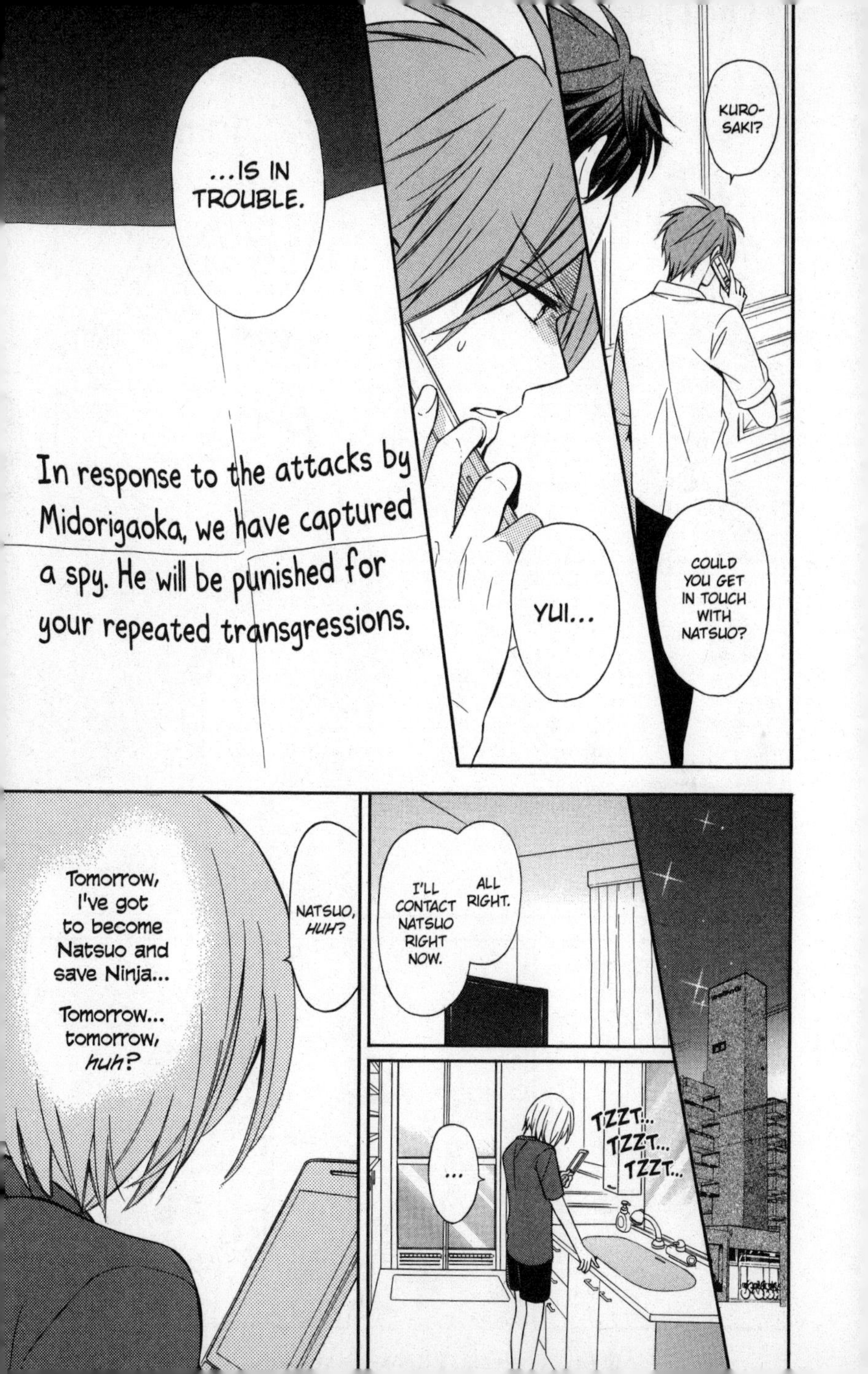
KURO-SAKI?
COULD YOU GET IN TOUCH WITH NATSUO?
YUI...
...IS IN TROUBLE.
In response to the attacks by Midorigaoka, we have captured a spy. He will be punished for your repeated transgressions.
ALL RIGHT.
I'LL CONTACT NATSUO RIGHT NOW.
TZZT... TZZT... TZZT...
...
NATSUO, *HUH?*
Tomorrow, I've got to become Natsuo and save Ninja...
Tomorrow... tomorrow, *huh?*

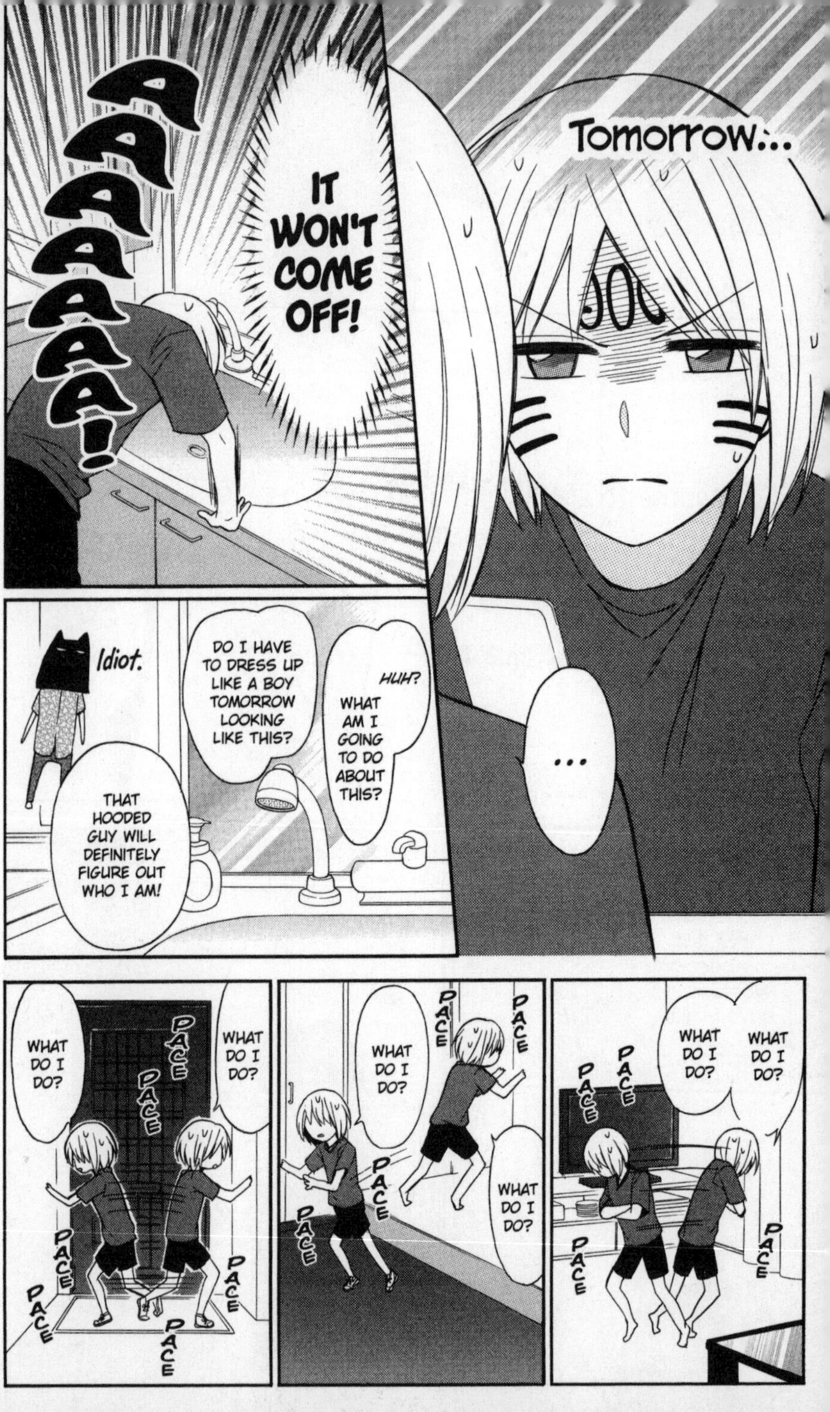
Tomorrow...
...
IT WON'T COME OFF!
AAAAAAA!
HUH? WHAT AM I GOING TO DO ABOUT THIS?
DO I HAVE TO DRESS UP LIKE A BOY TOMORROW LOOKING LIKE THIS?
Idiot.
THAT HOODED GUY WILL DEFINITELY FIGURE OUT WHO I AM!
WHAT DO I DO?
WHAT DO I DO?
PACE PACE
PACE PACE
PACE
WHAT DO I DO?
WHAT DO I DO?
PACE PACE PACE PACE
WHAT DO I DO?
WHAT DO I DO?
PACE PACE
PACE PACE PACE PACE

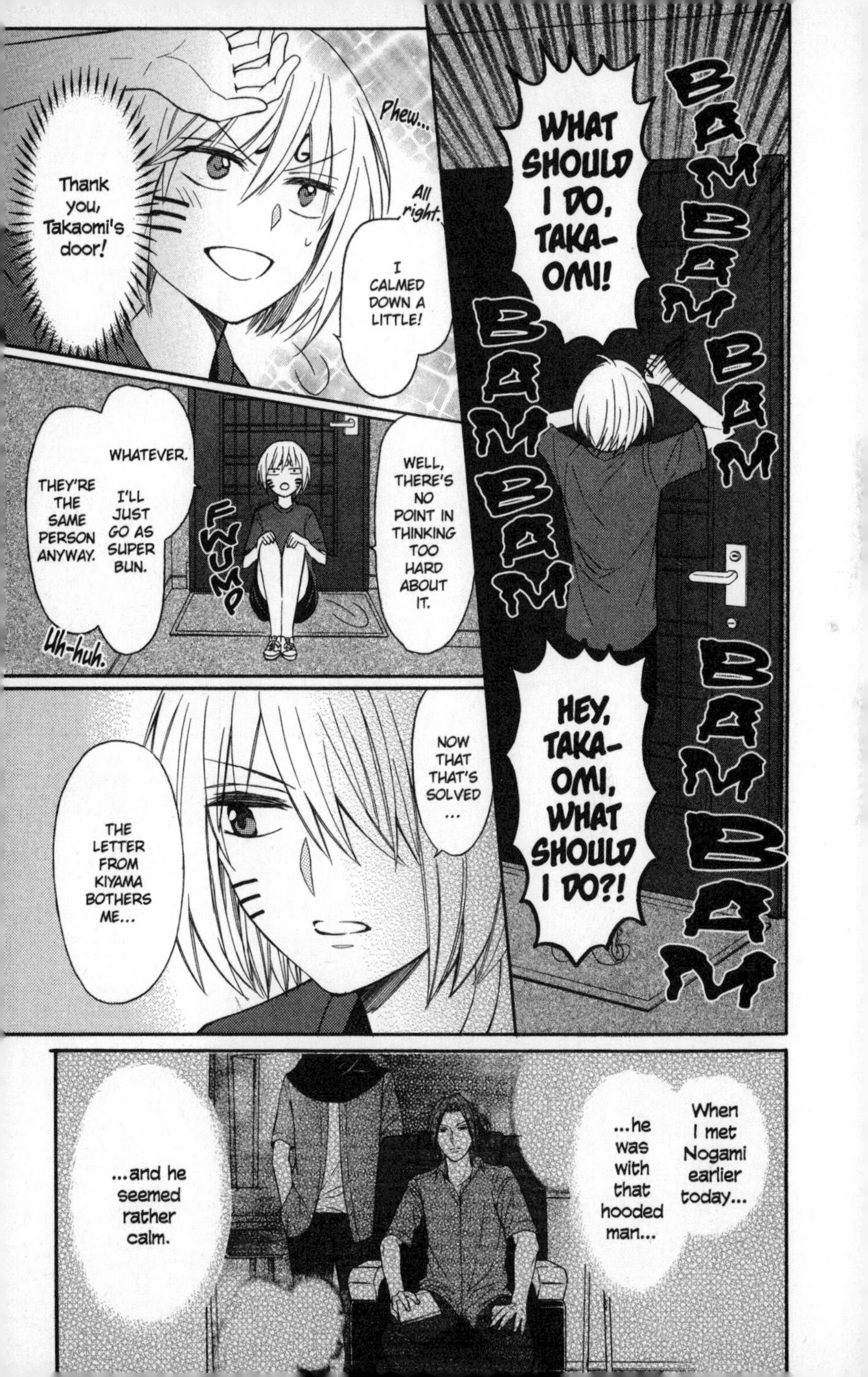
BAM BAM
WHAT SHOULD I DO, TAKAOMI!
BAM
BAM BAM BAM BAM
BAM BAM BAM
HEY, TAKAOMI, WHAT SHOULD I DO?!
Phew...
All right.
I CALMED DOWN A LITTLE!
Thank you, Takaomi's door!
WELL, THERE'S NO POINT IN THINKING TOO HARD ABOUT IT.
FWUMP
WHATEVER.
I'LL JUST GO AS SUPER BUN.
THEY'RE THE SAME PERSON ANYWAY.
Uh-huh.
NOW THAT THAT'S SOLVED ...
THE LETTER FROM KIYAMA BOTHERS ME...
When I met Nogami earlier today...
...he was with that hooded man...
...and he seemed rather calm.

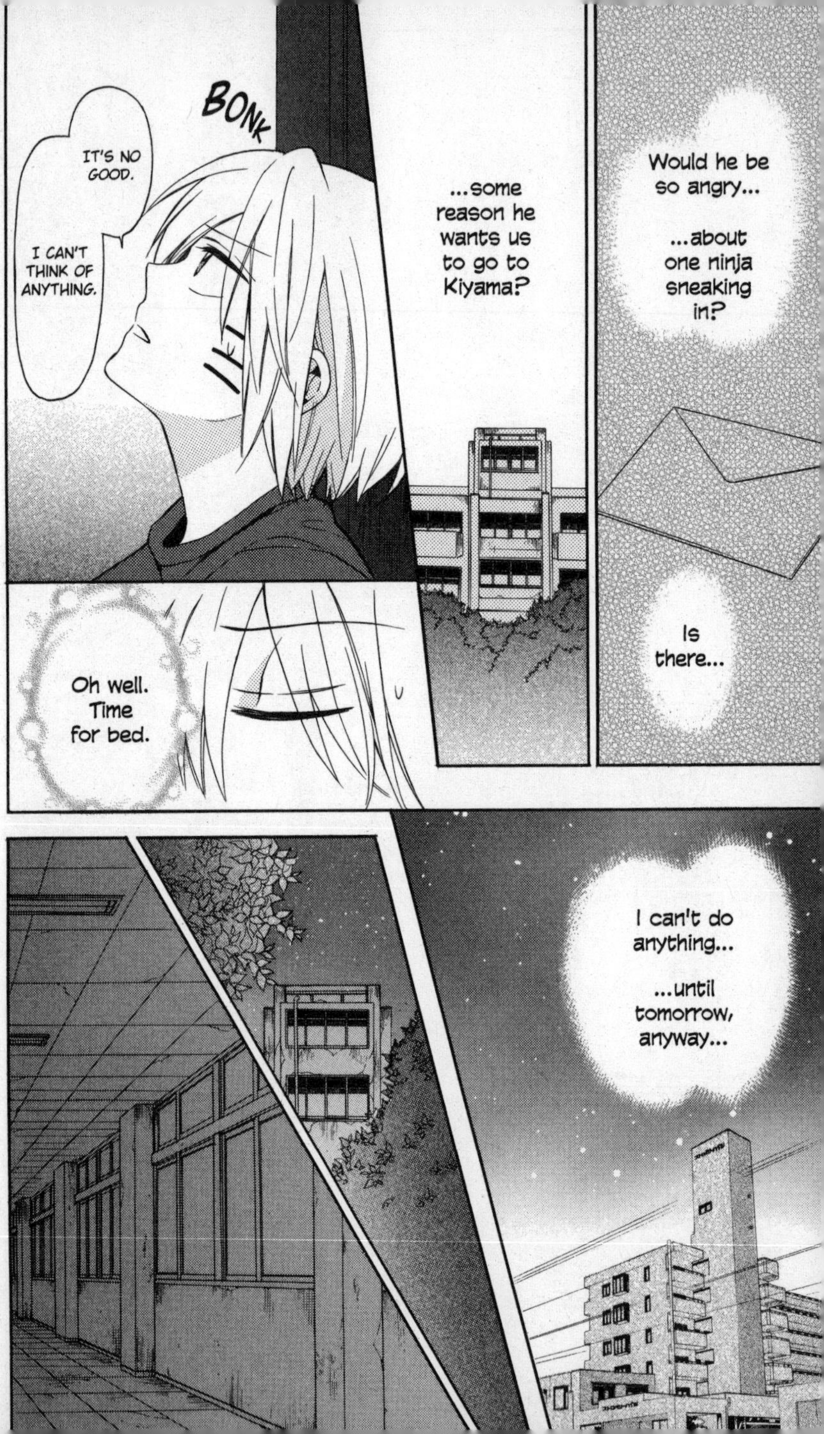
Would he be so angry...
...about one ninja sneaking in?
Is there...
...some reason he wants us to go to Kiyama?
BONK
IT'S NO GOOD.
I CAN'T THINK OF ANYTHING.
Oh well. Time for bed.
I can't do anything...
...until tomorrow, anyway...

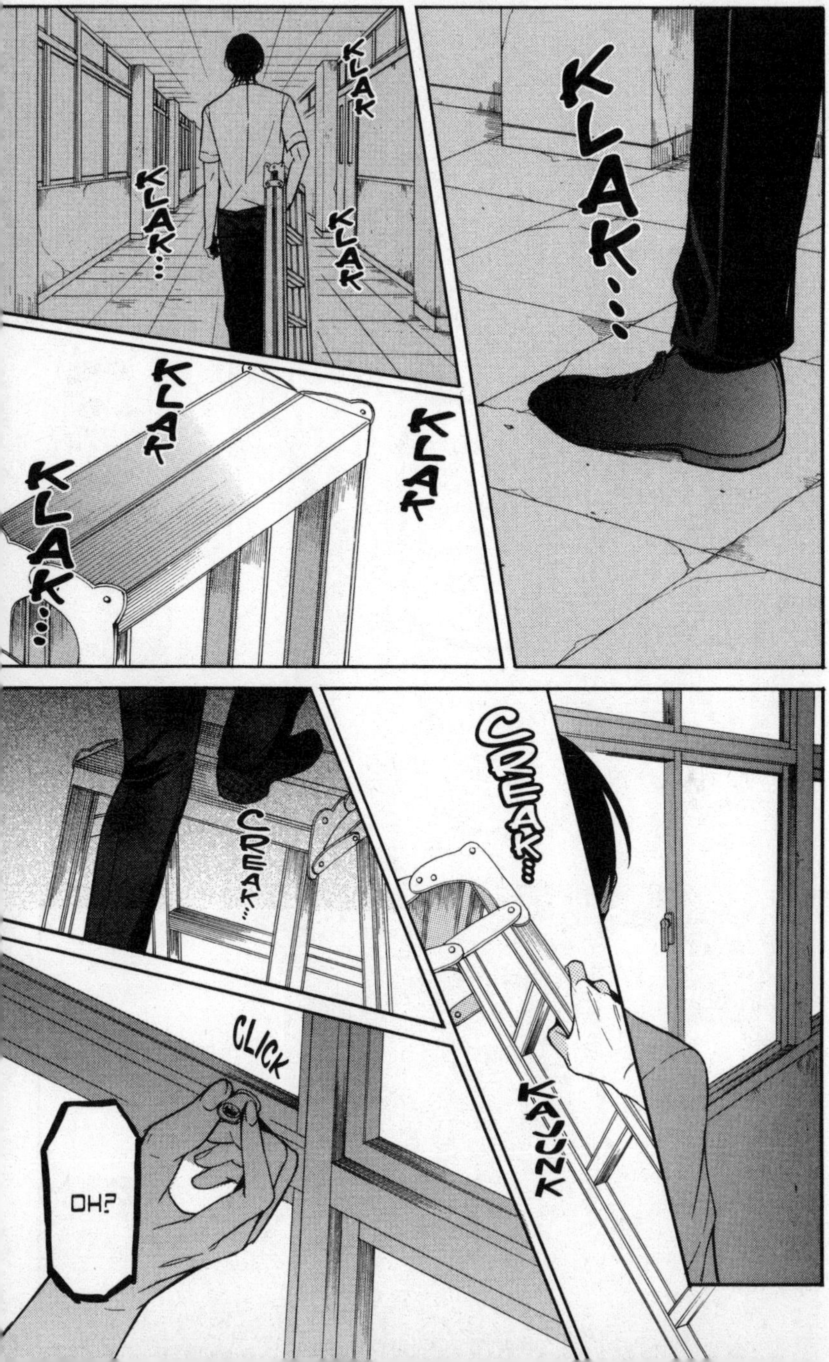
KLAK...
KLAK
KLAK...
KLAK
KLAK
KLAK
KLAK...
CREAK...
KAJUNK
CREAK...
CLICK
OH?

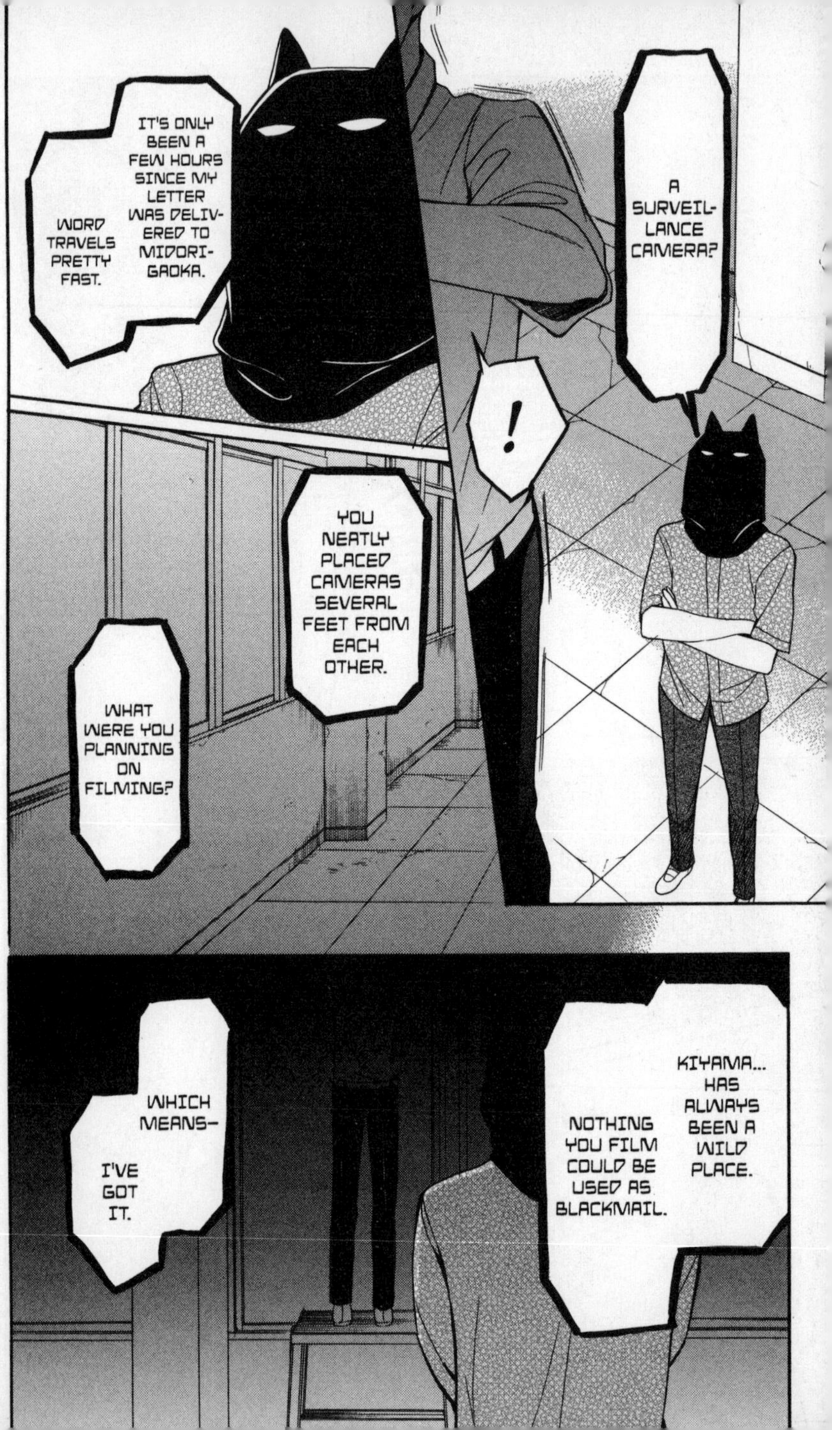
A SURVEILLANCE CAMERA?
!
IT'S ONLY BEEN A FEW HOURS SINCE MY LETTER WAS DELIVERED TO MIDORIGAOKA.
WORD TRAVELS PRETTY FAST.
YOU NEATLY PLACED CAMERAS SEVERAL FEET FROM EACH OTHER.
WHAT WERE YOU PLANNING ON FILMING?
KIYAMA... HAS ALWAYS BEEN A WILD PLACE.
NOTHING YOU FILM COULD BE USED AS BLACKMAIL.
WHICH MEANS—
I'VE GOT IT.

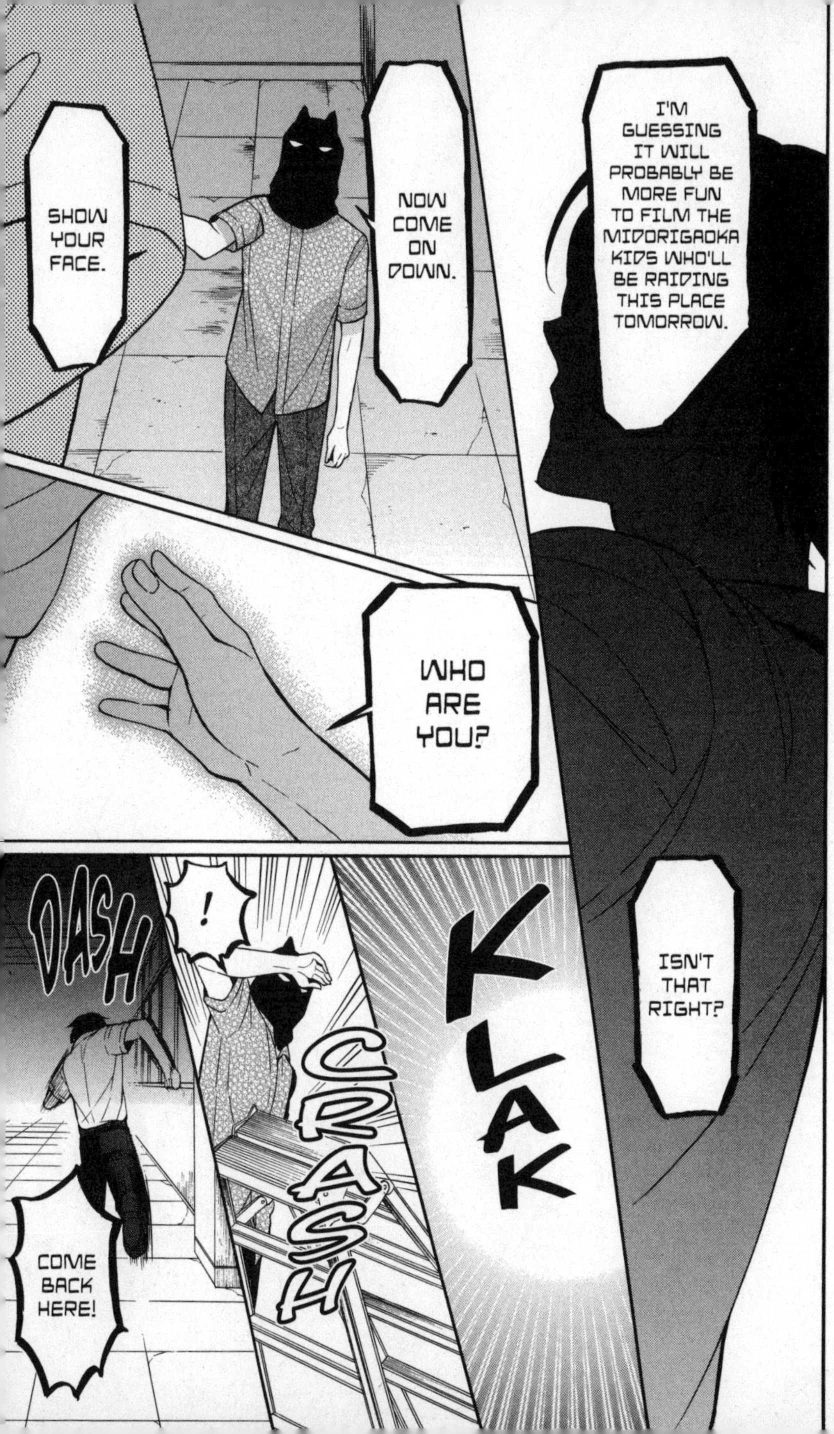
I'M GUESSING IT WILL PROBABLY BE MORE FUN TO FILM THE MIDORIGAOKA KIDS WHO'LL BE RAIDING THIS PLACE TOMORROW.
ISN'T THAT RIGHT?
NOW COME ON DOWN.
SHOW YOUR FACE.
WHO ARE YOU?
KLAK
CRASH
!
DASH
COME BACK HERE!

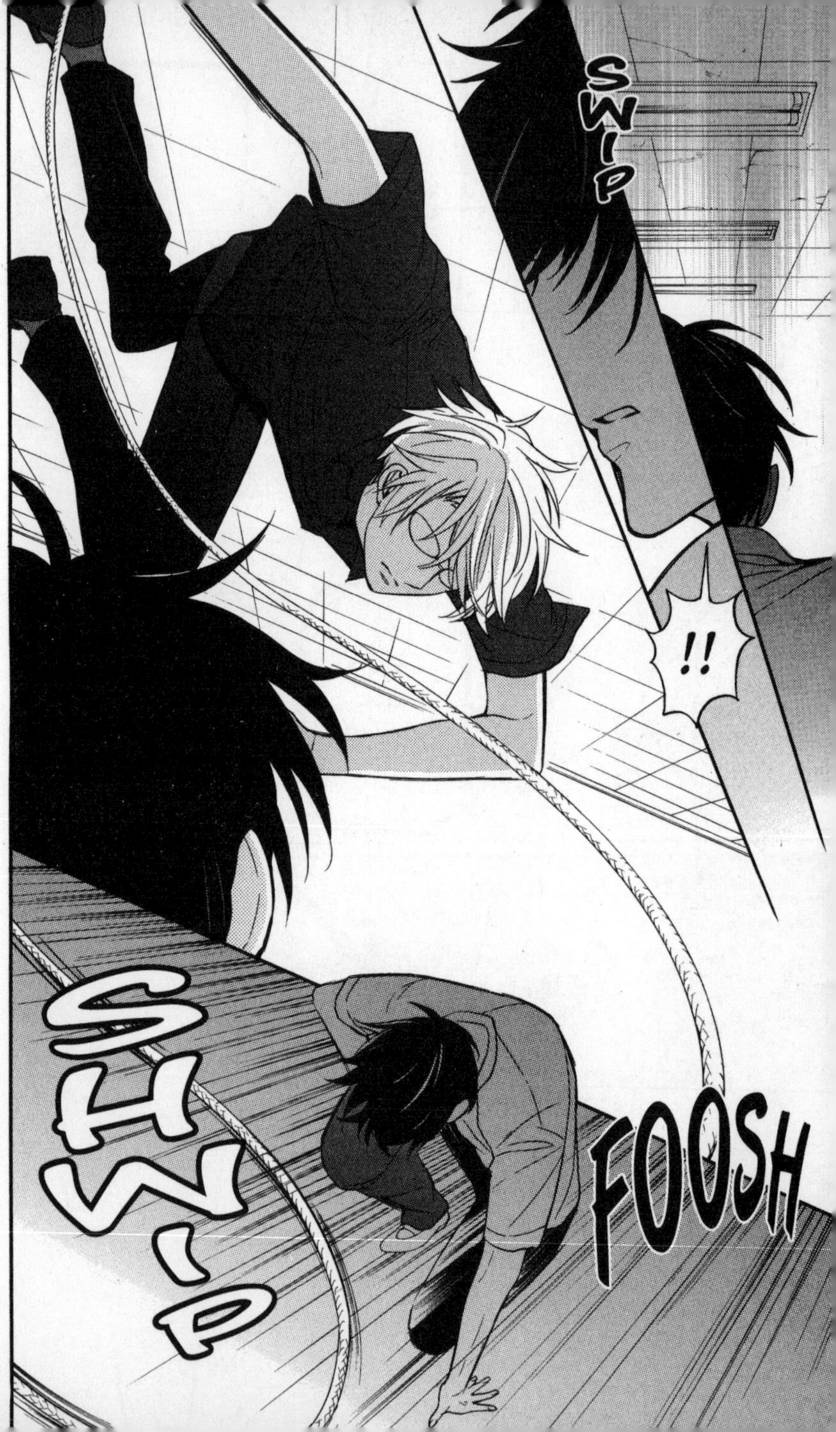
SWIP
!!
FOOSH
SHWIP

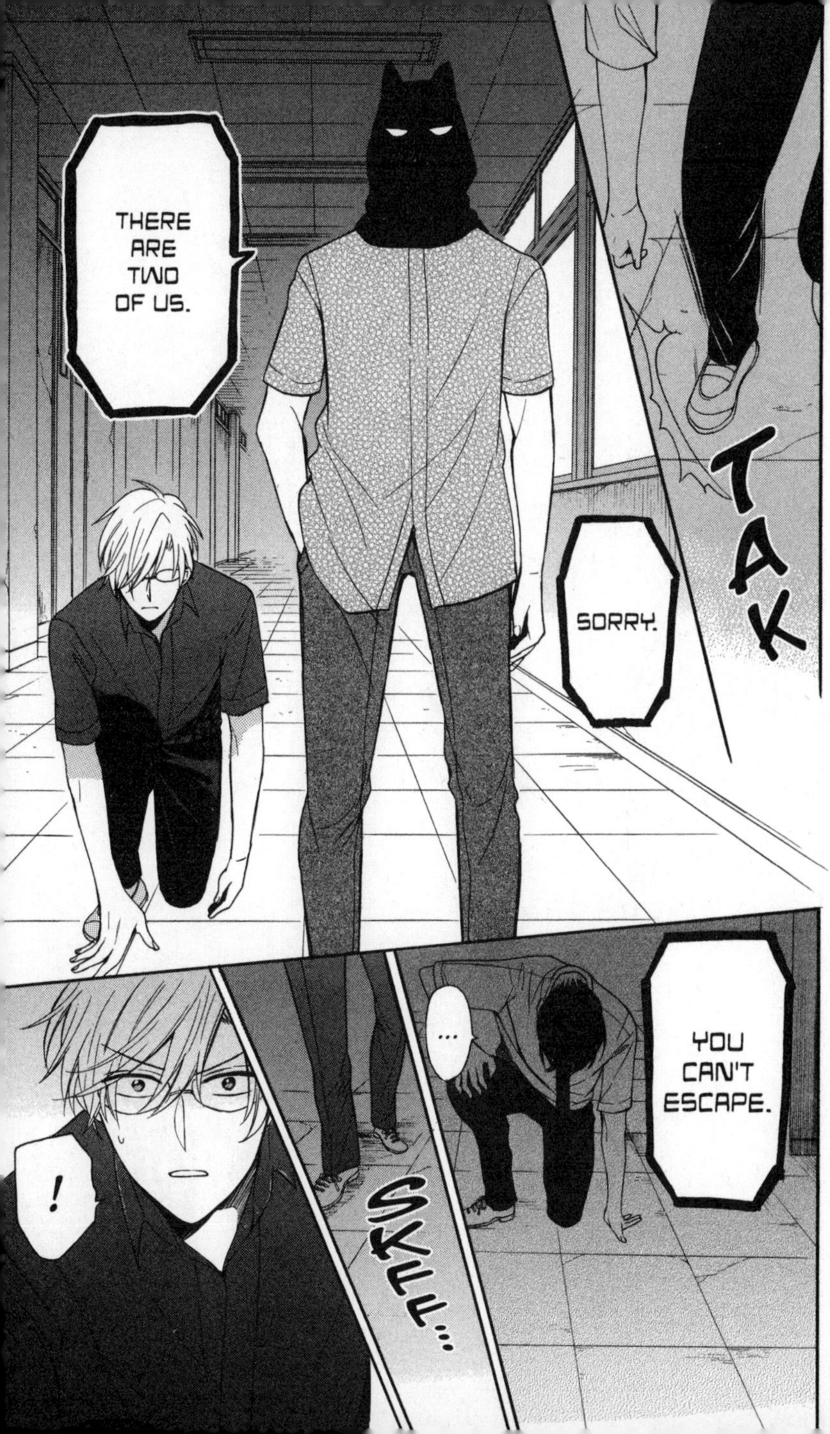
TAK
SORRY.
THERE ARE TWO OF US.
YOU CAN'T ESCAPE.
...
SKFF...
!

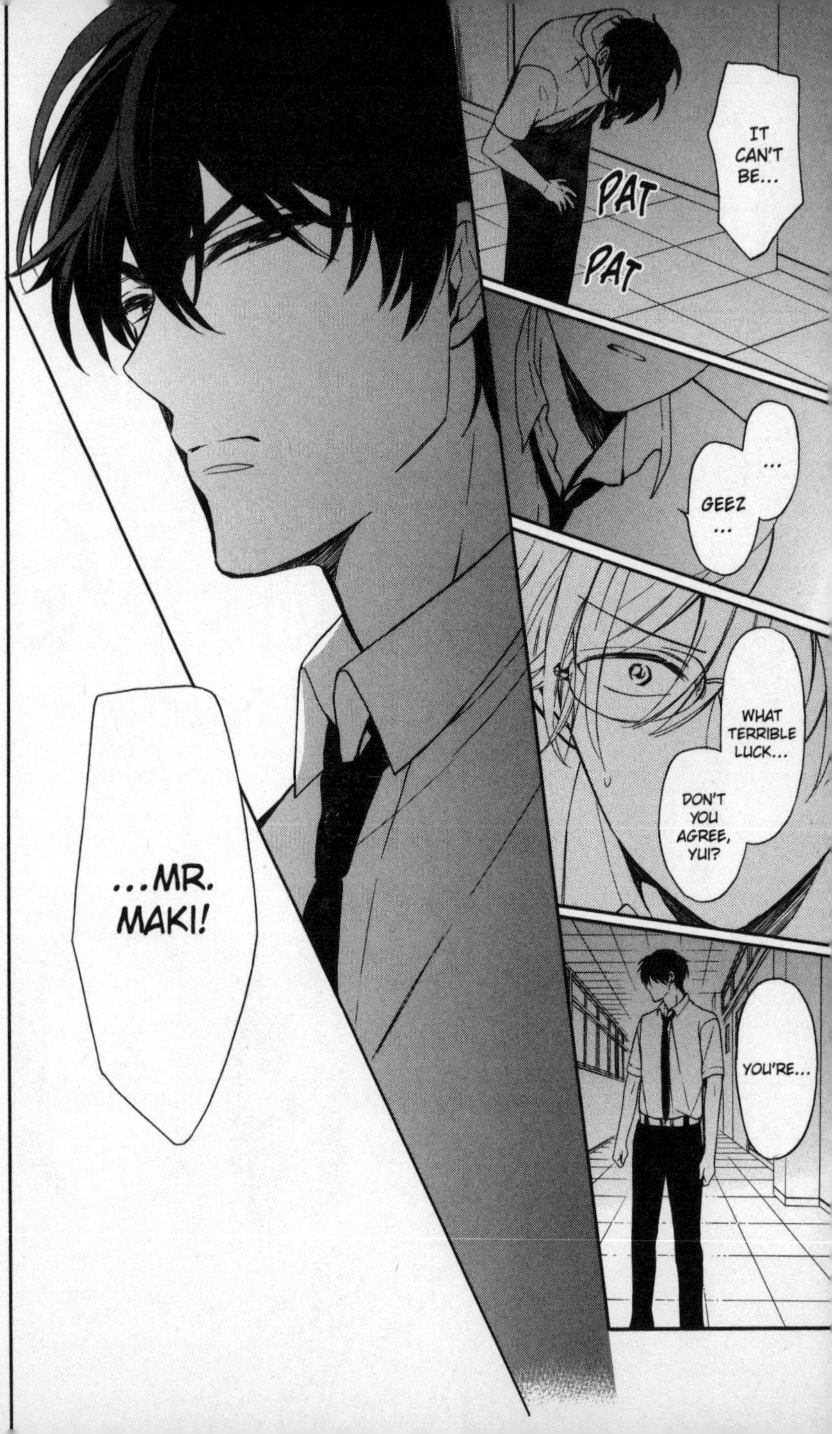
IT CAN'T BE...
PAT
PAT
... GEEZ ...
WHAT TERRIBLE LUCK...
DON'T YOU AGREE, YUI?
YOU'RE...
...MR. MAKI!

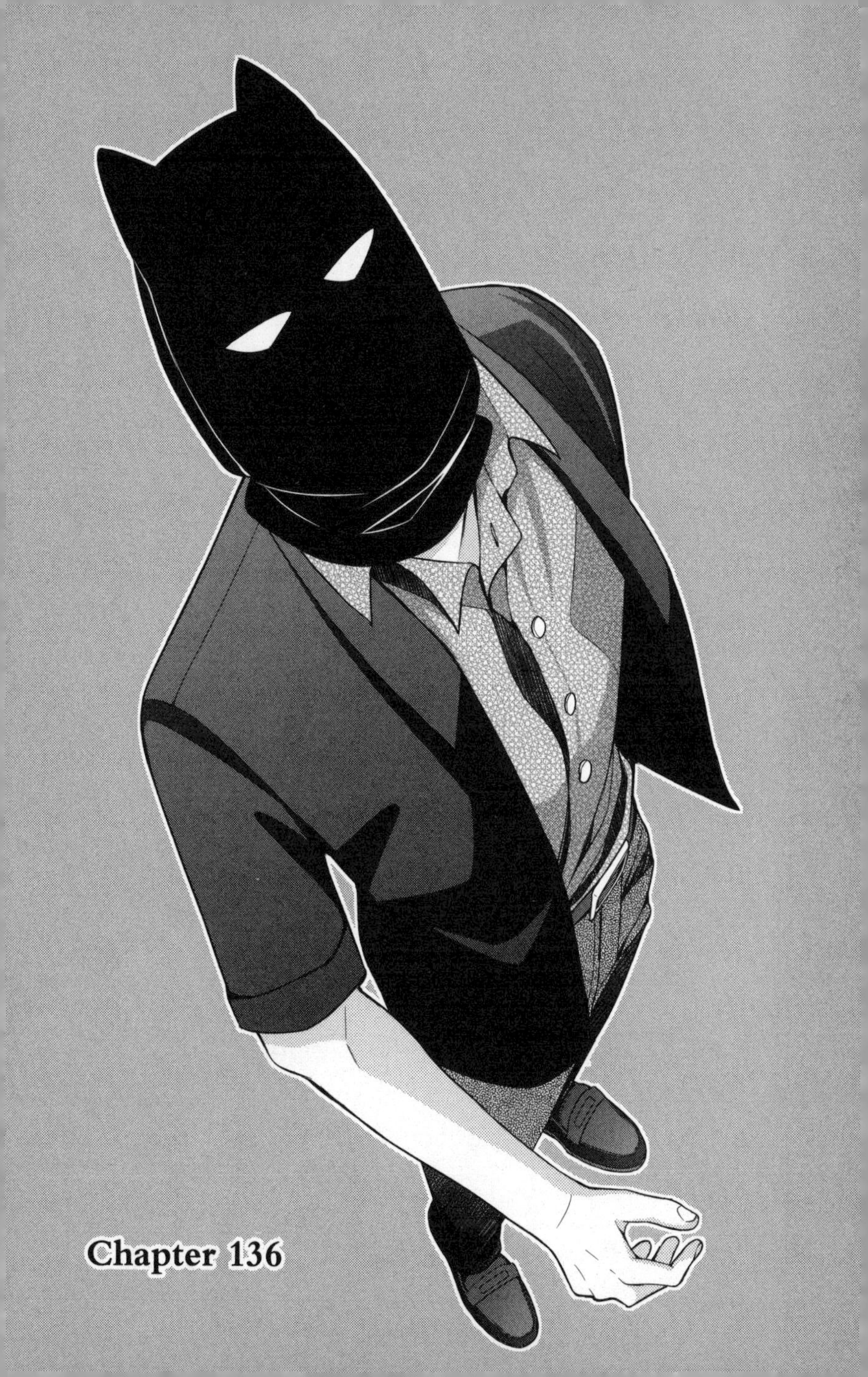

Chapter 136

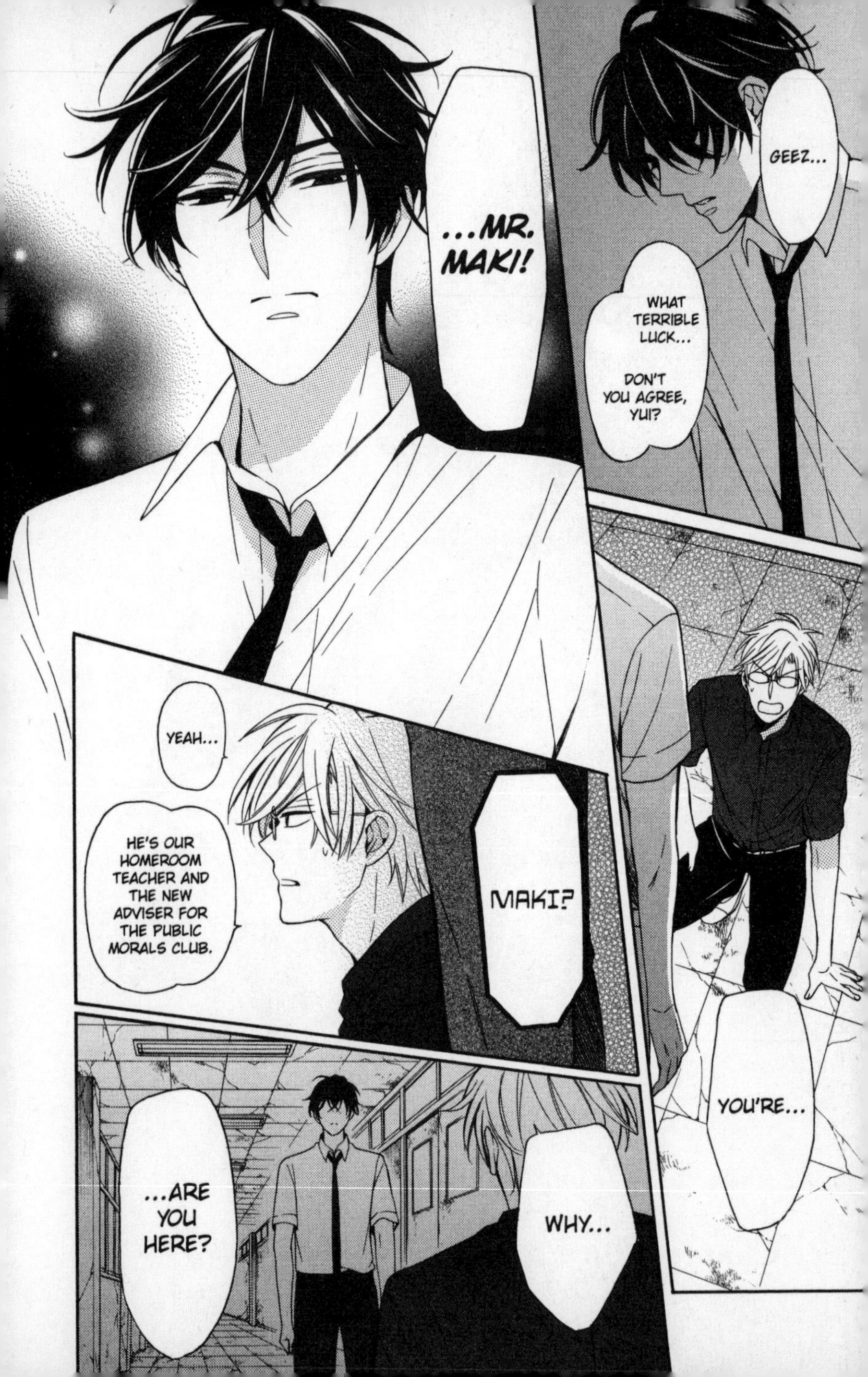
GEEZ...
WHAT TERRIBLE LUCK...
DON'T YOU AGREE, YUI?
...MR. MAKI!
MAKI?
YEAH...
HE'S OUR HOMEROOM TEACHER AND THE NEW ADVISER FOR THE PUBLIC MORALS CLUB.
YOU'RE...
WHY...
...ARE YOU HERE?

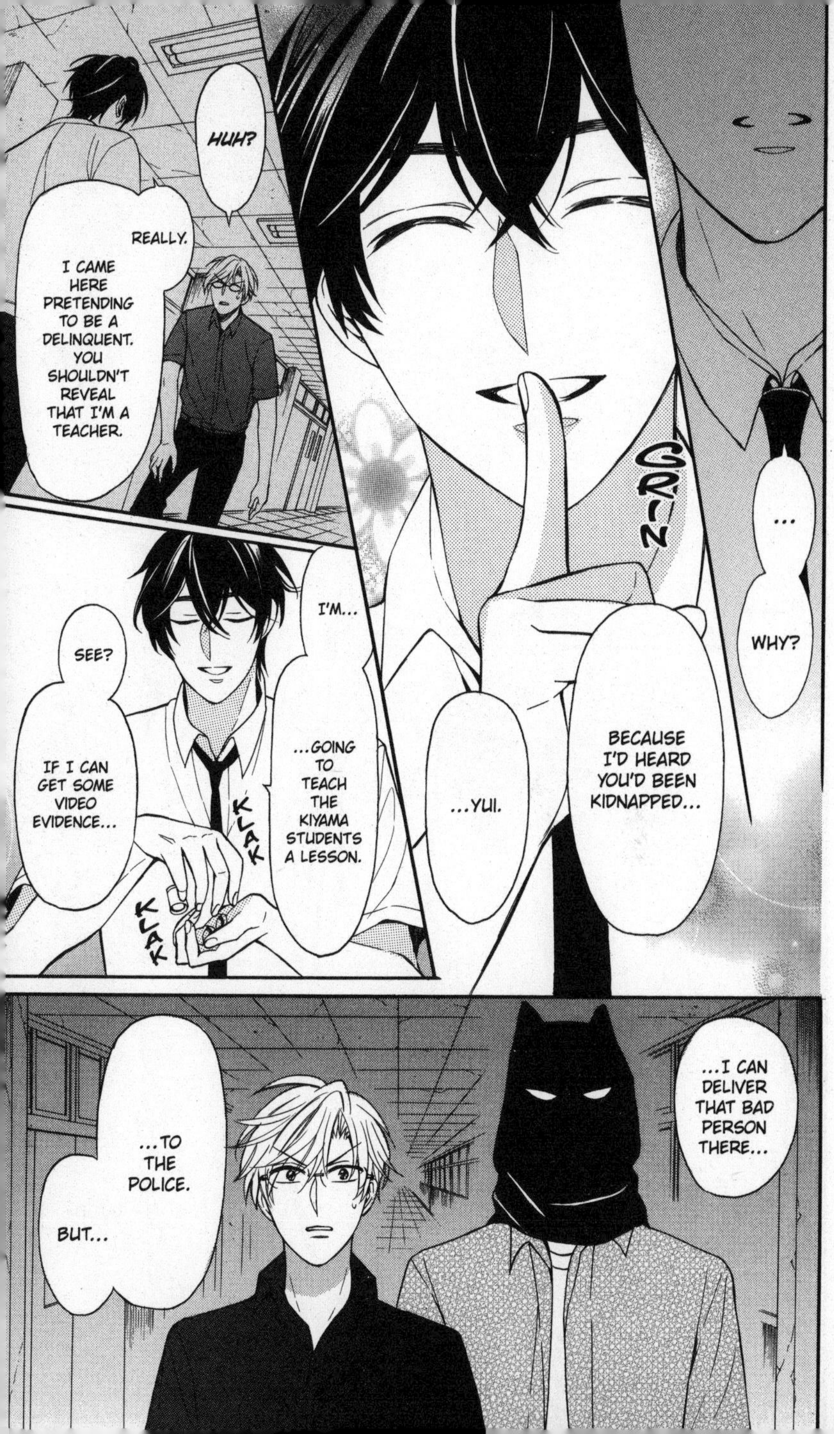
GRIN
...
WHY?
BECAUSE I'D HEARD YOU'D BEEN KIDNAPPED...
...YUI.
HUH?
REALLY.
I CAME HERE PRETENDING TO BE A DELINQUENT. YOU SHOULDN'T REVEAL THAT I'M A TEACHER.
I'M...
...GOING TO TEACH THE KIYAMA STUDENTS A LESSON.
SEE?
IF I CAN GET SOME VIDEO EVIDENCE...
KLAK
KLAK
...I CAN DELIVER THAT BAD PERSON THERE...
...TO THE POLICE.
BUT...

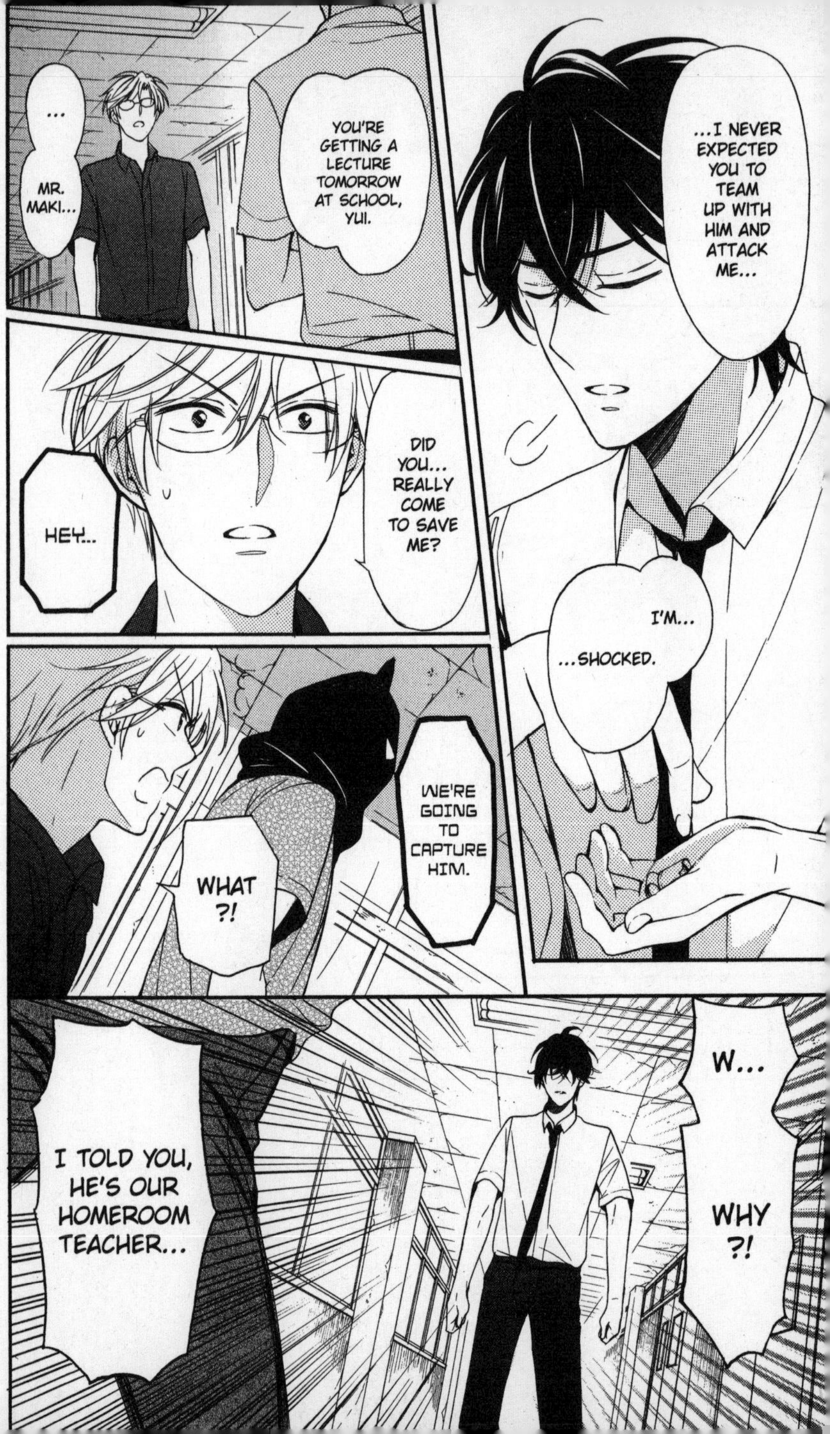
...I NEVER EXPECTED YOU TO TEAM UP WITH HIM AND ATTACK ME...
I'M...
...SHOCKED.
YOU'RE GETTING A LECTURE TOMORROW AT SCHOOL, YUI.
...
MR. MAKI...
DID YOU... REALLY COME TO SAVE ME?
HEY...
WE'RE GOING TO CAPTURE HIM.
WHAT ?!
W...
WHY ?!
I TOLD YOU, HE'S OUR HOMEROOM TEACHER...

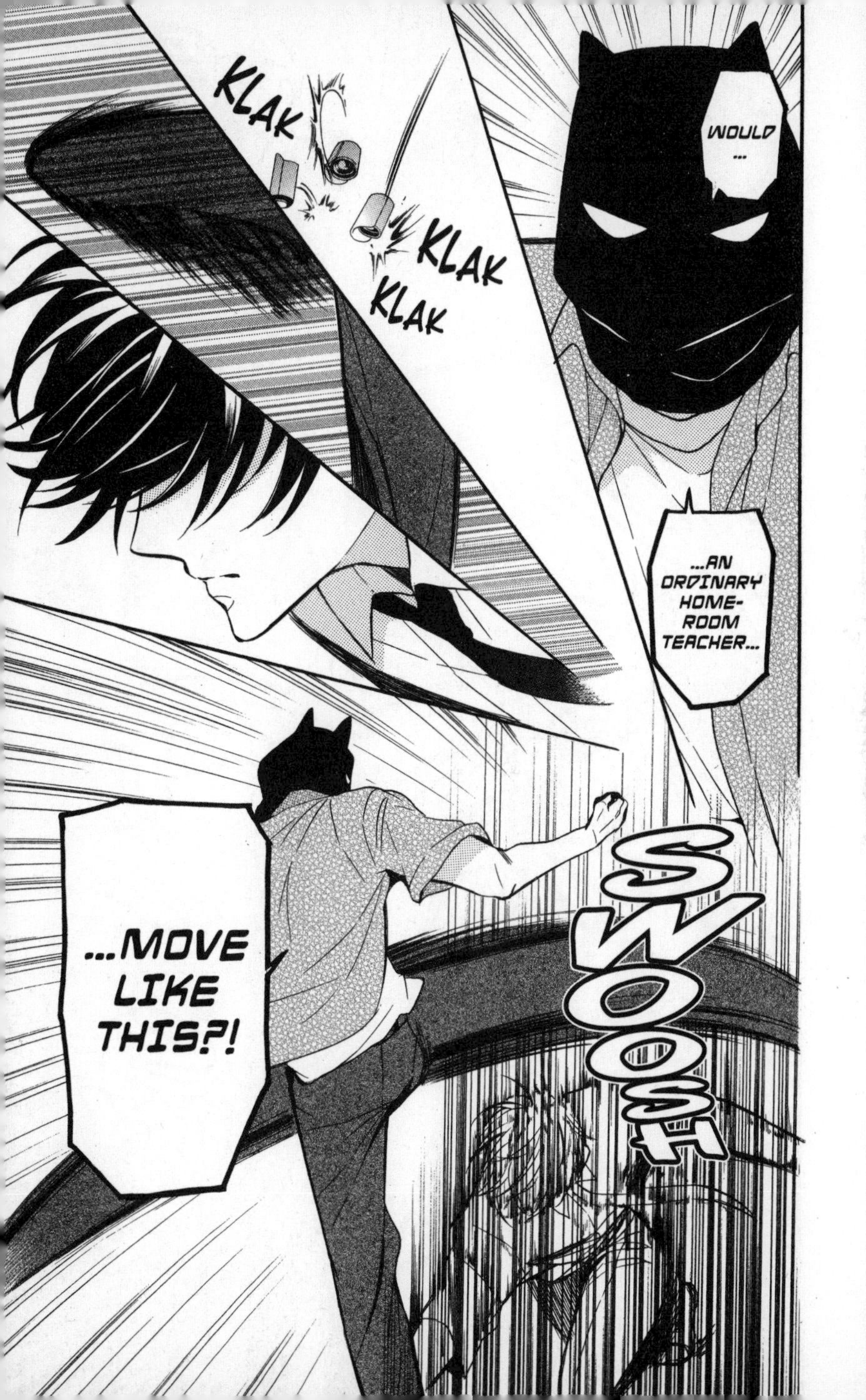
WOULD ...
KLAK
KLAK
KLAK
...AN ORDINARY HOME-ROOM TEACHER...
...MOVE LIKE THIS?!
SWOOSH

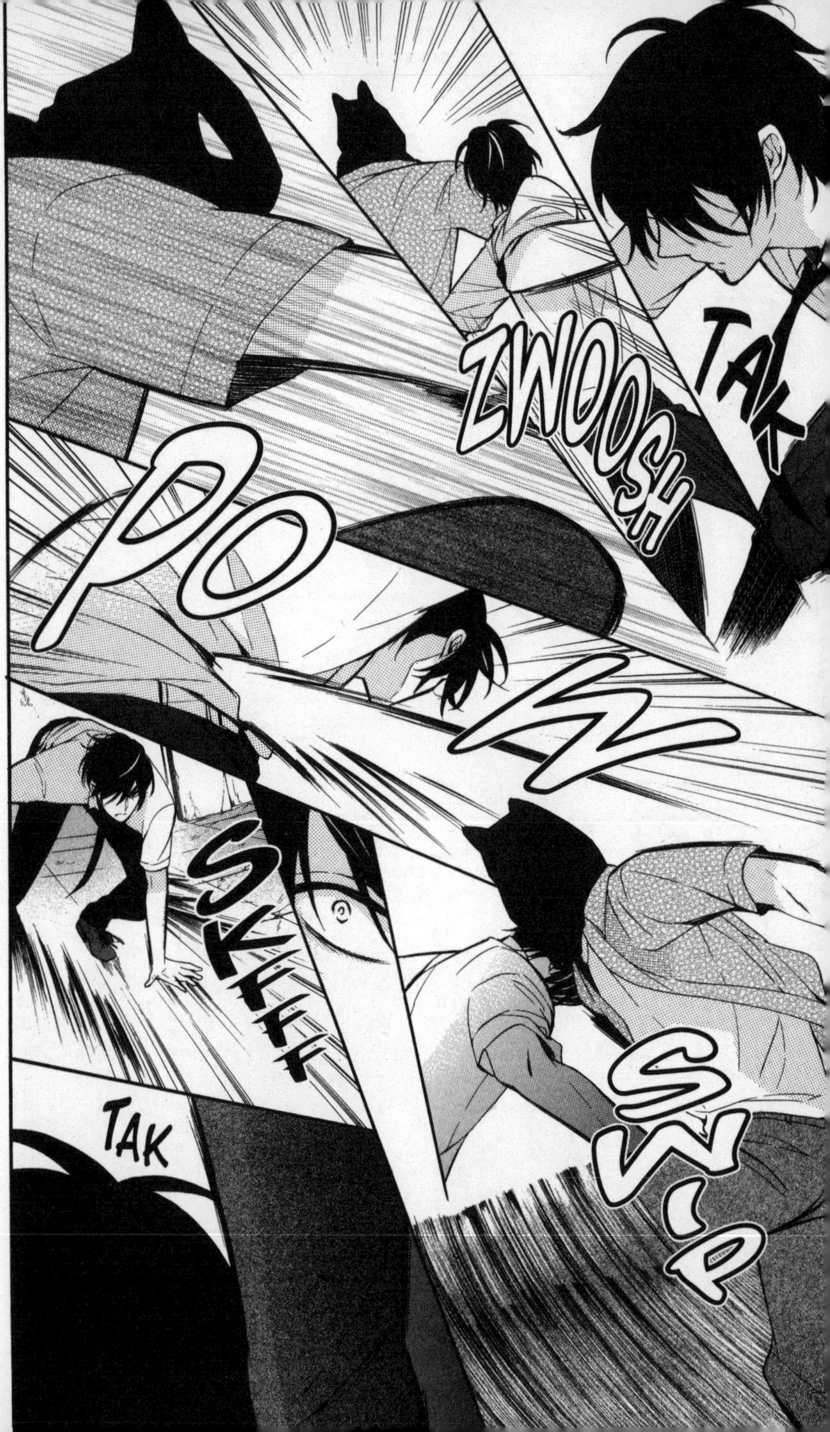
TAK
ZWOOSH
POW
SWIP
SKFFFF
TAK

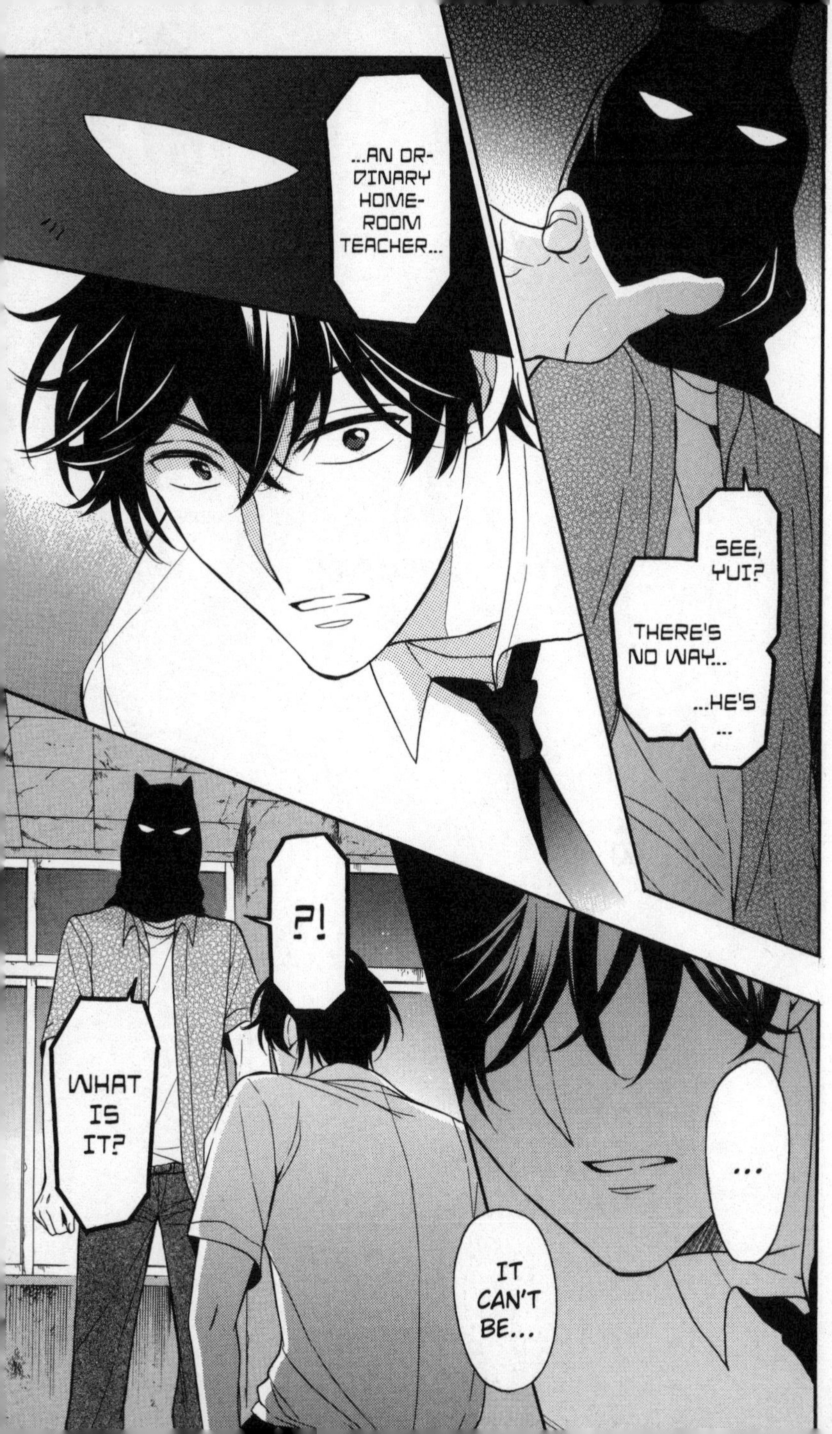
SEE, YUI?
THERE'S NO WAY...
...HE'S ...
...AN OR-DINARY HOME-ROOM TEACHER...
...
IT CAN'T BE...
?!
WHAT IS IT?

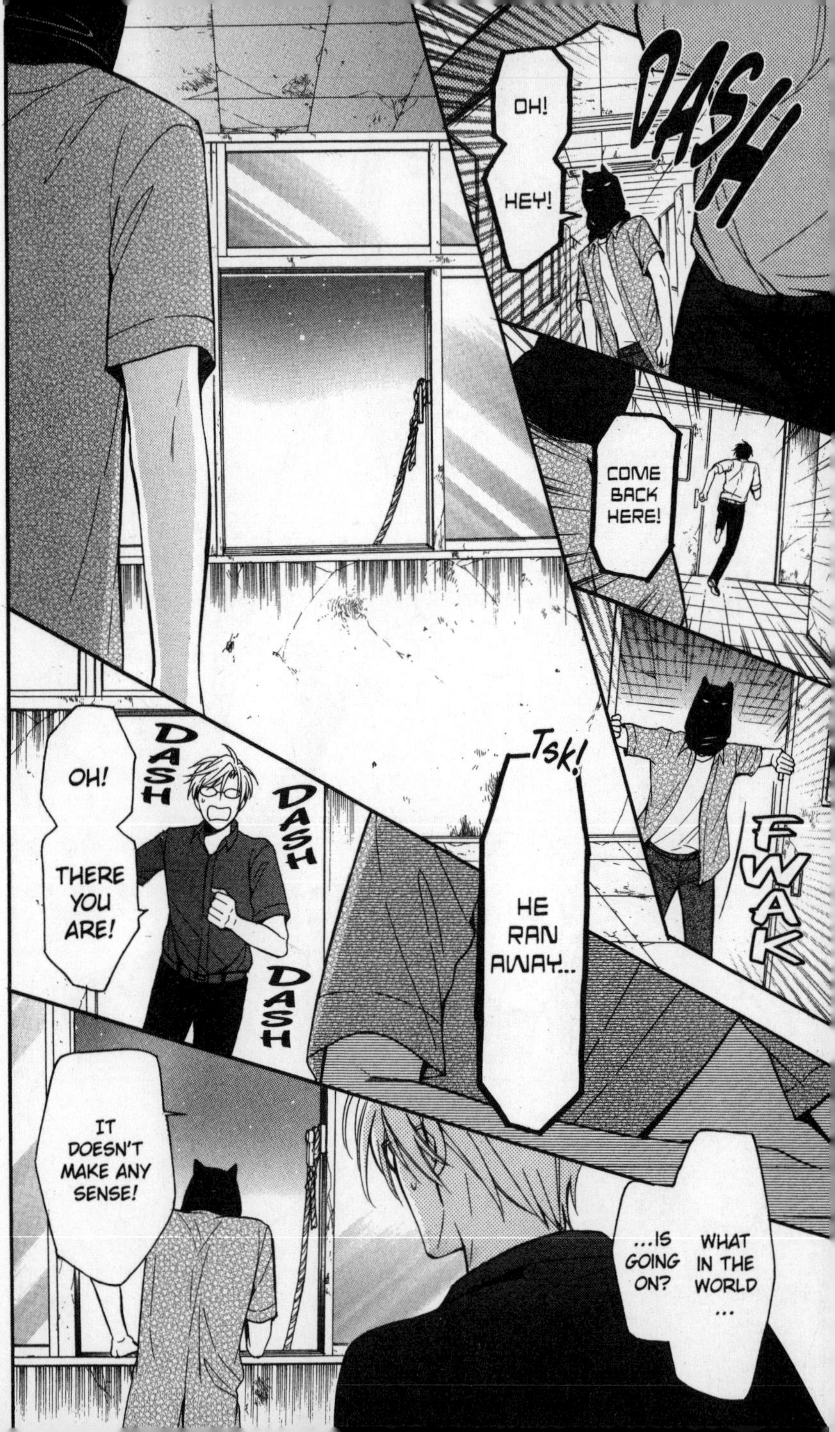
DASH
OH!
HEY!
COME BACK HERE!
FWAK
Tsk!
HE RAN AWAY...
OH!
THERE YOU ARE!
DASH
DASH
DASH
WHAT IN THE WORLD...
...IS GOING ON?
IT DOESN'T MAKE ANY SENSE!

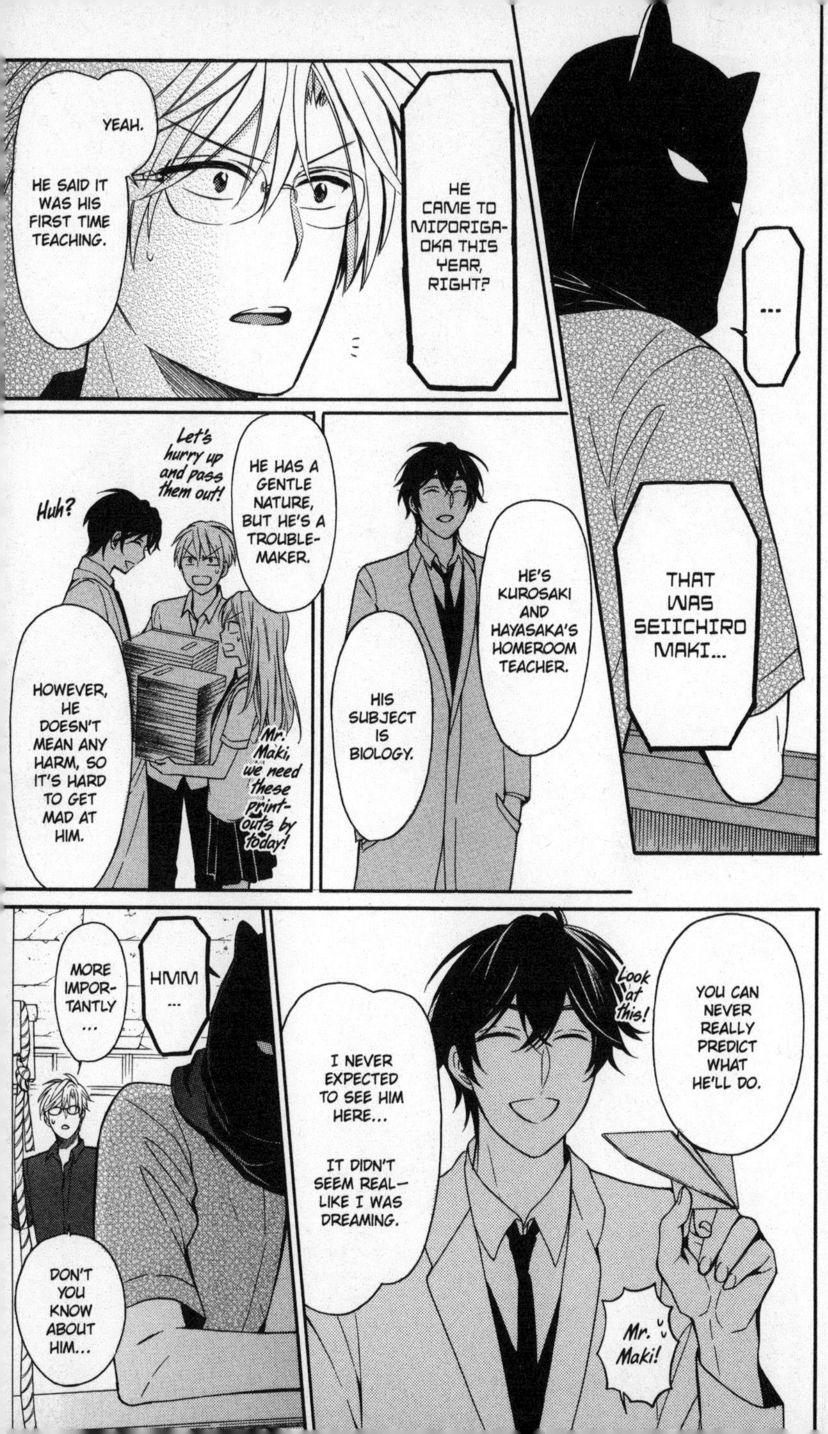
...
THAT WAS SEIICHIRO MAKI...
HE CAME TO MIDORIGAOKA THIS YEAR, RIGHT?
YEAH.
HE SAID IT WAS HIS FIRST TIME TEACHING.
HE'S KUROSAKI AND HAYASAKA'S HOMEROOM TEACHER.
HIS SUBJECT IS BIOLOGY.
HE HAS A GENTLE NATURE, BUT HE'S A TROUBLEMAKER.
Let's hurry up and pass them out!
Huh?
Mr. Maki, we need these printouts by today!
HOWEVER, HE DOESN'T MEAN ANY HARM, SO IT'S HARD TO GET MAD AT HIM.
YOU CAN NEVER REALLY PREDICT WHAT HE'LL DO.
Look at this!
I NEVER EXPECTED TO SEE HIM HERE...
IT DIDN'T SEEM REAL-LIKE I WAS DREAMING.
Mr. Maki!
HMM...
MORE IMPORTANTLY...
DON'T YOU KNOW ABOUT HIM...

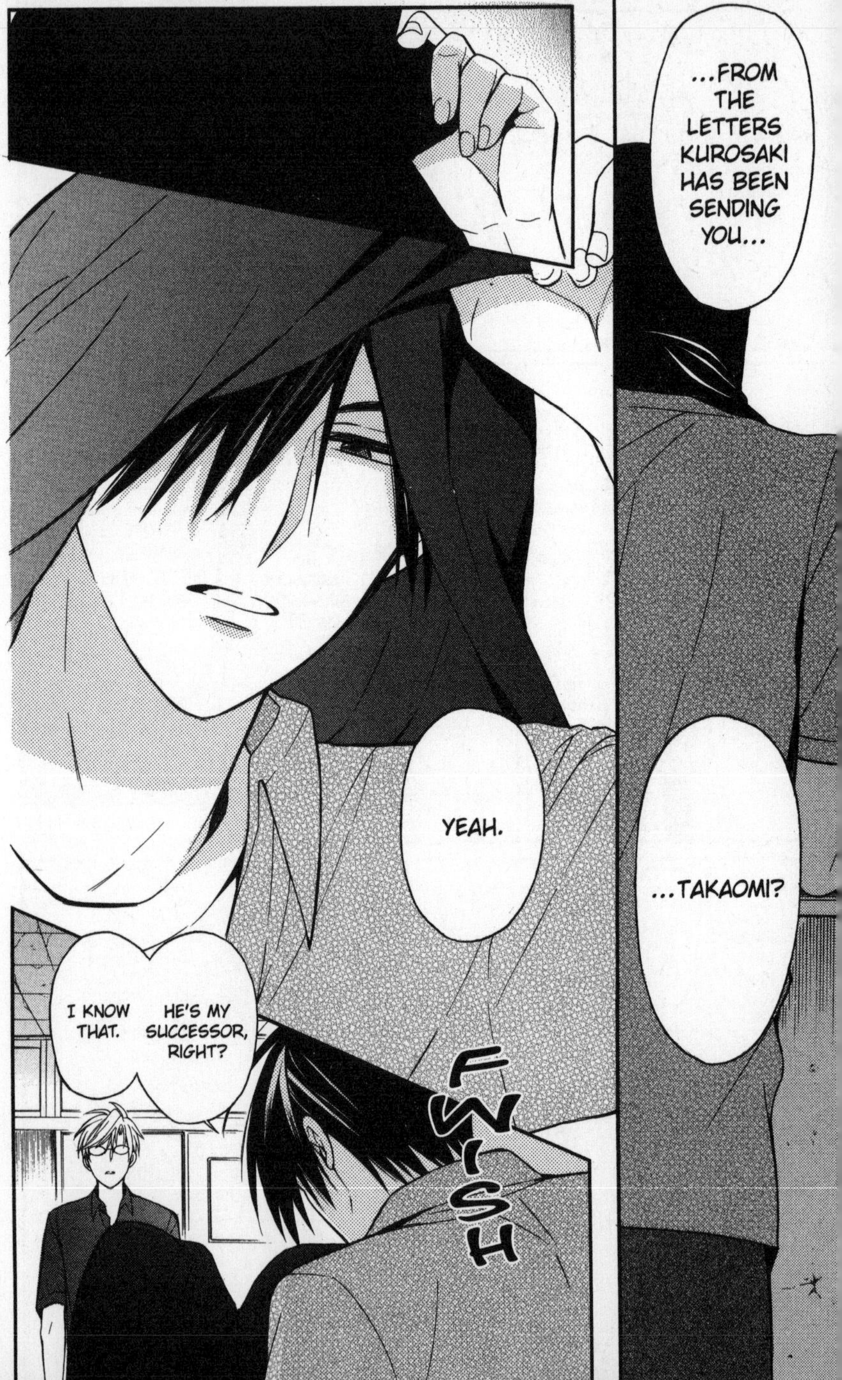
...FROM THE LETTERS KUROSAKI HAS BEEN SENDING YOU...
...TAKAOMI?
YEAH.
I KNOW THAT. HE'S MY SUCCESSOR, RIGHT?
FWISH

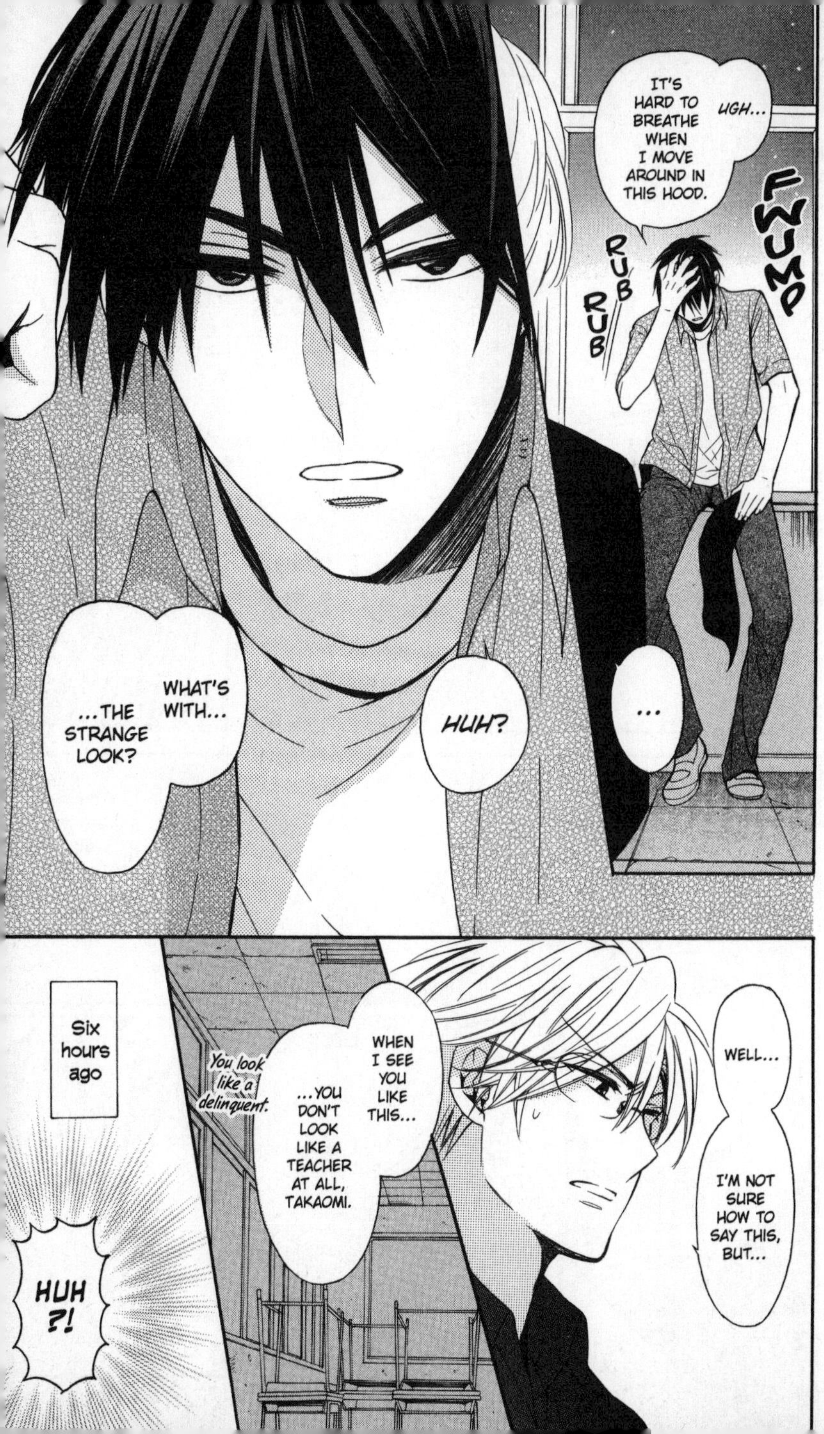
UGH...
IT'S HARD TO BREATHE WHEN I MOVE AROUND IN THIS HOOD.
FWUMP
RUB RUB
...
HUH?
WHAT'S WITH...
...THE STRANGE LOOK?
WELL...
I'M NOT SURE HOW TO SAY THIS, BUT...
WHEN I SEE YOU LIKE THIS...
...YOU DON'T LOOK LIKE A TEACHER AT ALL, TAKAOMI.
You look like a delinquent.
Six hours ago
HUH?!

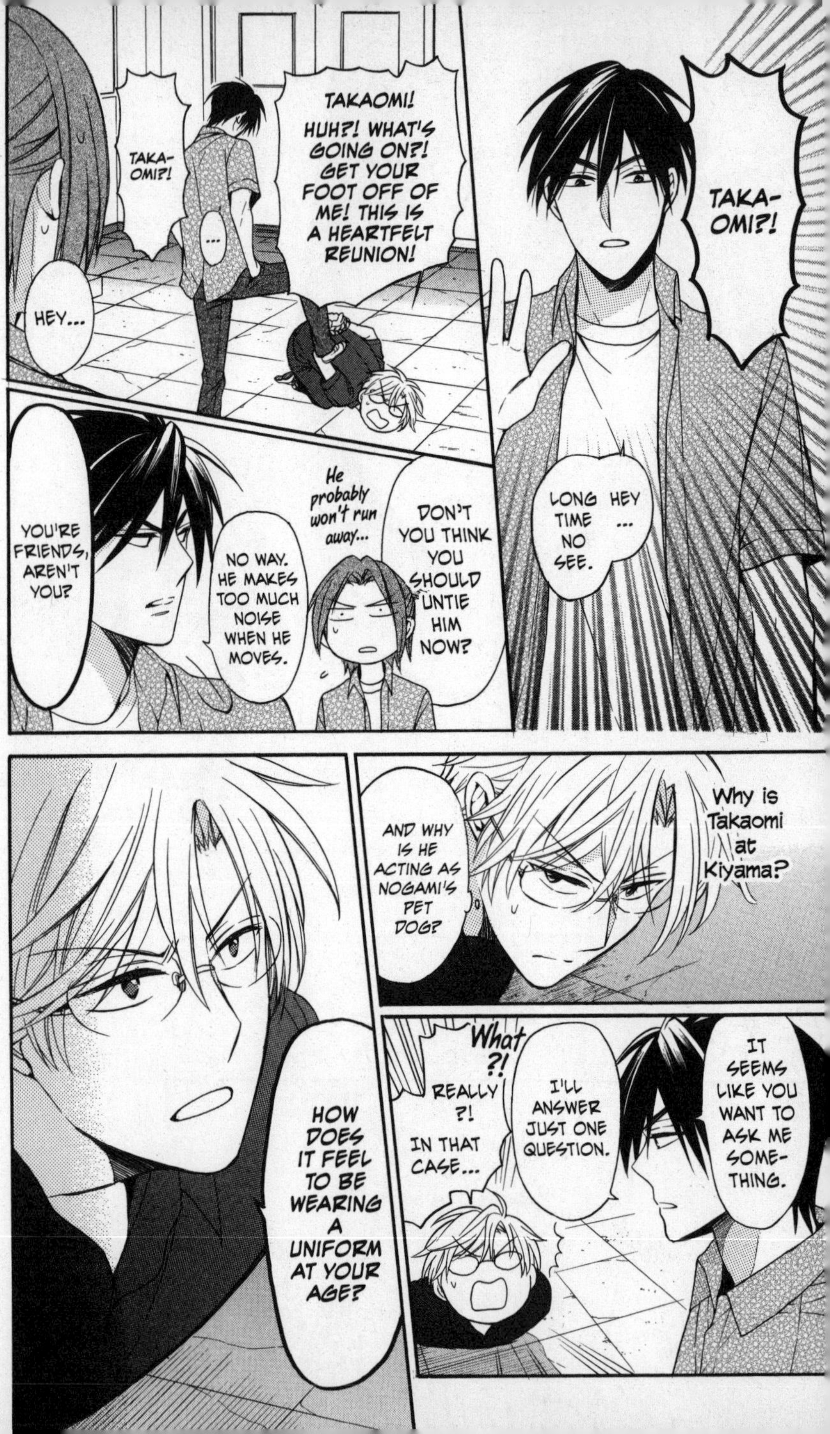
TAKA-OMI?!
HEY ... LONG TIME NO SEE.
TAKAOMI!
HUH?! WHAT'S GOING ON?! GET YOUR FOOT OFF OF ME! THIS IS A HEARTFELT REUNION!
TAKA-OMI?!
...
HEY...
DON'T YOU THINK YOU SHOULD UNTIE HIM NOW?
He probably won't run away...
NO WAY. HE MAKES TOO MUCH NOISE WHEN HE MOVES.
YOU'RE FRIENDS, AREN'T YOU?
Why is Takaomi at Kiyama?
AND WHY IS HE ACTING AS NOGAMI'S PET DOG?
IT SEEMS LIKE YOU WANT TO ASK ME SOME-THING.
I'LL ANSWER JUST ONE QUESTION.
What?!
REALLY?!
IN THAT CASE...
HOW DOES IT FEEL TO BE WEARING A UNIFORM AT YOUR AGE?

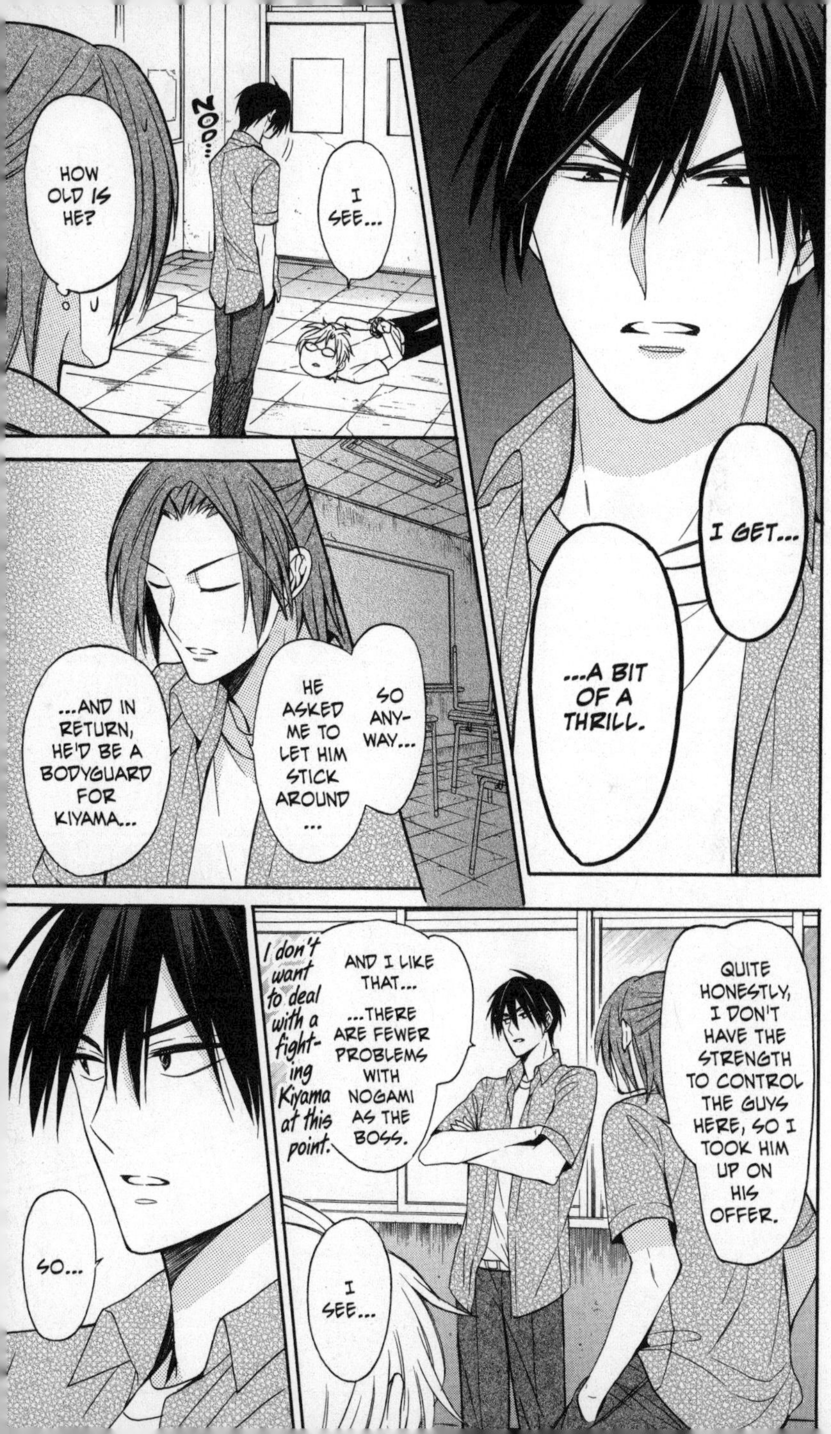
I GET...
...A BIT OF A THRILL.
I SEE...
NOD...
HOW OLD IS HE?
SO ANYWAY...
HE ASKED ME TO LET HIM STICK AROUND...
...AND IN RETURN, HE'D BE A BODYGUARD FOR KIYAMA...
QUITE HONESTLY, I DON'T HAVE THE STRENGTH TO CONTROL THE GUYS HERE, SO I TOOK HIM UP ON HIS OFFER.
AND I LIKE THAT...
...THERE ARE FEWER PROBLEMS WITH NOGAMI AS THE BOSS.
I don't want to deal with a fight-ing Kiyama at this point.
I SEE...
SO...

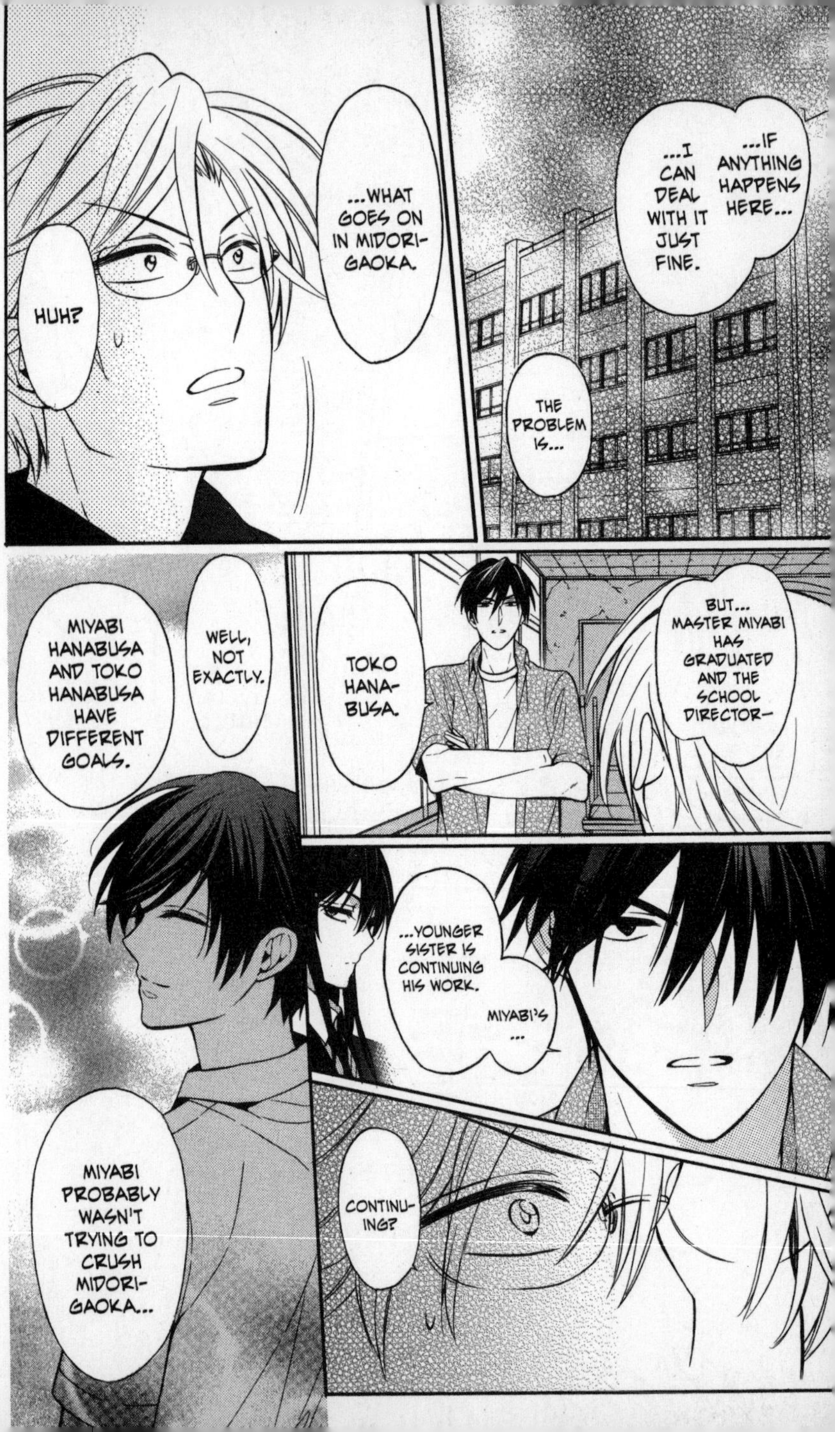
...IF ANYTHING HAPPENS HERE...
...I CAN DEAL WITH IT JUST FINE.
THE PROBLEM IS...
...WHAT GOES ON IN MIDORI-GAOKA.
HUH?
BUT... MASTER MIYABI HAS GRADUATED AND THE SCHOOL DIRECTOR—
TOKO HANA-BUSA.
MIYABI'S ...
...YOUNGER SISTER IS CONTINUING HIS WORK.
CONTINU-ING?
WELL, NOT EXACTLY.
MIYABI HANABUSA AND TOKO HANABUSA HAVE DIFFERENT GOALS.
MIYABI PROBABLY WASN'T TRYING TO CRUSH MIDORI-GAOKA...

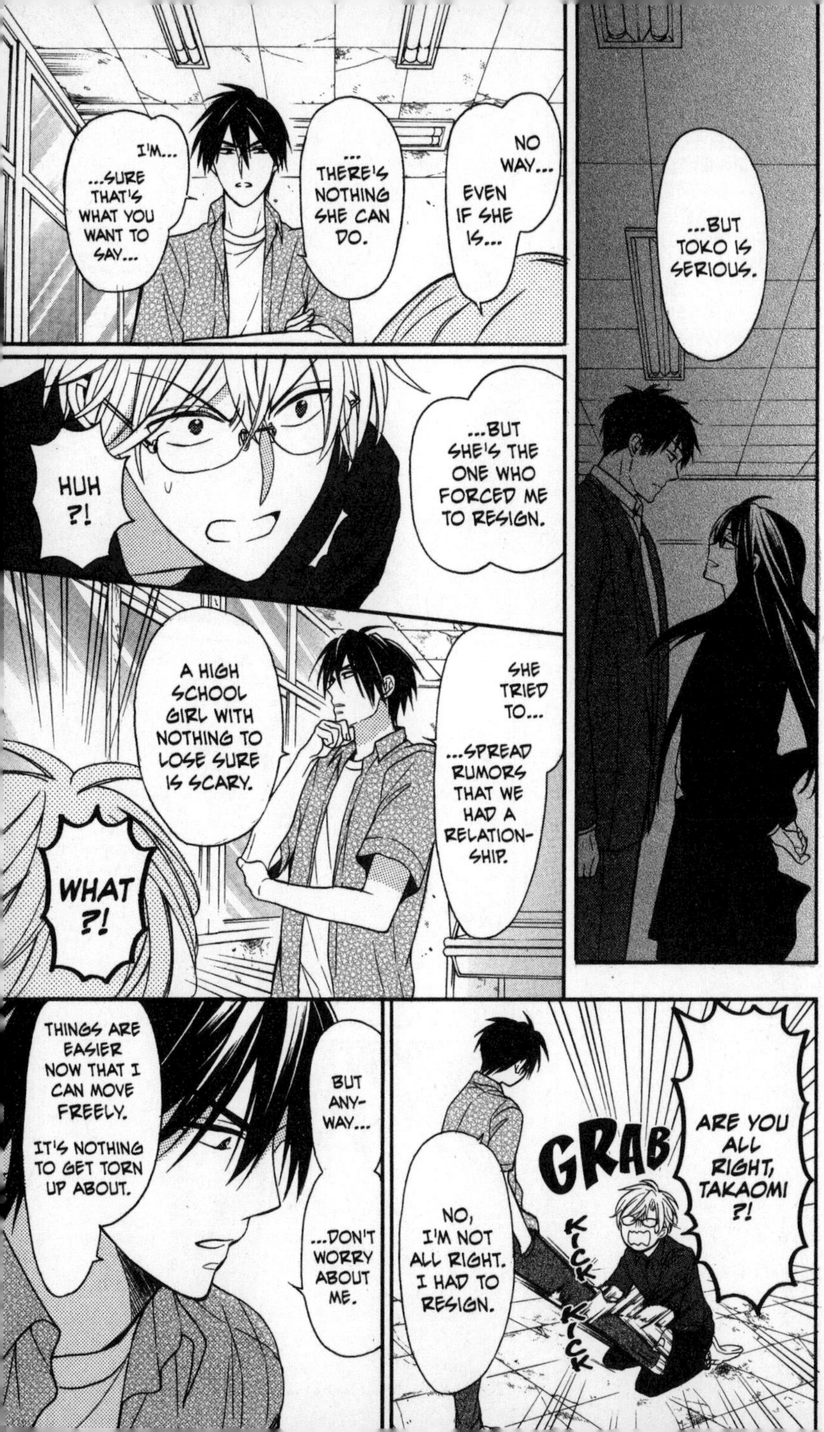
...BUT TOKO IS SERIOUS.
NO WAY... EVEN IF SHE IS...
... THERE'S NOTHING SHE CAN DO.
I'M... ...SURE THAT'S WHAT YOU WANT TO SAY...
...BUT SHE'S THE ONE WHO FORCED ME TO RESIGN.
HUH ?!
SHE TRIED TO... ...SPREAD RUMORS THAT WE HAD A RELATION-SHIP.
A HIGH SCHOOL GIRL WITH NOTHING TO LOSE SURE IS SCARY.
WHAT ?!
ARE YOU ALL RIGHT, TAKAOMI ?!
GRAB
KICK KICK
NO, I'M NOT ALL RIGHT. I HAD TO RESIGN.
BUT ANYWAY... ...DON'T WORRY ABOUT ME.
THINGS ARE EASIER NOW THAT I CAN MOVE FREELY.
IT'S NOTHING TO GET TORN UP ABOUT.

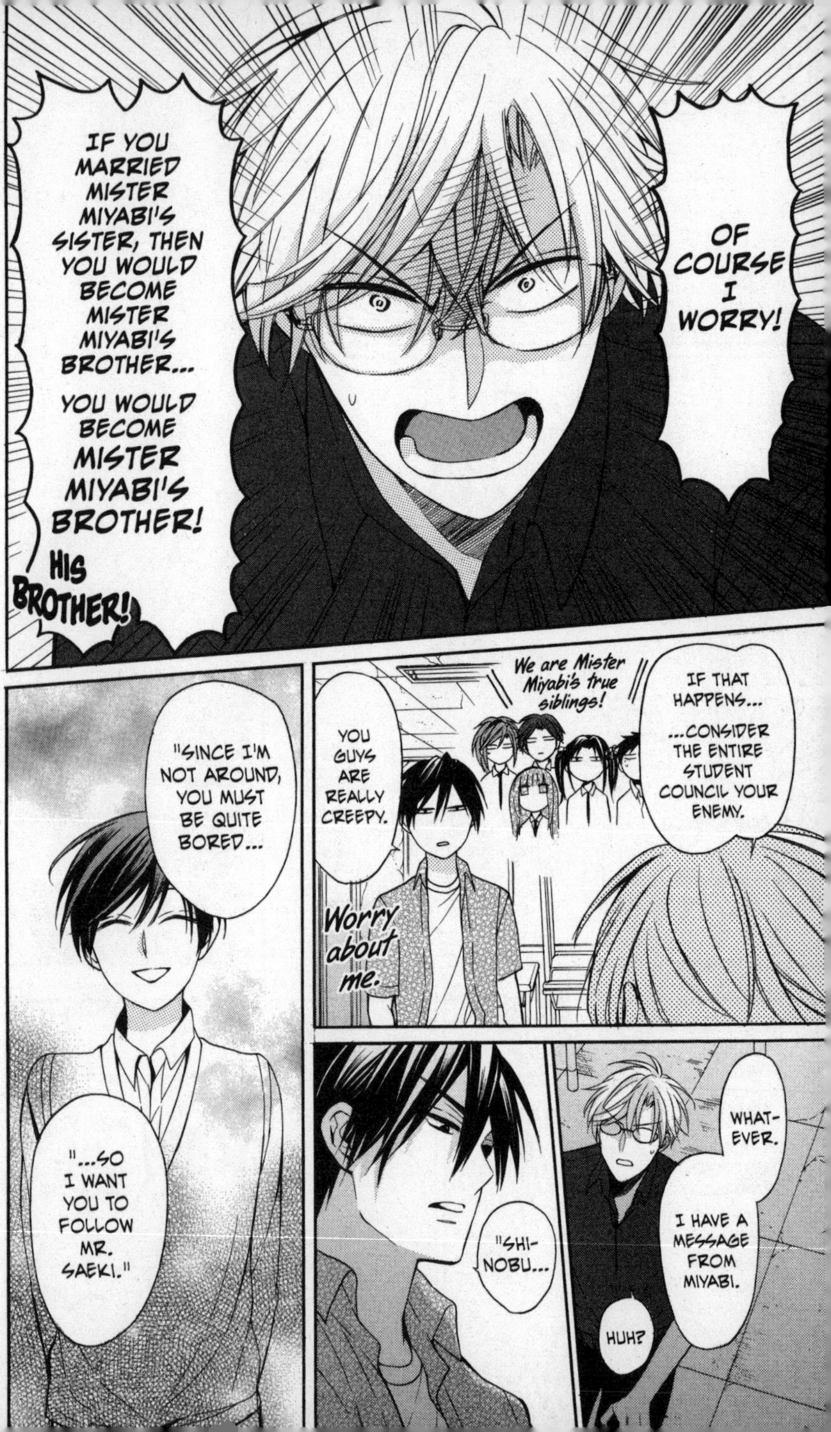
OF COURSE I WORRY!
IF YOU MARRIED MISTER MIYABI'S SISTER, THEN YOU WOULD BECOME MISTER MIYABI'S BROTHER...
YOU WOULD BECOME MISTER MIYABI'S BROTHER!
HIS BROTHER!
IF THAT HAPPENS...
...CONSIDER THE ENTIRE STUDENT COUNCIL YOUR ENEMY.
We are Mister Miyabi's true siblings!
YOU GUYS ARE REALLY CREEPY.
Worry about me.
WHAT-EVER.
I HAVE A MESSAGE FROM MIYABI.
HUH?
"SHI-NOBU...
"SINCE I'M NOT AROUND, YOU MUST BE QUITE BORED...
"...SO I WANT YOU TO FOLLOW MR. SAEKI."

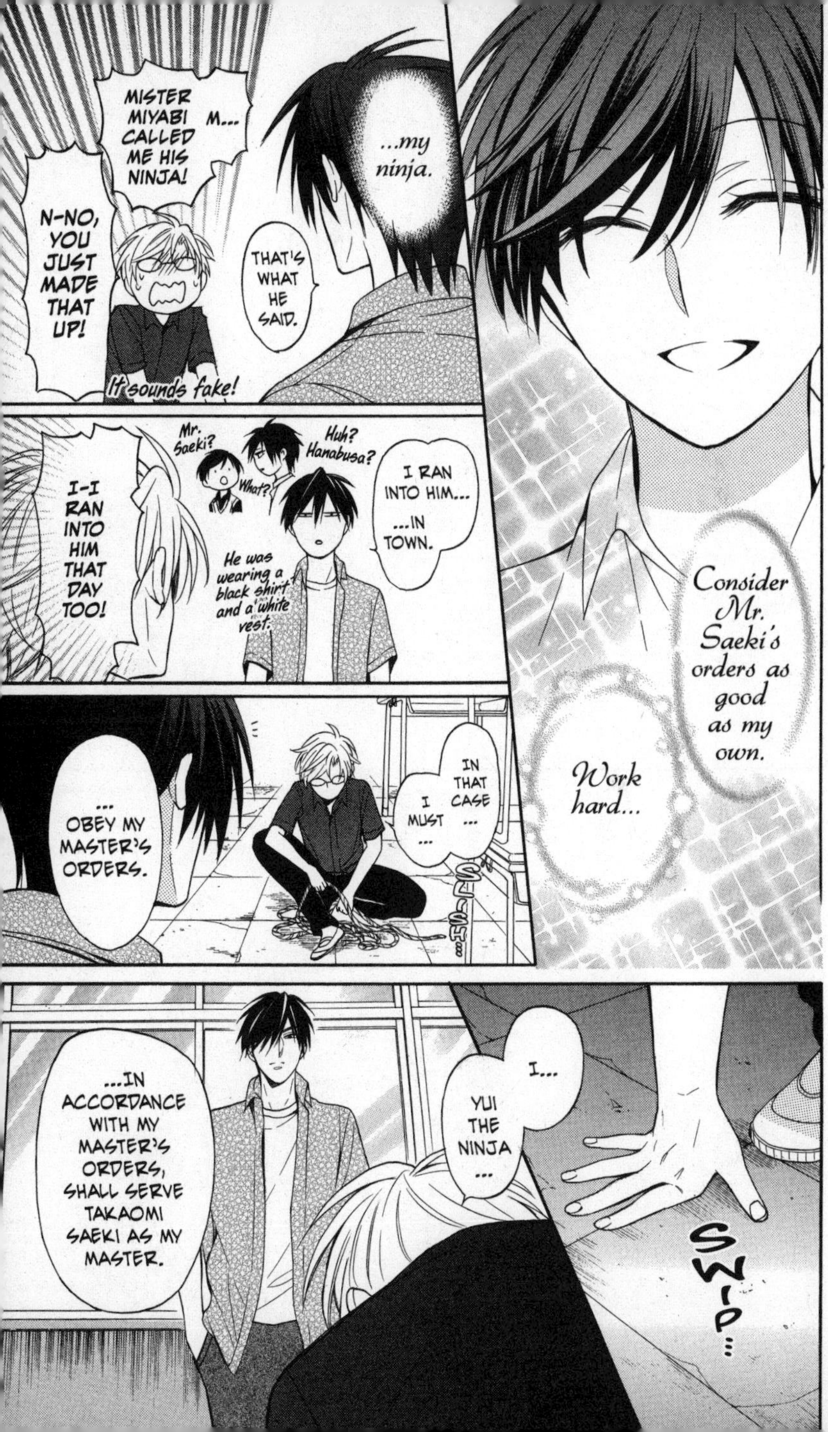
Consider Mr. Saeki's orders as good as my own.
Work hard...
...my ninja.
M...
MISTER MIYABI CALLED ME HIS NINJA!
THAT'S WHAT HE SAID.
N-NO, YOU JUST MADE THAT UP!
It sounds fake!
Huh? Hanabusa?
Mr. Saeki?
What?
I RAN INTO HIM... ...IN TOWN.
I-I RAN INTO HIM THAT DAY TOO!
He was wearing a black shirt and a white vest.
IN THAT CASE...
I MUST...
SLASH...
...OBEY MY MASTER'S ORDERS.
I...
YUI THE NINJA...
SWIP...
...IN ACCORDANCE WITH MY MASTER'S ORDERS, SHALL SERVE TAKAOMI SAEKI AS MY MASTER.

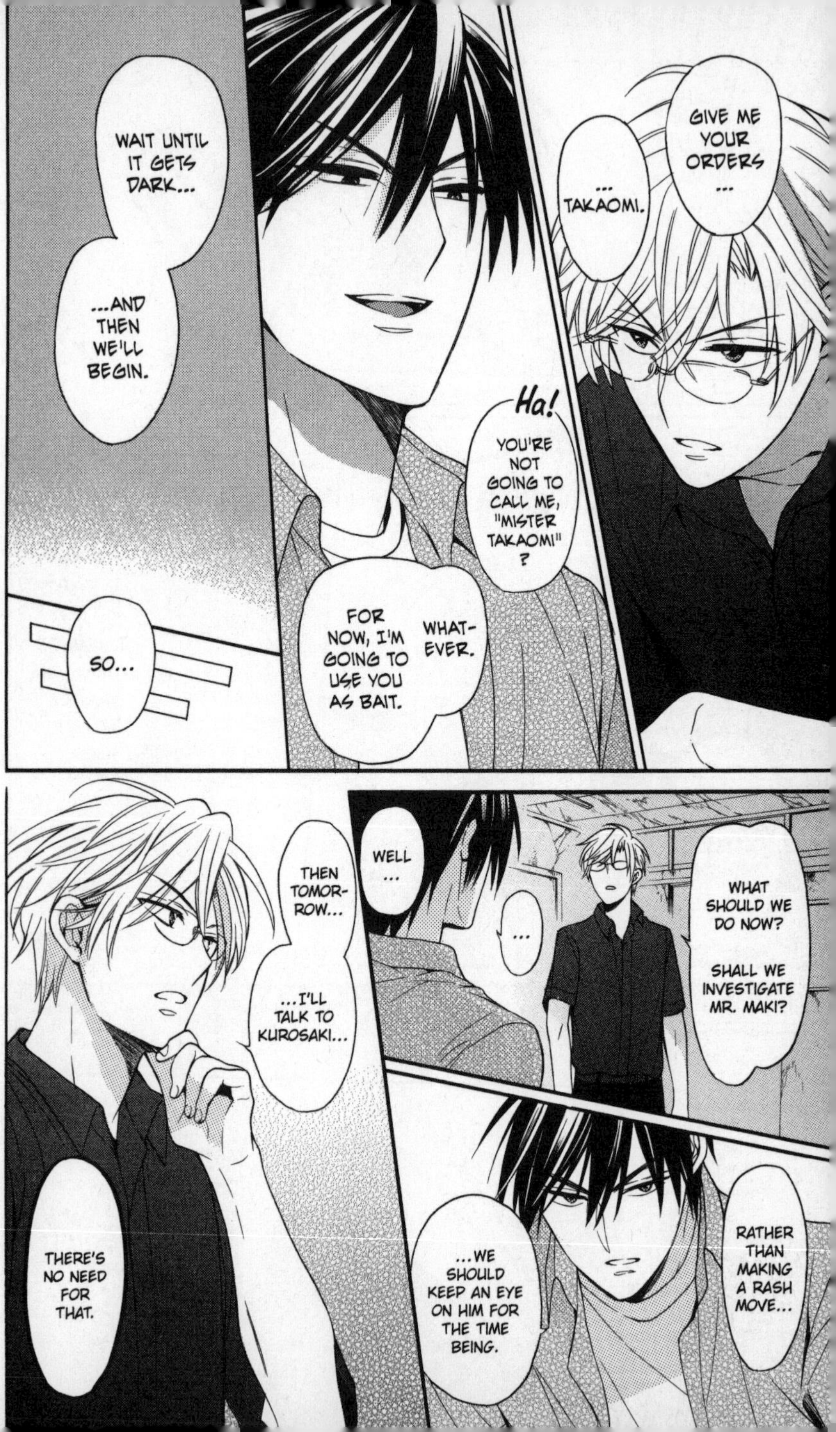
GIVE ME YOUR ORDERS ...
... TAKAOMI.
Ha!
YOU'RE NOT GOING TO CALL ME, "MISTER TAKAOMI"?
WHAT-EVER.
FOR NOW, I'M GOING TO USE YOU AS BAIT.
WAIT UNTIL IT GETS DARK...
...AND THEN WE'LL BEGIN.
SO...
WHAT SHOULD WE DO NOW?
SHALL WE INVESTIGATE MR. MAKI?
...
WELL ...
RATHER THAN MAKING A RASH MOVE...
...WE SHOULD KEEP AN EYE ON HIM FOR THE TIME BEING.
THEN TOMORROW...
...I'LL TALK TO KUROSAKI...
THERE'S NO NEED FOR THAT.

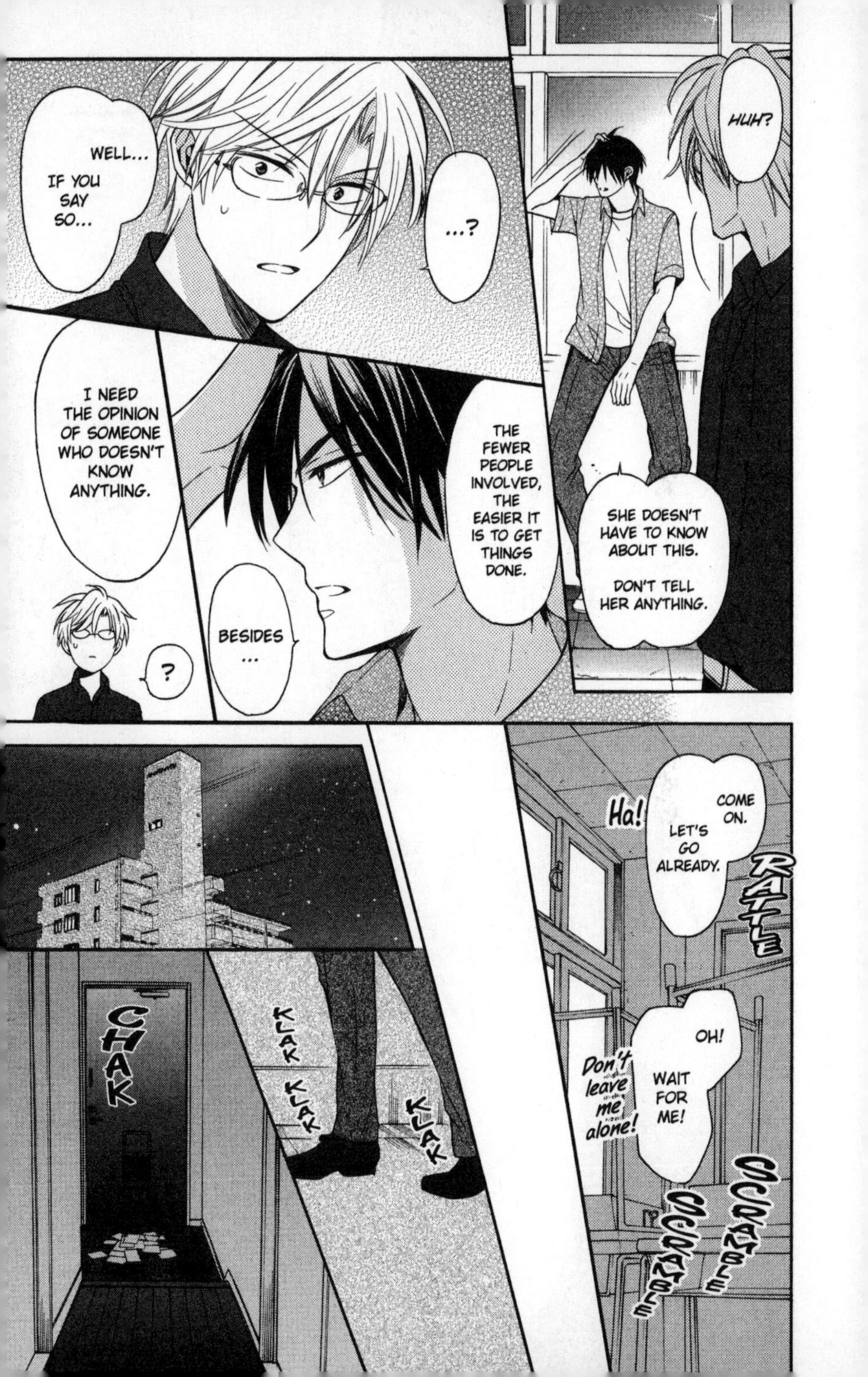
HUH?
...
SHE DOESN'T HAVE TO KNOW ABOUT THIS.
DON'T TELL HER ANYTHING.
...?
WELL... IF YOU SAY SO...
THE FEWER PEOPLE INVOLVED, THE EASIER IT IS TO GET THINGS DONE.
I NEED THE OPINION OF SOMEONE WHO DOESN'T KNOW ANYTHING.
BESIDES ...
?
Ha!
COME ON. LET'S GO ALREADY.
RATTLE
OH! WAIT FOR ME!
Don't leave me alone!
SCRAMBLE
SCRAMBLE
KLAK KLAK KLAK
CHAK

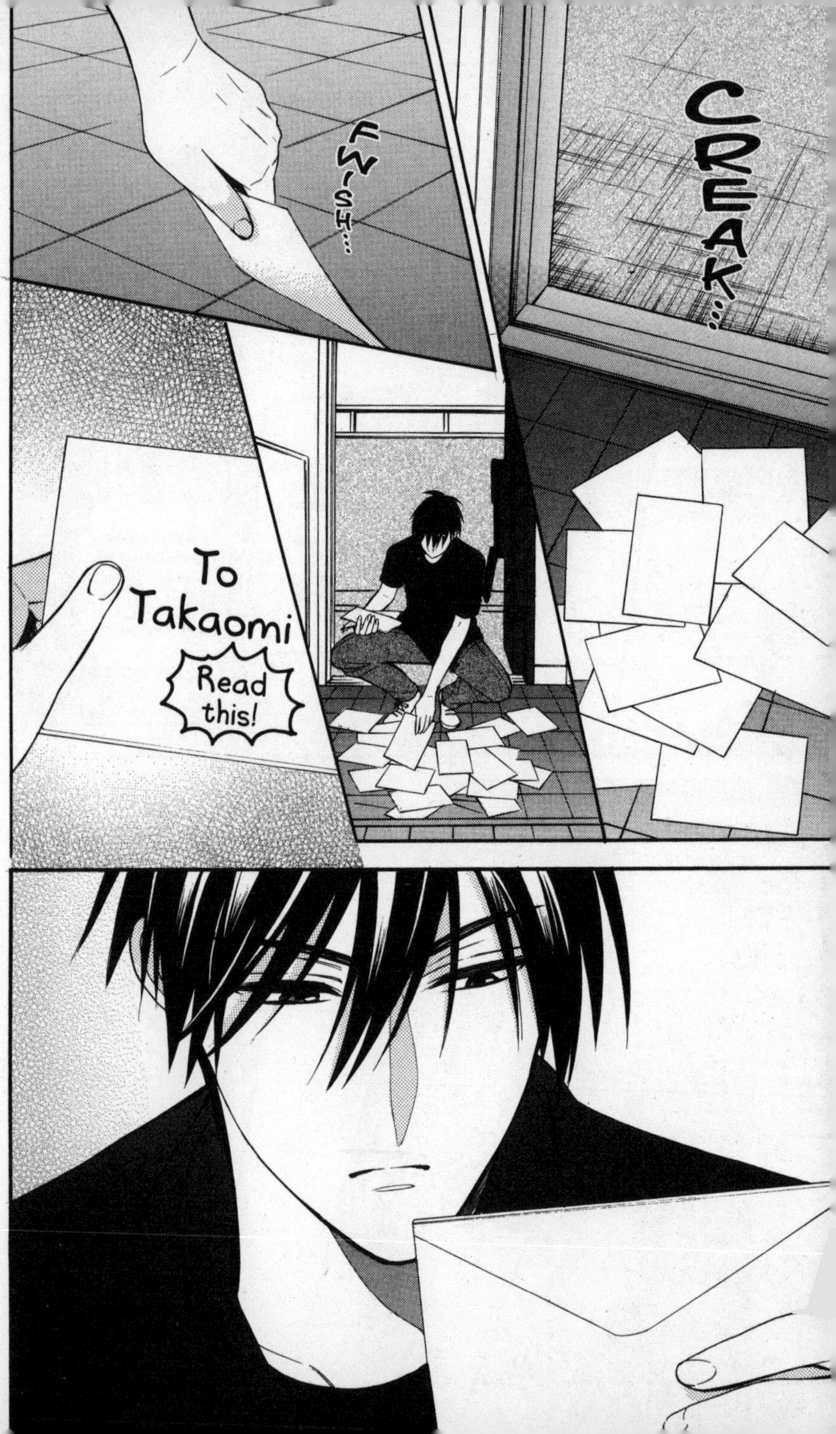
CREAK...
FWISH...
To Takaomi
Read this!

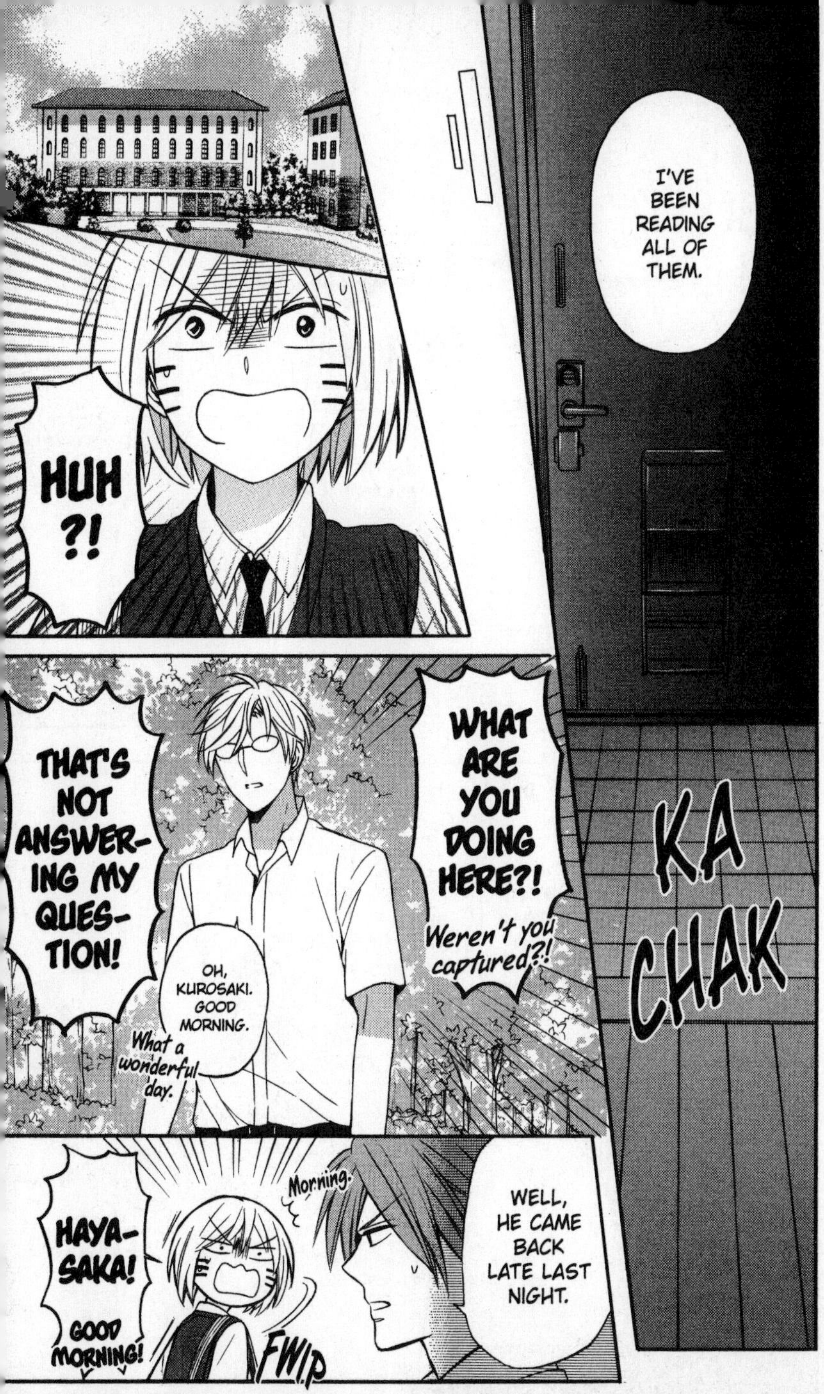
I'VE BEEN READING ALL OF THEM.
KA CHAK
HUH?!
WHAT ARE YOU DOING HERE?!
Weren't you captured?!
OH, KUROSAKI. GOOD MORNING.
What a wonderful day.
THAT'S NOT ANSWERING MY QUESTION!
WELL, HE CAME BACK LATE LAST NIGHT.
Morning.
HAYASAKA!
GOOD MORNING!
FWIP

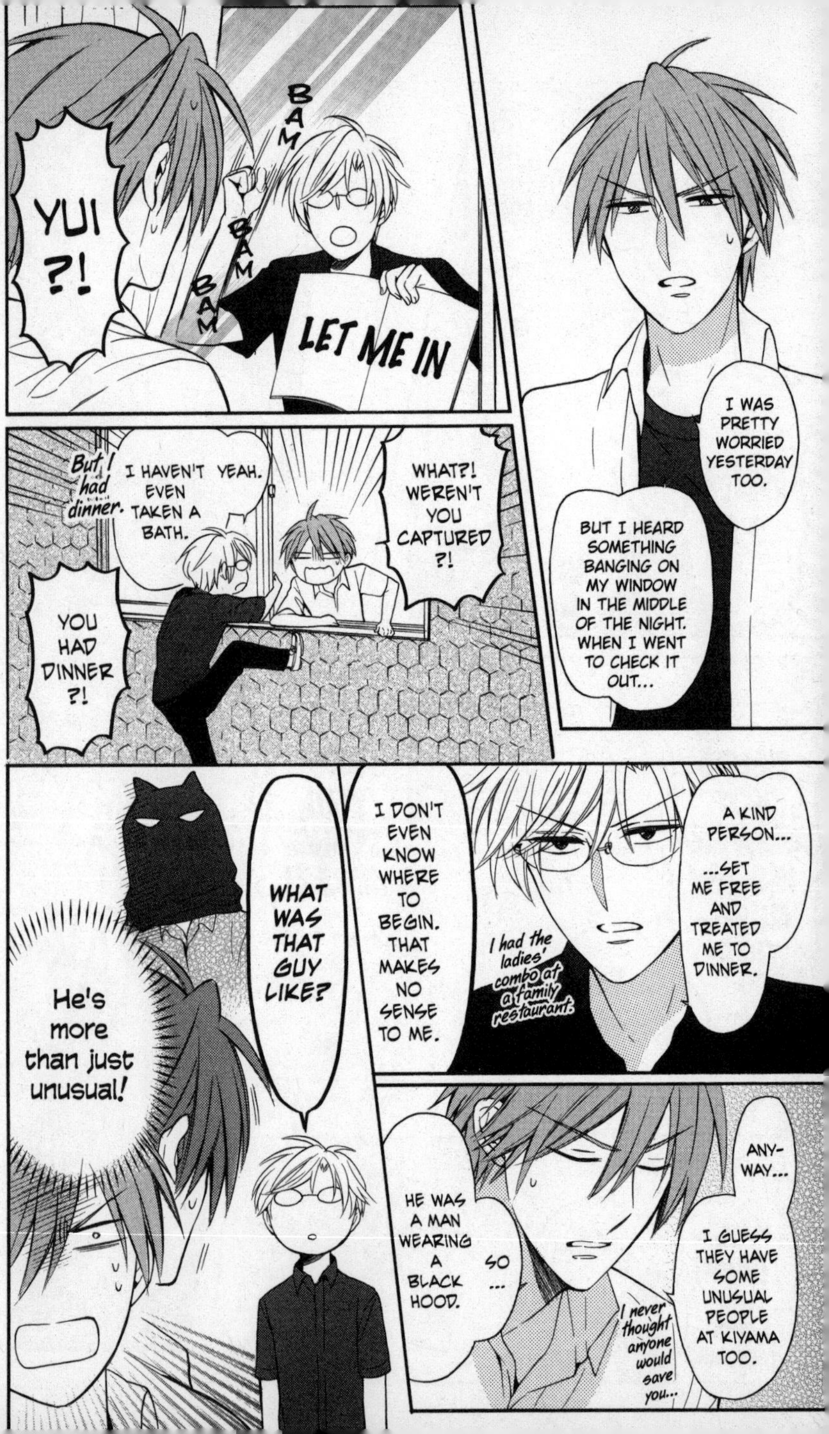
I WAS PRETTY WORRIED YESTERDAY TOO.
BUT I HEARD SOMETHING BANGING ON MY WINDOW IN THE MIDDLE OF THE NIGHT. WHEN I WENT TO CHECK IT OUT...
BAM
BAM
BAM
LET ME IN
YUI ?!
WHAT?! WEREN'T YOU CAPTURED ?!
YEAH.
I HAVEN'T EVEN TAKEN A BATH.
But I had dinner.
YOU HAD DINNER ?!
A KIND PERSON...
...SET ME FREE AND TREATED ME TO DINNER.
I had the ladies' combo at a family restaurant.
I DON'T EVEN KNOW WHERE TO BEGIN. THAT MAKES NO SENSE TO ME.
ANY-WAY...
I GUESS THEY HAVE SOME UNUSUAL PEOPLE AT KIYAMA TOO.
I never thought anyone would save you...
SO ...
HE WAS A MAN WEARING A BLACK HOOD.
WHAT WAS THAT GUY LIKE?
He's more than just unusual!

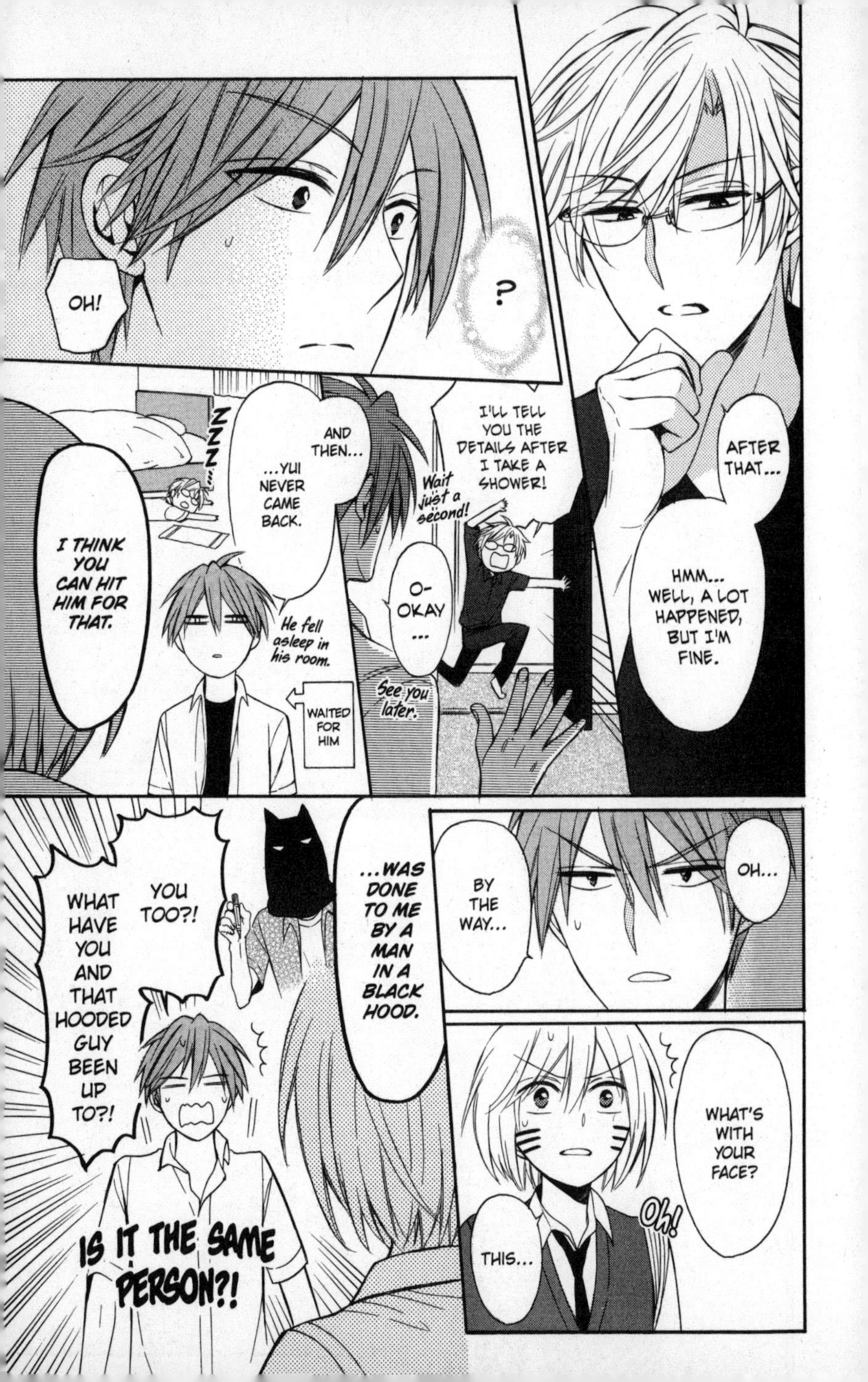
AFTER THAT...
HMM... WELL, A LOT HAPPENED, BUT I'M FINE.
?
OH!
I'LL TELL YOU THE DETAILS AFTER I TAKE A SHOWER!
Wait just a second!
O-OKAY...
See you later.
AND THEN...
...YUI NEVER CAME BACK.
ZZZ...
He fell asleep in his room.
WAITED FOR HIM
I THINK YOU CAN HIT HIM FOR THAT.
OH...
BY THE WAY...
WHAT'S WITH YOUR FACE?
Oh!
THIS...
...WAS DONE TO ME BY A MAN IN A BLACK HOOD.
YOU TOO?!
WHAT HAVE YOU AND THAT HOODED GUY BEEN UP TO?!
IS IT THE SAME PERSON?!

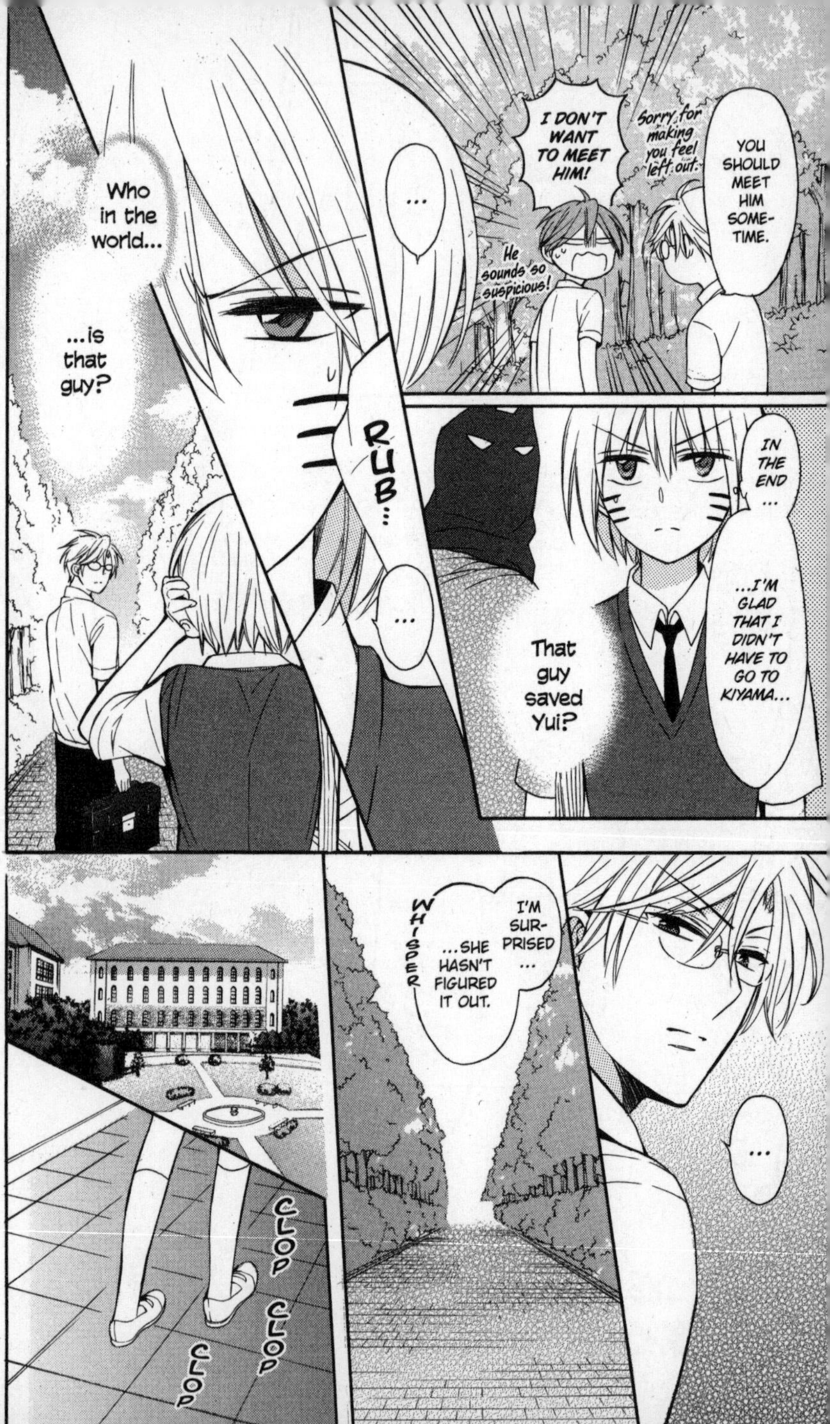
YOU SHOULD MEET HIM SOME-TIME.
Sorry for making you feel left out.
I DON'T WANT TO MEET HIM!
He sounds so suspicious!
...
IN THE END...
...I'M GLAD THAT I DIDN'T HAVE TO GO TO KIYAMA...
That guy saved Yui?
RUB...
...
Who in the world...
...is that guy?
I'M SUR-PRISED...
...SHE HASN'T FIGURED IT OUT.
WHISPER
...
CLOP
CLOP
CLOP

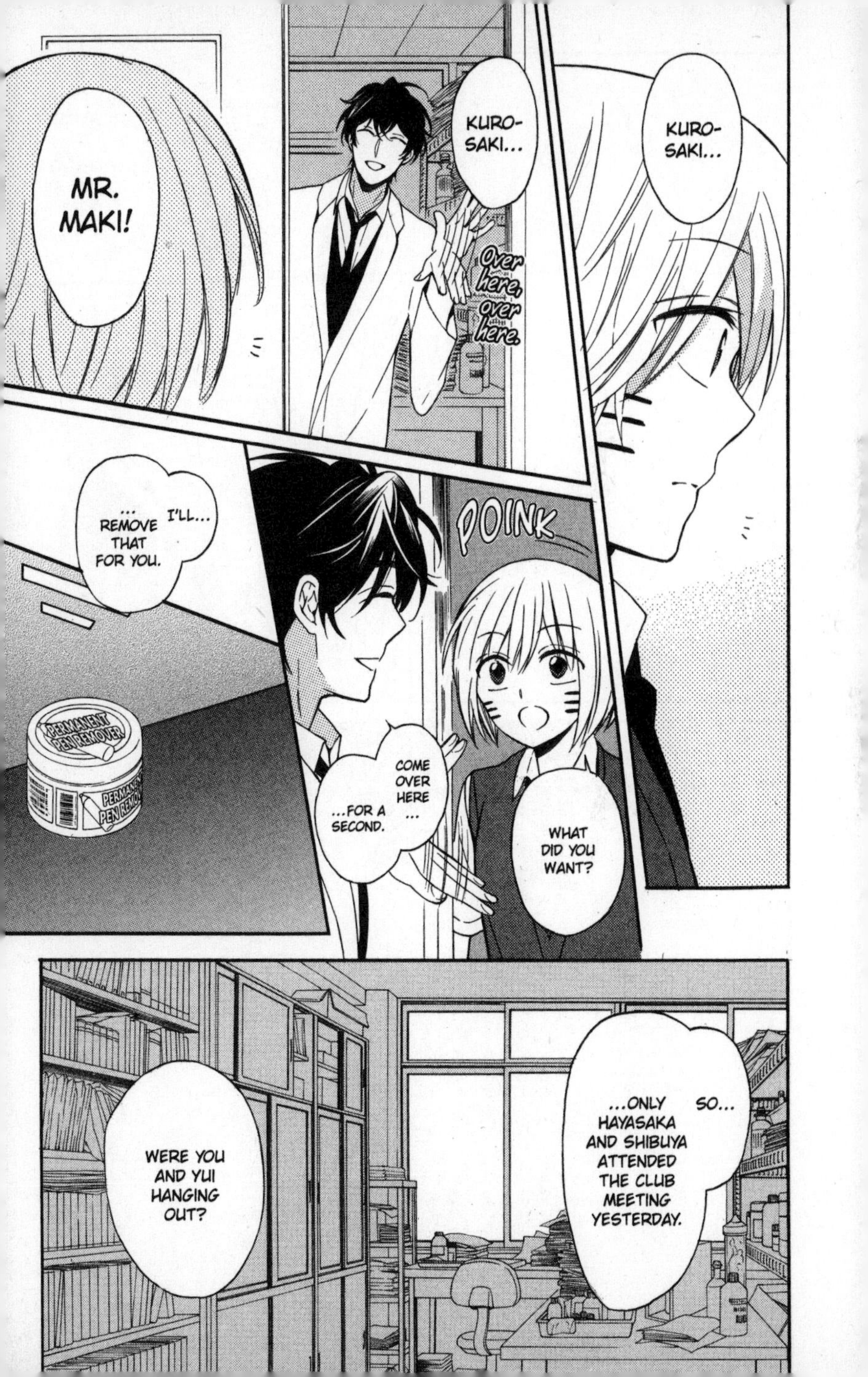
KURO-SAKI...
KURO-SAKI...
Over here, over here.
MR. MAKI!
POINK
WHAT DID YOU WANT?
COME OVER HERE ...
...FOR A SECOND.
I'LL...
...REMOVE THAT FOR YOU.
PERMANENT PEN REMOVER
SO...
...ONLY HAYASAKA AND SHIBUYA ATTENDED THE CLUB MEETING YESTERDAY.
WERE YOU AND YUI HANGING OUT?

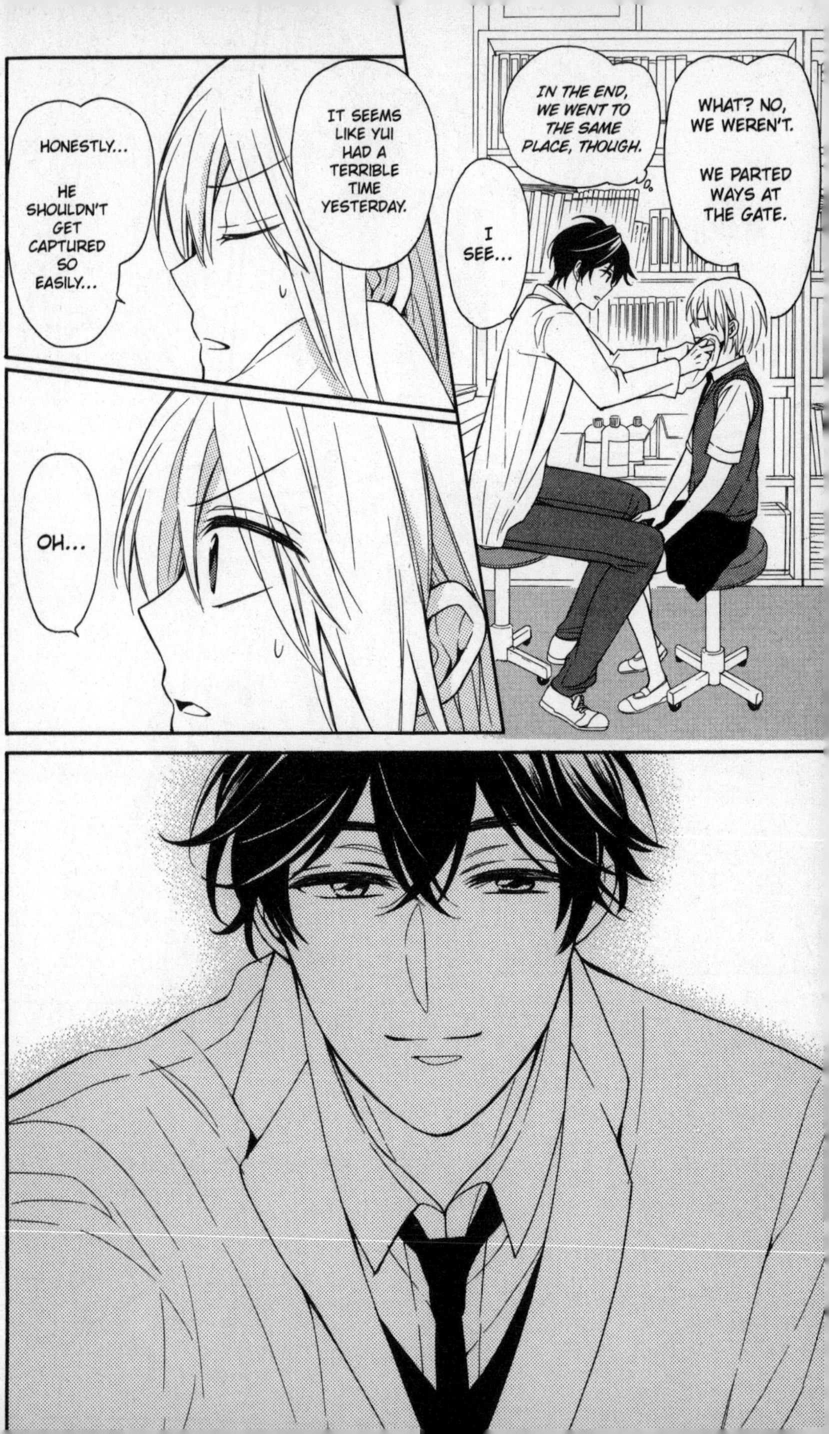
WHAT? NO, WE WEREN'T.
WE PARTED WAYS AT THE GATE.
IN THE END, WE WENT TO THE SAME PLACE, THOUGH.
I SEE...
IT SEEMS LIKE YUI HAD A TERRIBLE TIME YESTERDAY.
HONESTLY...
HE SHOULDN'T GET CAPTURED SO EASILY...
OH...

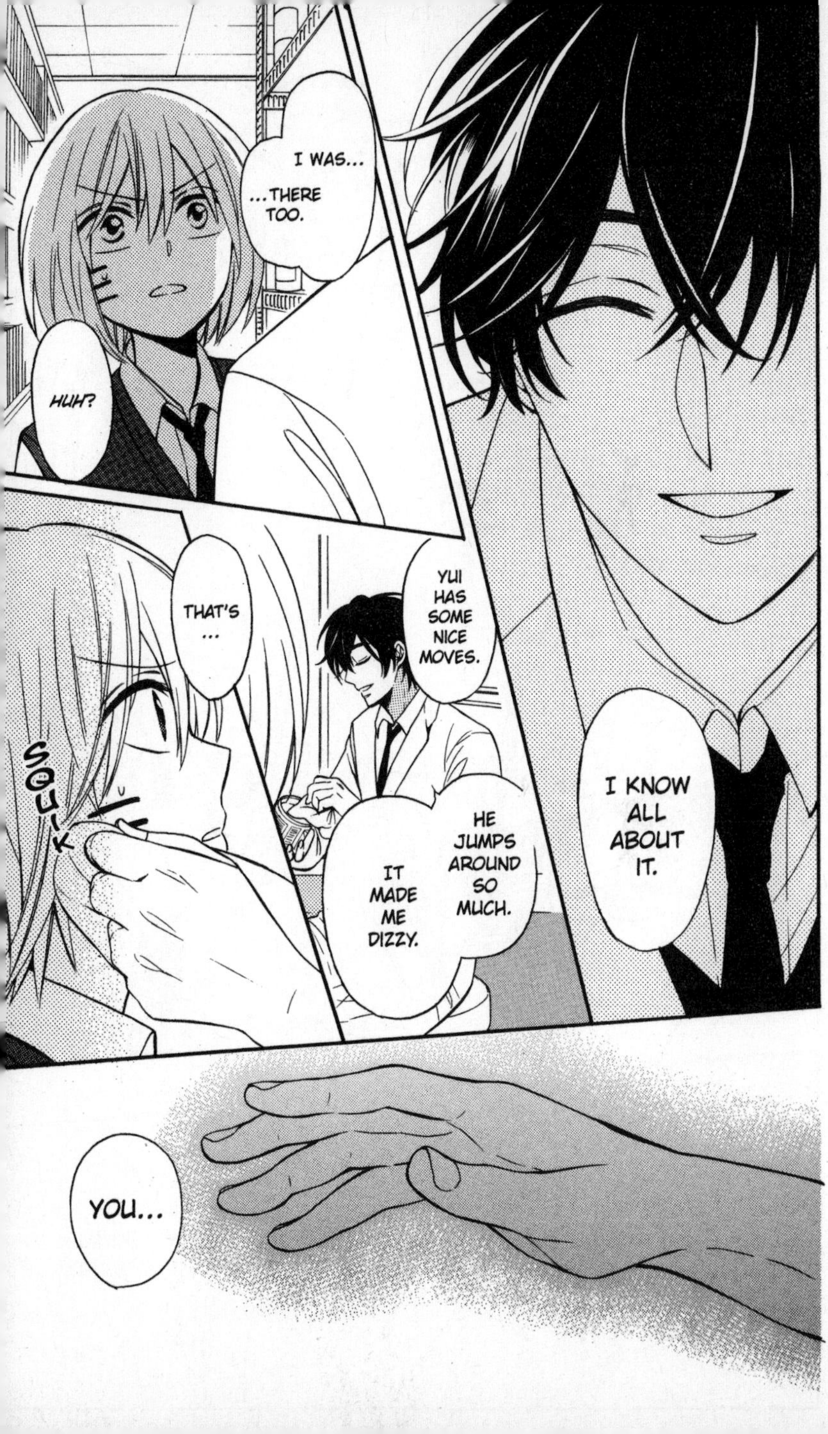
I KNOW ALL ABOUT IT.
I WAS...
...THERE TOO.
HUH?
YUI HAS SOME NICE MOVES.
HE JUMPS AROUND SO MUCH.
IT MADE ME DIZZY.
THAT'S...
SQUIK
YOU...

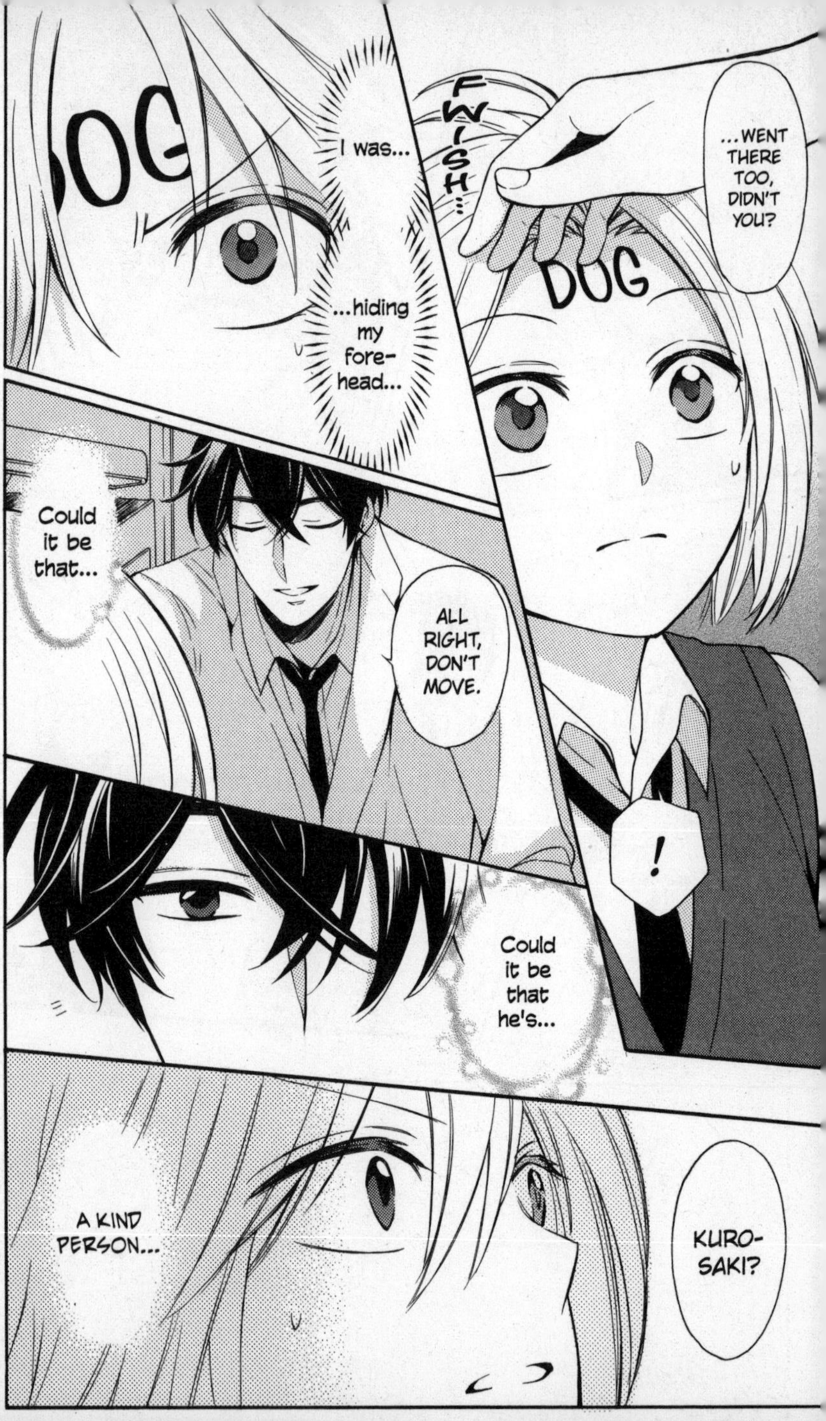
FWISH...
...WENT THERE TOO, DIDN'T YOU?
DOG
!
OG
I was...
...hiding my fore-head...
Could it be that...
ALL RIGHT, DON'T MOVE.
Could it be that he's...
KURO-SAKI?
A KIND PERSON...

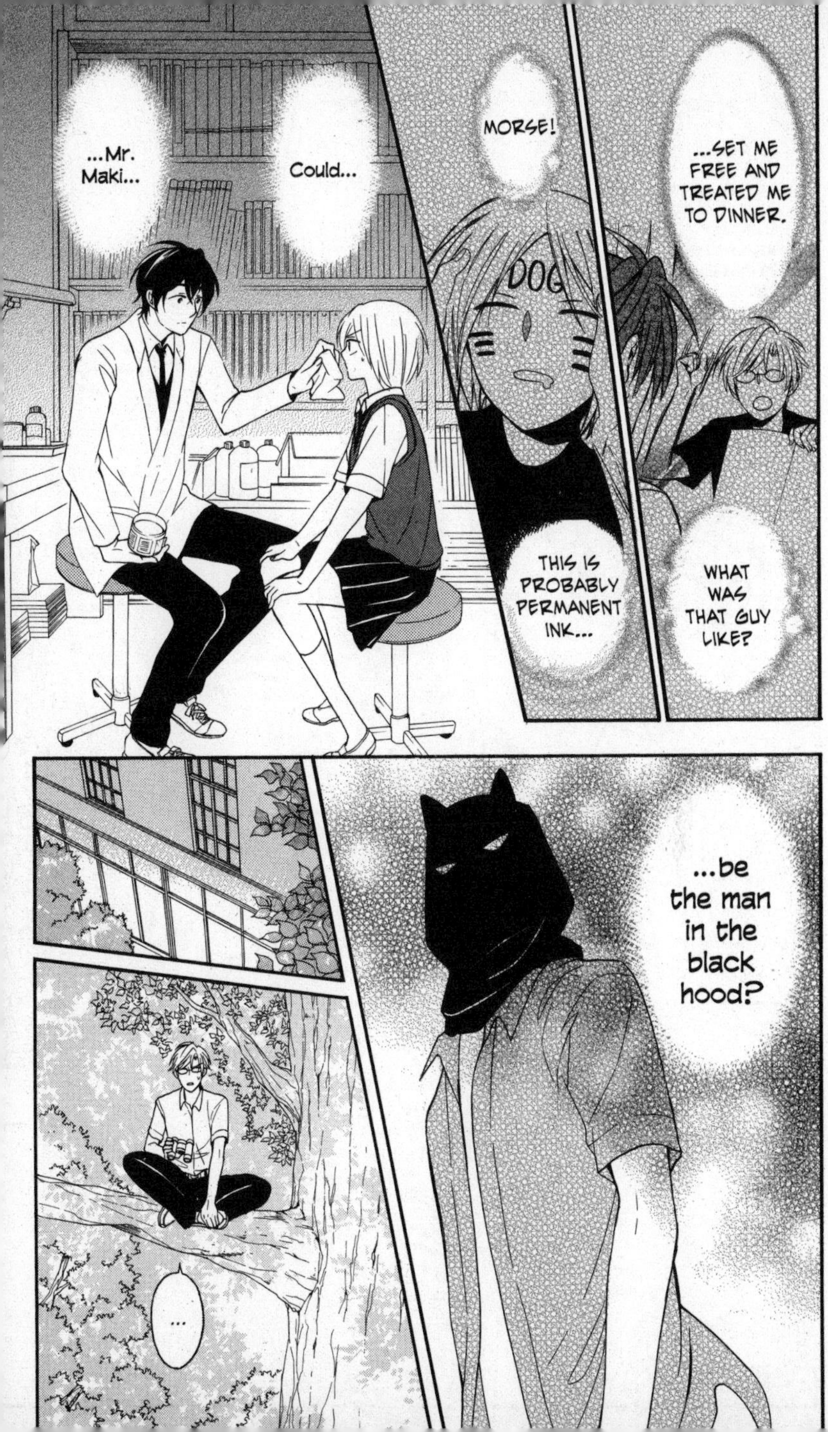
...SET ME FREE AND TREATED ME TO DINNER.
WHAT WAS THAT GUY LIKE?
MORSE!
DOG
THIS IS PROBABLY PERMANENT INK...
...Mr. Maki...
Could...
...be the man in the black hood?
...

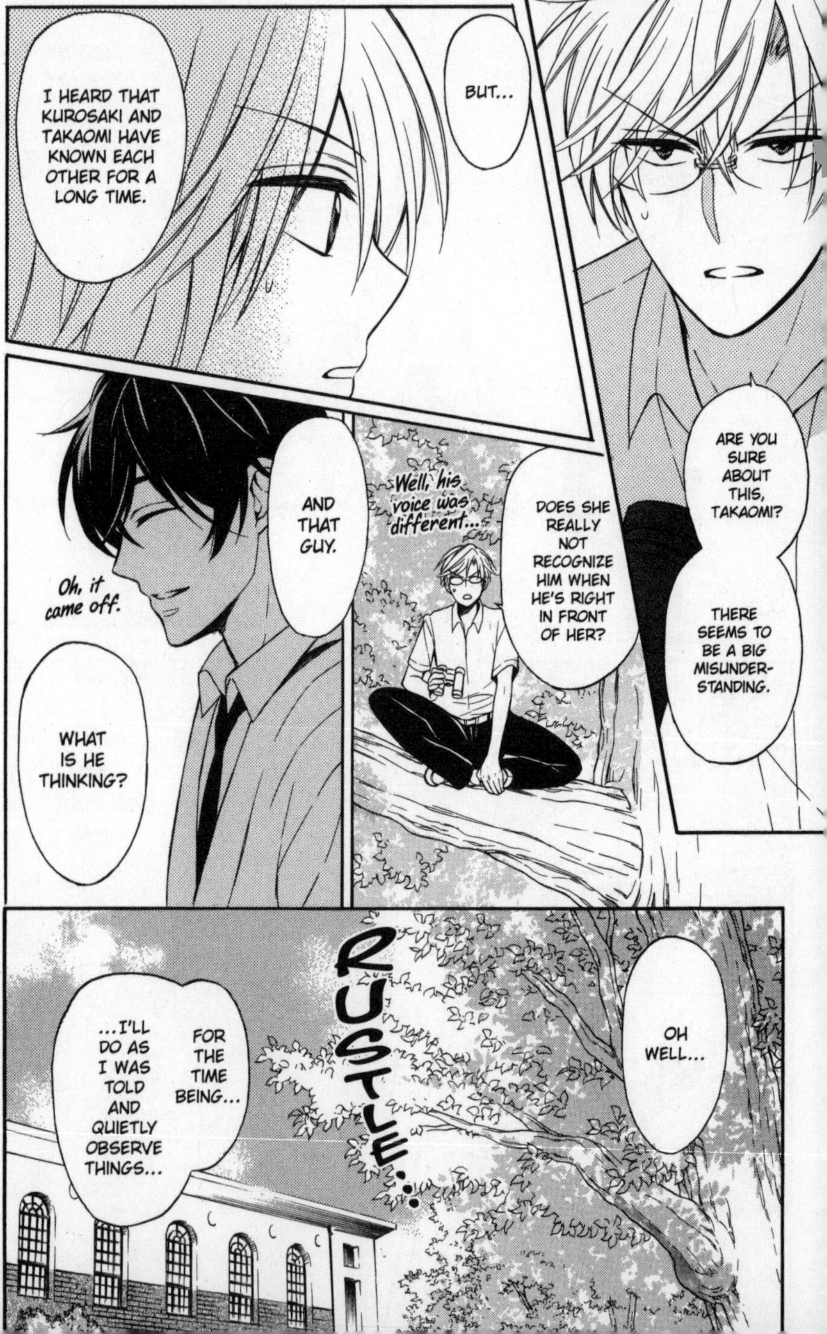
ARE YOU SURE ABOUT THIS, TAKAOMI?
THERE SEEMS TO BE A BIG MISUNDER-STANDING.
BUT...
I HEARD THAT KUROSAKI AND TAKAOMI HAVE KNOWN EACH OTHER FOR A LONG TIME.
DOES SHE REALLY NOT RECOGNIZE HIM WHEN HE'S RIGHT IN FRONT OF HER?
Well, his voice was different...
AND THAT GUY.
Oh, it came off.
WHAT IS HE THINKING?
OH WELL...
RUSTLE...
FOR THE TIME BEING...
...I'LL DO AS I WAS TOLD AND QUIETLY OBSERVE THINGS...

THE PATH TO CREATING INUZUKA

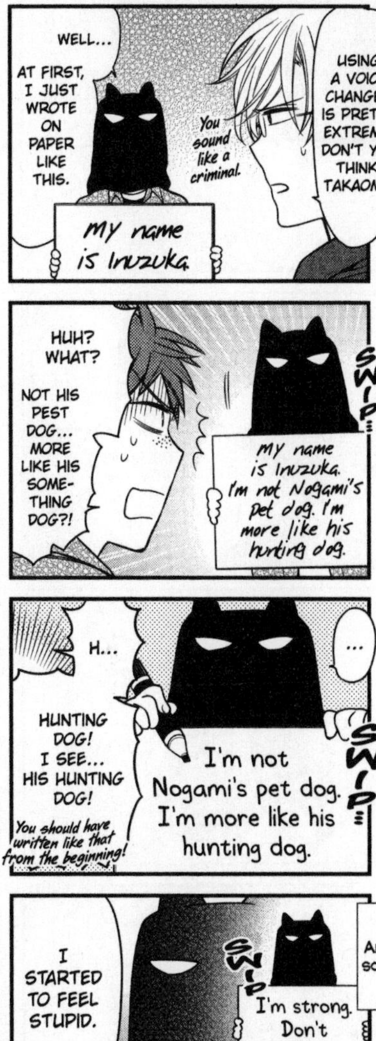
USING A VOICE CHANGER IS PRETTY EXTREME, DON'T YOU THINK, TAKAOMI?
You sound like a criminal.
WELL...
AT FIRST, I JUST WROTE ON PAPER LIKE THIS.
My name is Inuzuka
SWIP
My name is Inuzuka. I'm not Nogami's pet dog. I'm more like his hunting dog.
HUH? WHAT?
NOT HIS PEST DOG... MORE LIKE HIS SOMETHING DOG?!
...
SWIP
I'm not Nogami's pet dog. I'm more like his hunting dog.
H...
HUNTING DOG! I SEE... HIS HUNTING DOG!
You should have written like that from the beginning!
And so...
SWIP
I'm strong. Don't defy me.
I STARTED TO FEEL STUPID.
So I stopped writing things out.

SPECTACULAR PRIVATE LESSONS

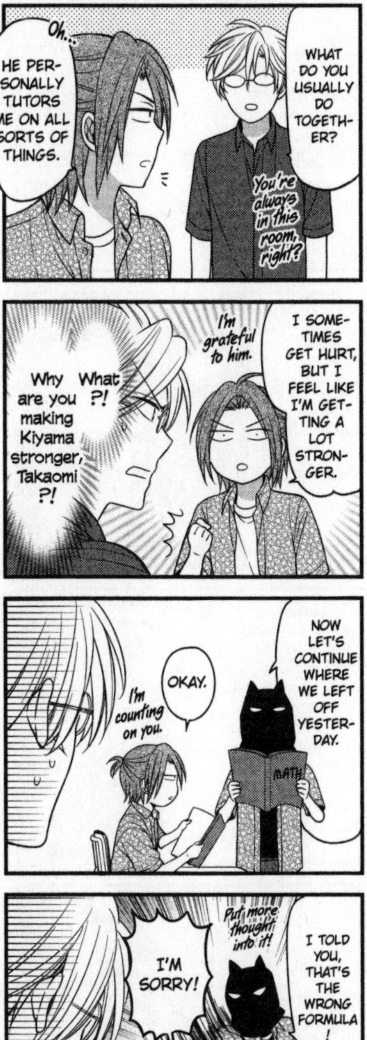
WHAT DO YOU USUALLY DO TOGETHER?
You're always in this room, right?
Oh...
HE PERSONALLY TUTORS ME ON ALL SORTS OF THINGS.
I SOMETIMES GET HURT, BUT I FEEL LIKE I'M GETTING A LOT STRONGER.
I'm grateful to him.
What?!
Why are you making Kiyama stronger, Takaomi?!
NOW LET'S CONTINUE WHERE WE LEFT OFF YESTERDAY.
MATH
OKAY.
I'm counting on you.
I TOLD YOU, THAT'S THE WRONG FORMULA!
Put more thought into it!
I'M SORRY!
WHAP
BONK

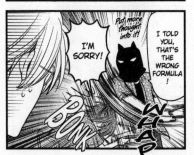

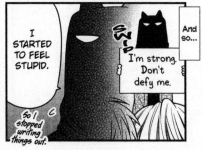

A GOOD ENVIRONMENT FOR STUDYING

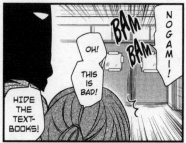

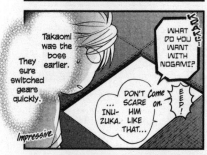

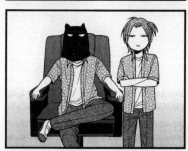

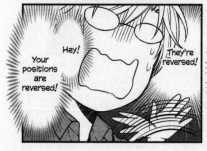

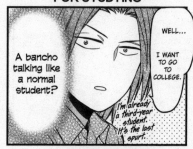

WELL...
I WANT TO GO TO COLLEGE.
I'm already a third-year student. It's the last spurt.
A bancho talking like a normal student?
THE SUMMER OF YOUR THIRD YEAR...
...IS AN IMPORTANT TIME FOR STUDENTS LIKE YOU...
A hooded man talking like a normal teacher?
HOW IS THIS OKAY?!
WHY ARE YOU ACTING LIKE IT'S NORMAL?!
Isn't this supposed to be a bad school?!
THERE'S ALWAYS FIGHTS BREAKING OUT AT SCHOOL.
I always get called out.
I...
I SEE!
So you still fight!
WELL...
IT'S IMPORTANT TO GET PROPER EXERCISE.
He tries to participate in one every two hours.
?!
That's his refresh time?!

ACTING NATURAL

NOGAMI!
BAM
BAM
OH!
THIS IS BAD!
HIDE THE TEXT-BOOKS!
KRAK!
WHAT DO YOU WANT WITH NOGAMI?
EEP!
Come on.
DON'T SCARE HIM LIKE THAT...
...INU-ZUKA.
Takaomi was the boss earlier.
They sure switched gears quickly.
Impressive.
They're reversed!
Hey!
Your positions are reversed!

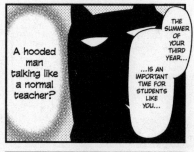

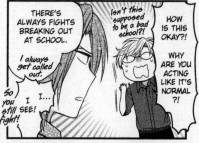

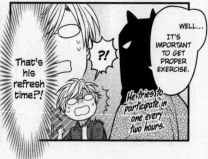

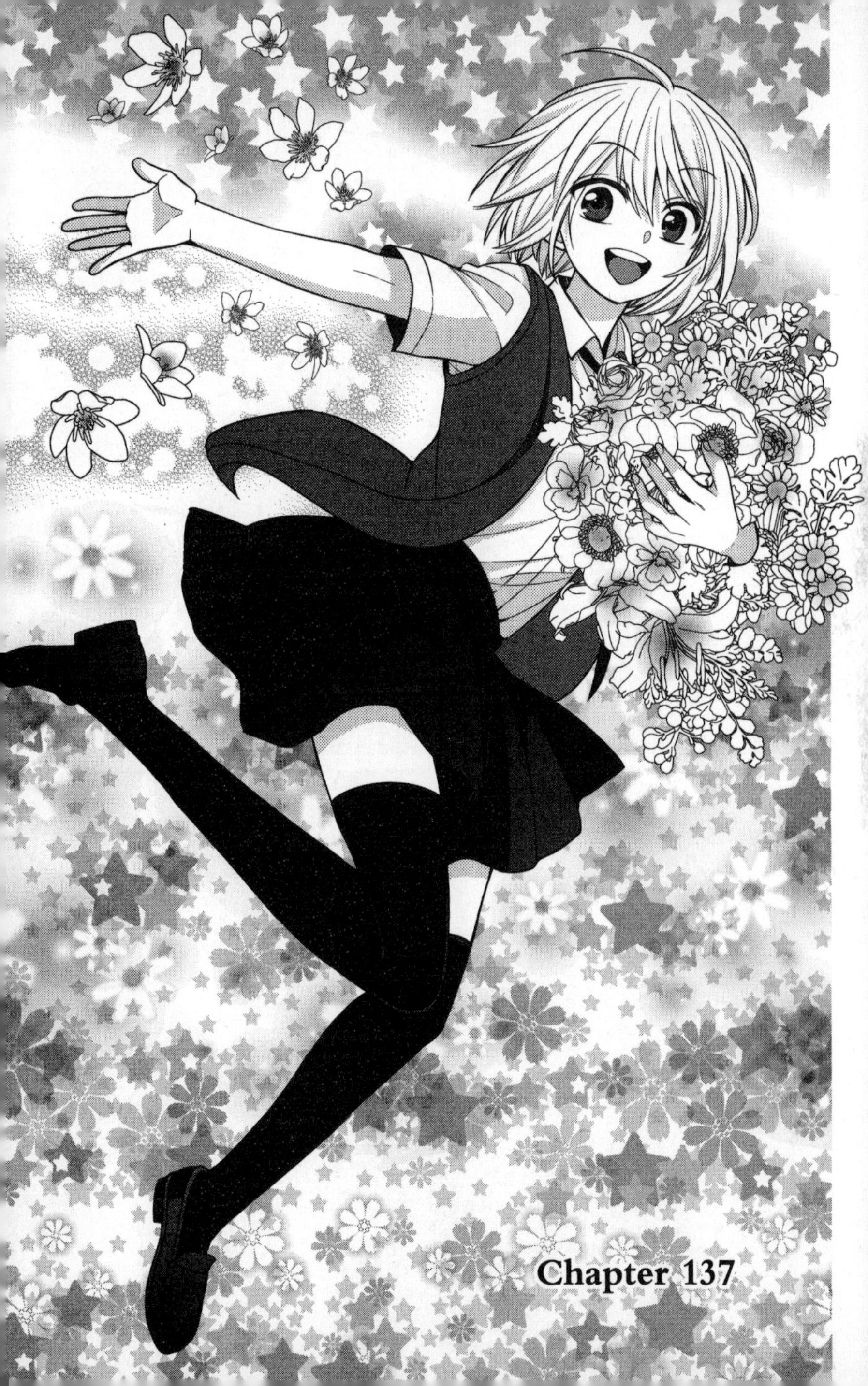
Chapter 137

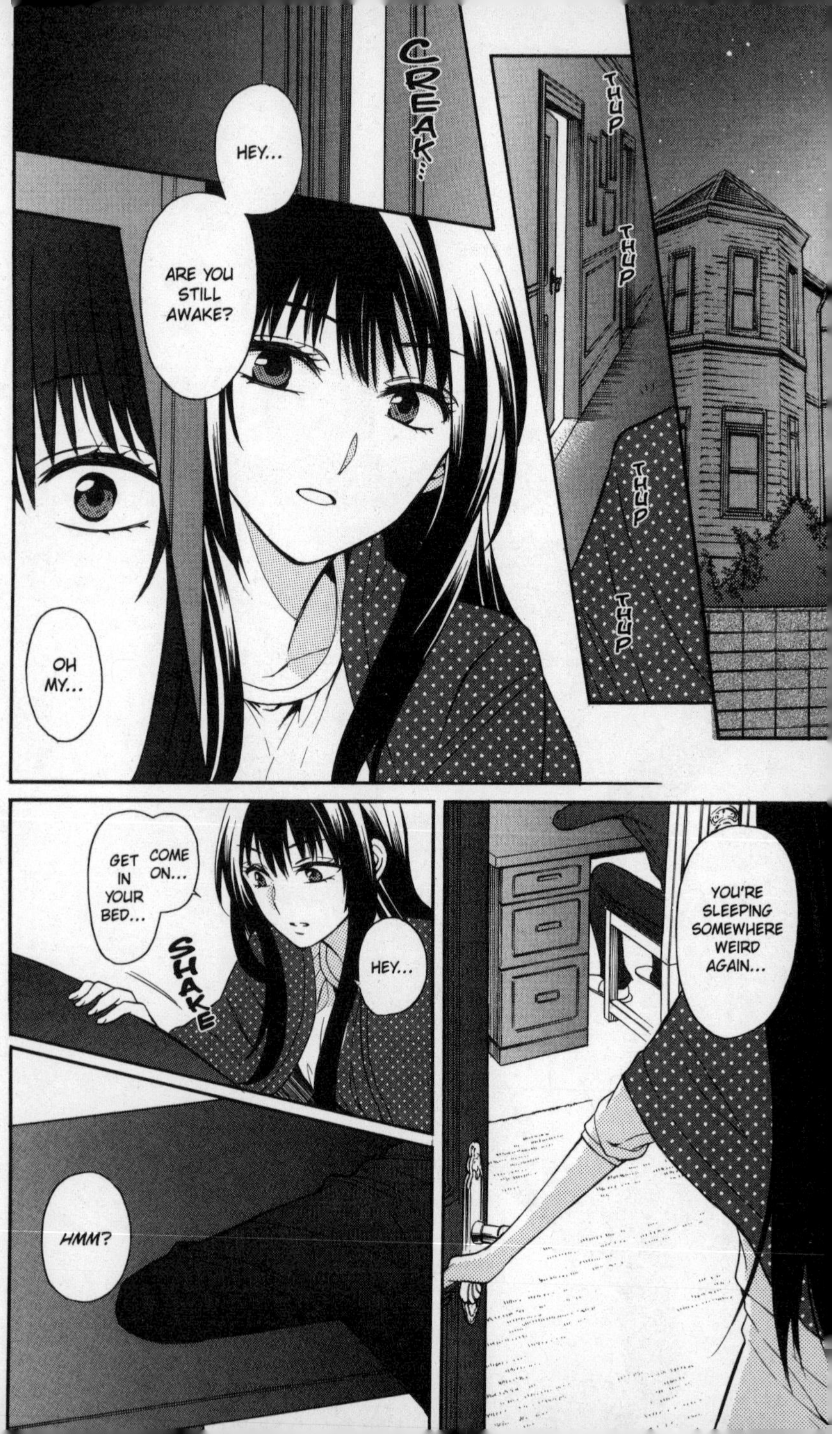
THUP
THUP
THUP
THUP
CREAK...
HEY...
ARE YOU STILL AWAKE?
OH MY...
YOU'RE SLEEPING SOMEWHERE WEIRD AGAIN...
HEY...
SHAKE
COME ON... GET IN YOUR BED...
HMM?

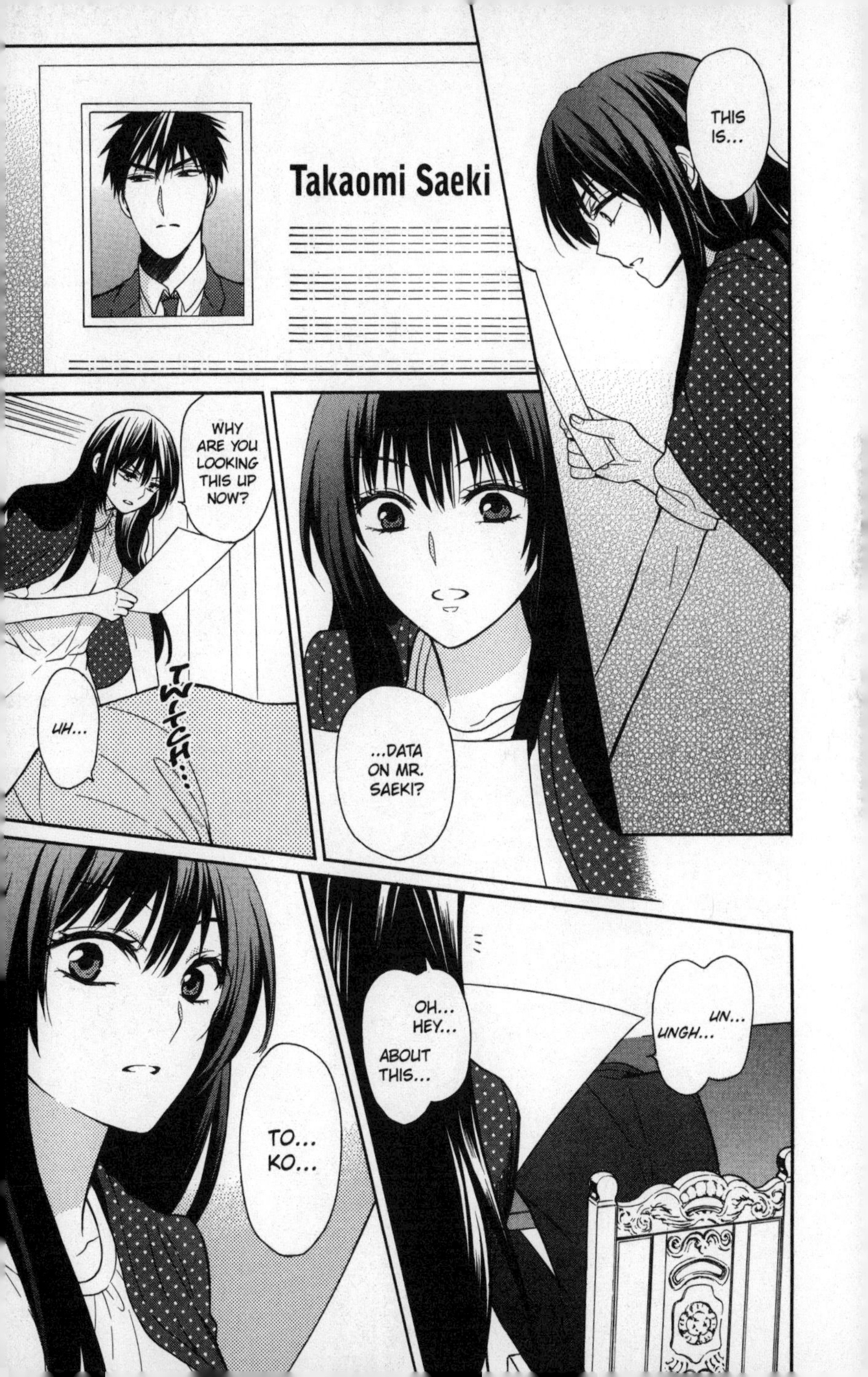
THIS IS...
Takaomi Saeki
...DATA ON MR. SAEKI?
WHY ARE YOU LOOKING THIS UP NOW?
TWITCH...
UH...
UN... UNGH...
OH... HEY... ABOUT THIS...
TO... KO...

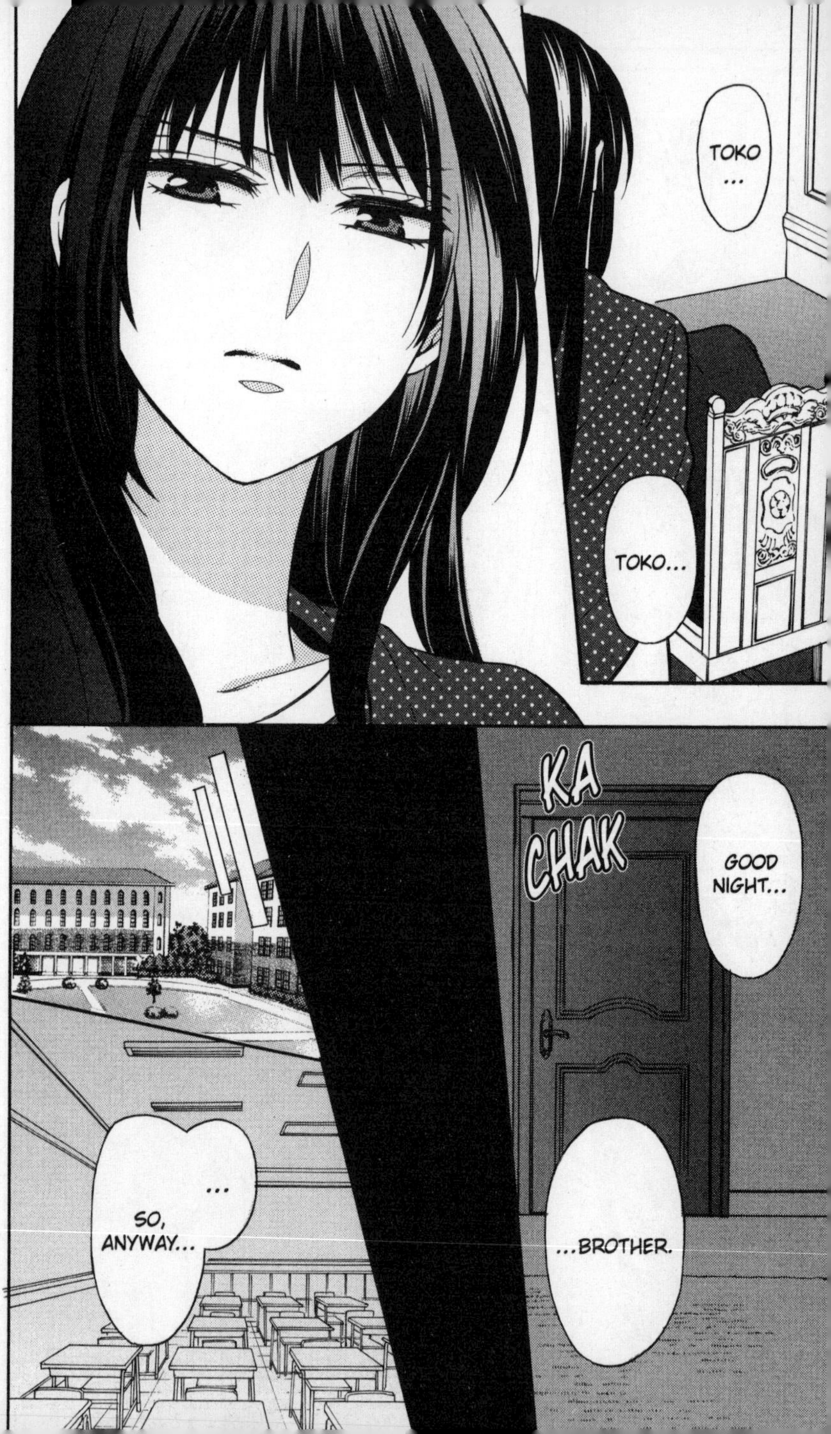
TOKO ...
TOKO...
KA CHAK
GOOD NIGHT...
...BROTHER.
...
SO, ANYWAY...

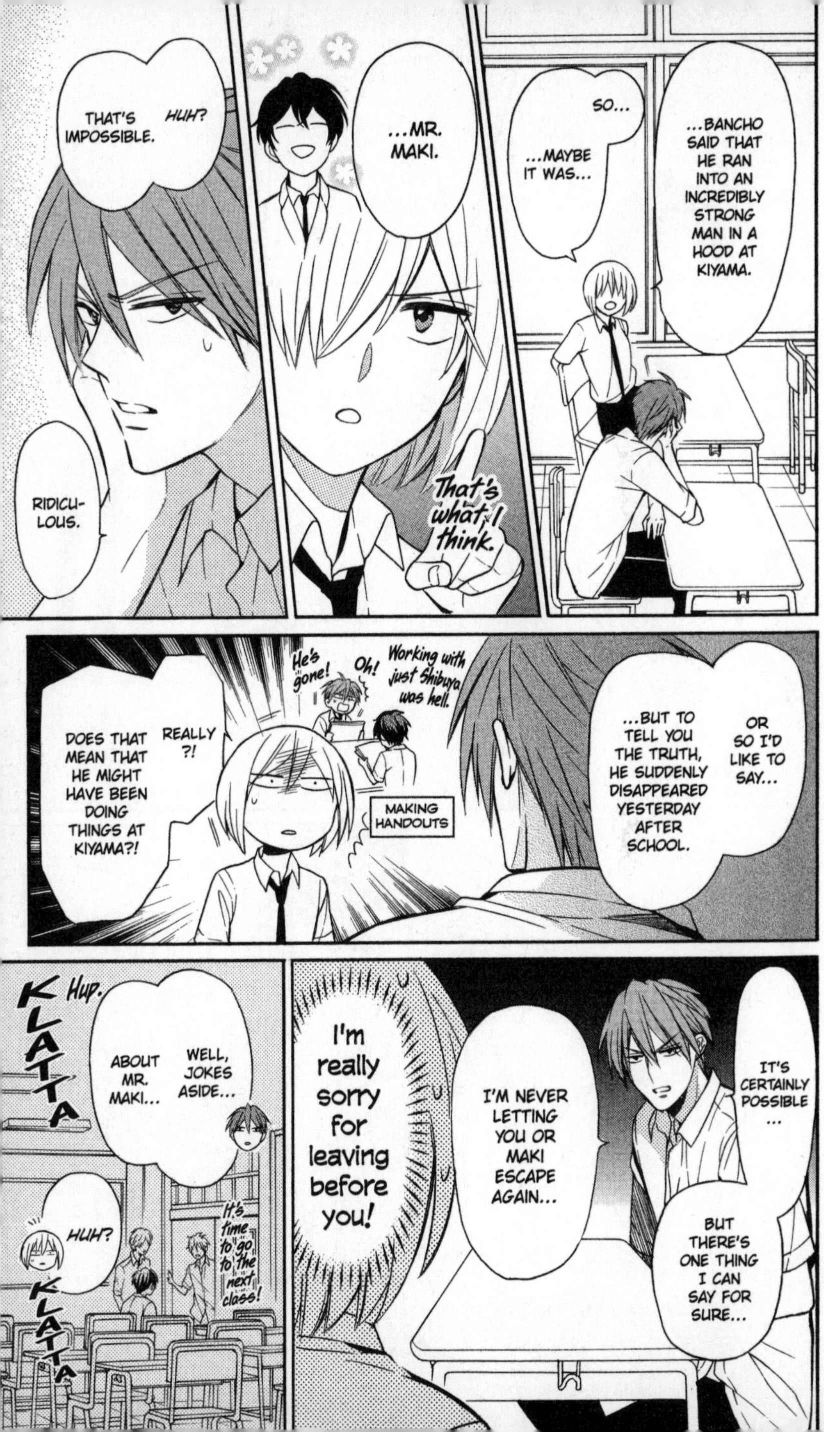
...BANCHO SAID THAT HE RAN INTO AN INCREDIBLY STRONG MAN IN A HOOD AT KIYAMA.
SO...
...MAYBE IT WAS...
...MR. MAKI.
That's what I think.
HUH?
THAT'S IMPOSSIBLE.
RIDICULOUS.
OR SO I'D LIKE TO SAY...
...BUT TO TELL YOU THE TRUTH, HE SUDDENLY DISAPPEARED YESTERDAY AFTER SCHOOL.
Working with just Shibuya was hell.
Oh!
He's gone!
MAKING HANDOUTS
REALLY?!
DOES THAT MEAN THAT HE MIGHT HAVE BEEN DOING THINGS AT KIYAMA?!
IT'S CERTAINLY POSSIBLE...
BUT THERE'S ONE THING I CAN SAY FOR SURE...
I'M NEVER LETTING YOU OR MAKI ESCAPE AGAIN...
I'm really sorry for leaving before you!
WELL, JOKES ASIDE...
ABOUT MR. MAKI...
Hup.
KLATTA
HUH?
It's time to go to the next class!
KLATTA

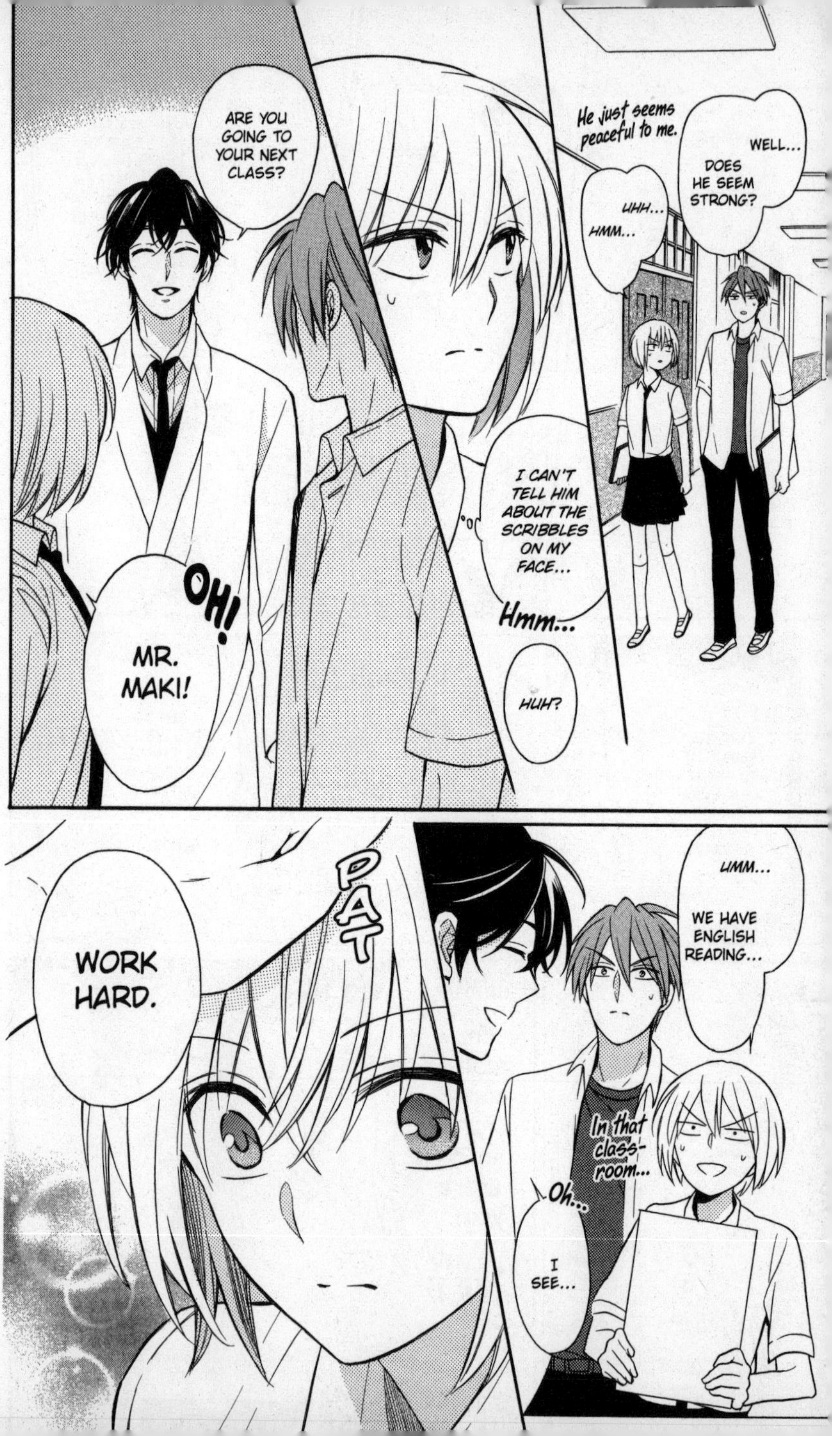
WELL... DOES HE SEEM STRONG?
UHH... HMM...
He just seems peaceful to me.
I CAN'T TELL HIM ABOUT THE SCRIBBLES ON MY FACE...
Hmm...
HUH?
ARE YOU GOING TO YOUR NEXT CLASS?
OH!
MR. MAKI!
UMM...
WE HAVE ENGLISH READING...
In that class-room...
Oh...
I SEE...
PAT
WORK HARD.

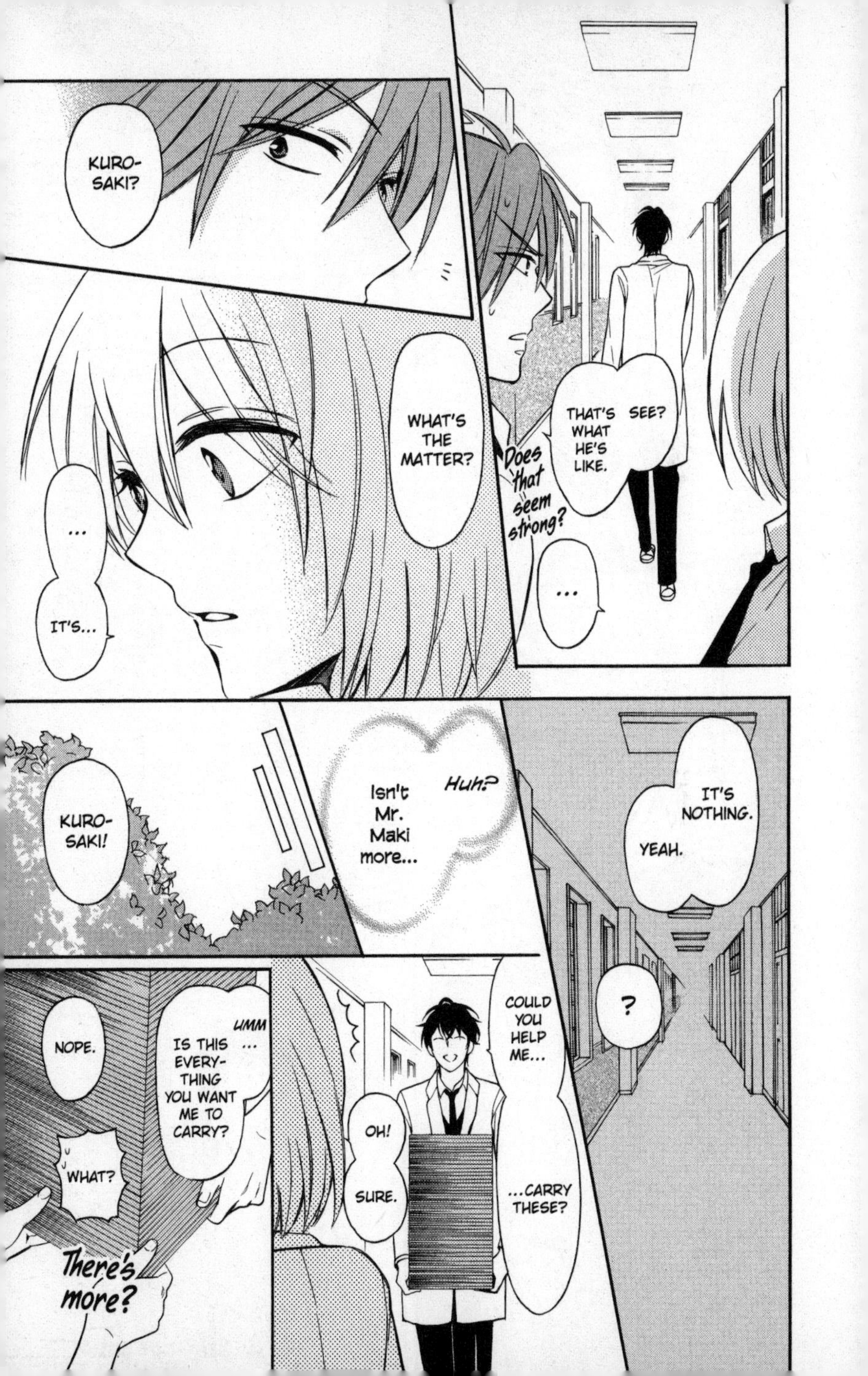
SEE?
THAT'S WHAT HE'S LIKE.
Does that seem strong?
...
KURO-SAKI?
WHAT'S THE MATTER?
...
IT'S...
IT'S NOTHING.
YEAH.
?
Huh?
Isn't Mr. Maki more...
KURO-SAKI!
COULD YOU HELP ME...
...CARRY THESE?
OH!
SURE.
UMM ...
IS THIS EVERY-THING YOU WANT ME TO CARRY?
NOPE.
WHAT?
There's more?

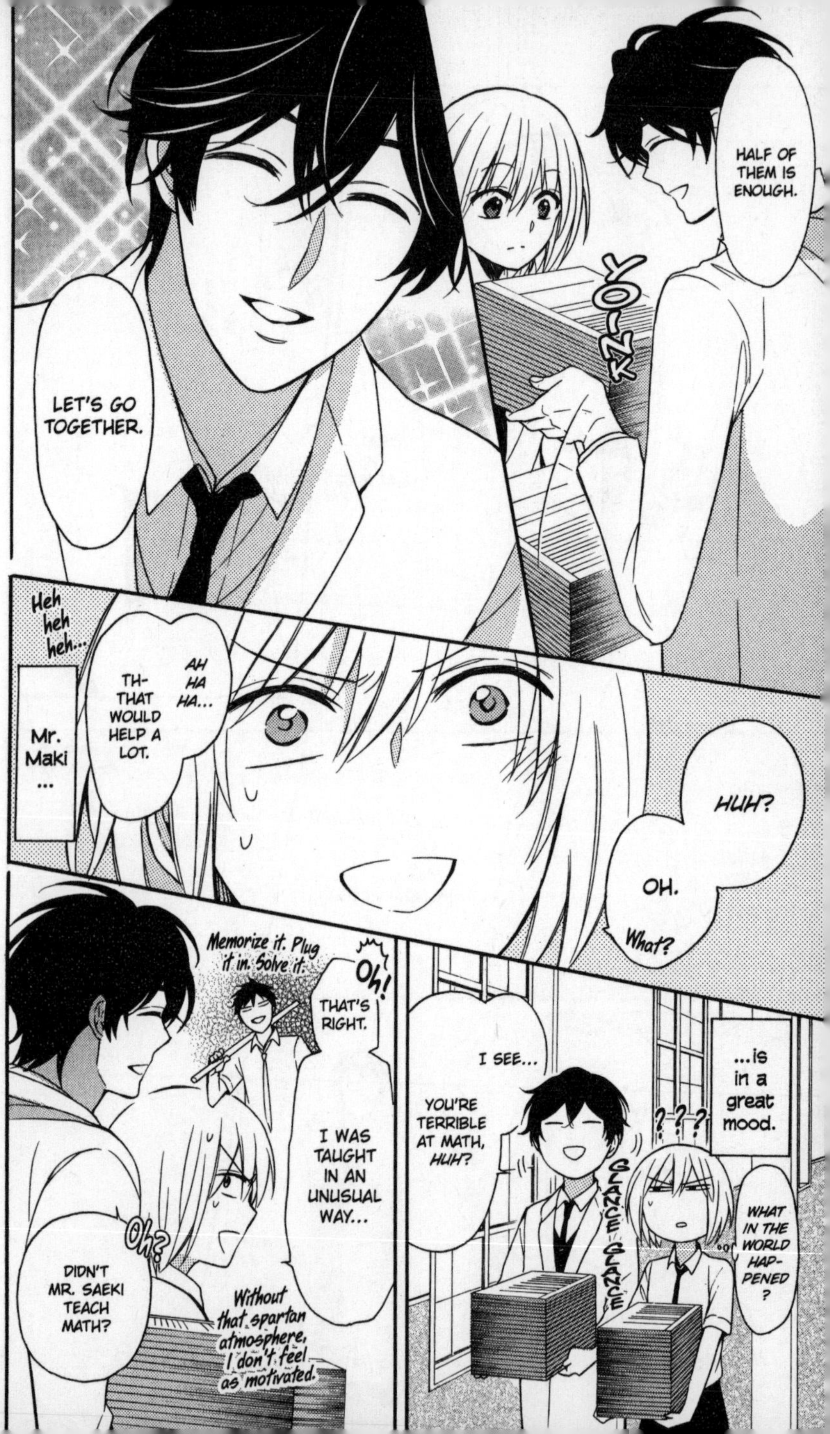
HALF OF THEM IS ENOUGH.
YOINK
LET'S GO TOGETHER.
HUH?
OH.
What?
AH HA HA...
TH-THAT WOULD HELP A LOT.
Heh heh heh...
Mr. Maki...
...is in a great mood.
I SEE...
YOU'RE TERRIBLE AT MATH, HUH?
???
GLANCE GLANCE
WHAT IN THE WORLD HAPPENED?
Oh!
THAT'S RIGHT.
Memorize it. Plug it in. Solve it.
I WAS TAUGHT IN AN UNUSUAL WAY...
Oh?
DIDN'T MR. SAEKI TEACH MATH?
Without that spartan atmosphere, I don't feel as motivated.

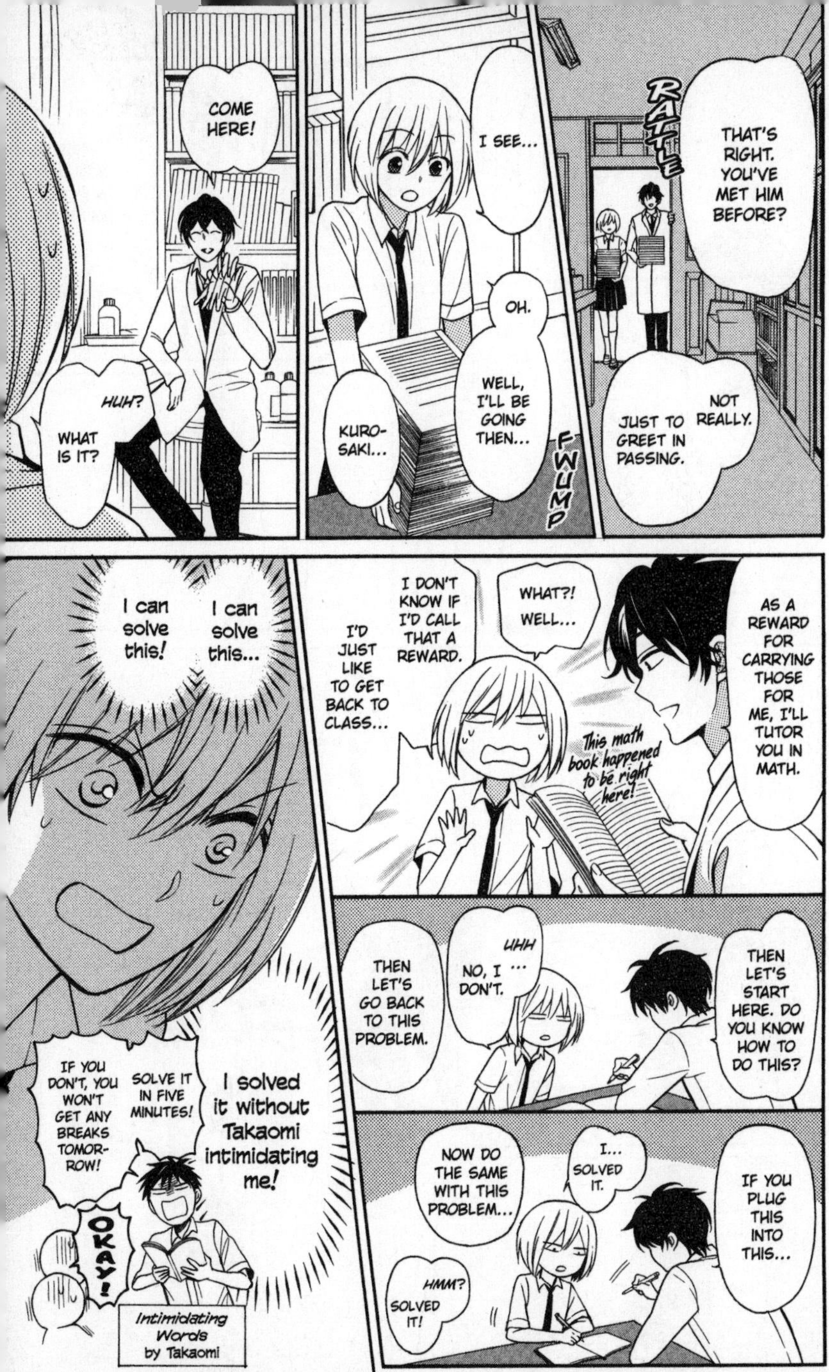
THAT'S RIGHT. YOU'VE MET HIM BEFORE?
RATTLE
NOT REALLY.
JUST TO GREET IN PASSING.
I SEE...
OH.
WELL, I'LL BE GOING THEN...
FWUMP
KURO-SAKI...
COME HERE!
HUH?
WHAT IS IT?
AS A REWARD FOR CARRYING THOSE FOR ME, I'LL TUTOR YOU IN MATH.
WHAT?! WELL...
I DON'T KNOW IF I'D CALL THAT A REWARD.
I'D JUST LIKE TO GET BACK TO CLASS...
This math book happened to be right here!
THEN LET'S START HERE. DO YOU KNOW HOW TO DO THIS?
UHH...
NO, I DON'T.
THEN LET'S GO BACK TO THIS PROBLEM.
IF YOU PLUG THIS INTO THIS...
I... SOLVED IT.
NOW DO THE SAME WITH THIS PROBLEM...
HMM?
SOLVED IT!
I can solve this...
I can solve this!
I solved it without Takaomi intimidating me!
SOLVE IT IN FIVE MINUTES!
IF YOU DON'T, YOU WON'T GET ANY BREAKS TOMORROW!
OKAY!
Intimidating Words by Takaomi

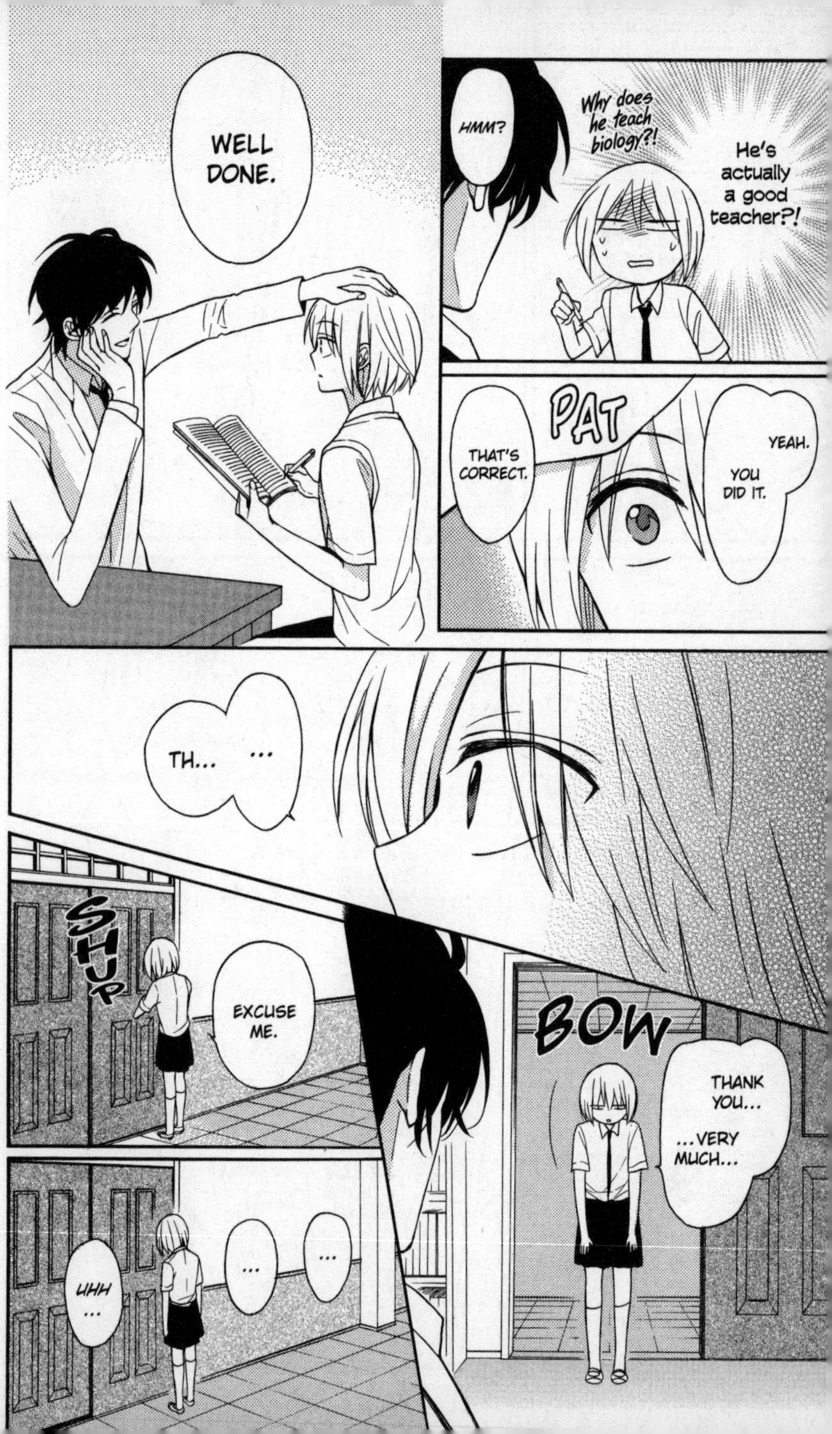
He's actually a good teacher?!
Why does he teach biology?!
HMM?
YEAH.
YOU DID IT.
PAT
THAT'S CORRECT.
WELL DONE.
...
TH...
BOW
THANK YOU...
...VERY MUCH...
SHUP
EXCUSE ME.
...
...
UHH ...

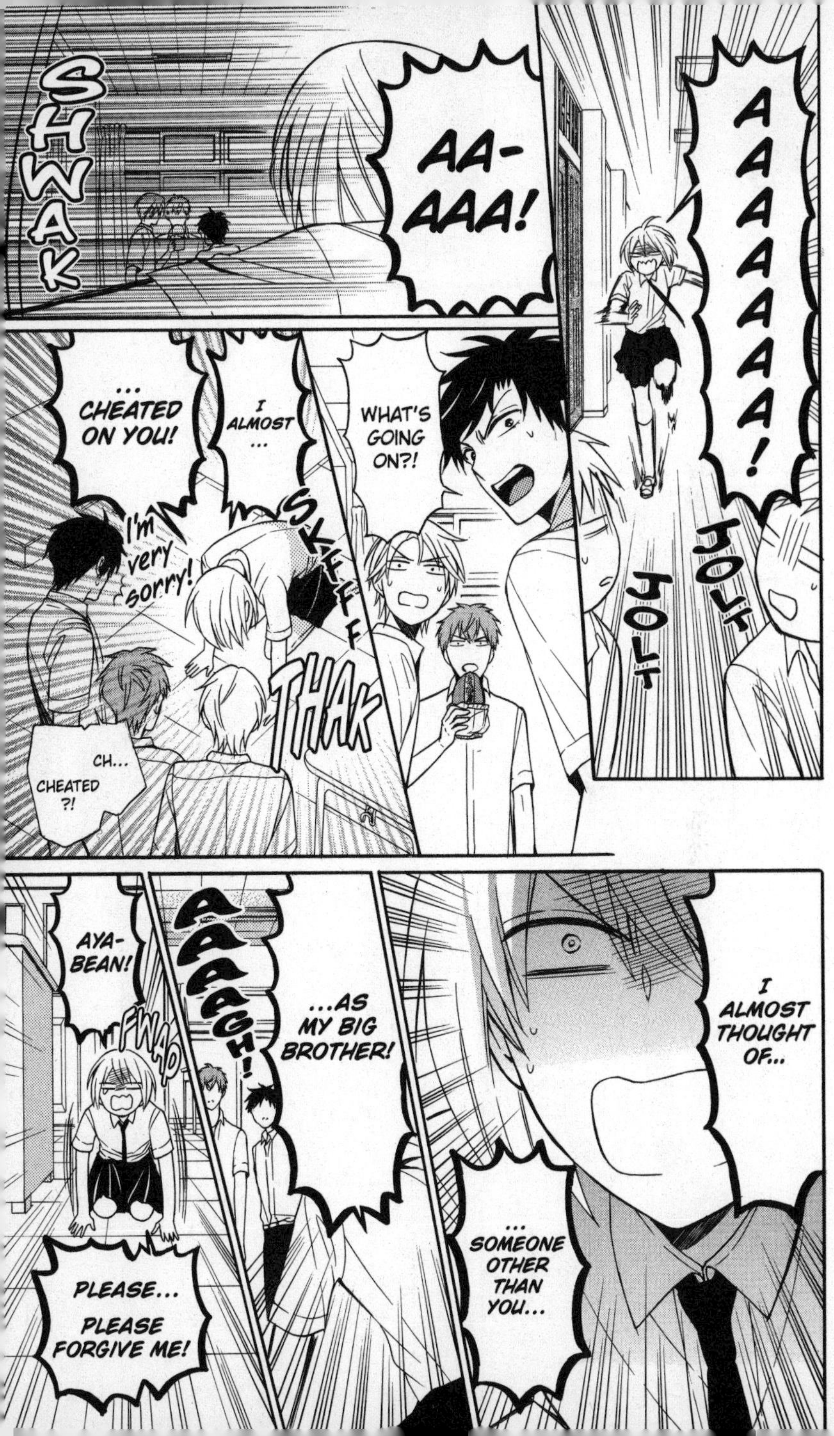
AAAAAAAAA!
JOLT
JOLT
AA-AAA!
SHWAK
WHAT'S GOING ON?!
I ALMOST ...
... CHEATED ON YOU!
I'm very sorry!
SKFFF
THAK
CH... CHEATED ?!
I ALMOST THOUGHT OF...
... SOMEONE OTHER THAN YOU...
...AS MY BIG BROTHER!
AAAAGH!
AYA-BEAN!
FWAP
PLEASE... PLEASE FORGIVE ME!

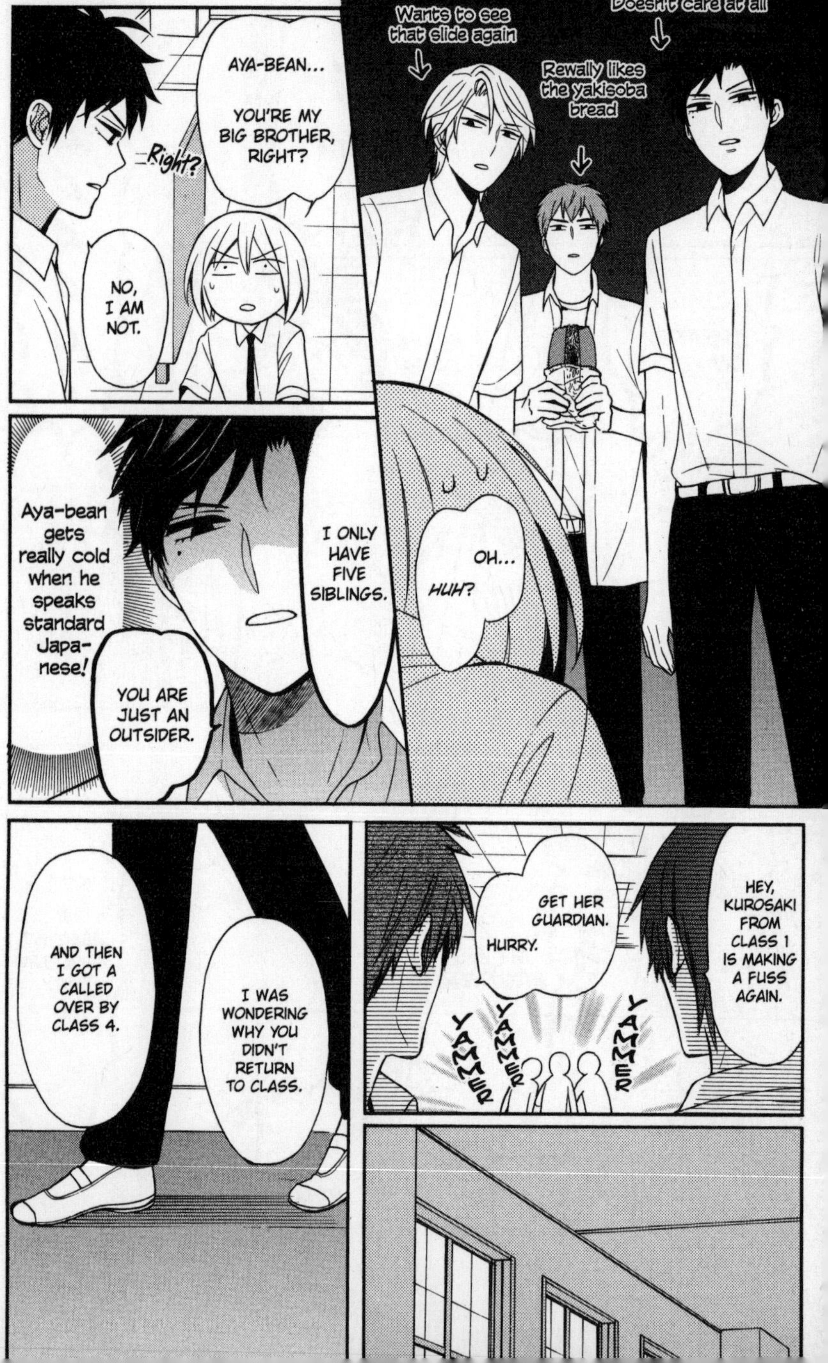
Doesn't care at all
Rewally likes the yakisoba bread
Wants to see that slide again
OH... HUH?
AYA-BEAN... YOU'RE MY BIG BROTHER, RIGHT?
Right?
NO, I AM NOT.
I ONLY HAVE FIVE SIBLINGS.
Aya-bean gets really cold when he speaks standard Japa-nese!
YOU ARE JUST AN OUTSIDER.
HEY, KUROSAKI FROM CLASS 1 IS MAKING A FUSS AGAIN.
GET HER GUARDIAN. HURRY.
YAMMER
YAMMER
YAMMER
I WAS WONDERING WHY YOU DIDN'T RETURN TO CLASS.
AND THEN I GOT A CALLED OVER BY CLASS 4.

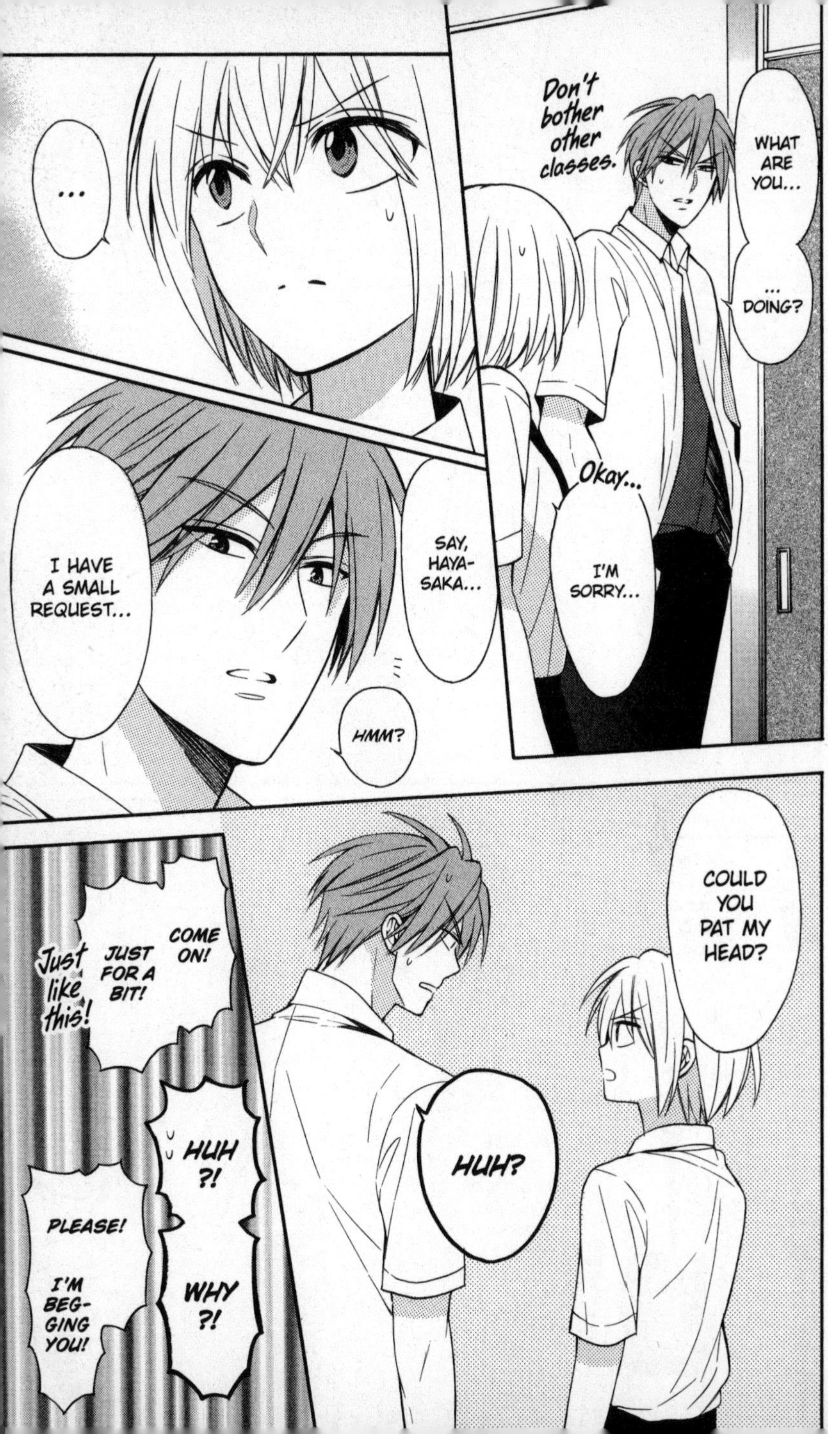
WHAT ARE YOU...
... DOING?
Don't bother other classes.
Okay...
I'M SORRY...
...
SAY, HAYA-SAKA...
HMM?
I HAVE A SMALL REQUEST...
COULD YOU PAT MY HEAD?
HUH?
HUH ?!
WHY ?!
COME ON!
JUST FOR A BIT!
Just like this!
PLEASE!
I'M BEG-GING YOU!

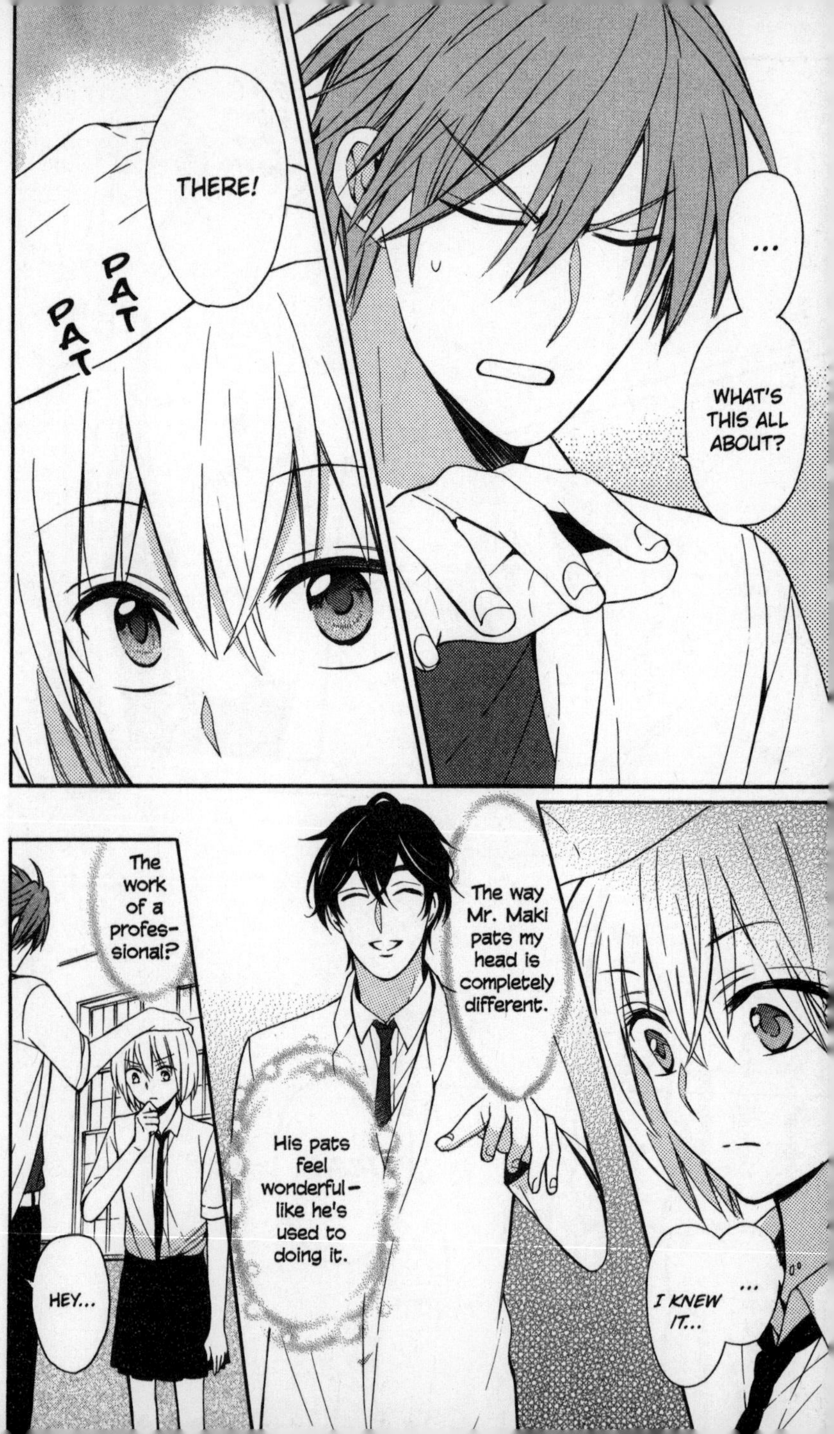
...
WHAT'S THIS ALL ABOUT?
THERE!
PAT PAT
...
I KNEW IT...
The way Mr. Maki pats my head is completely different.
His pats feel wonderful—like he's used to doing it.
The work of a profes-sional?
HEY...

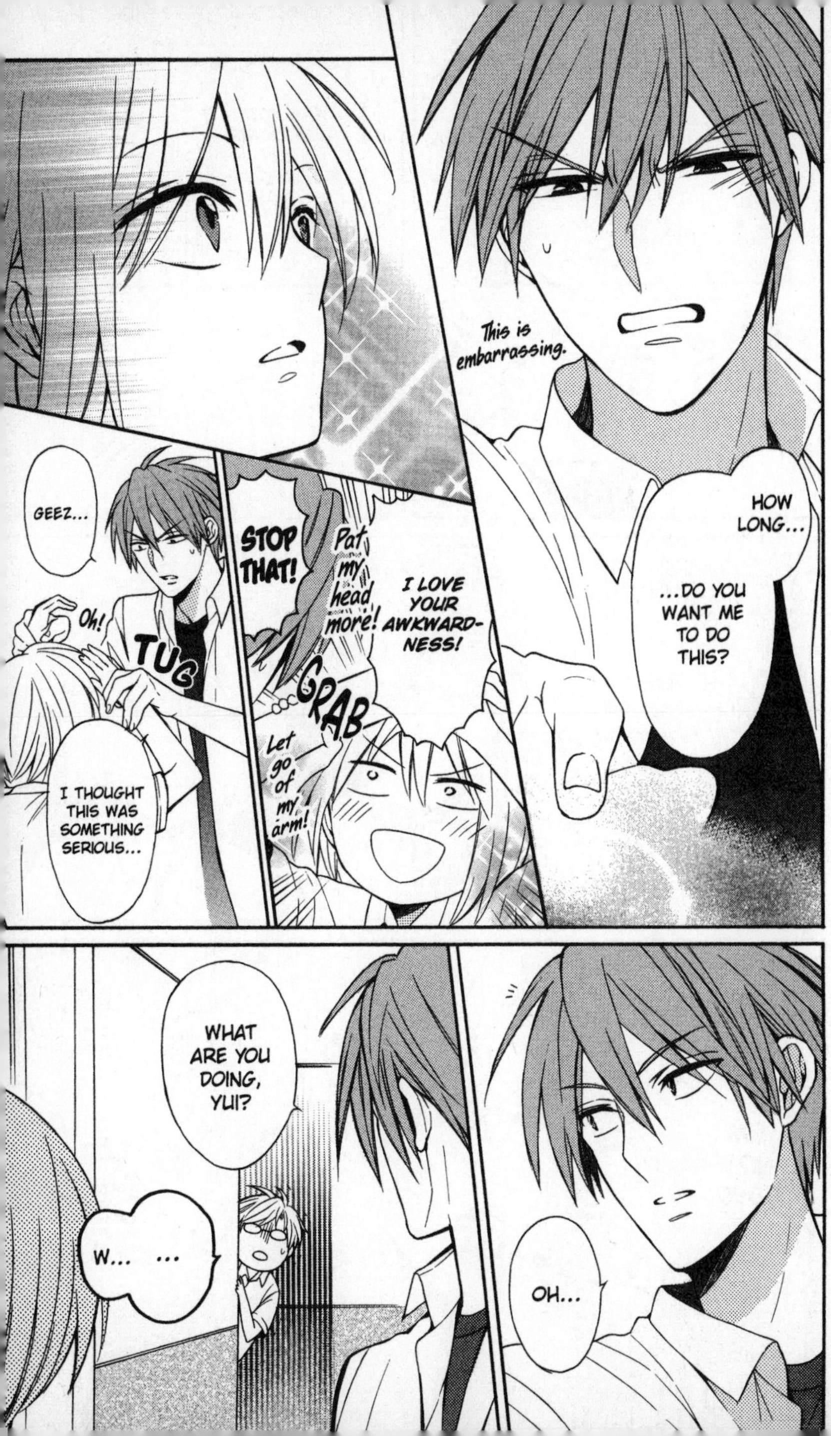
This is embarrassing.
HOW LONG...
...DO YOU WANT ME TO DO THIS?
STOP THAT!
Pat my head more!
I LOVE YOUR AWKWARDNESS!
GRAB
Let go of my arm!
GEEZ...
Oh!
TUG
I THOUGHT THIS WAS SOMETHING SERIOUS...
OH...
WHAT ARE YOU DOING, YUI?
W... ...

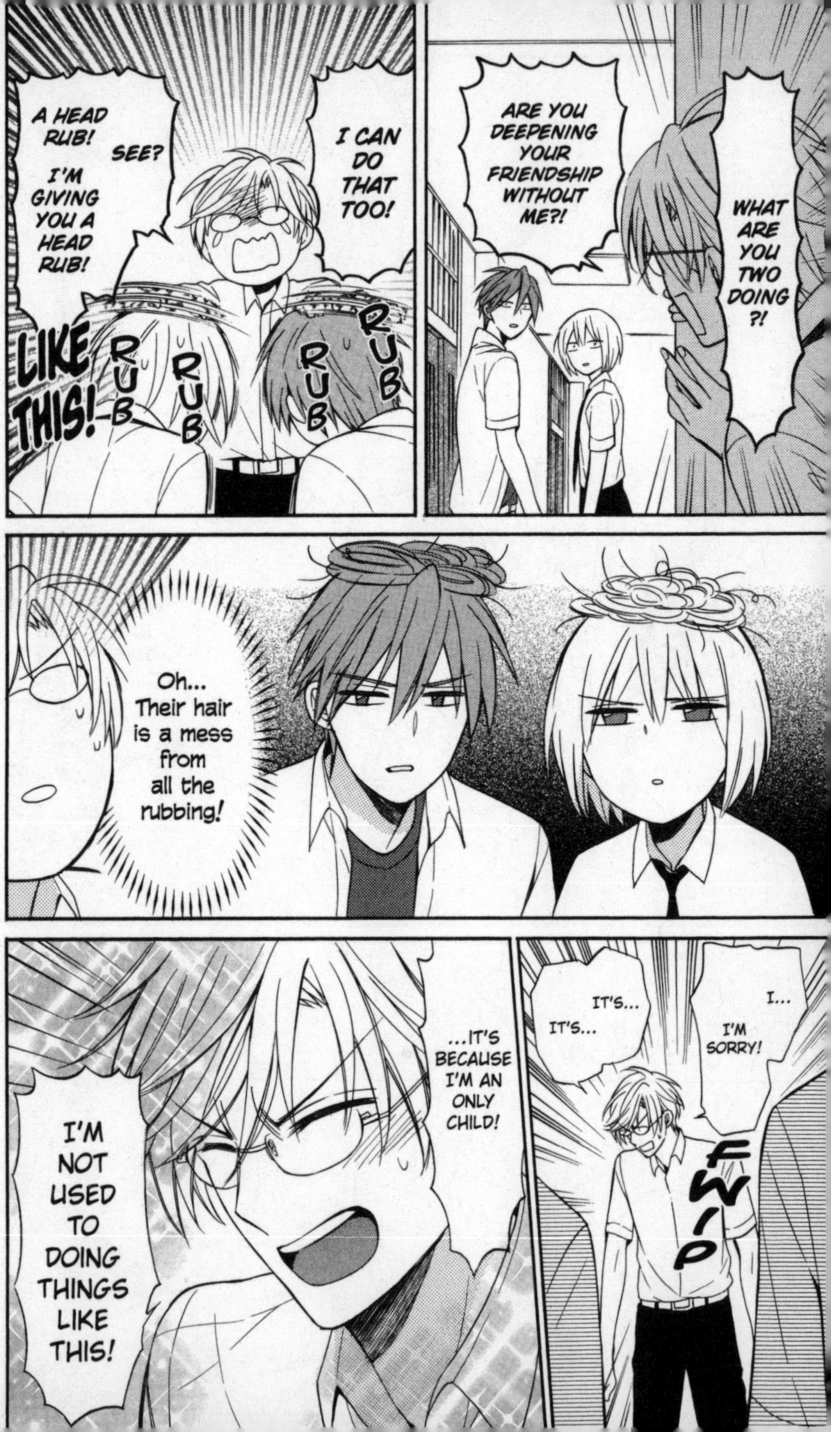
WHAT ARE YOU TWO DOING?!
ARE YOU DEEPENING YOUR FRIENDSHIP WITHOUT ME?!
I CAN DO THAT TOO!
RUB RUB
A HEAD RUB! SEE?
I'M GIVING YOU A HEAD RUB!
RUB RUB
LIKE THIS!
Oh... Their hair is a mess from all the rubbing!
I...
I'M SORRY!
IT'S...
IT'S...
FWIP
...IT'S BECAUSE I'M AN ONLY CHILD!
I'M NOT USED TO DOING THINGS LIKE THIS!

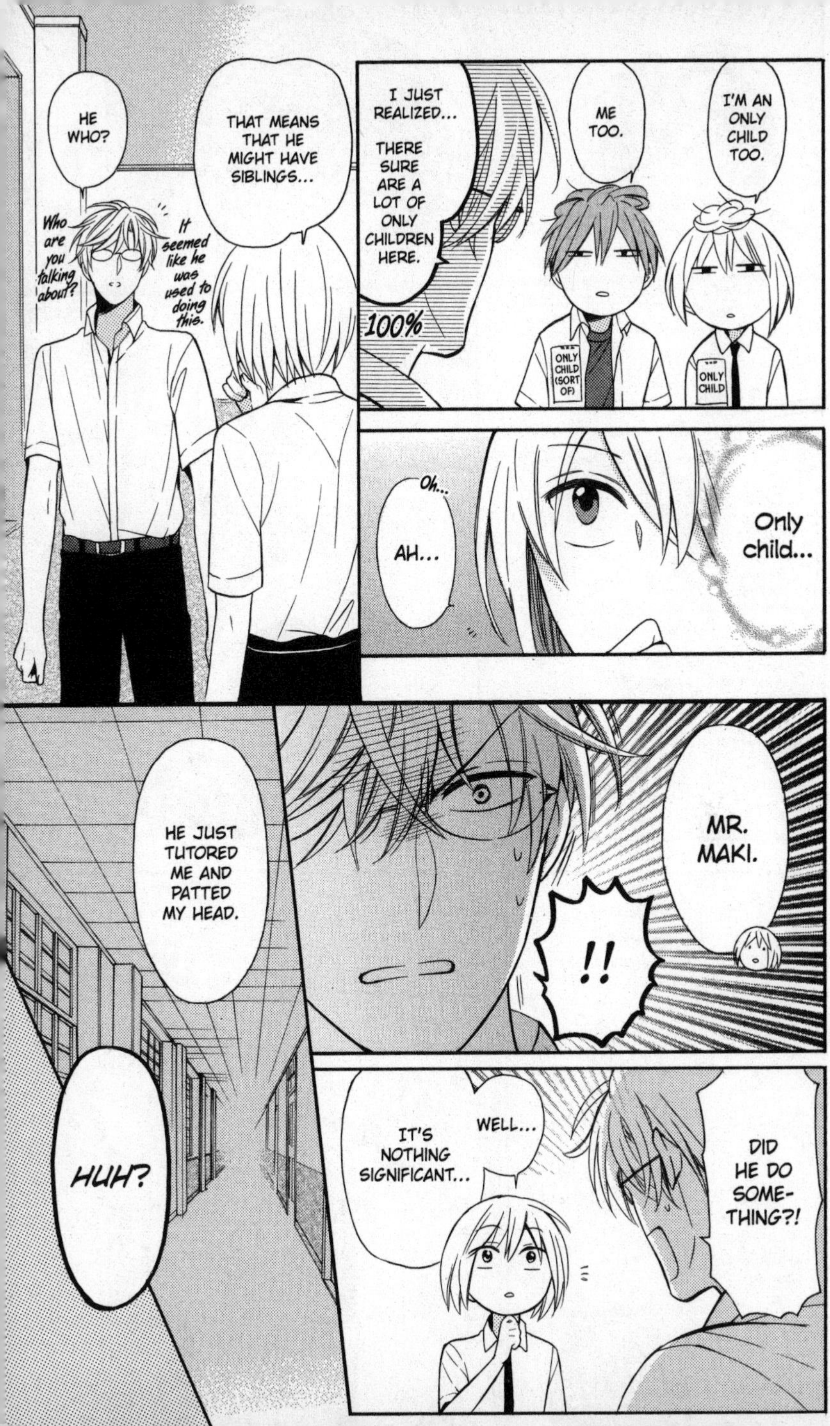
I'M AN ONLY CHILD TOO.
ME TOO.
I JUST REALIZED... THERE SURE ARE A LOT OF ONLY CHILDREN HERE.
100%
ONLY CHILD
ONLY CHILD (SORT OF)
Only child...
Oh... AH...
THAT MEANS THAT HE MIGHT HAVE SIBLINGS...
It seemed like he was used to doing this.
HE WHO?
Who are you talking about?
MR. MAKI.
!!
DID HE DO SOME-THING?!
WELL...
IT'S NOTHING SIGNIFICANT...
HE JUST TUTORED ME AND PATTED MY HEAD.
HUH?

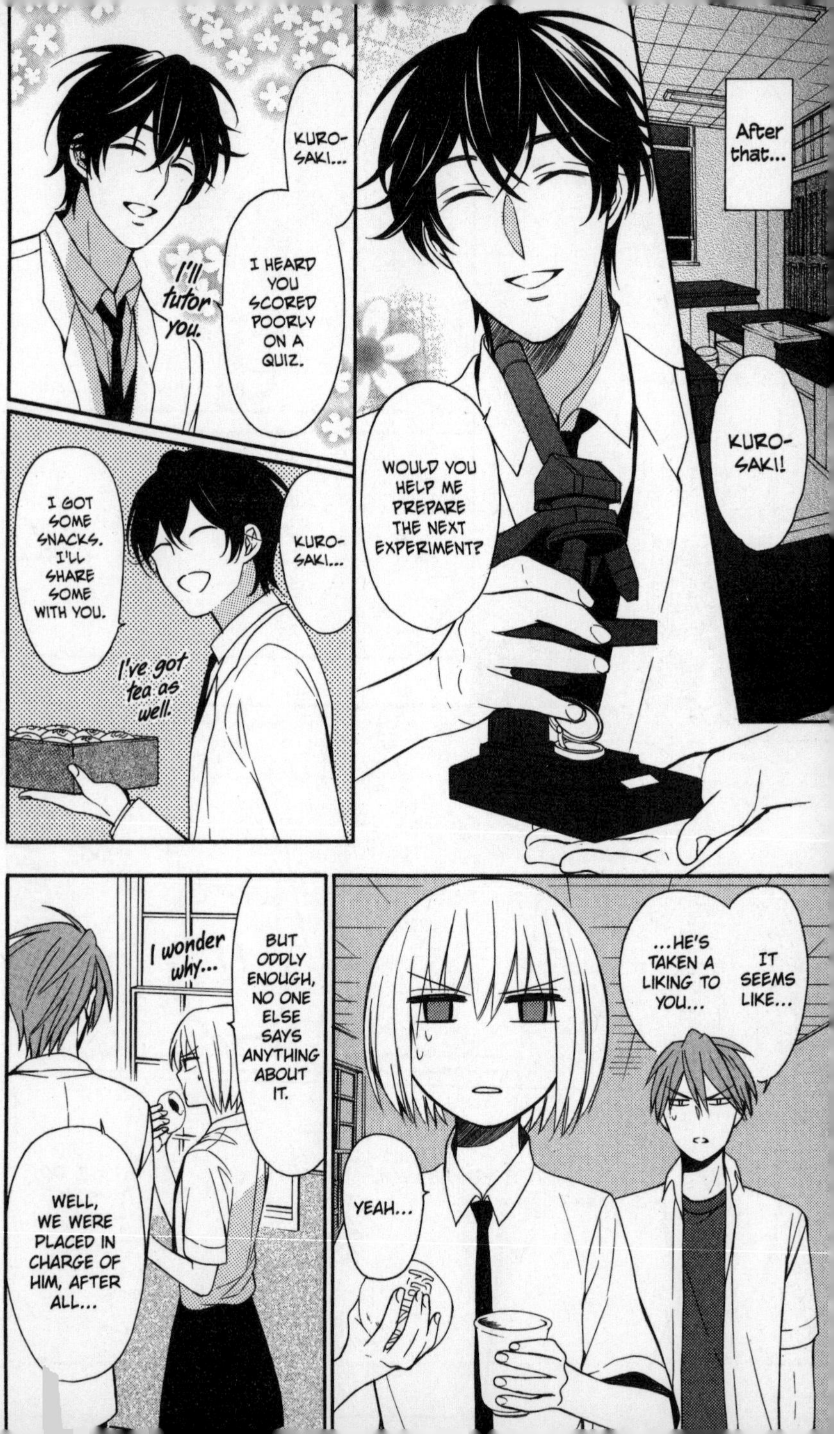
After that...
KURO-SAKI!
WOULD YOU HELP ME PREPARE THE NEXT EXPERIMENT?
KURO-SAKI...
I HEARD YOU SCORED POORLY ON A QUIZ.
I'll tutor you.
KURO-SAKI...
I GOT SOME SNACKS. I'LL SHARE SOME WITH YOU.
I've got tea as well.
IT SEEMS LIKE...
...HE'S TAKEN A LIKING TO YOU...
YEAH...
BUT ODDLY ENOUGH, NO ONE ELSE SAYS ANYTHING ABOUT IT.
I wonder why...
WELL, WE WERE PLACED IN CHARGE OF HIM, AFTER ALL...

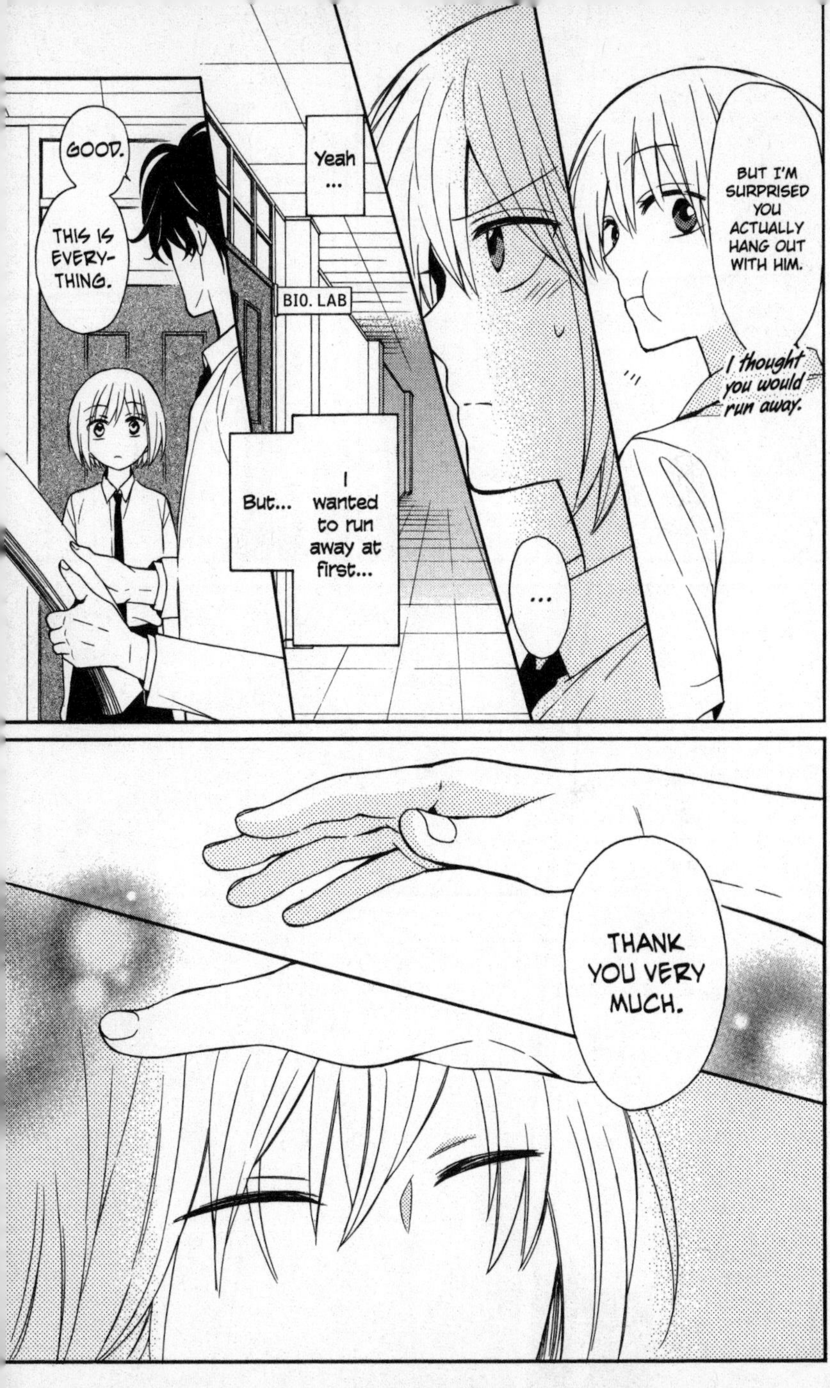
BUT I'M SURPRISED YOU ACTUALLY HANG OUT WITH HIM.
I thought you would run away.
...
Yeah...
I wanted to run away at first...
But...
BIO. LAB
GOOD.
THIS IS EVERY-THING.
THANK YOU VERY MUCH.

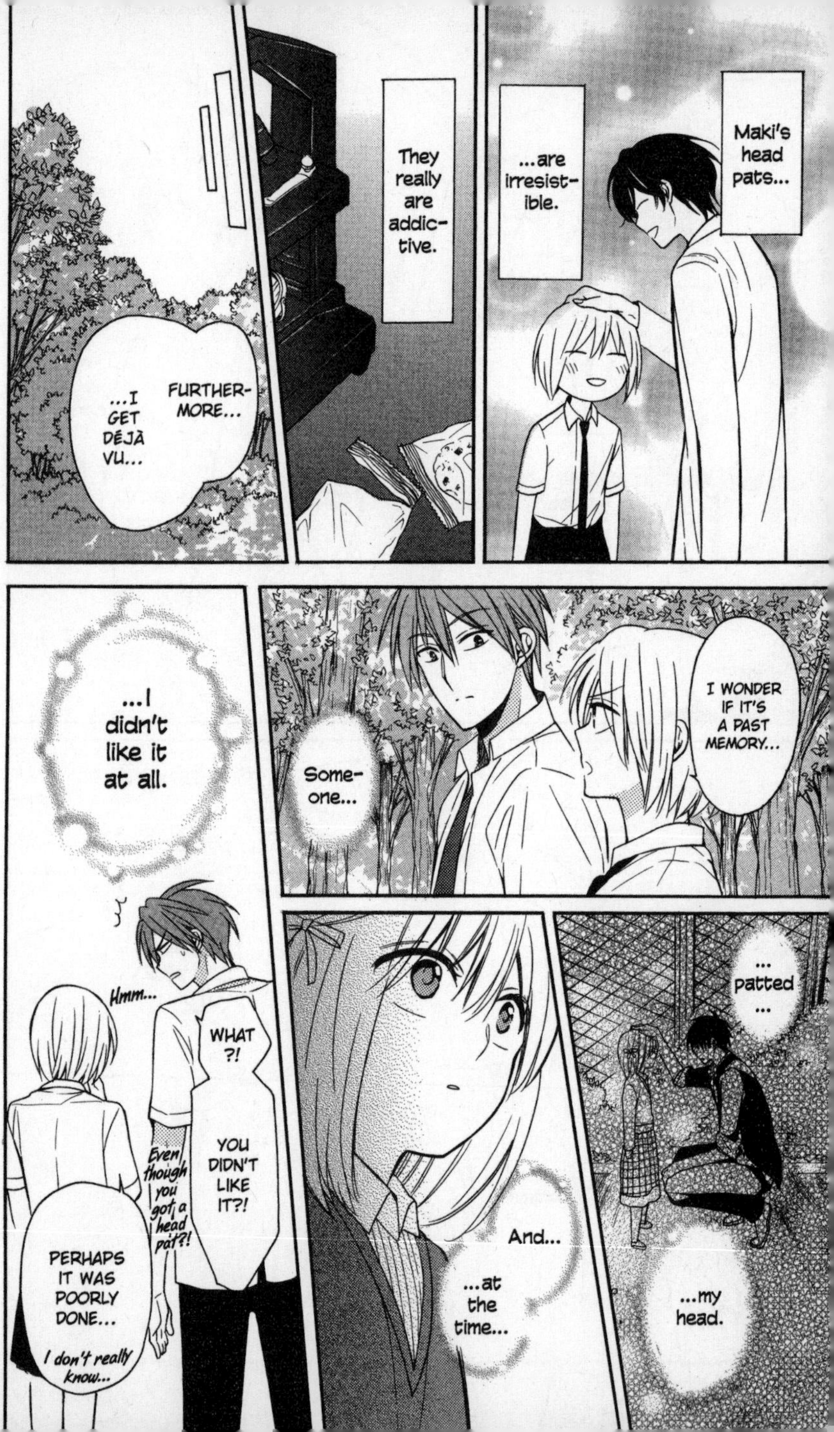

Maki's head pats...
...are irresistible.
They really are addictive.
FURTHERMORE...
...I GET DÉJÀ VU...
I WONDER IF IT'S A PAST MEMORY...
Someone...
...patted...
...my head.
And...
...at the time...
...I didn't like it at all.
Hmm...
WHAT?!
YOU DIDN'T LIKE IT?!
Even though you got a head pat?!
PERHAPS IT WAS POORLY DONE...
I don't really know...

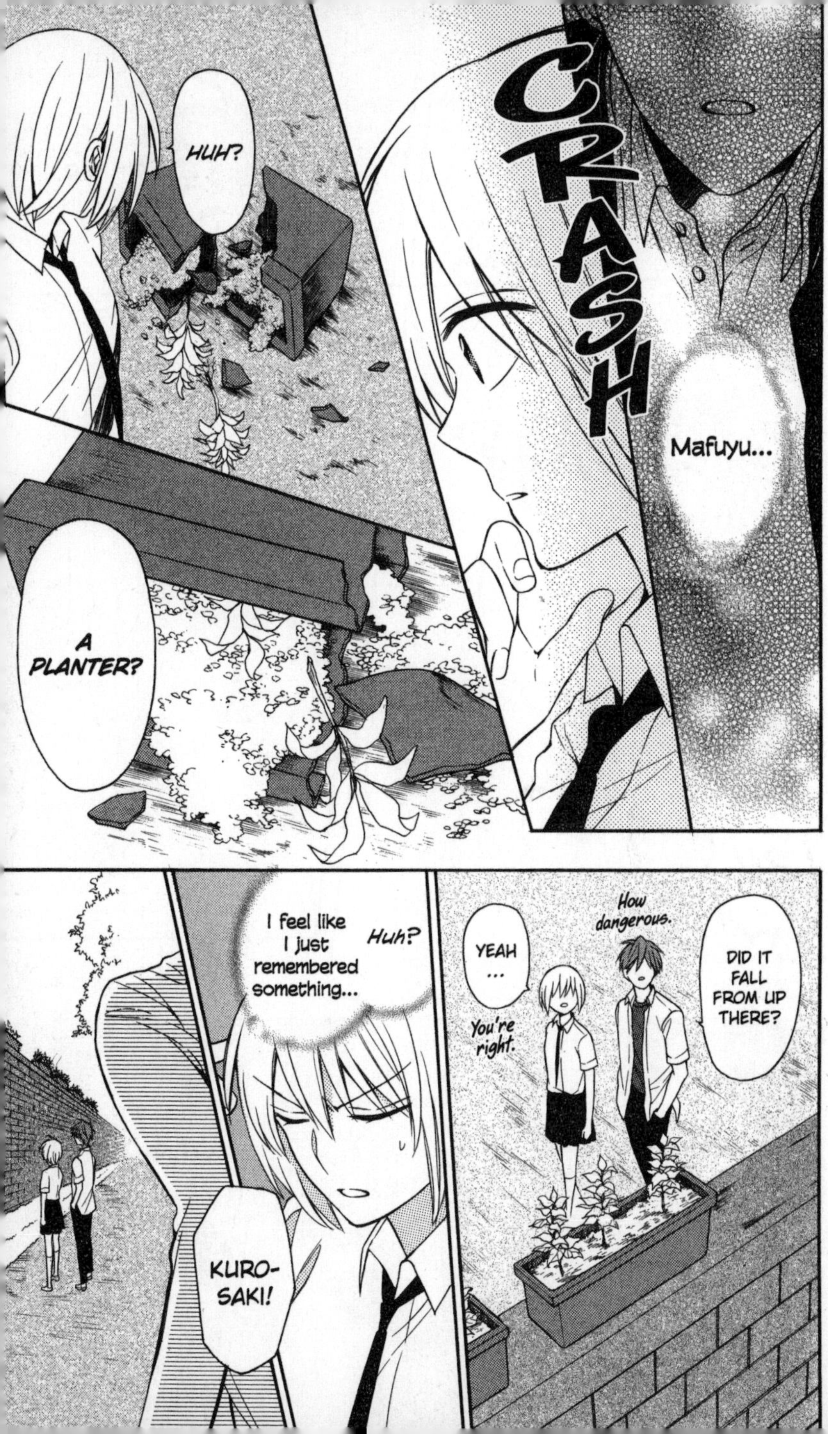
CRASH
Mafuyu...
HUH?
A PLANTER?
DID IT FALL FROM UP THERE?
How dangerous.
YEAH...
You're right.
Huh?
I feel like I just remembered something...
KURO-SAKI!

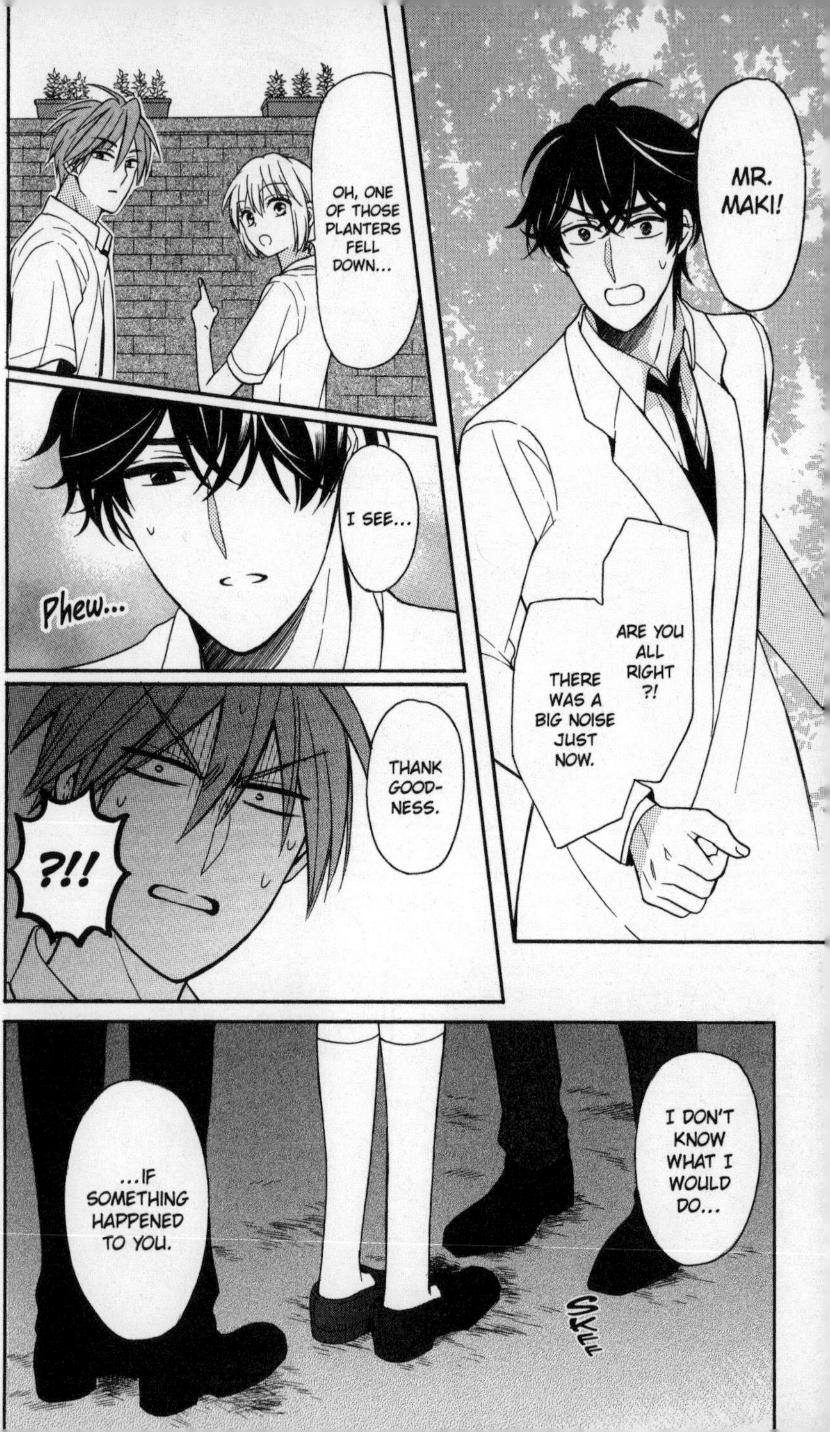
MR. MAKI!
ARE YOU ALL RIGHT ?!
THERE WAS A BIG NOISE JUST NOW.
OH, ONE OF THOSE PLANTERS FELL DOWN...
I SEE...
Phew...
THANK GOODNESS.
?!!
I DON'T KNOW WHAT I WOULD DO...
...IF SOMETHING HAPPENED TO YOU.
SKFF

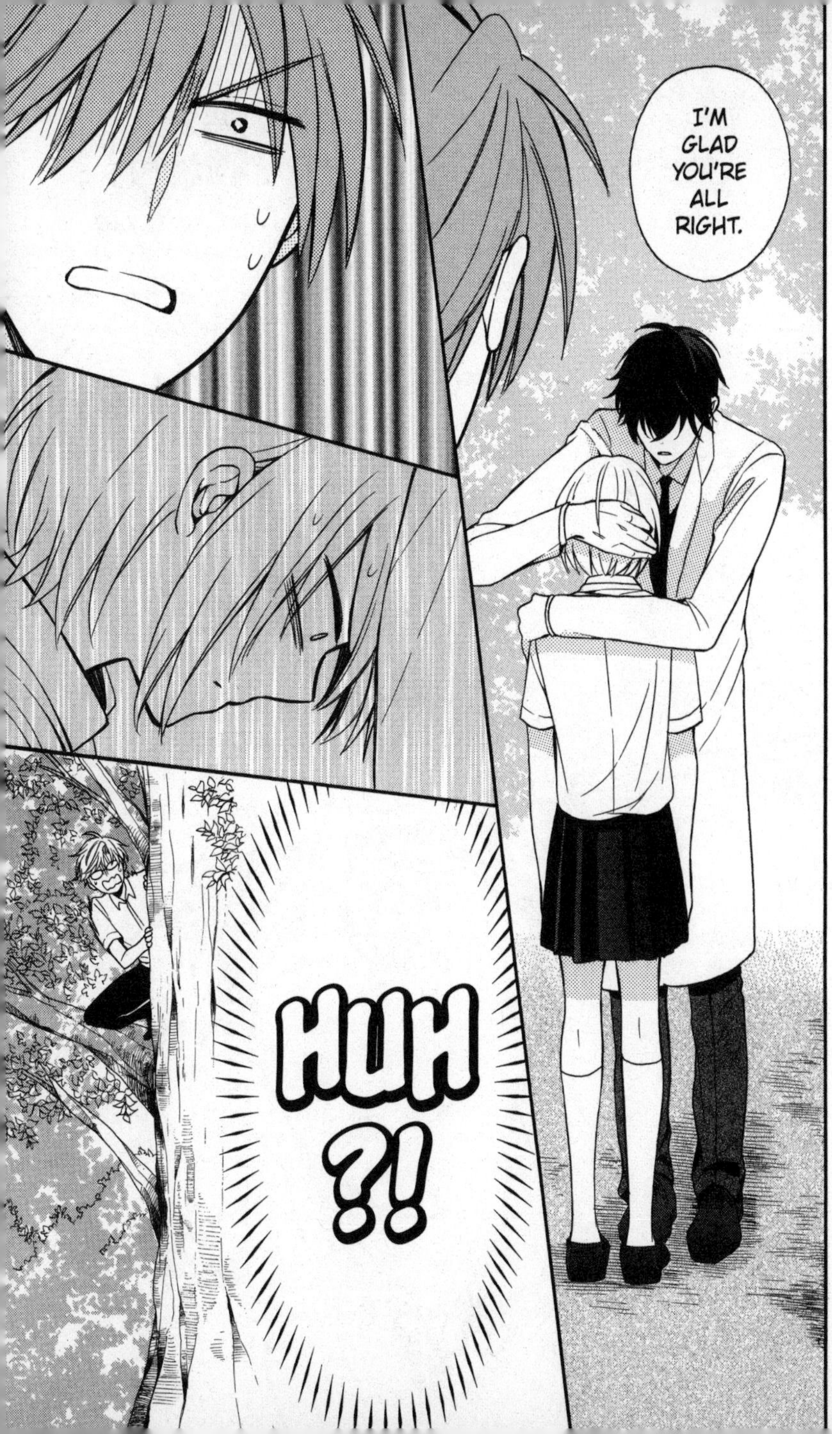
I'M GLAD YOU'RE ALL RIGHT.
HUH ?!

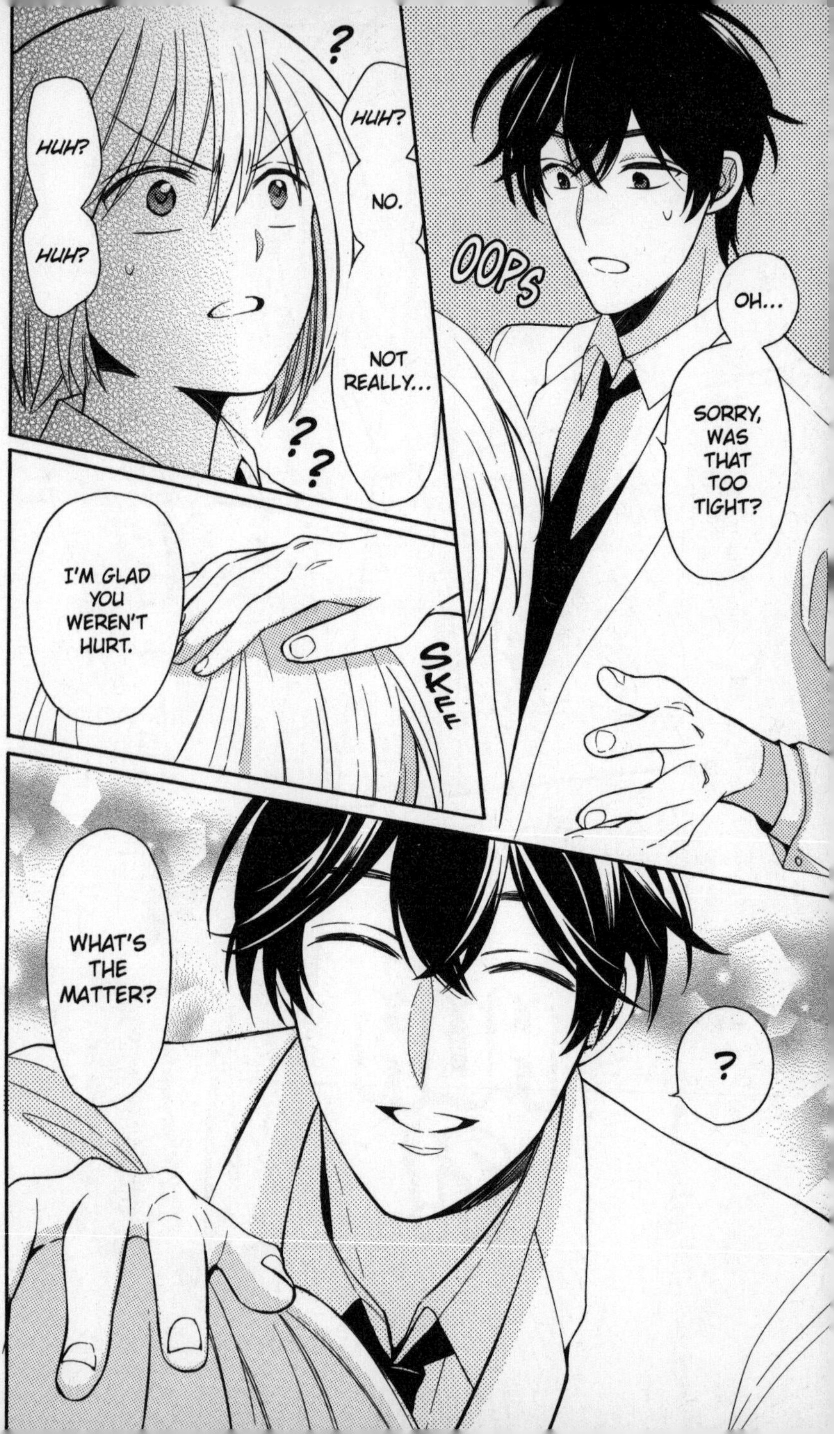
OOPS
OH...
SORRY, WAS THAT TOO TIGHT?
?
HUH?
NO.
NOT REALLY...
??
HUH?
HUH?
I'M GLAD YOU WEREN'T HURT.
SKFF
?
WHAT'S THE MATTER?

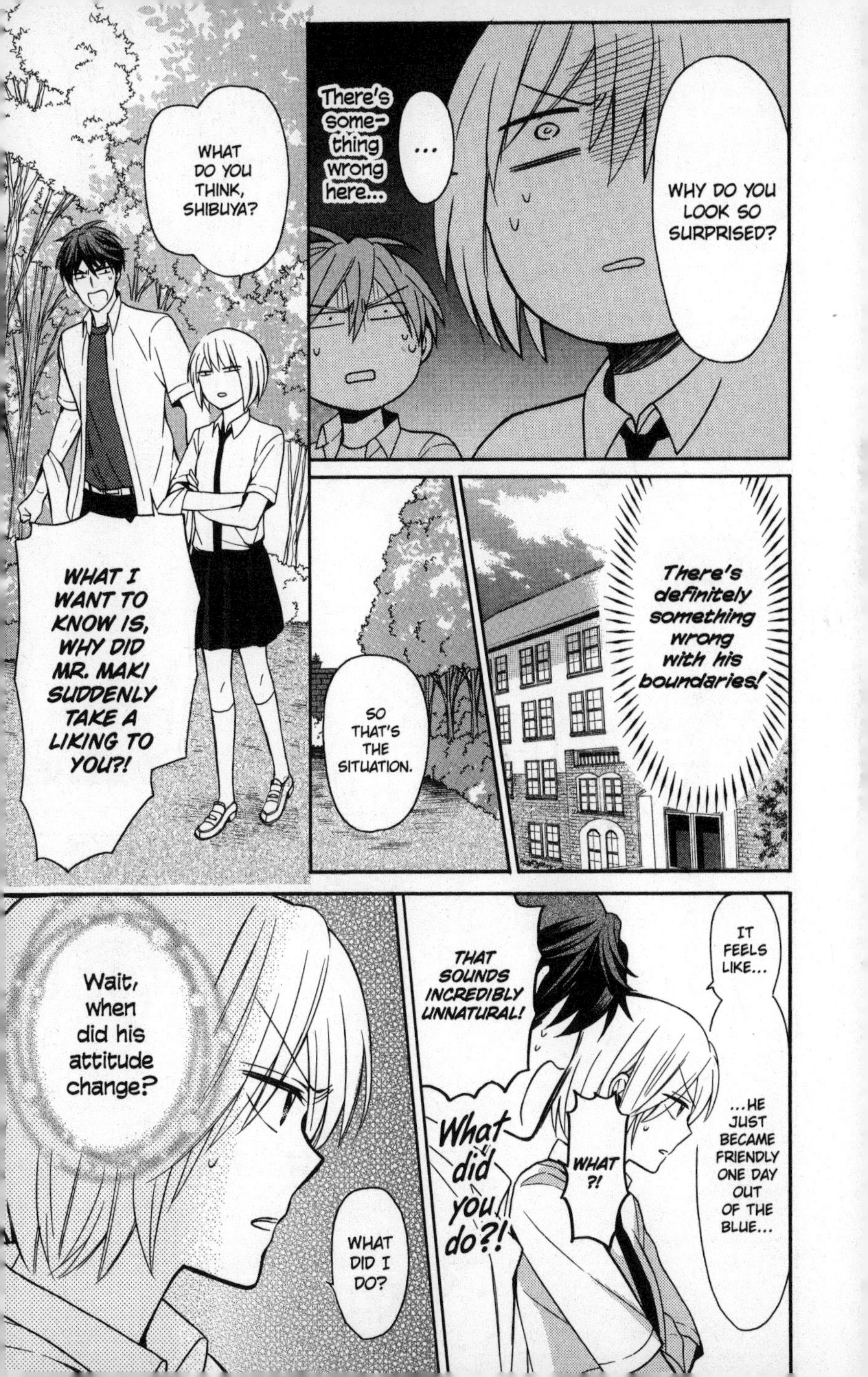
WHY DO YOU LOOK SO SURPRISED?
...
There's some-thing wrong here...
There's definitely something wrong with his boundaries!
SO THAT'S THE SITUATION.
WHAT DO YOU THINK, SHIBUYA?
WHAT I WANT TO KNOW IS, WHY DID MR. MAKI SUDDENLY TAKE A LIKING TO YOU?!
IT FEELS LIKE...
THAT SOUNDS INCREDIBLY UNNATURAL!
...HE JUST BECAME FRIENDLY ONE DAY OUT OF THE BLUE...
WHAT?!
What did you do?!
Wait, when did his attitude change?
WHAT DID I DO?

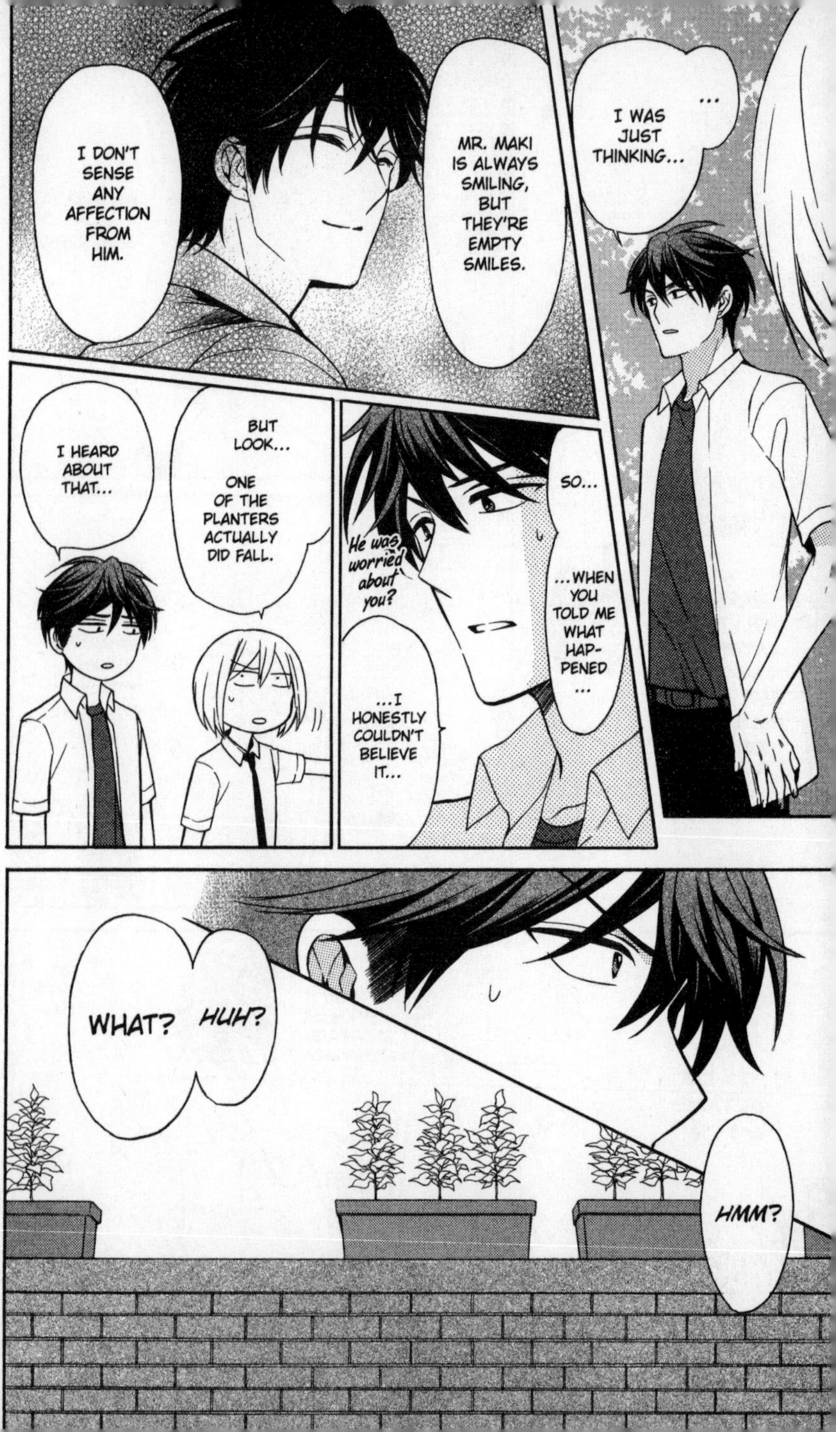
...
I WAS JUST THINKING...
MR. MAKI IS ALWAYS SMILING, BUT THEY'RE EMPTY SMILES.
I DON'T SENSE ANY AFFECTION FROM HIM.
SO...
...WHEN YOU TOLD ME WHAT HAP-PENED...
He was worried about you?
...I HONESTLY COULDN'T BELIEVE IT...
BUT LOOK...
ONE OF THE PLANTERS ACTUALLY DID FALL.
I HEARD ABOUT THAT...
HMM?
WHAT?
HUH?

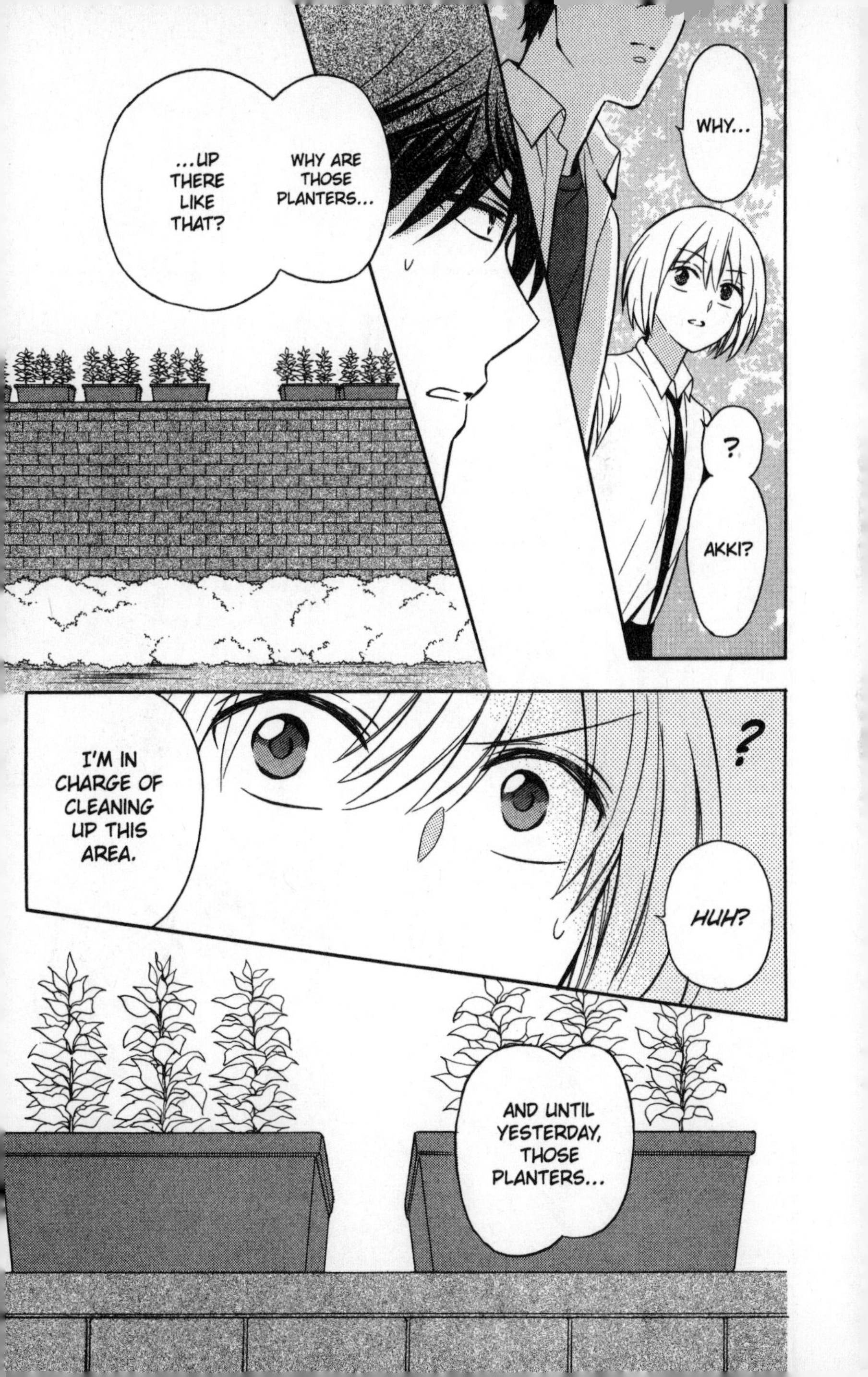
WHY...
?
AKKI?
WHY ARE THOSE PLANTERS...
...UP THERE LIKE THAT?
?
HUH?
I'M IN CHARGE OF CLEANING UP THIS AREA.
AND UNTIL YESTERDAY, THOSE PLANTERS...

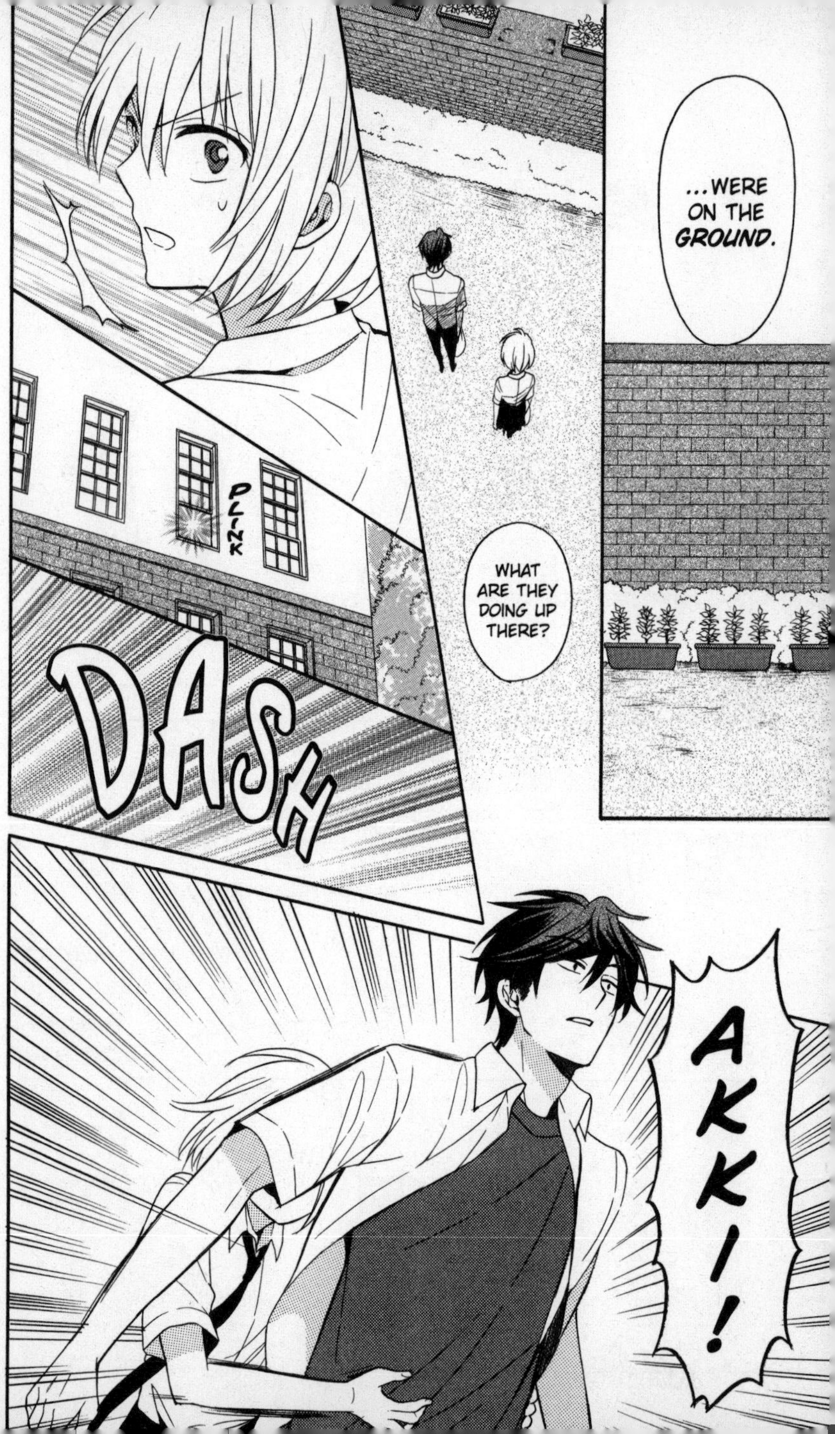
...WERE ON THE GROUND.
WHAT ARE THEY DOING UP THERE?
PLINK
DASH
AKKI!

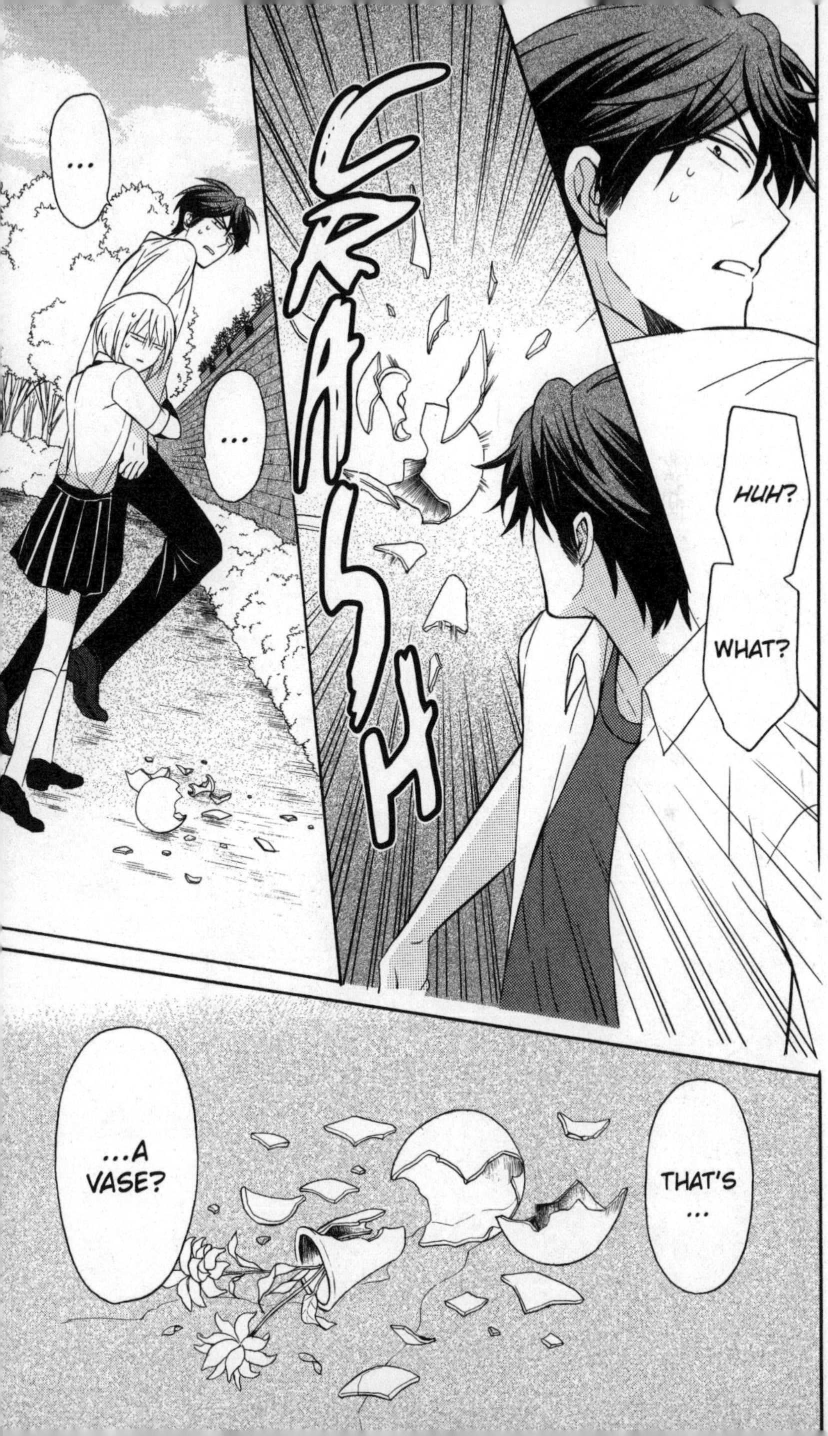
HUH?
WHAT?
CRASH
...
...
THAT'S ...
...A VASE?

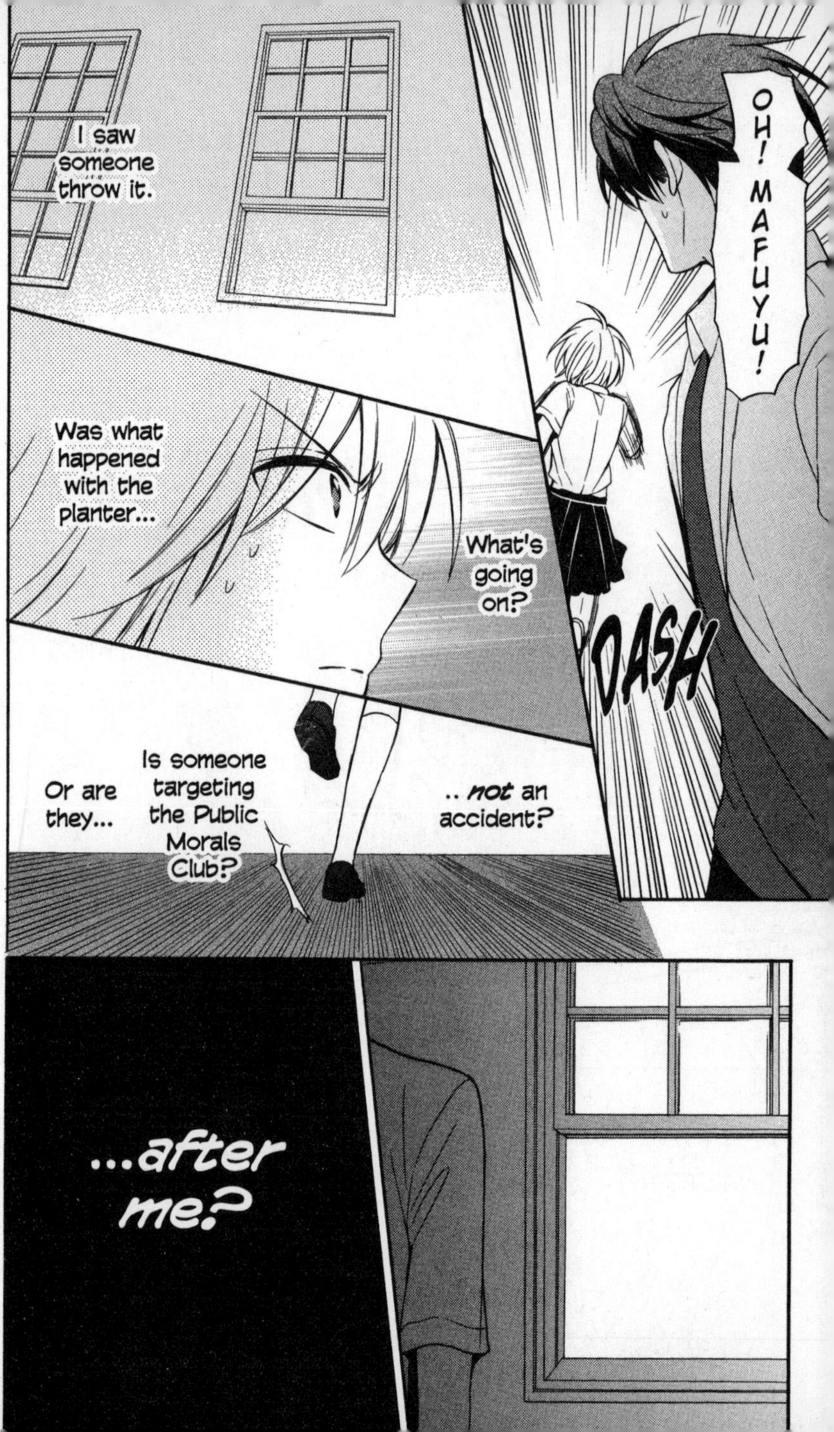
OH! MAFUYU!
DASH
I saw someone throw it.
Was what happened with the planter...
What's going on?
.. *not* an accident?
Is someone targeting the Public Morals Club?
Or are they...
...after me?

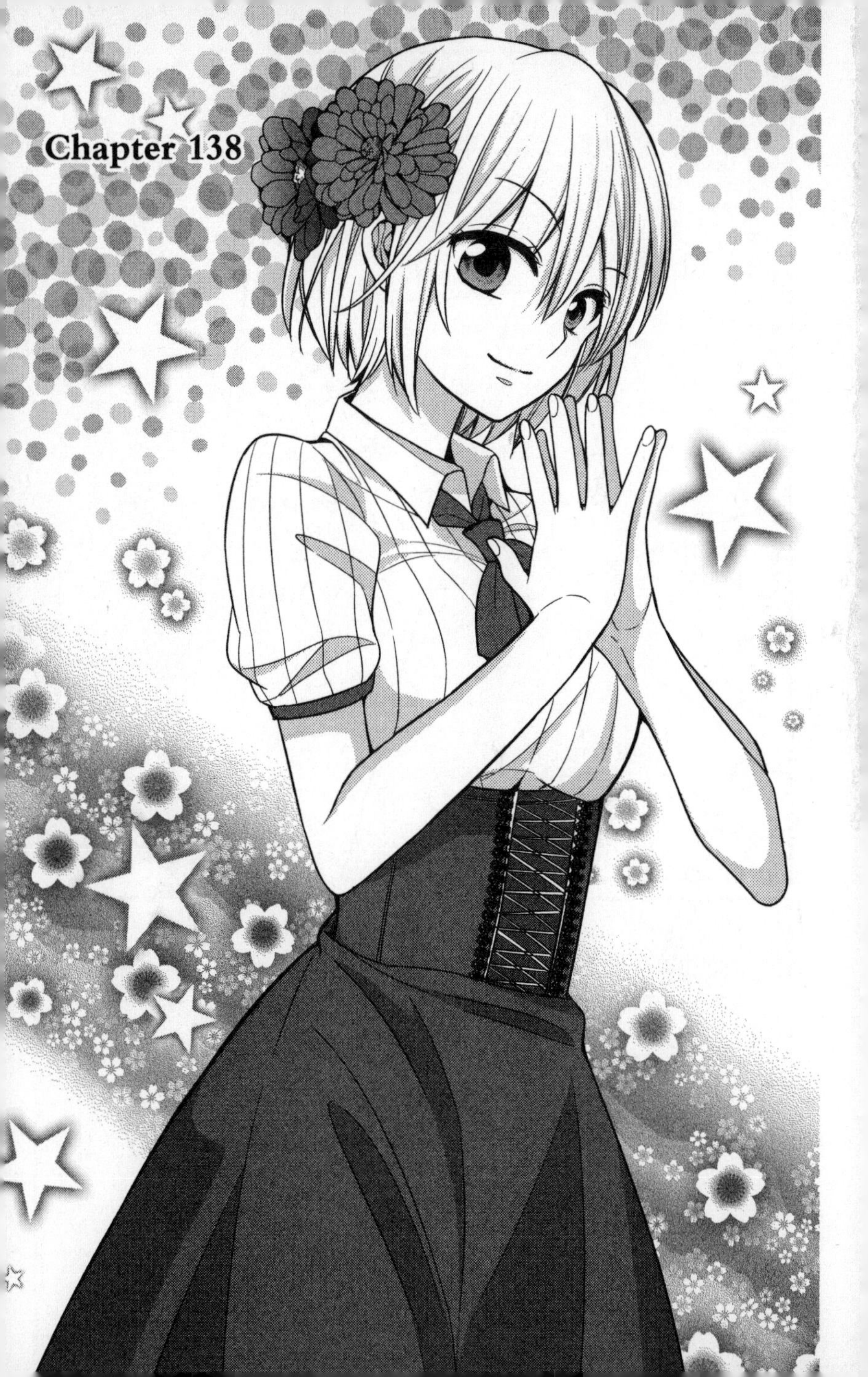
Chapter 138

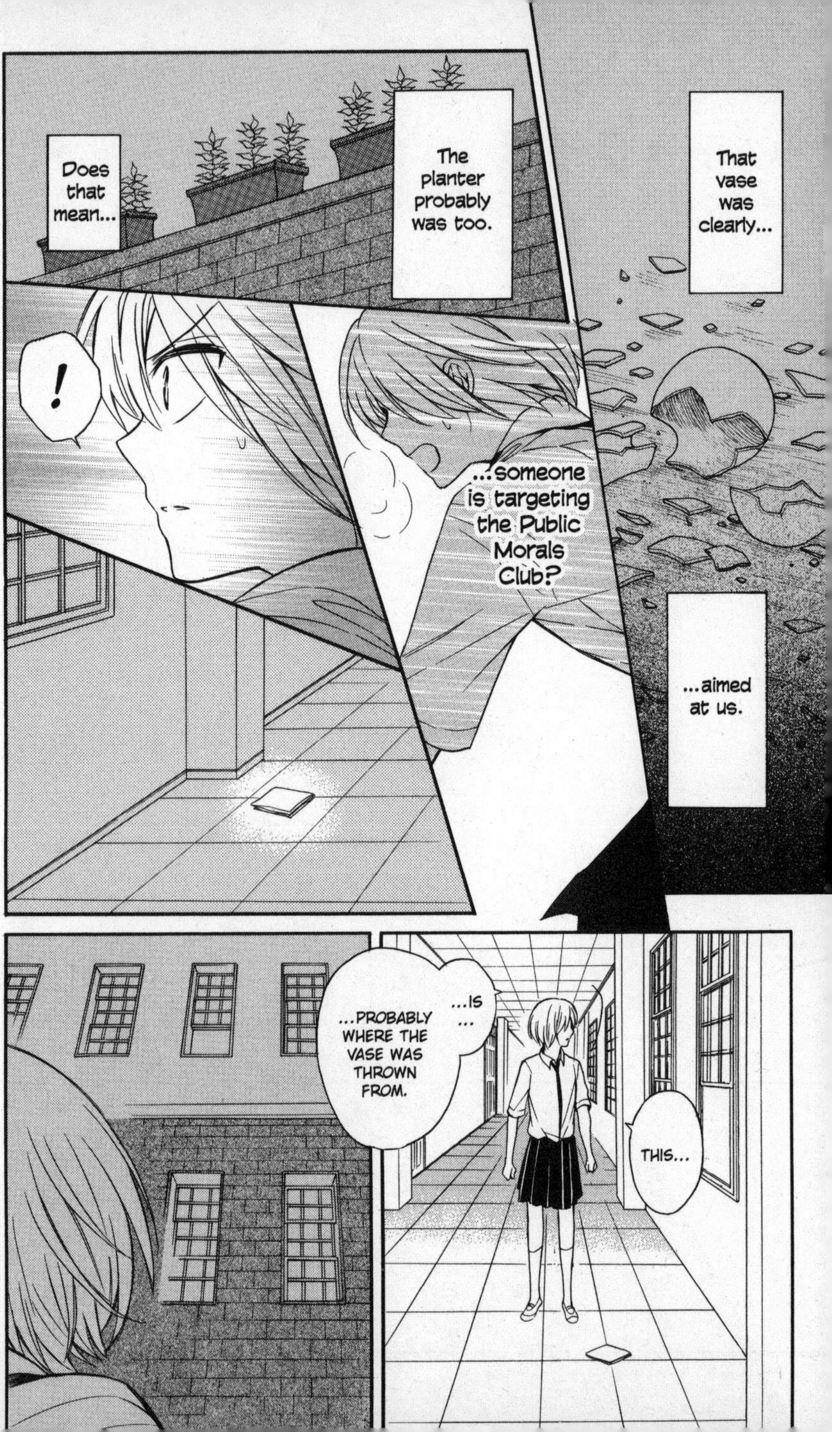
That vase was clearly...
...aimed at us.
The planter probably was too.
Does that mean...
...someone is targeting the Public Morals Club?
!
THIS...
...IS ...
...PROBABLY WHERE THE VASE WAS THROWN FROM.

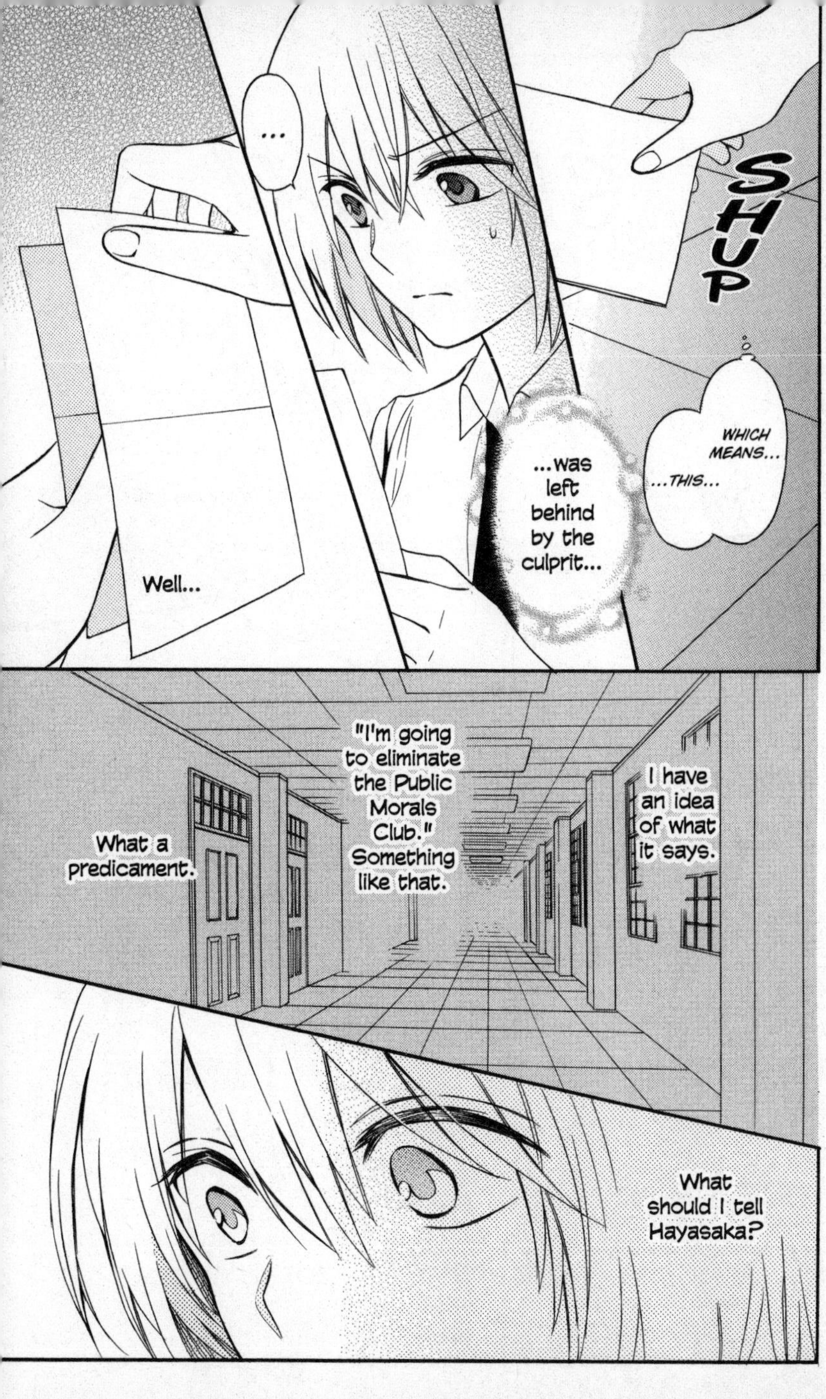
SHUP
WHICH MEANS... ...THIS...
...was left behind by the culprit...
...
Well...
I have an idea of what it says.
"I'm going to eliminate the Public Morals Club." Something like that.
What a predicament.
What should I tell Hayasaka?

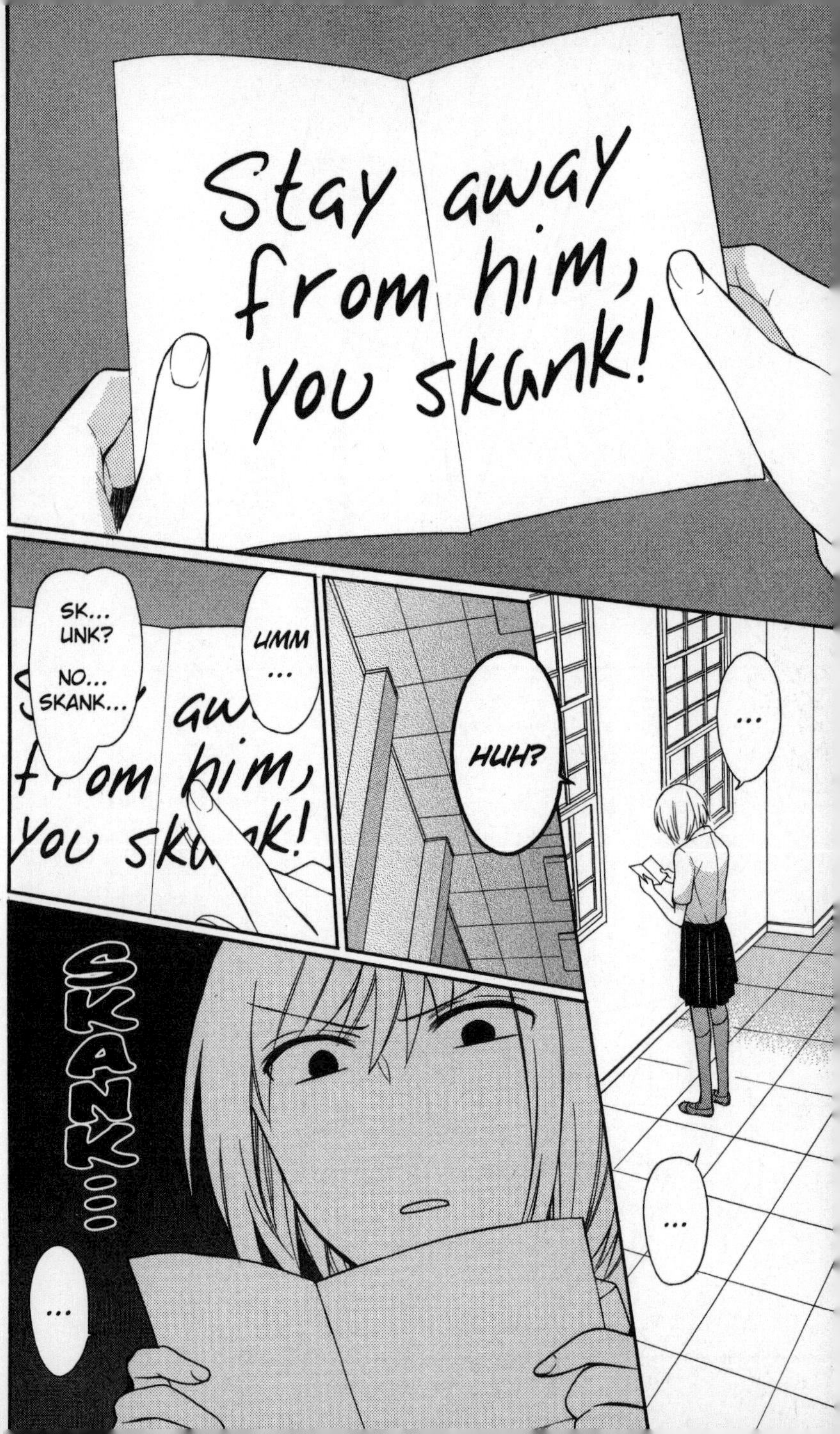

Stay away from him, you skank!
...
...
HUH?
UMM ...
SK... UNK?
NO... SKANK...
SKANK...
...

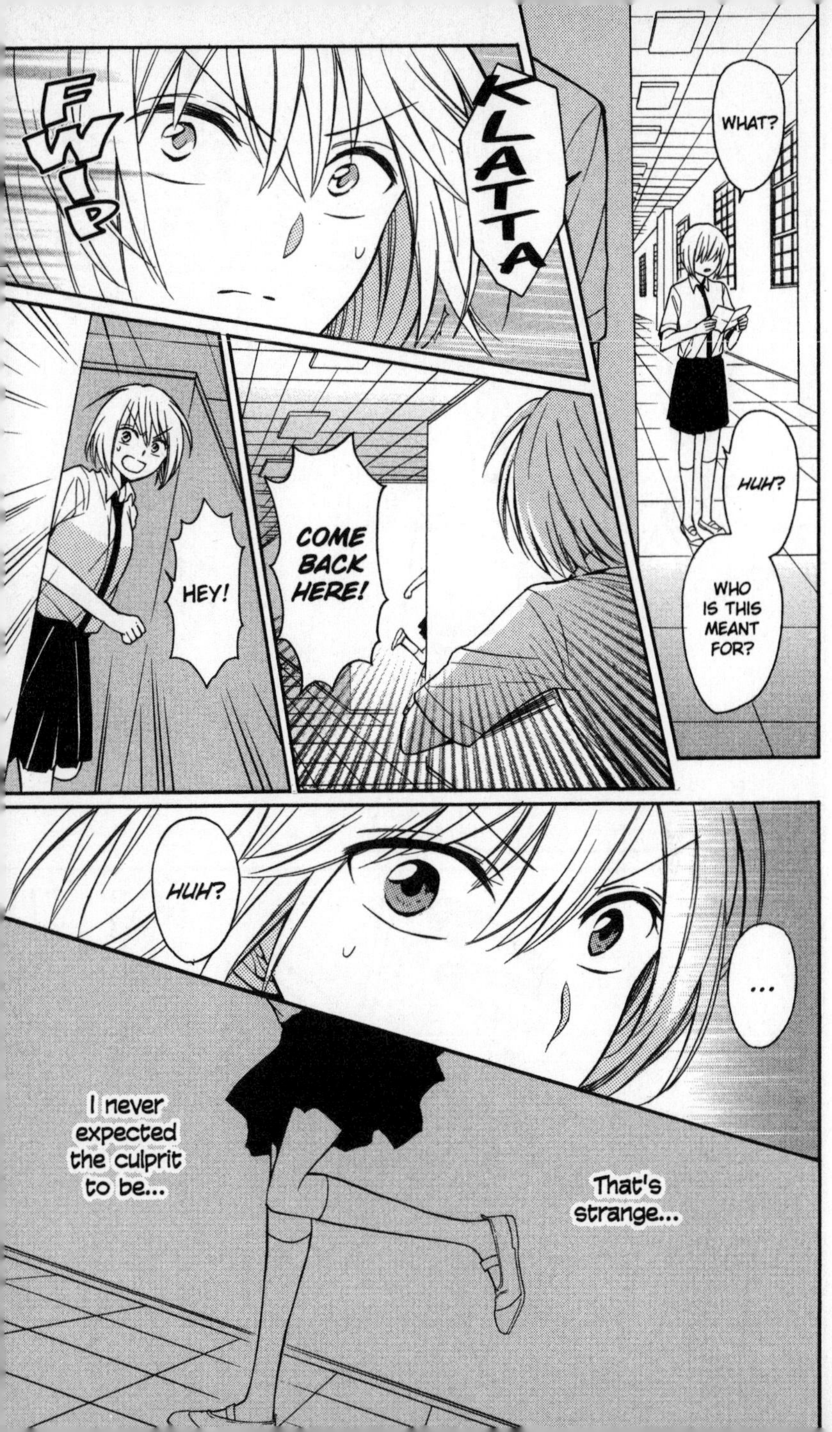
WHAT?
HUH?
WHO IS THIS MEANT FOR?
KLATTA
FWIP
COME BACK HERE!
HEY!
HUH?
...
That's strange...
I never expected the culprit to be...

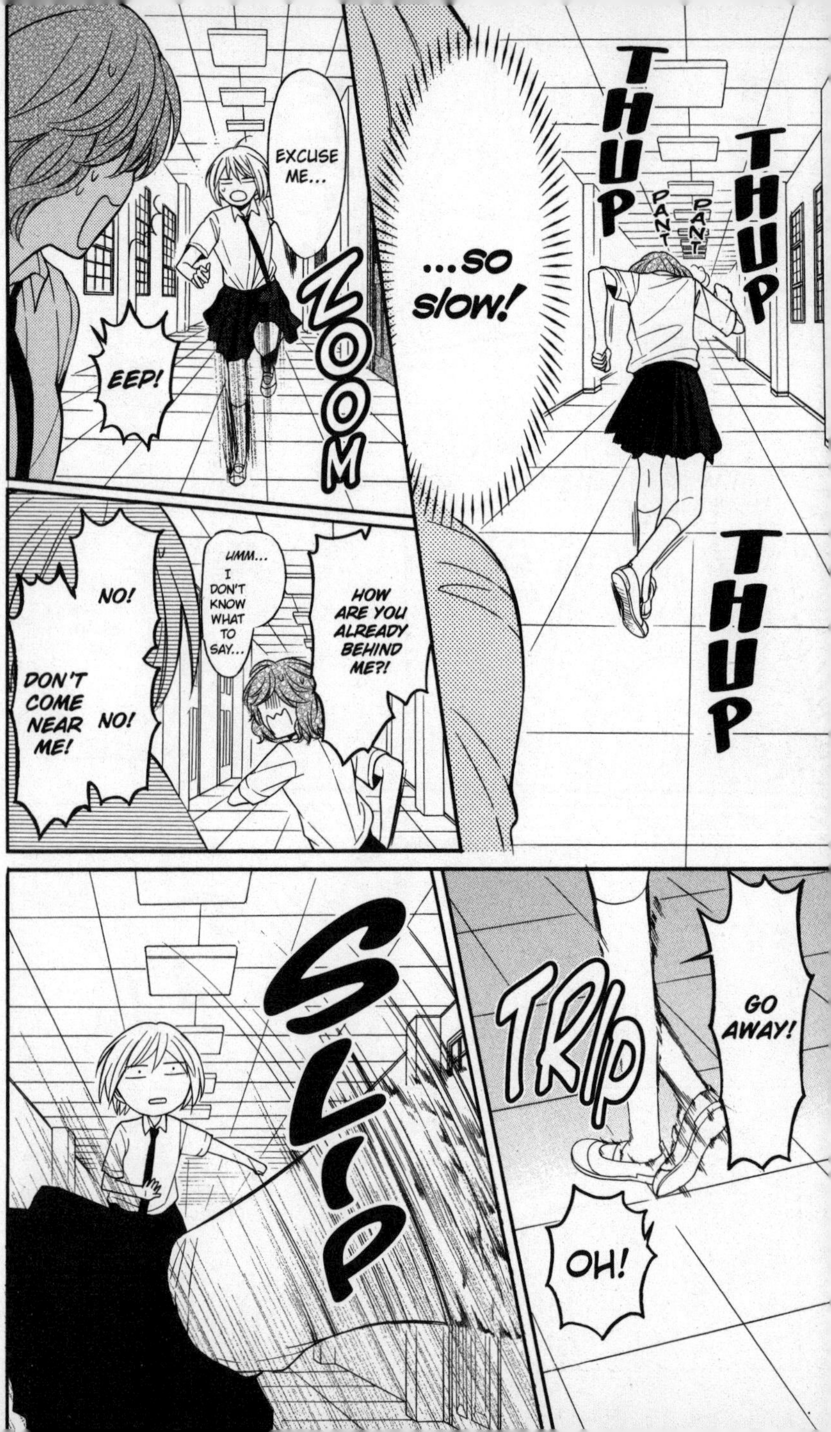
THUP
THUP
PANT
PANT
...so slow!
THUP
THUP
EXCUSE ME...
ZOOM
EEP!
HOW ARE YOU ALREADY BEHIND ME?!
UMM... I DON'T KNOW WHAT TO SAY...
NO!
NO!
DON'T COME NEAR ME!
GO AWAY!
TRIP
OH!
SLIP

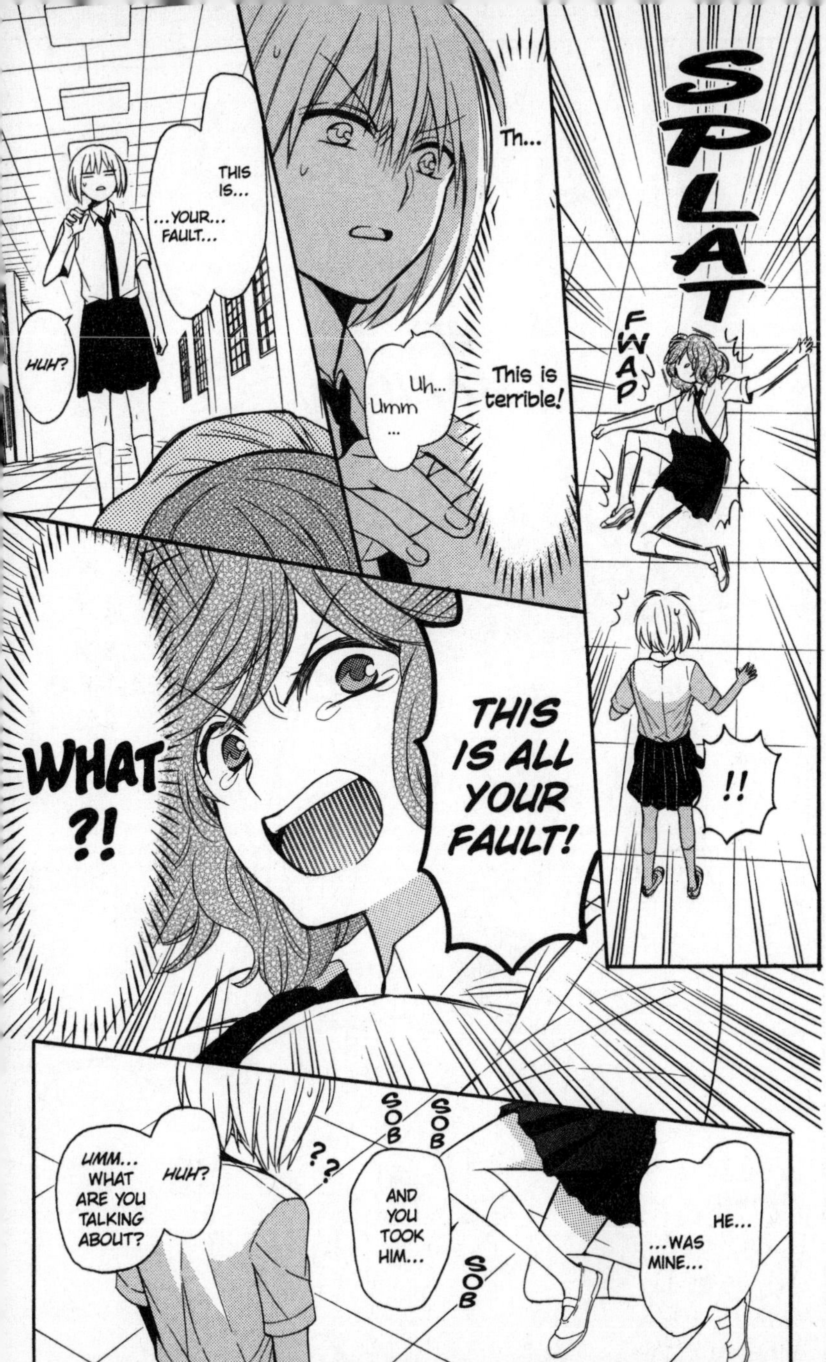
SPLAT
FWAP
!!
Th...
This is terrible!
Uh... Umm ...
THIS IS... ...YOUR... FAULT...
HUH?
THIS IS ALL YOUR FAULT!
WHAT?!
HE... ...WAS MINE...
SOB SOB
AND YOU TOOK HIM...
SOB
??
HUH?
UMM... WHAT ARE YOU TALKING ABOUT?

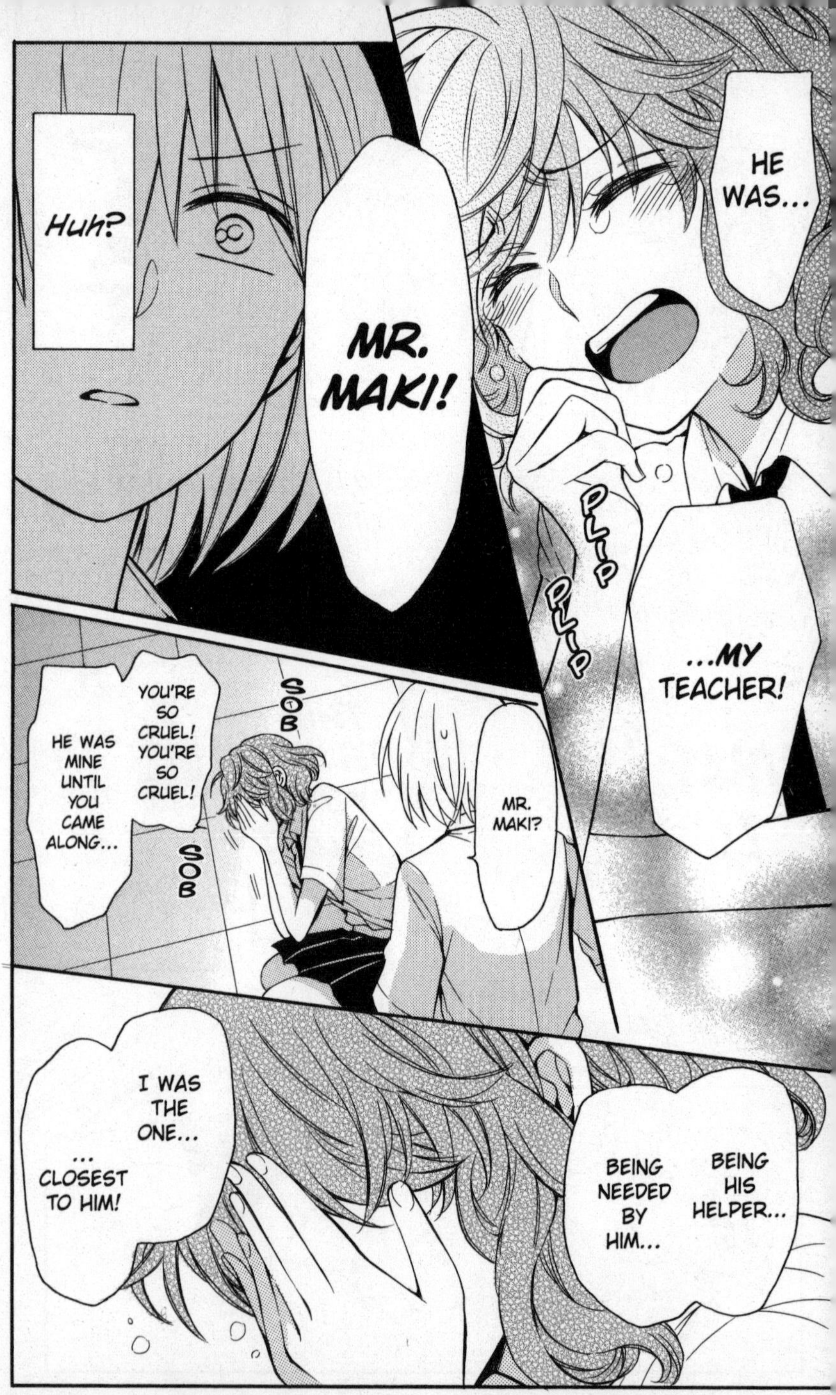
HE WAS...
MR. MAKI!
PLIP PLIP
...MY TEACHER!
Huh?
MR. MAKI?
SOB SOB
YOU'RE SO CRUEL! YOU'RE SO CRUEL!
HE WAS MINE UNTIL YOU CAME ALONG...
BEING HIS HELPER...
BEING NEEDED BY HIM...
I WAS THE ONE...
... CLOSEST TO HIM!

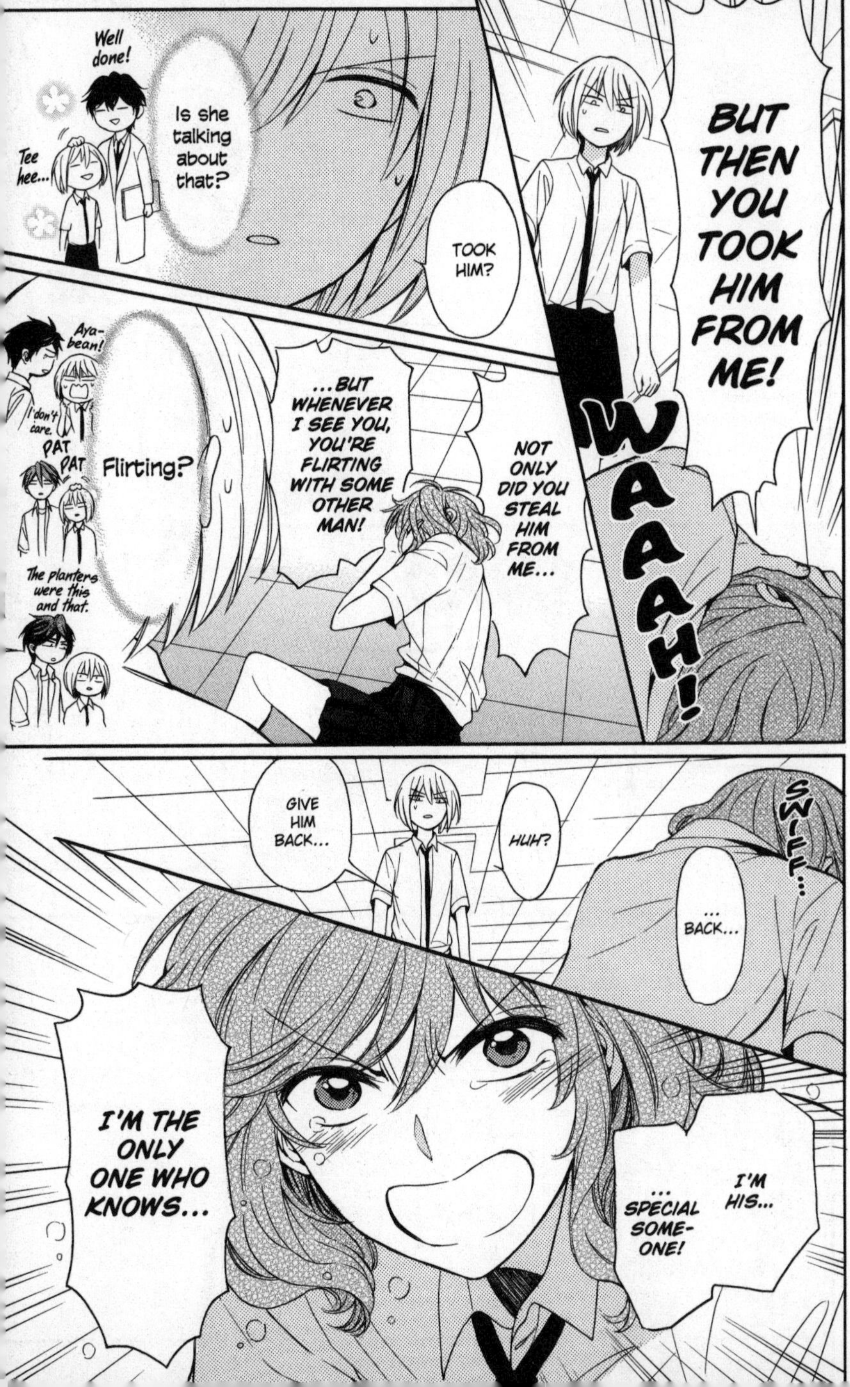
BUT THEN YOU TOOK HIM FROM ME!
TOOK HIM?
Is she talking about that?
Well done!
Tee hee...
NOT ONLY DID YOU STEAL HIM FROM ME...
...BUT WHENEVER I SEE YOU, YOU'RE FLIRTING WITH SOME OTHER MAN!
WAAAH!
Flirting?
Aya-bean!
I don't care.
PAT PAT
The planters were this and that.
SWIFF...
...BACK...
HUH?
GIVE HIM BACK...
I'M HIS...
...SPECIAL SOME-ONE!
I'M THE ONLY ONE WHO KNOWS...

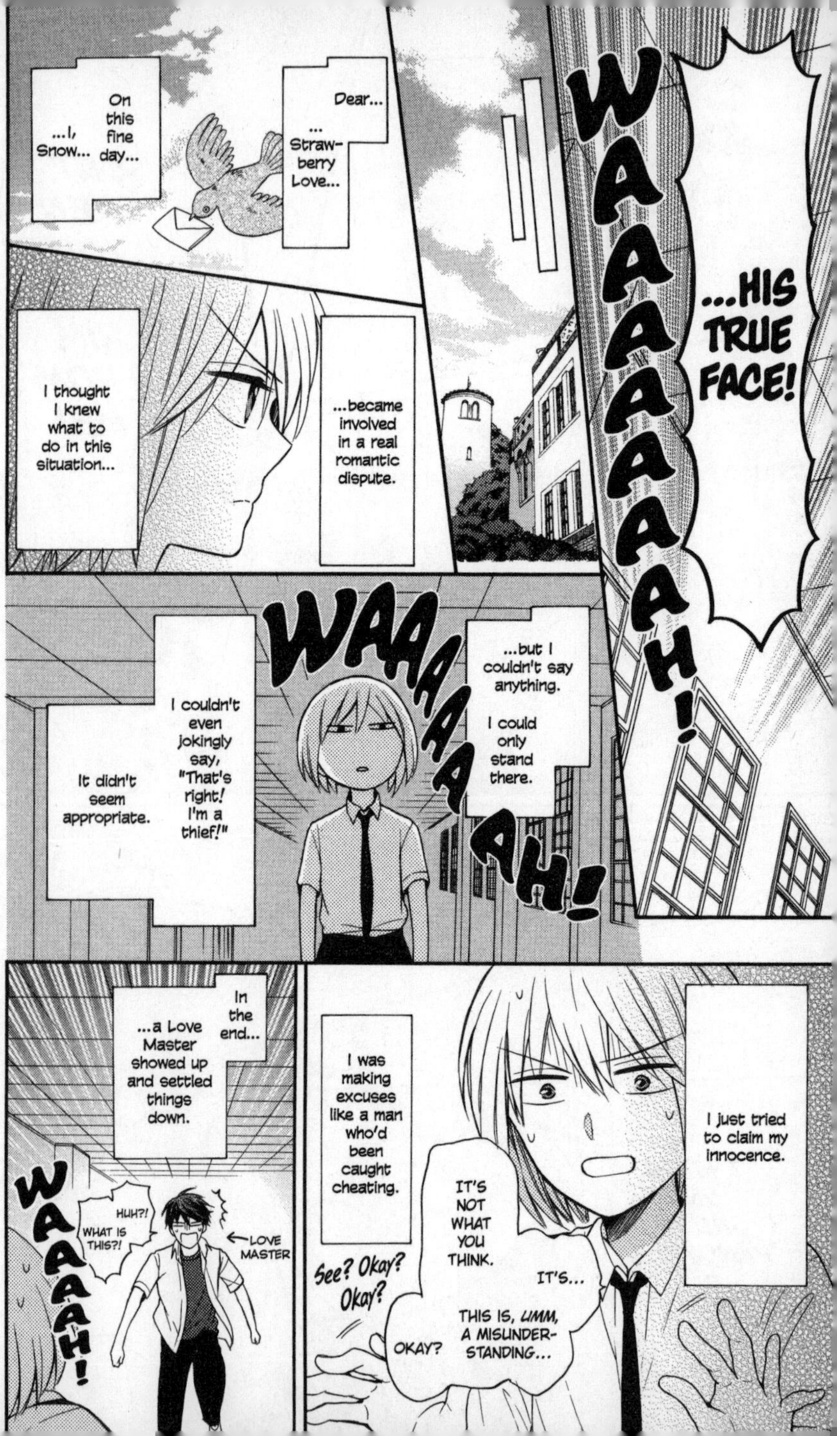
WAAAAAAAAH!
...HIS TRUE FACE!
Dear... ... Strawberry Love...
On this fine day...
...I, Snow...
...became involved in a real romantic dispute.
I thought I knew what to do in this situation...
...but I couldn't say anything.
I could only stand there.
WAAAAAAH!
I couldn't even jokingly say, "That's right! I'm a thief!"
It didn't seem appropriate.
I just tried to claim my innocence.
IT'S NOT WHAT YOU THINK.
IT'S...
THIS IS, UMM, A MISUNDERSTANDING...
OKAY?
See? Okay? Okay?
I was making excuses like a man who'd been caught cheating.
In the end...
...a Love Master showed up and settled things down.
HUH?! WHAT IS THIS?!
LOVE MASTER
WAAAAAH!

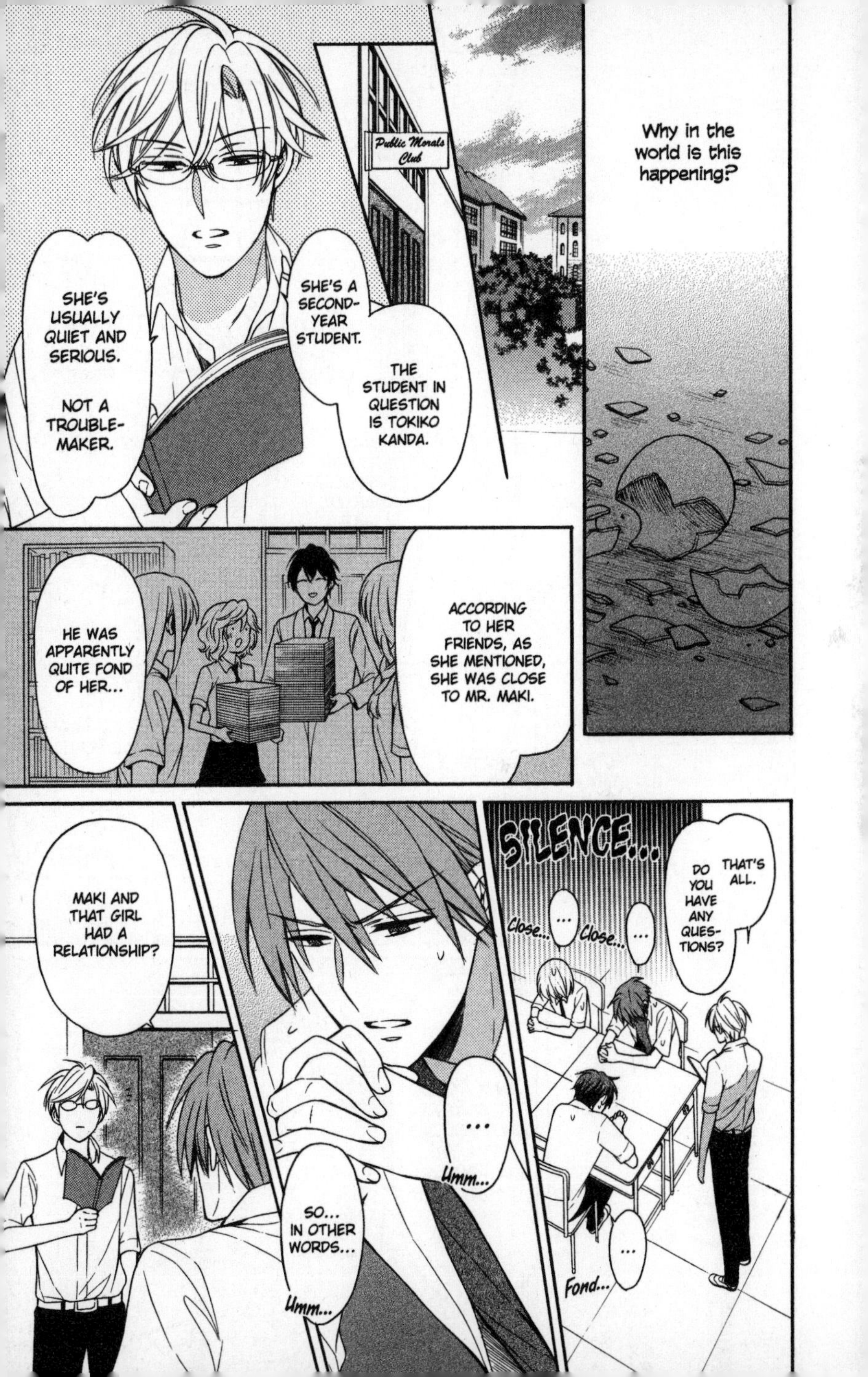
Why in the world is this happening?
Public Morals Club
SHE'S A SECOND-YEAR STUDENT.
THE STUDENT IN QUESTION IS TOKIKO KANDA.
SHE'S USUALLY QUIET AND SERIOUS.
NOT A TROUBLE-MAKER.
ACCORDING TO HER FRIENDS, AS SHE MENTIONED, SHE WAS CLOSE TO MR. MAKI.
HE WAS APPARENTLY QUITE FOND OF HER...
THAT'S ALL.
DO YOU HAVE ANY QUESTIONS?
SILENCE...
...
Close...
...
Close...
...
Fond...
...
Umm...
SO... IN OTHER WORDS...
Umm...
MAKI AND THAT GIRL HAD A RELATIONSHIP?

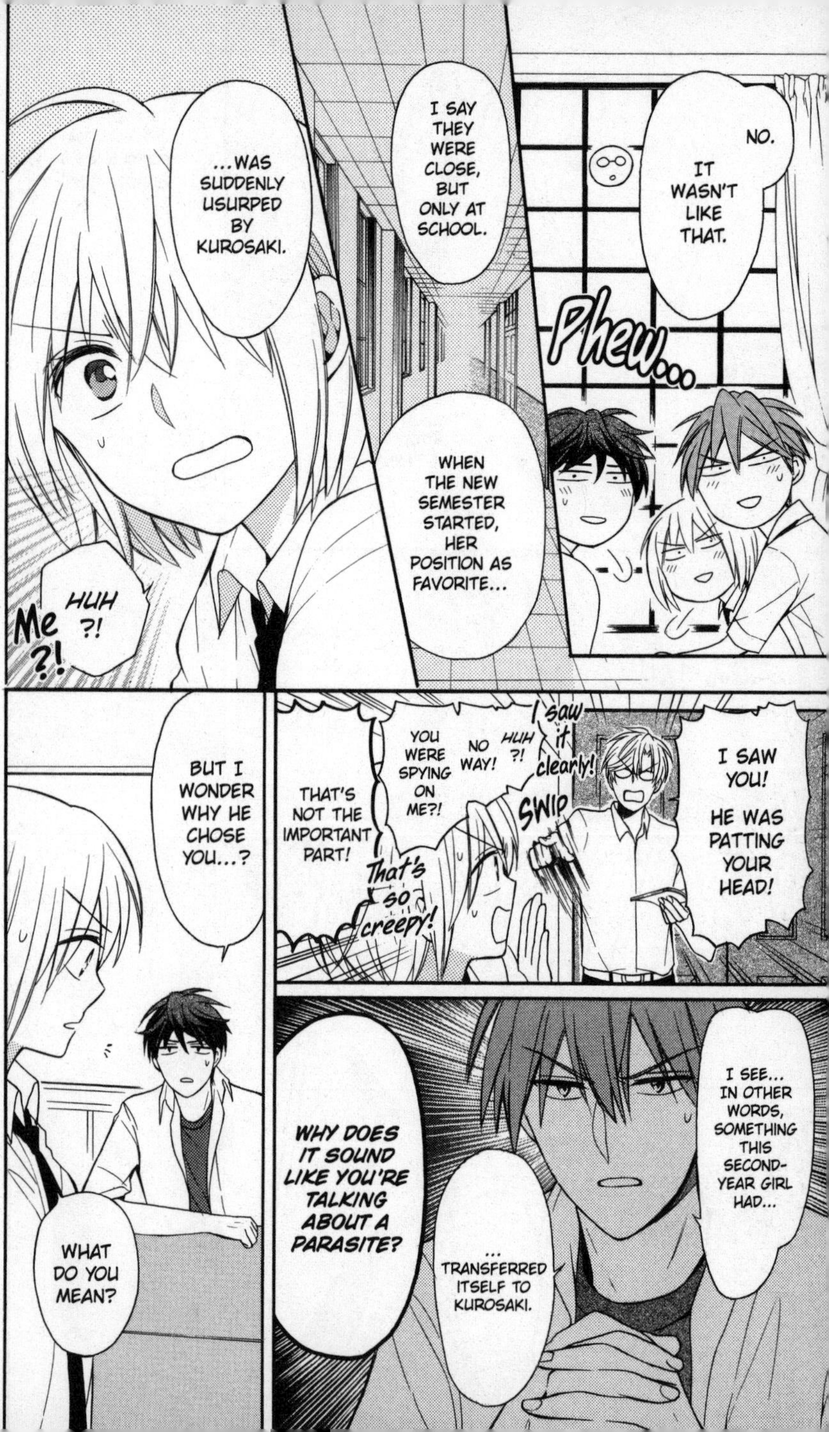
NO.
IT WASN'T LIKE THAT.
Phew...
I SAY THEY WERE CLOSE, BUT ONLY AT SCHOOL.
WHEN THE NEW SEMESTER STARTED, HER POSITION AS FAVORITE...
...WAS SUDDENLY USURPED BY KUROSAKI.
HUH ?!
Me ?!
I SAW YOU!
HE WAS PATTING YOUR HEAD!
I saw it clearly!
SWIP
HUH ?!
NO WAY!
YOU WERE SPYING ON ME?!
THAT'S NOT THE IMPORTANT PART!
That's so creepy!
I SEE... IN OTHER WORDS, SOMETHING THIS SECOND-YEAR GIRL HAD...
...TRANSFERRED ITSELF TO KUROSAKI.
WHY DOES IT SOUND LIKE YOU'RE TALKING ABOUT A PARASITE?
BUT I WONDER WHY HE CHOSE YOU...?
WHAT DO YOU MEAN?

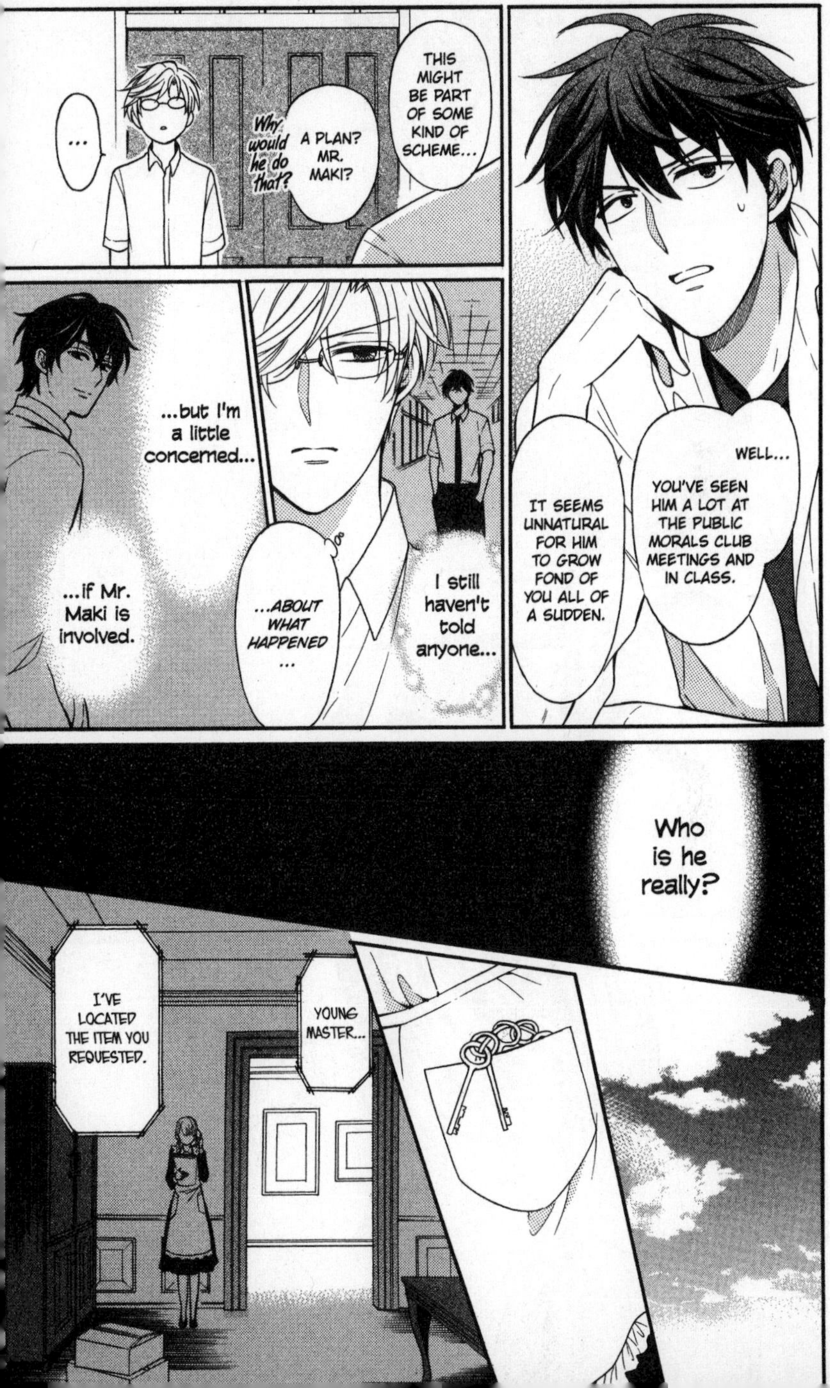
WELL...
YOU'VE SEEN HIM A LOT AT THE PUBLIC MORALS CLUB MEETINGS AND IN CLASS.
IT SEEMS UNNATURAL FOR HIM TO GROW FOND OF YOU ALL OF A SUDDEN.
THIS MIGHT BE PART OF SOME KIND OF SCHEME...
A PLAN? MR. MAKI?
Why would he do that?
...
I still haven't told anyone...
...ABOUT WHAT HAPPENED...
...but I'm a little concerned...
...if Mr. Maki is involved.
Who is he really?
YOUNG MASTER...
I'VE LOCATED THE ITEM YOU REQUESTED.

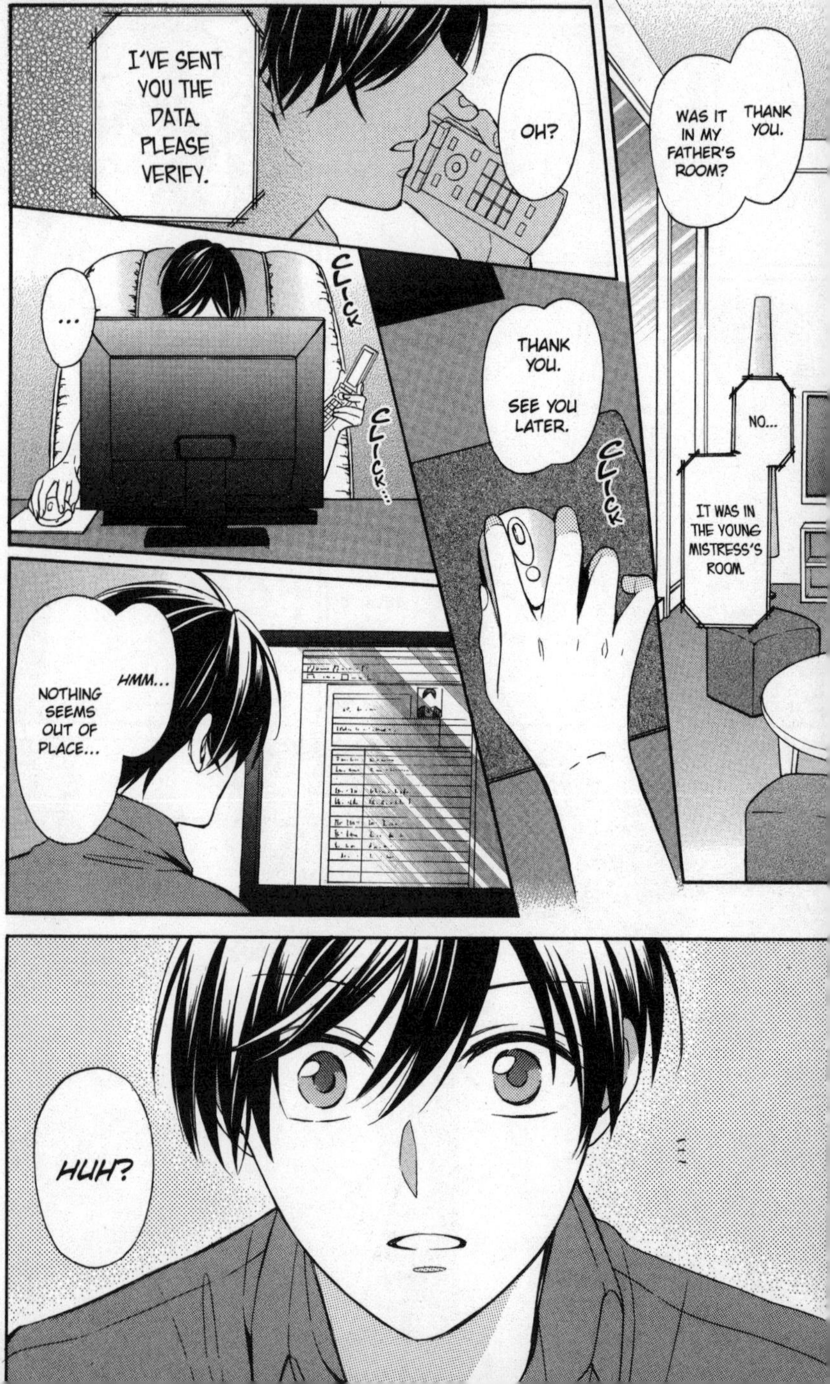
THANK YOU.
WAS IT IN MY FATHER'S ROOM?
NO...
IT WAS IN THE YOUNG MISTRESS'S ROOM.
OH?
I'VE SENT YOU THE DATA. PLEASE VERIFY.
THANK YOU.
SEE YOU LATER.
CLICK
CLICK
...
CLICK...
HMM...
NOTHING SEEMS OUT OF PLACE...
HUH?

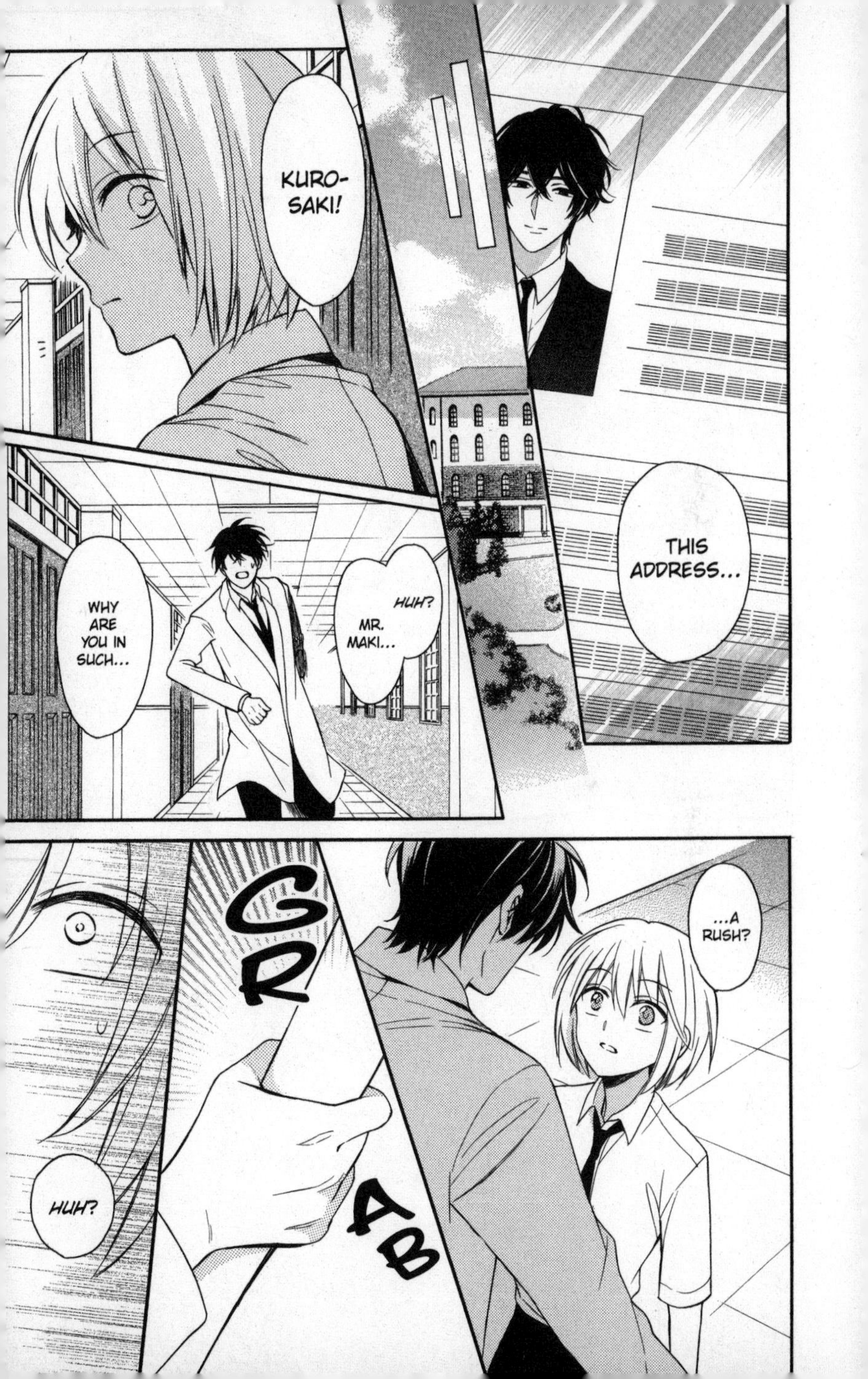
THIS ADDRESS...
KURO-SAKI!
HUH? MR. MAKI...
WHY ARE YOU IN SUCH...
...A RUSH?
GRAB
HUH?

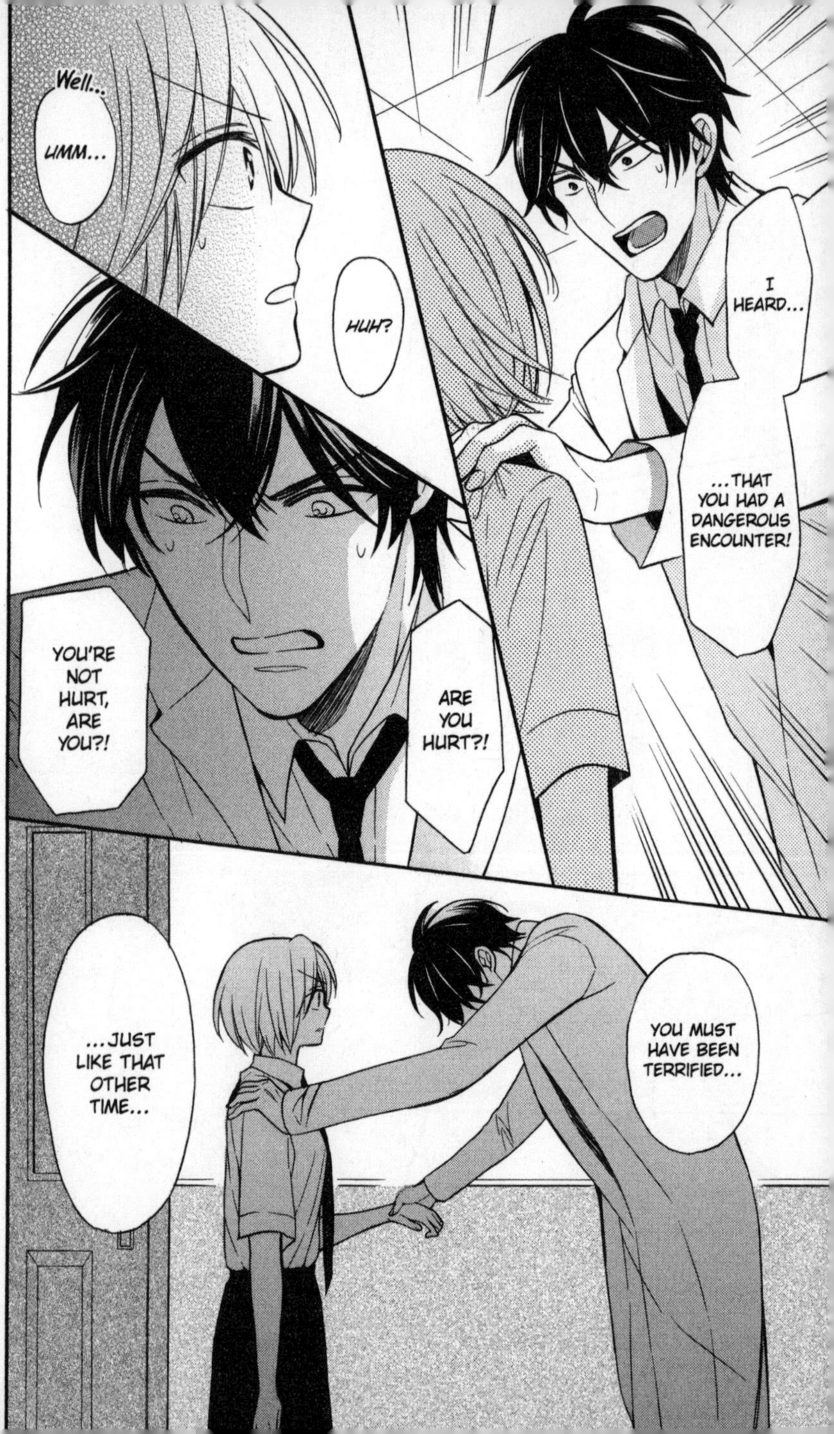
I HEARD...
...THAT YOU HAD A DANGEROUS ENCOUNTER!
HUH?
Well... UMM...
ARE YOU HURT?!
YOU'RE NOT HURT, ARE YOU?!
YOU MUST HAVE BEEN TERRIFIED...
...JUST LIKE THAT OTHER TIME...

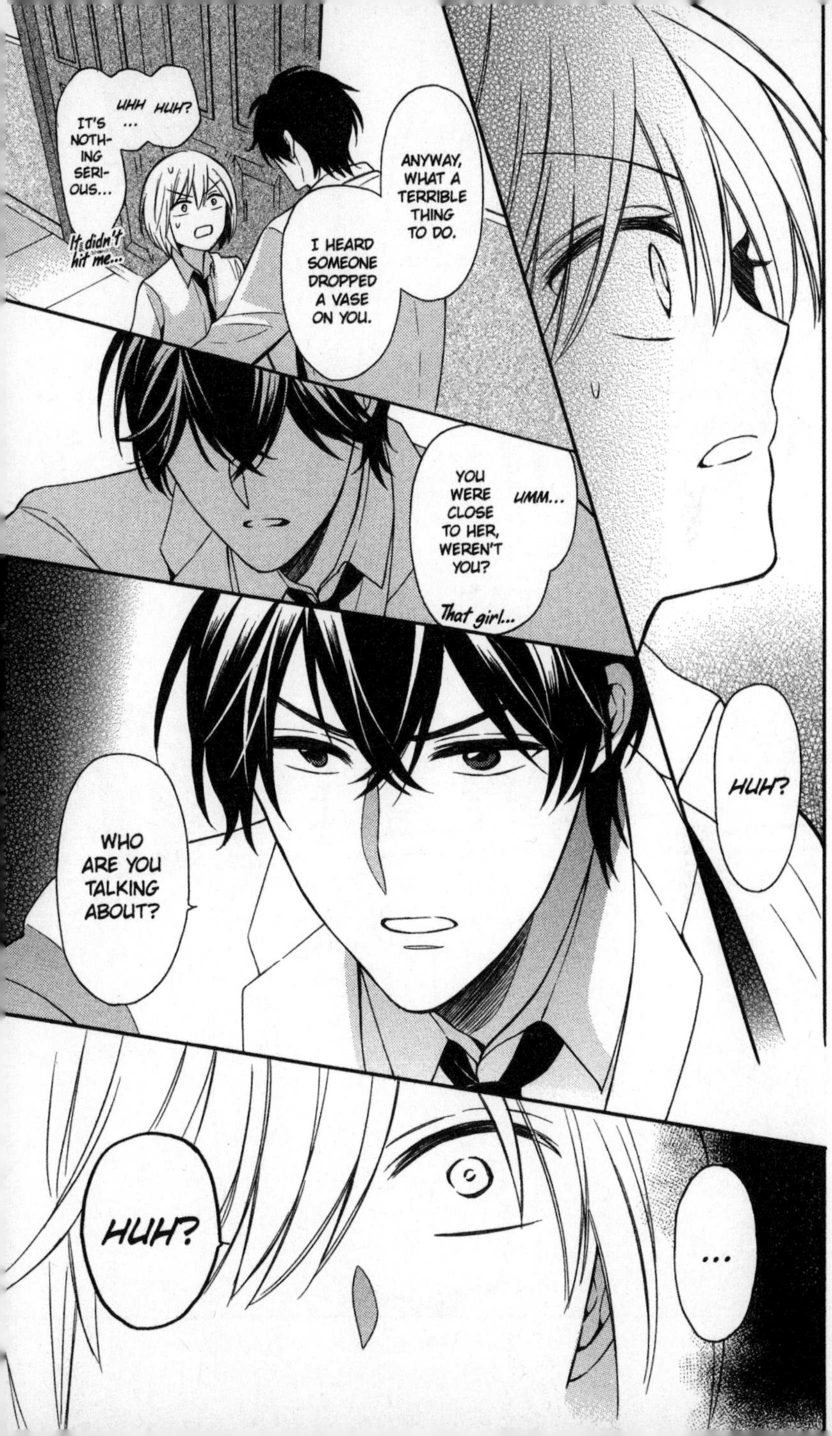
ANYWAY, WHAT A TERRIBLE THING TO DO.
I HEARD SOMEONE DROPPED A VASE ON YOU.
UHH ... HUH?
IT'S NOTHING SERIOUS...
It didn't hit me...
That girl...
YOU WERE CLOSE TO HER, WEREN'T YOU?
UMM...
HUH?
WHO ARE YOU TALKING ABOUT?
...
HUH?

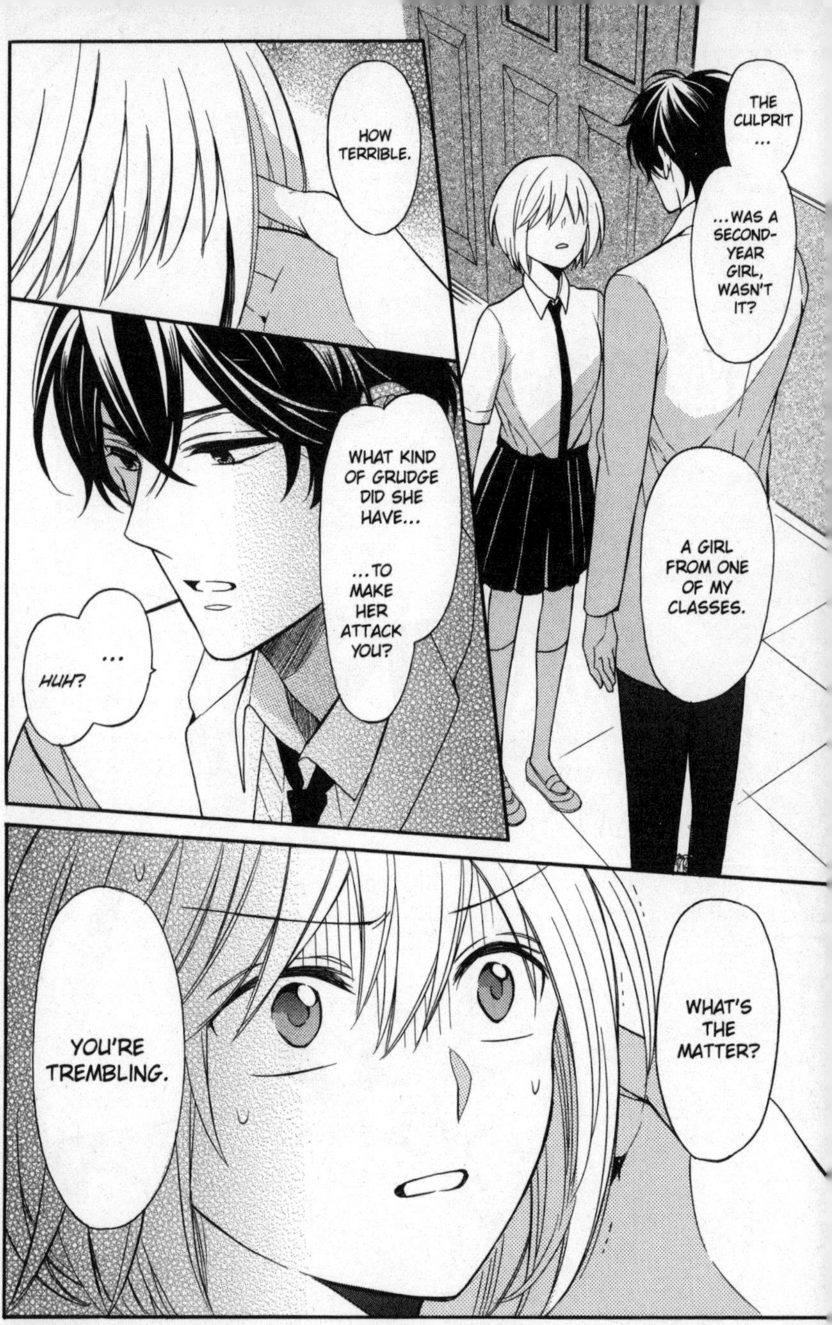
THE CULPRIT ...
...WAS A SECOND-YEAR GIRL, WASN'T IT?
A GIRL FROM ONE OF MY CLASSES.
HOW TERRIBLE.
WHAT KIND OF GRUDGE DID SHE HAVE...
...TO MAKE HER ATTACK YOU?
... HUH?
WHAT'S THE MATTER?
YOU'RE TREMBLING.

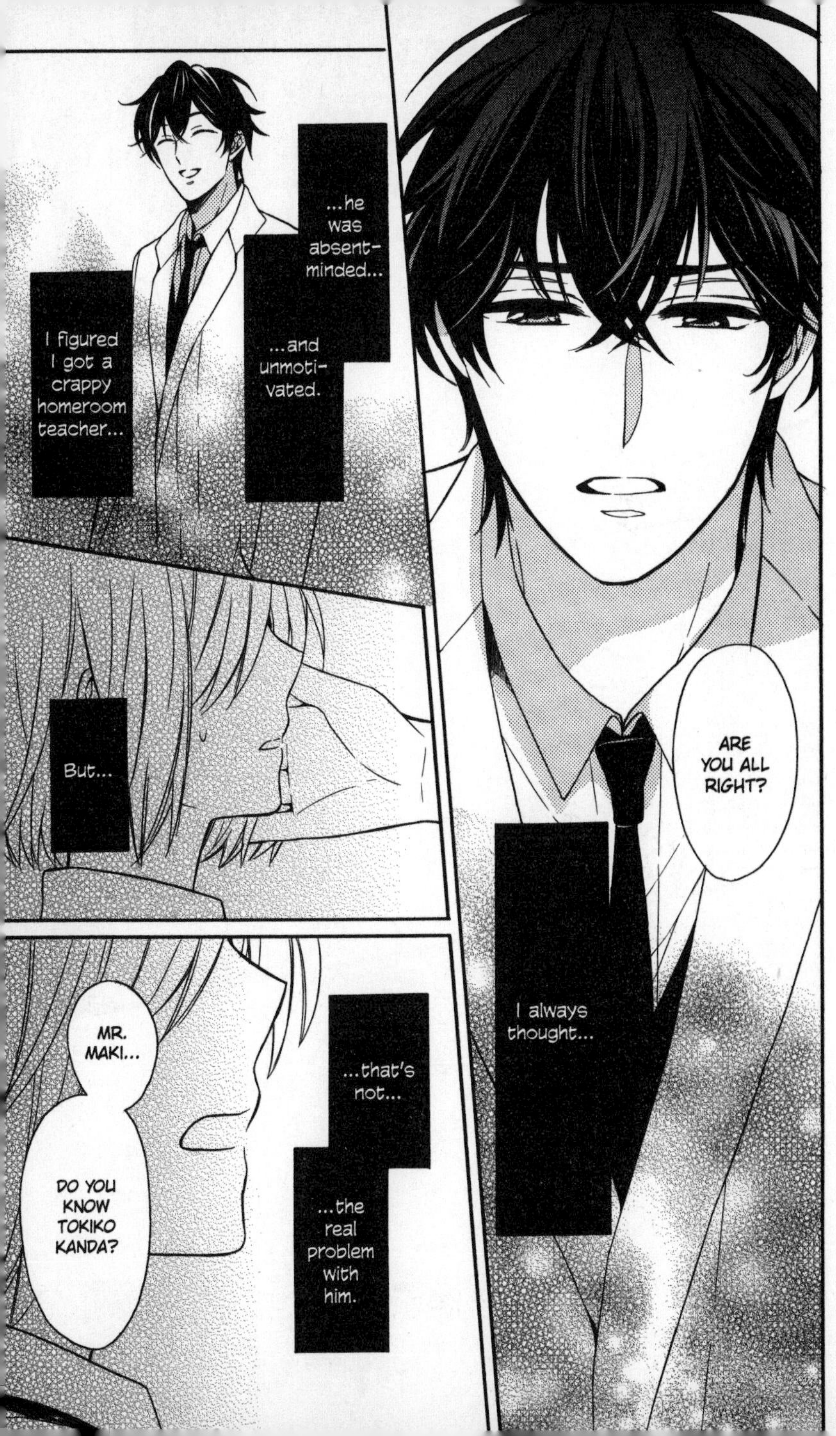

ARE YOU ALL RIGHT?
I always thought...
...he was absent-minded...
...and unmotivated.
I figured I got a crappy homeroom teacher...
But...
...that's not...
...the real problem with him.
MR. MAKI...
DO YOU KNOW TOKIKO KANDA?

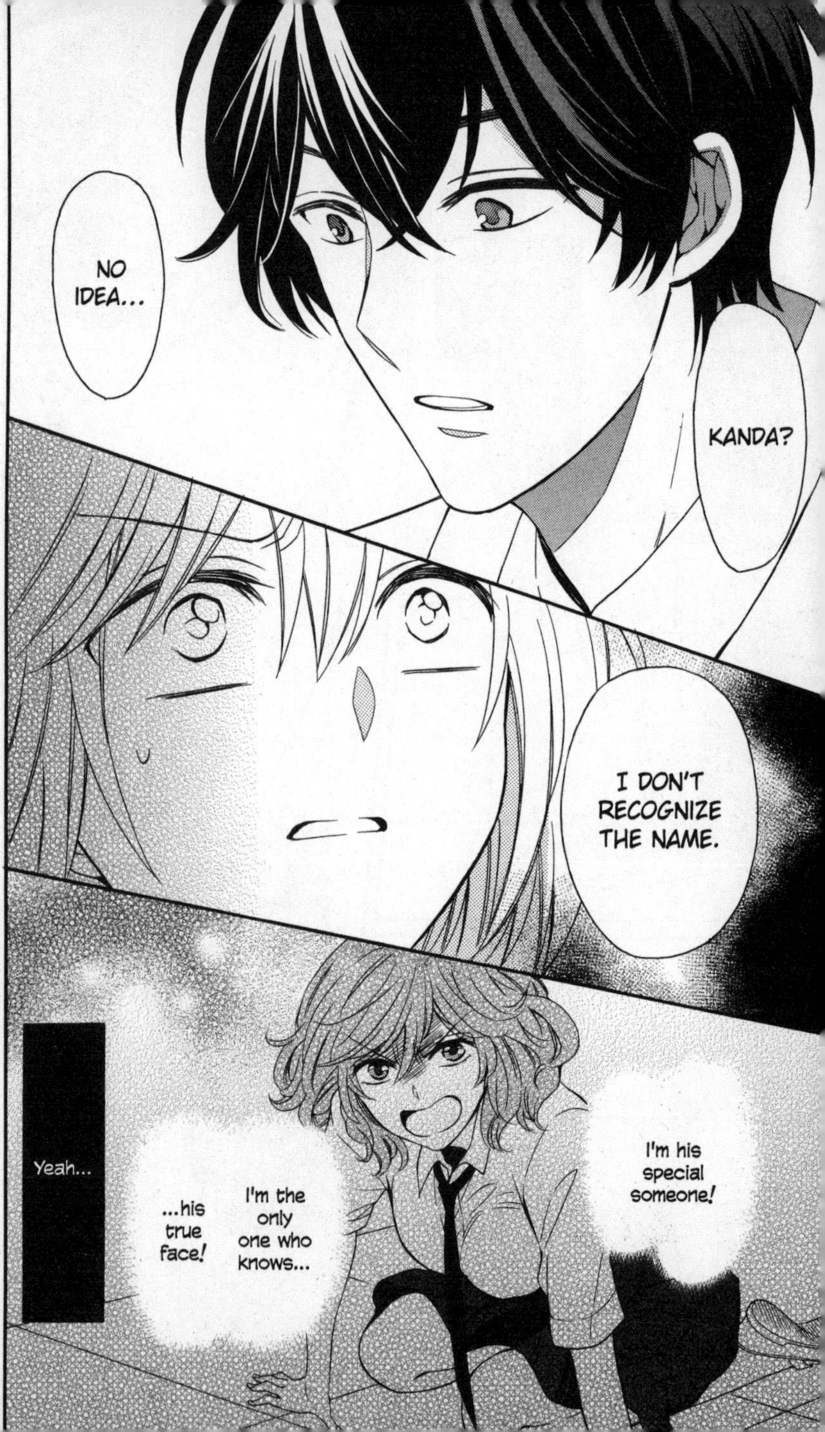
KANDA?
NO IDEA...
I DON'T RECOGNIZE THE NAME.
I'm his special someone!
I'm the only one who knows...
...his true face!
Yeah...

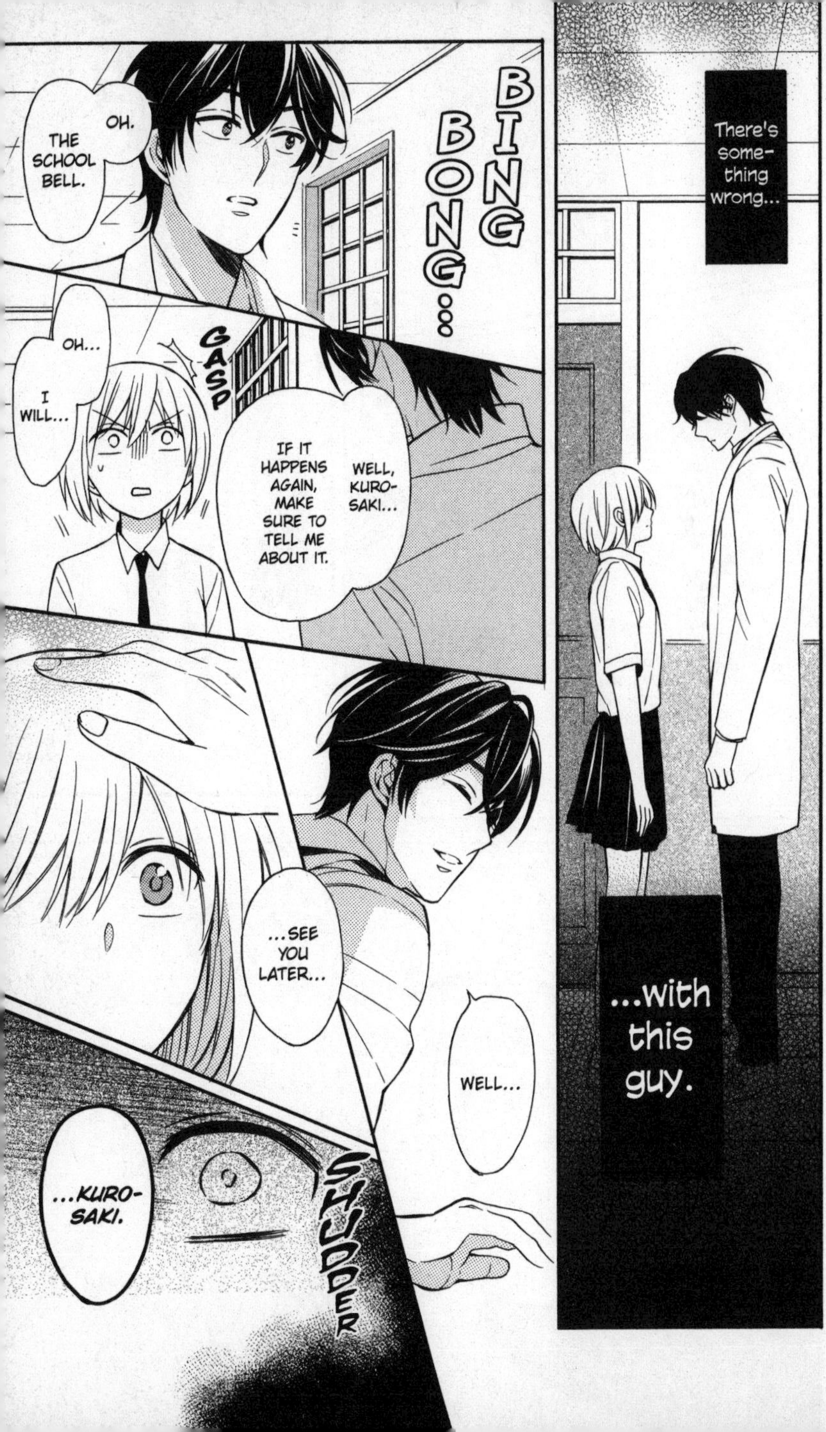
There's some-thing wrong...
...with this guy.
BING BONG...
OH. THE SCHOOL BELL.
WELL, KURO-SAKI...
IF IT HAPPENS AGAIN, MAKE SURE TO TELL ME ABOUT IT.
GASP
OH... I WILL...
...SEE YOU LATER...
WELL...
...KURO-SAKI.
SHUDDER

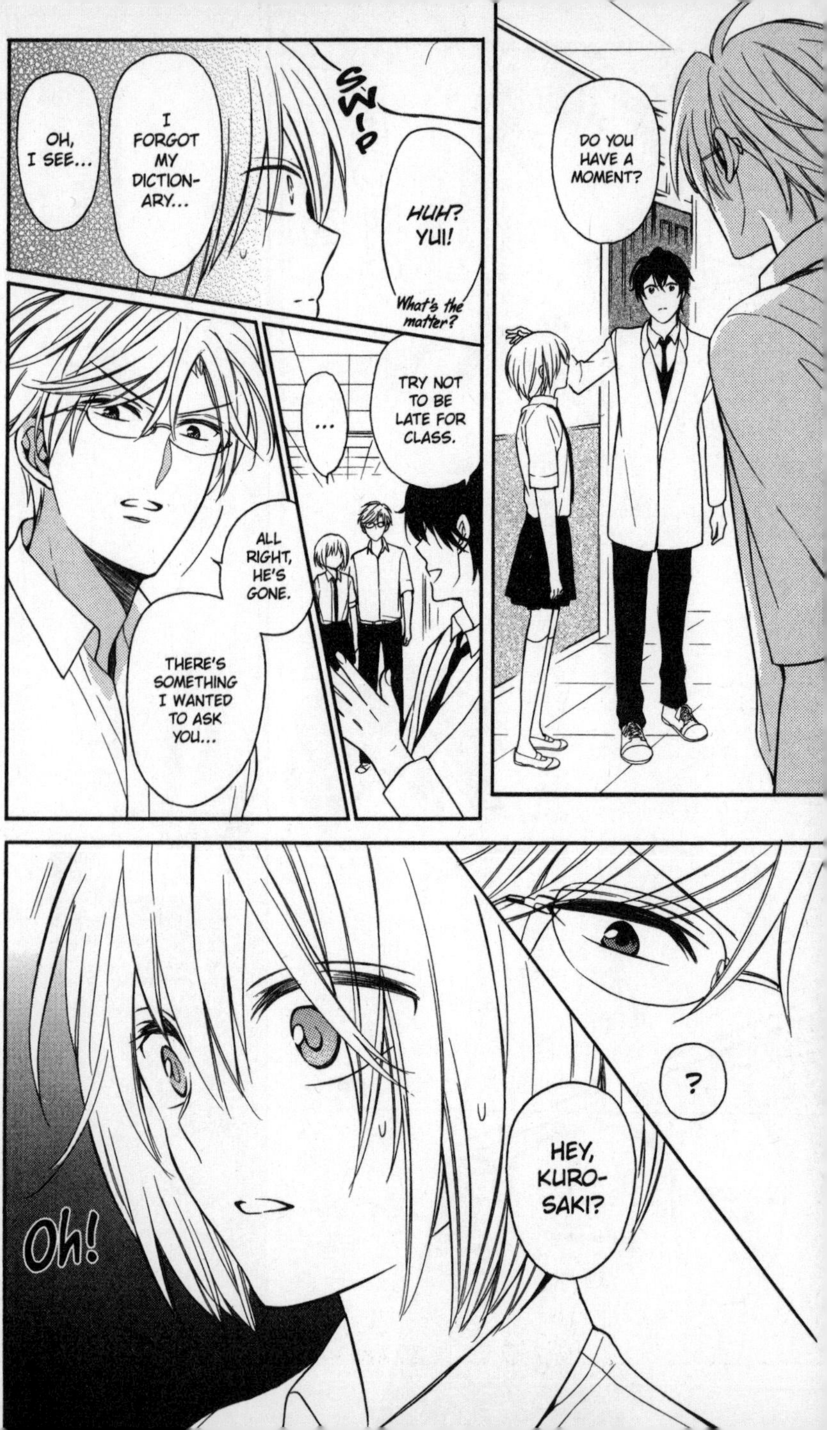
DO YOU HAVE A MOMENT?
HUH? YUI!
What's the matter?
SWIP
I FORGOT MY DICTIONARY...
OH, I SEE...
TRY NOT TO BE LATE FOR CLASS.
...
ALL RIGHT, HE'S GONE.
THERE'S SOMETHING I WANTED TO ASK YOU...
?
HEY, KUROSAKI?
Oh!

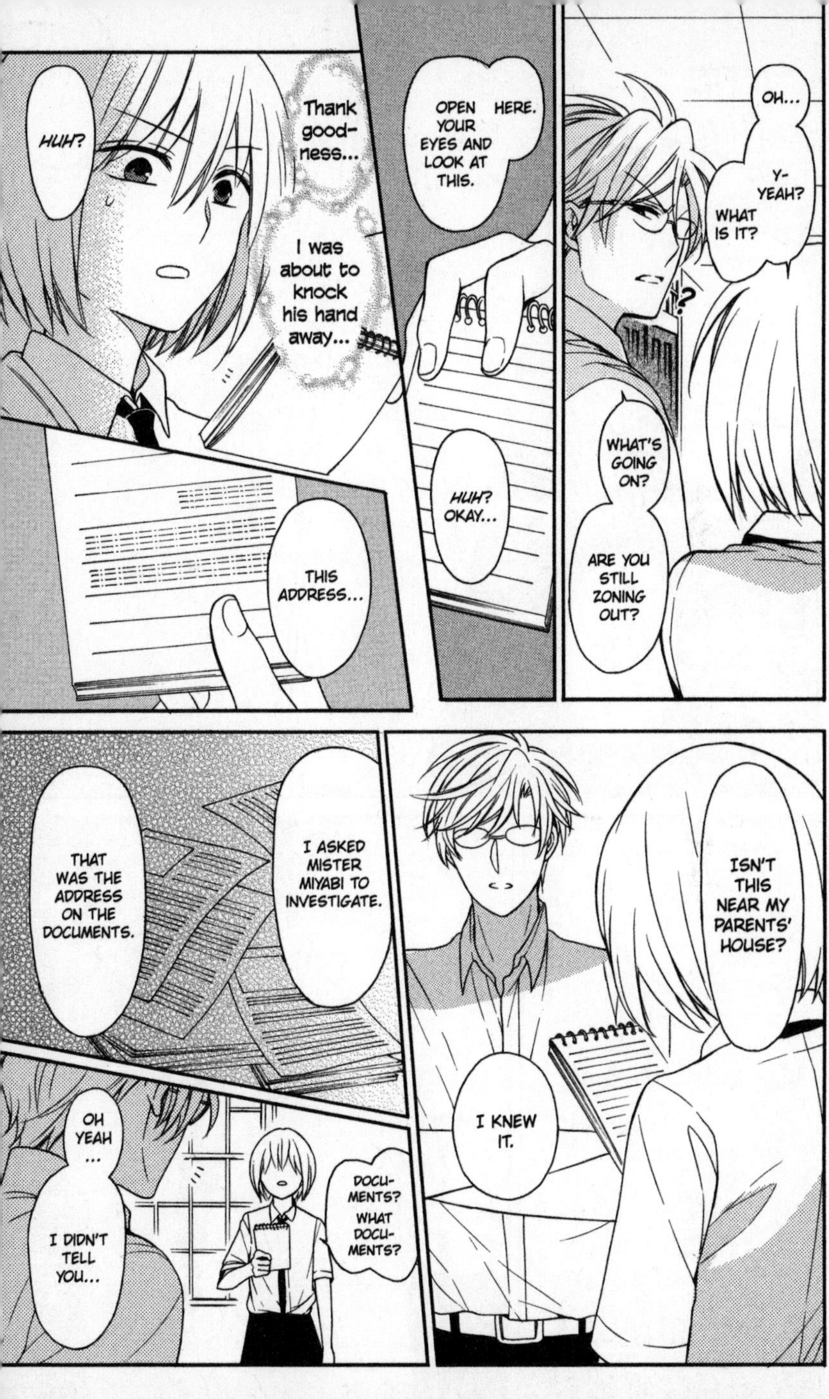
OH...
Y-YEAH? WHAT IS IT?
WHAT'S GOING ON?
ARE YOU STILL ZONING OUT?
HERE. OPEN YOUR EYES AND LOOK AT THIS.
HUH? OKAY...
Thank goodness...
I was about to knock his hand away...
HUH?
THIS ADDRESS...
ISN'T THIS NEAR MY PARENTS' HOUSE?
I KNEW IT.
I ASKED MISTER MIYABI TO INVESTIGATE.
THAT WAS THE ADDRESS ON THE DOCUMENTS.
DOCUMENTS? WHAT DOCUMENTS?
OH YEAH ...
I DIDN'T TELL YOU...

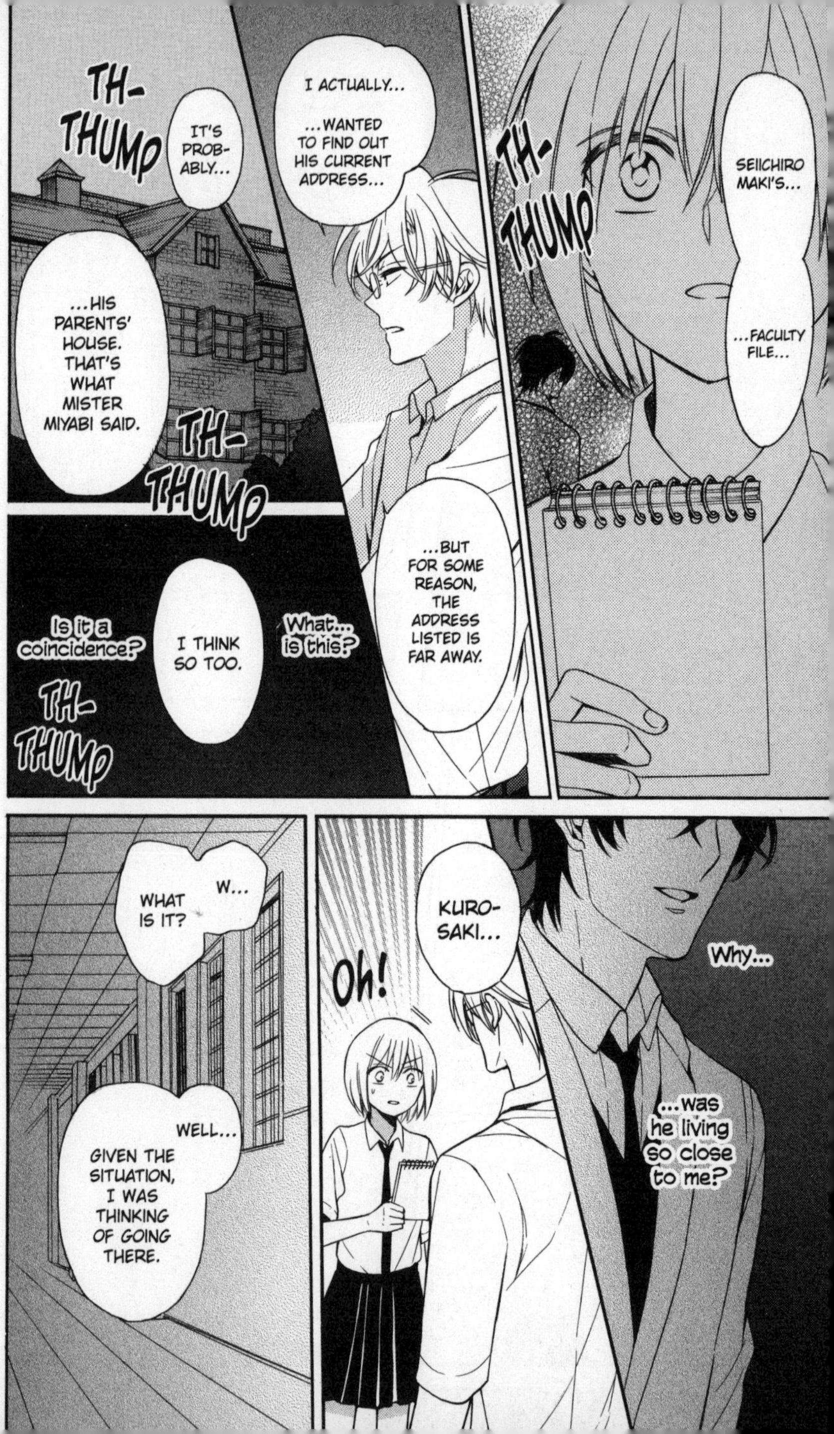

TH-THUMP
SEIICHIRO MAKI'S...
...FACULTY FILE...
I ACTUALLY...
...WANTED TO FIND OUT HIS CURRENT ADDRESS...
...BUT FOR SOME REASON, THE ADDRESS LISTED IS FAR AWAY.
TH-THUMP
IT'S PROBABLY...
...HIS PARENTS' HOUSE. THAT'S WHAT MISTER MIYABI SAID.
TH-THUMP
What... is this?
I THINK SO TOO.
Is it a coincidence?
TH-THUMP
Why...
...was he living so close to me?
KURO-SAKI...
Oh!
W...
WHAT IS IT?
WELL...
GIVEN THE SITUATION, I WAS THINKING OF GOING THERE.

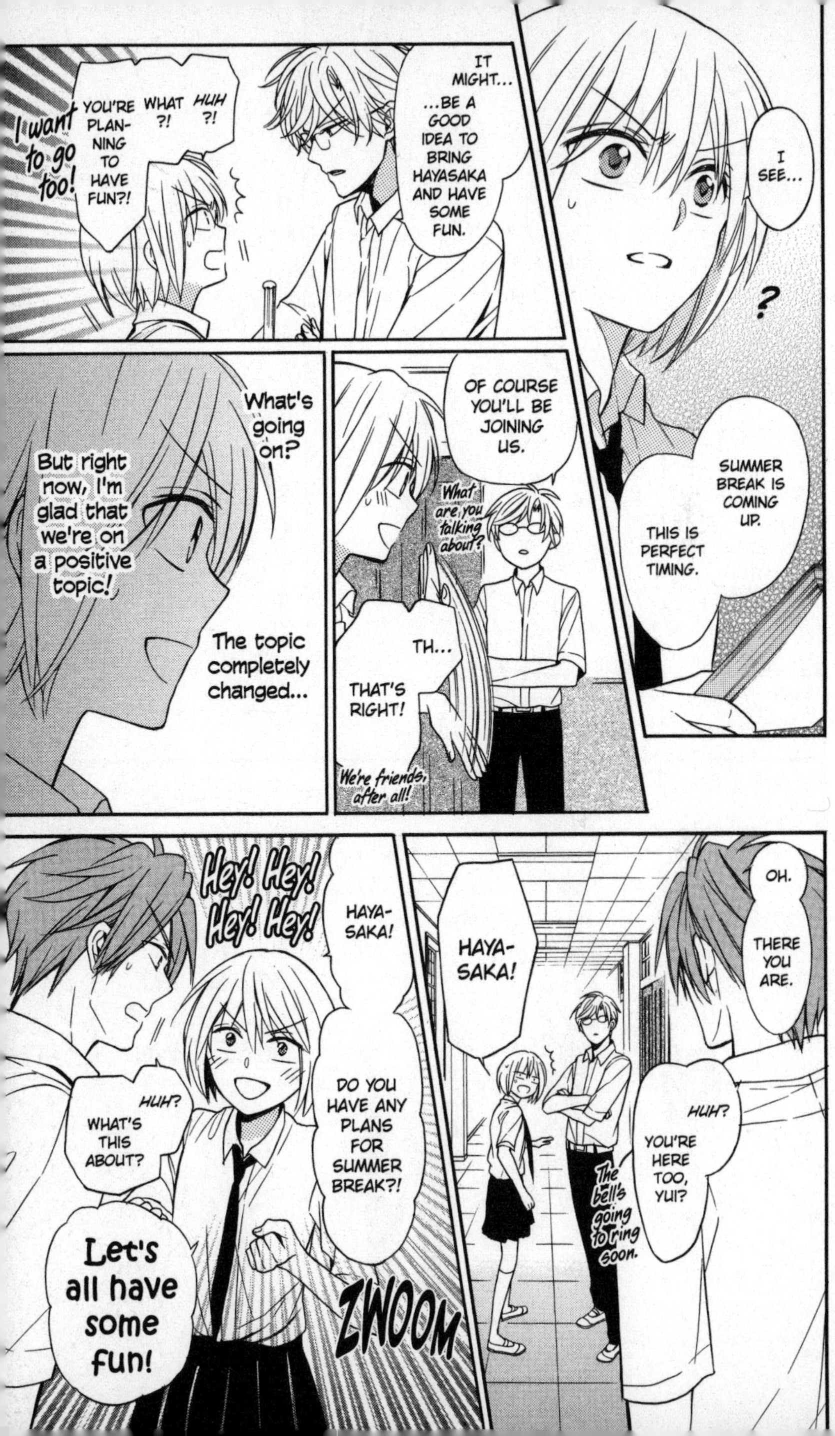
I SEE...
?
SUMMER BREAK IS COMING UP.
THIS IS PERFECT TIMING.
IT MIGHT...
...BE A GOOD IDEA TO BRING HAYASAKA AND HAVE SOME FUN.
HUH ?!
WHAT ?!
YOU'RE PLAN-NING TO HAVE FUN?!
I want to go too!
OF COURSE YOU'LL BE JOINING US.
What are you talking about?
TH...
THAT'S RIGHT!
We're friends, after all!
What's going on?
The topic completely changed...
But right now, I'm glad that we're on a positive topic!
OH.
THERE YOU ARE.
HUH?
YOU'RE HERE TOO, YUI?
HAYA-SAKA!
The bell's going to ring soon.
Hey! Hey! Hey! Hey!
HAYA-SAKA!
DO YOU HAVE ANY PLANS FOR SUMMER BREAK?!
HUH?
WHAT'S THIS ABOUT?
Let's all have some fun!
ZWOOM

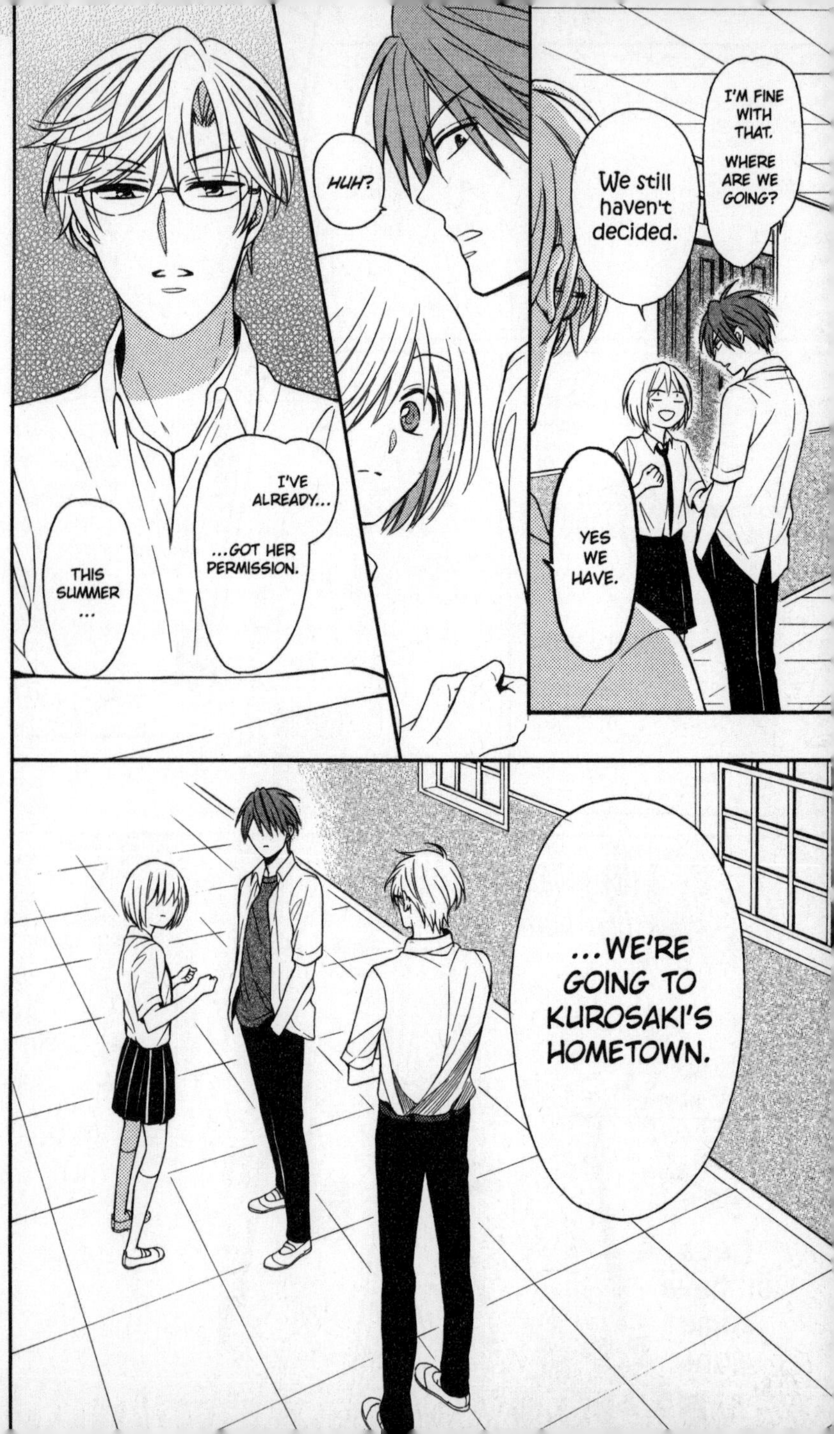
I'M FINE WITH THAT.
WHERE ARE WE GOING?
We still haven't decided.
YES WE HAVE.
HUH?
I'VE ALREADY...
...GOT HER PERMISSION.
THIS SUMMER...
...WE'RE GOING TO KUROSAKI'S HOMETOWN.

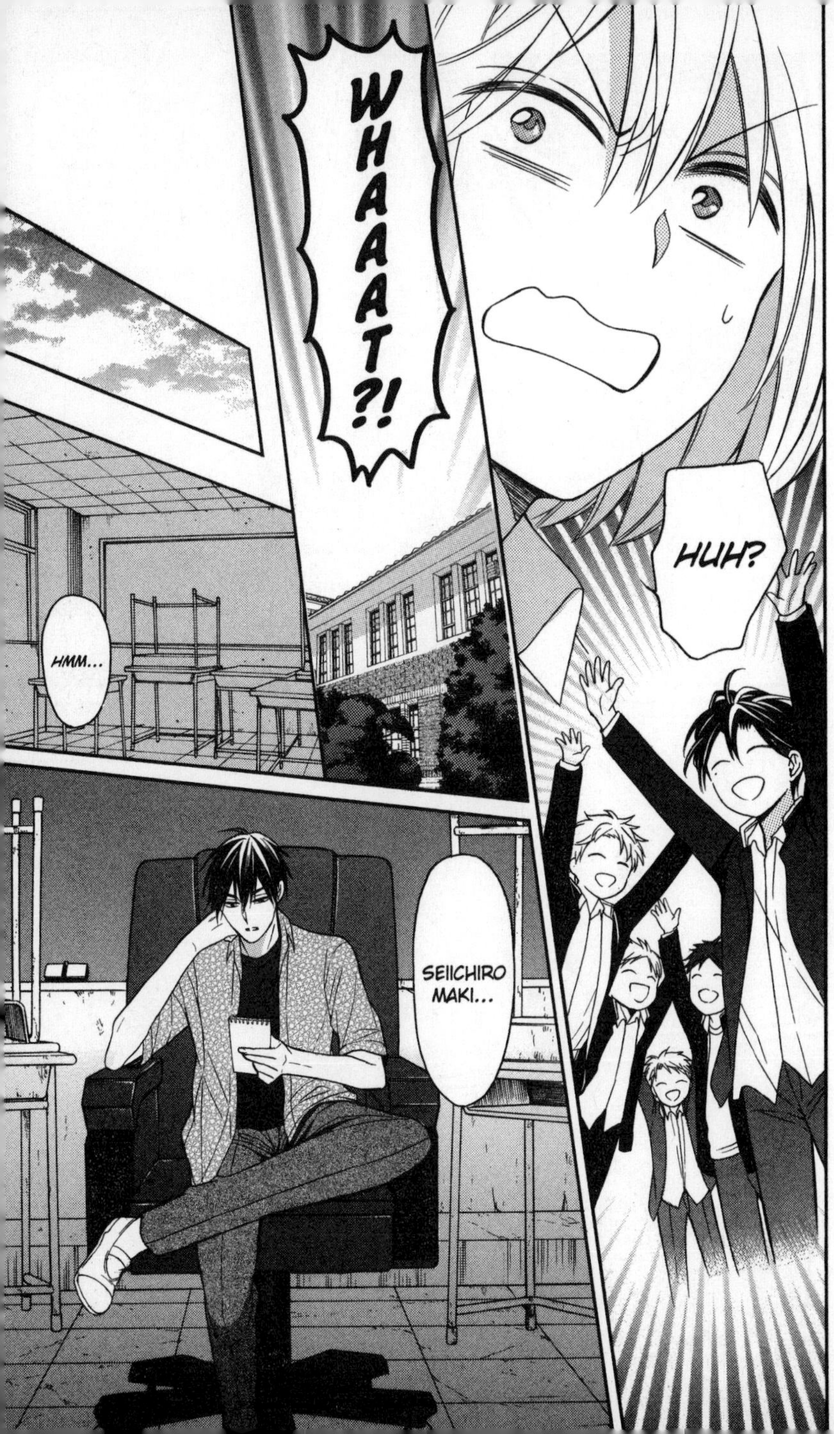
HUH?
WHAAAT?!
HMM...
SEIICHIRO MAKI...

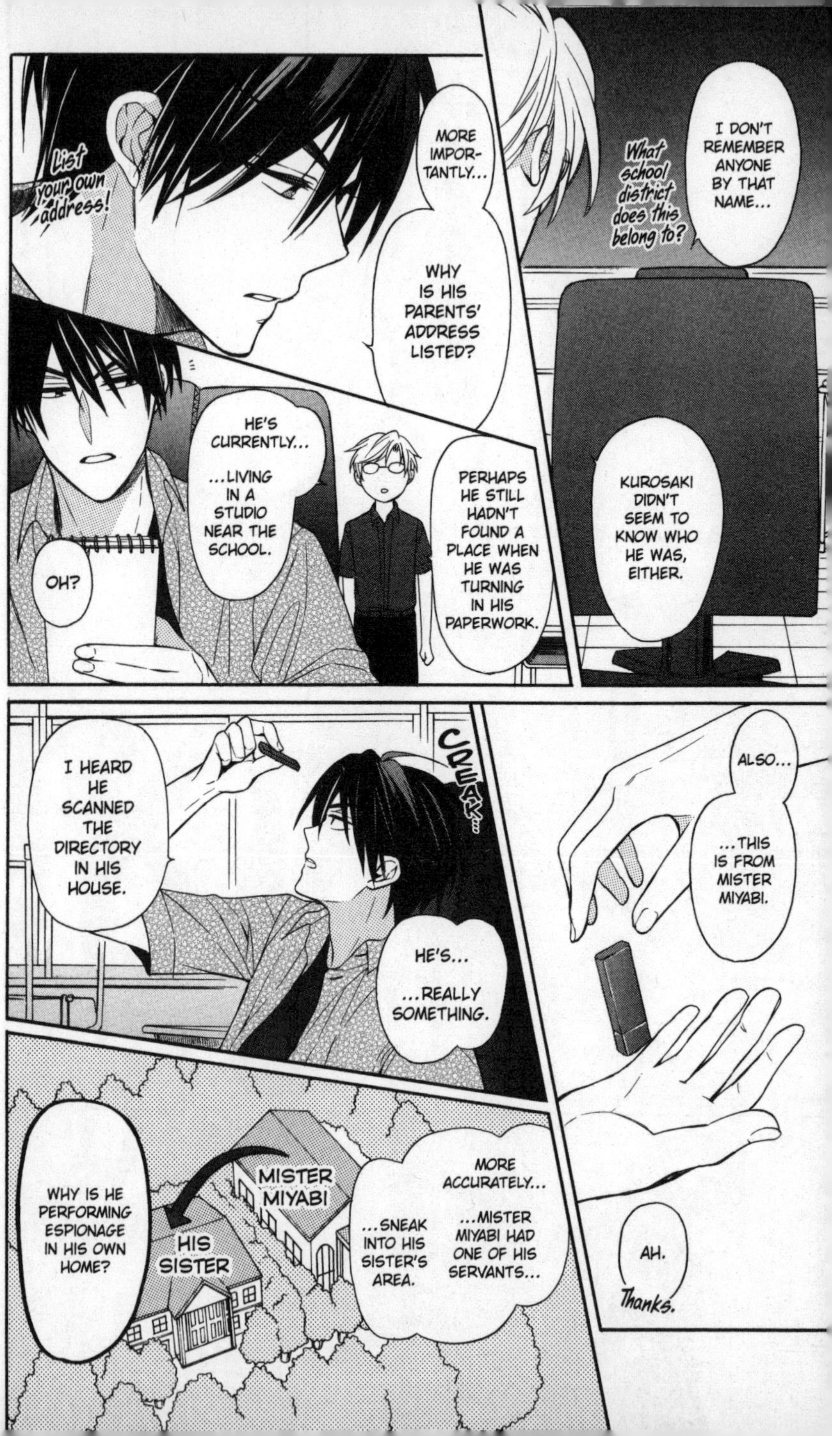
I DON'T REMEMBER ANYONE BY THAT NAME...
What school district does this belong to?
KUROSAKI DIDN'T SEEM TO KNOW WHO HE WAS, EITHER.
MORE IMPORTANTLY...
WHY IS HIS PARENTS' ADDRESS LISTED?
List your own address!
PERHAPS HE STILL HADN'T FOUND A PLACE WHEN HE WAS TURNING IN HIS PAPERWORK.
HE'S CURRENTLY...
...LIVING IN A STUDIO NEAR THE SCHOOL.
OH?
ALSO...
...THIS IS FROM MISTER MIYABI.
AH.
Thanks.
CREAK...
I HEARD HE SCANNED THE DIRECTORY IN HIS HOUSE.
HE'S...
...REALLY SOMETHING.
MORE ACCURATELY...
...MISTER MIYABI HAD ONE OF HIS SERVANTS...
...SNEAK INTO HIS SISTER'S AREA.
MISTER MIYABI
HIS SISTER
WHY IS HE PERFORMING ESPIONAGE IN HIS OWN HOME?

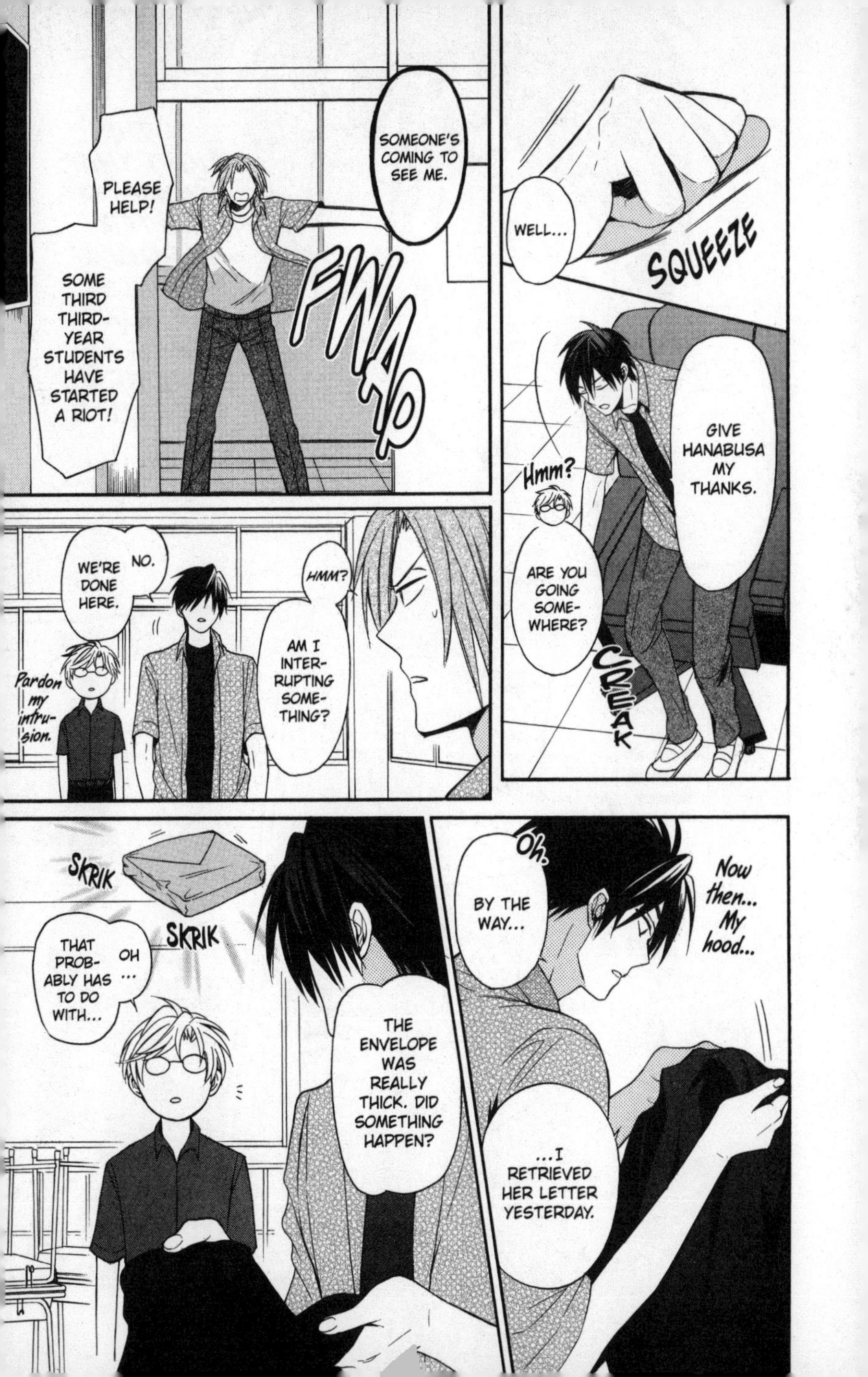
WELL...
SQUEEZE
GIVE HANABUSA MY THANKS.
Hmm?
ARE YOU GOING SOME-WHERE?
CREAK
SOMEONE'S COMING TO SEE ME.
FWAP
PLEASE HELP!
SOME THIRD THIRD-YEAR STUDENTS HAVE STARTED A RIOT!
HMM?
AM I INTER-RUPTING SOME-THING?
NO.
WE'RE DONE HERE.
Pardon my intru-sion.
Now then... My hood...
Oh.
BY THE WAY...
...I RETRIEVED HER LETTER YESTERDAY.
THE ENVELOPE WAS REALLY THICK. DID SOMETHING HAPPEN?
OH...
THAT PROB-ABLY HAS TO DO WITH...
SKRIK
SKRIK

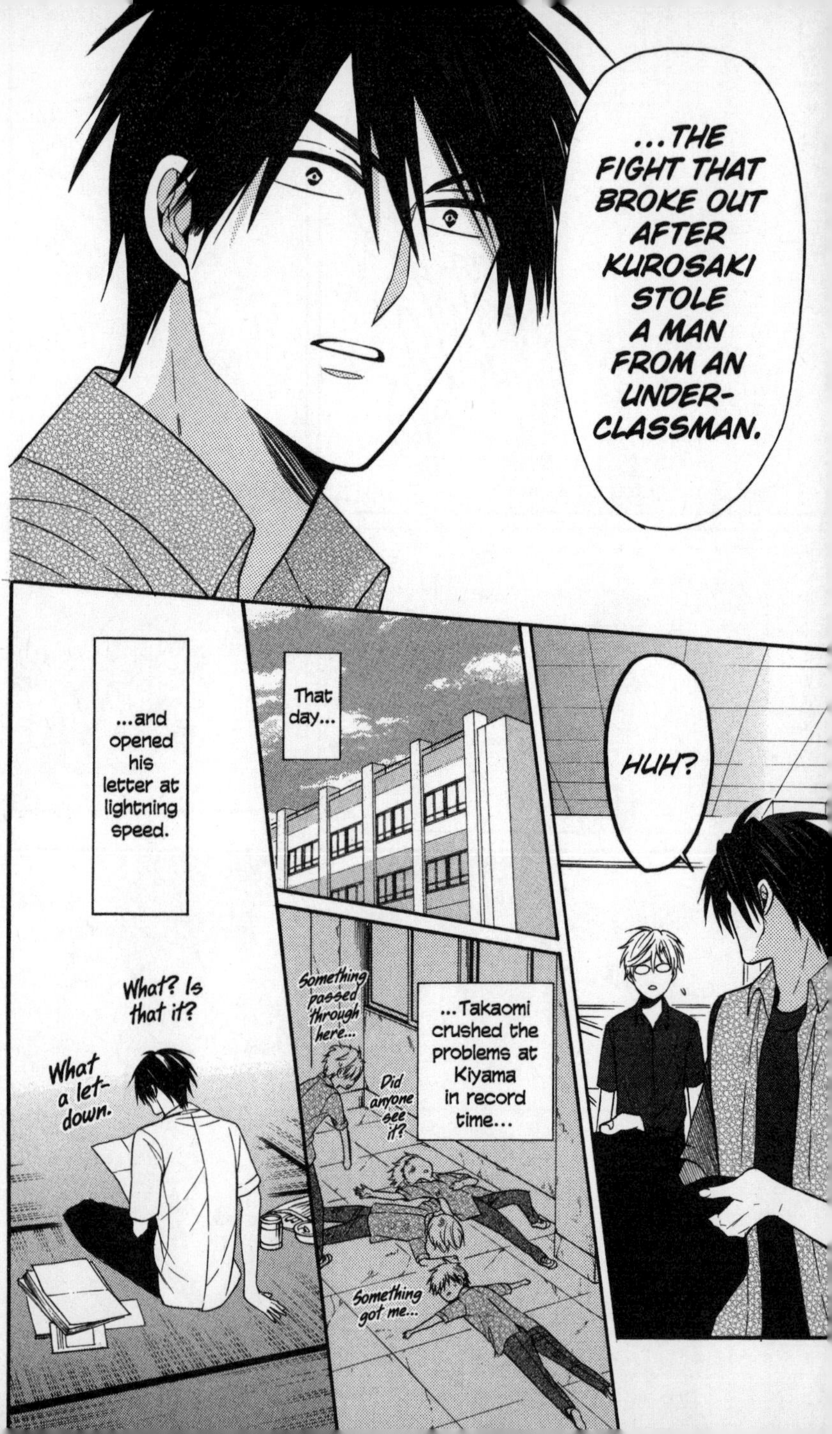
...THE FIGHT THAT BROKE OUT AFTER KUROSAKI STOLE A MAN FROM AN UNDER-CLASSMAN.
HUH?
That day...
...Takaomi crushed the problems at Kiyama in record time...
Something passed through here...
Did anyone see it?
Something got me...
...and opened his letter at lightning speed.
What? Is that it?
What a let-down.

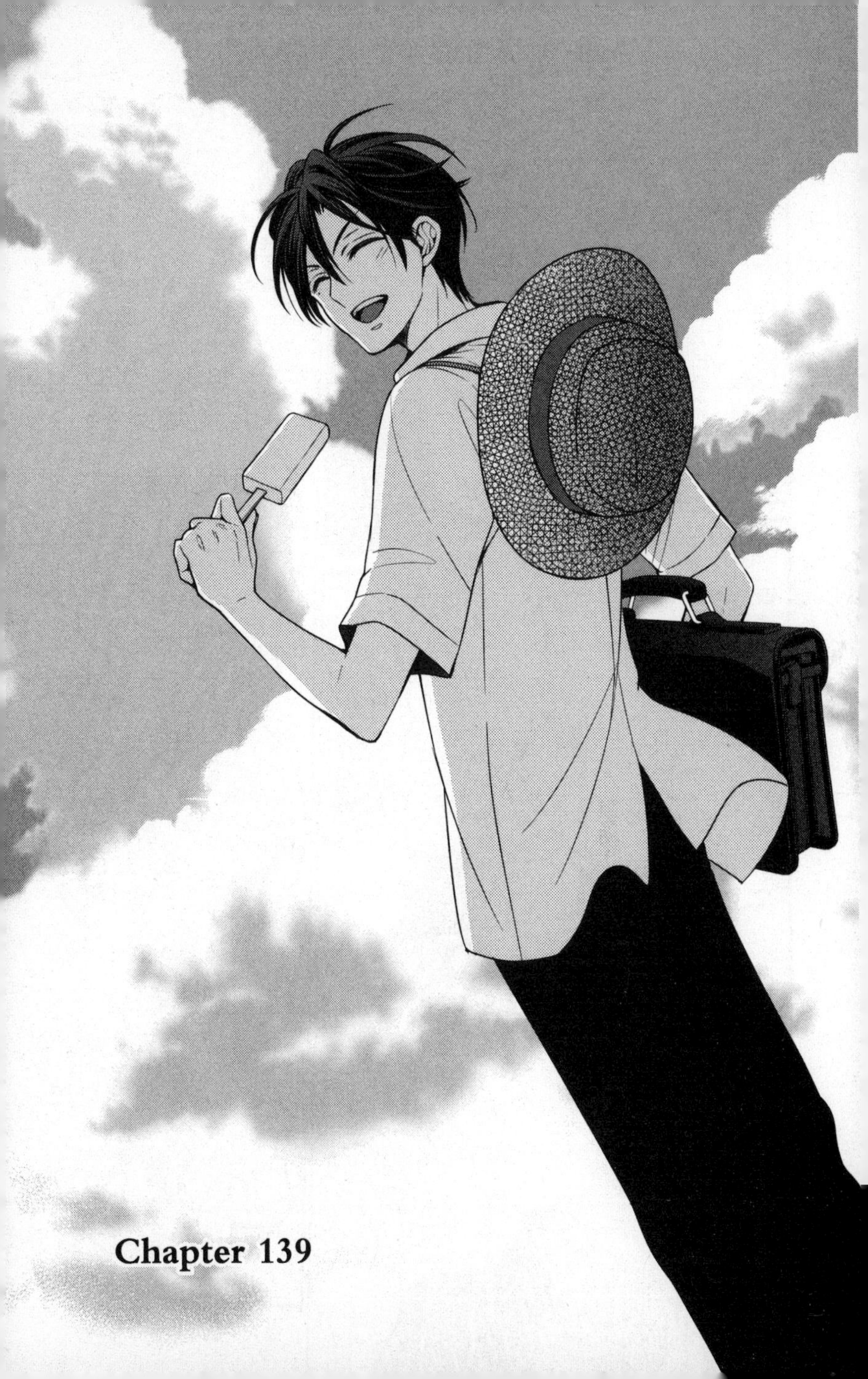

Chapter 139

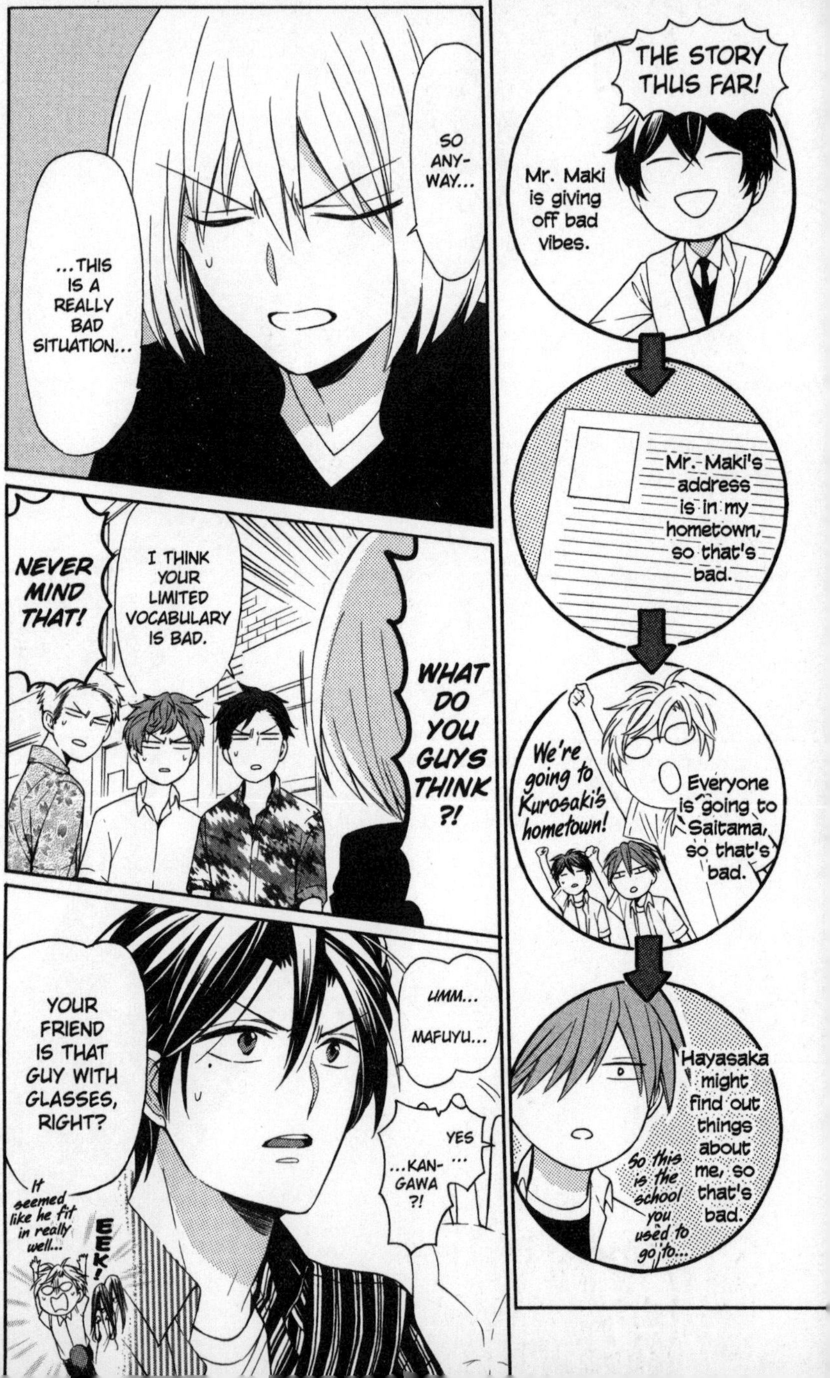
THE STORY THUS FAR!
Mr. Maki is giving off bad vibes.
Mr. Maki's address is in my hometown, so that's bad.
Everyone is going to Saitama, so that's bad.
We're going to Kurosaki's hometown!
Hayasaka might find out things about me, so that's bad.
So this is the school you used to go to...
SO ANYWAY...
...THIS IS A REALLY BAD SITUATION...
WHAT DO YOU GUYS THINK?!
I THINK YOUR LIMITED VOCABULARY IS BAD.
NEVER MIND THAT!
UMM...
MAFUYU...
YES...
...KANGAWA?!
YOUR FRIEND IS THAT GUY WITH GLASSES, RIGHT?
It seemed like he fit in really well...
EEK!

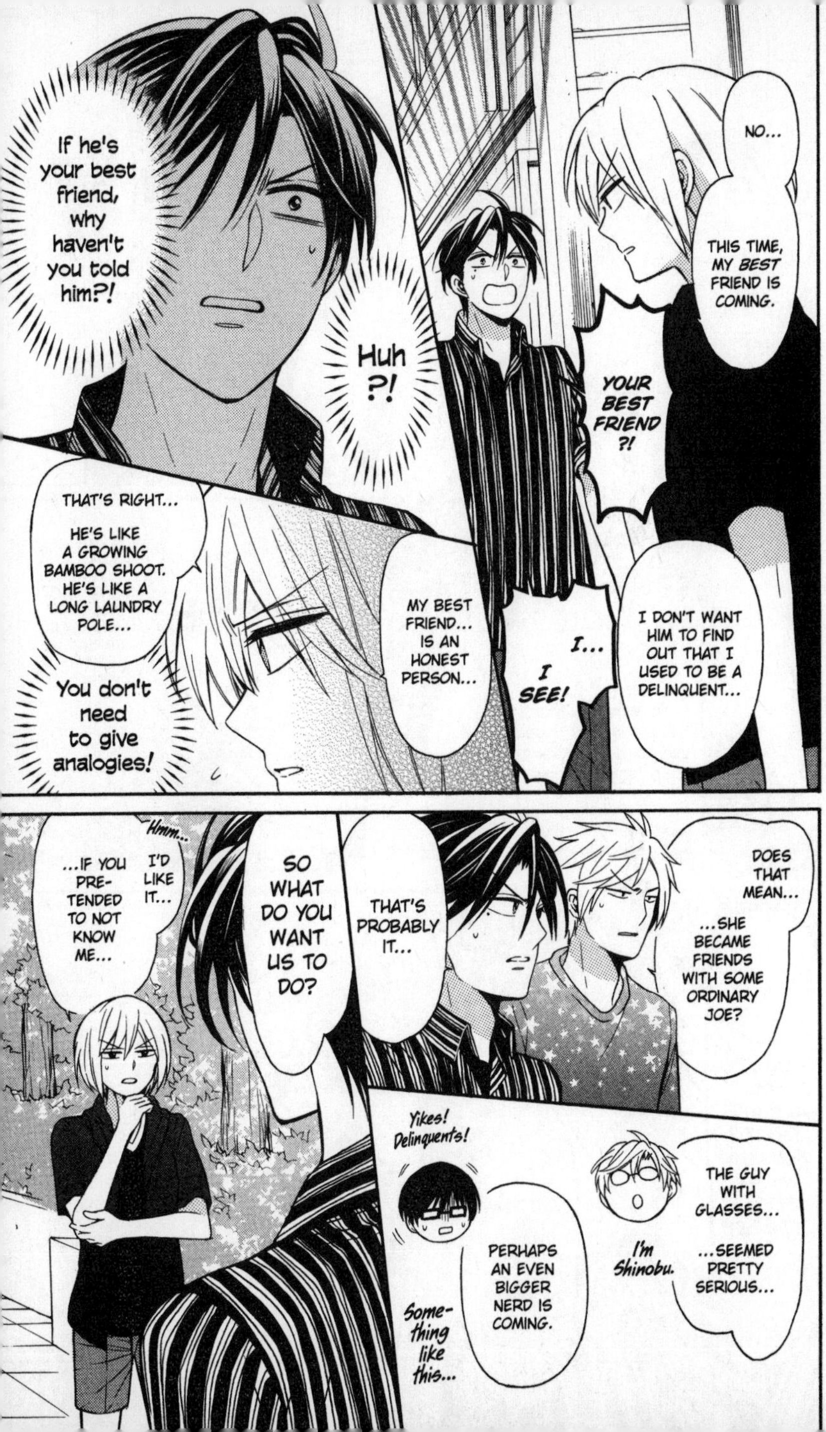
NO...
THIS TIME, MY *BEST* FRIEND IS COMING.
YOUR BEST FRIEND ?!
I DON'T WANT HIM TO FIND OUT THAT I USED TO BE A DELINQUENT...
I... I SEE!
If he's your best friend, why haven't you told him?!
Huh ?!
MY BEST FRIEND... IS AN HONEST PERSON...
THAT'S RIGHT... HE'S LIKE A GROWING BAMBOO SHOOT. HE'S LIKE A LONG LAUNDRY POLE...
You don't need to give analogies!
DOES THAT MEAN... ...SHE BECAME FRIENDS WITH SOME ORDINARY JOE?
THAT'S PROBABLY IT...
SO WHAT DO YOU WANT US TO DO?
Hmm...
I'D LIKE IT...
...IF YOU PRETENDED TO NOT KNOW ME...
THE GUY WITH GLASSES... ...SEEMED PRETTY SERIOUS...
I'm Shinobu.
PERHAPS AN EVEN BIGGER NERD IS COMING.
Yikes! Delinquents!
Something like this...

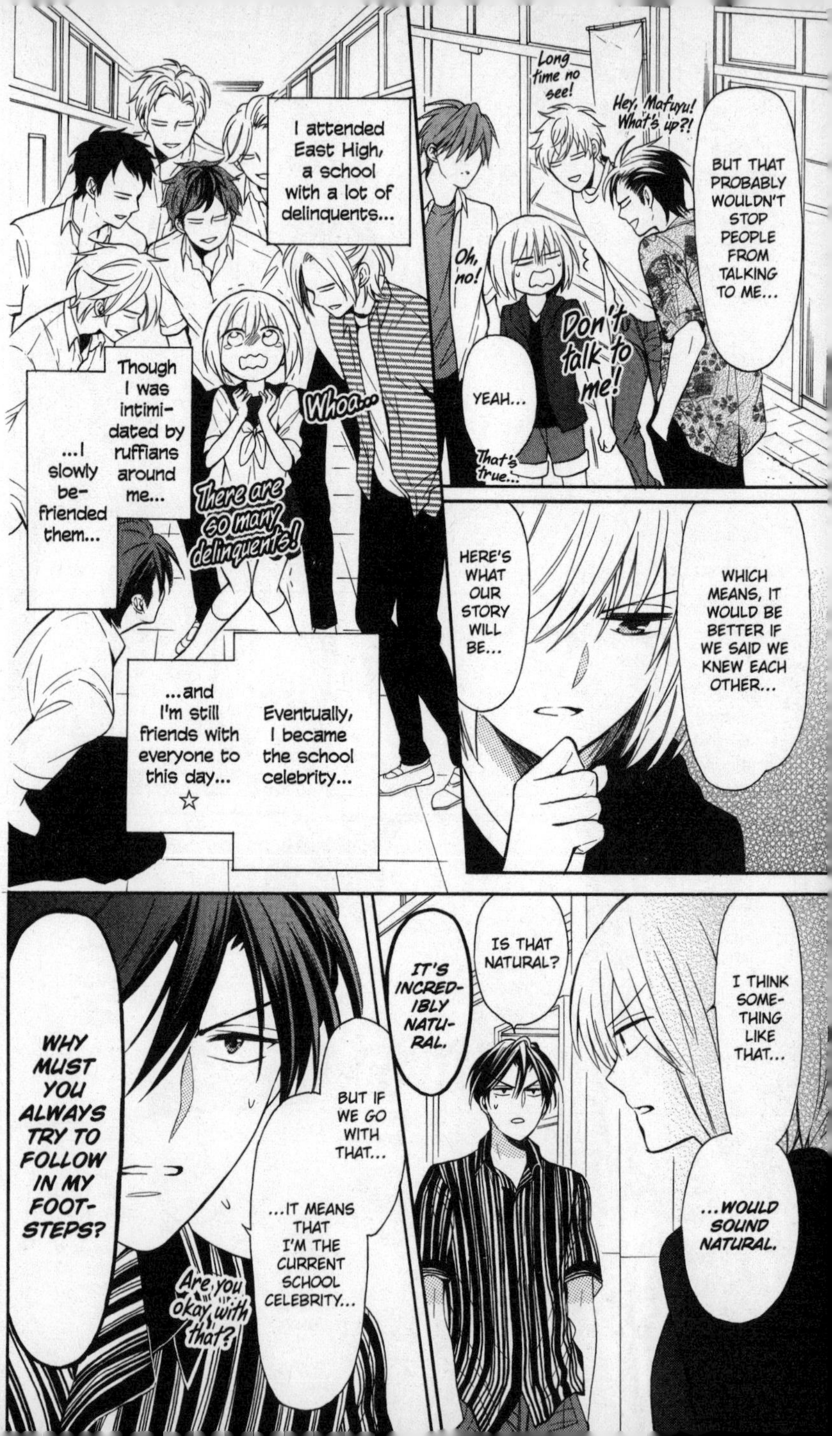
Hey, Mafuyu! What's up?!
Long time no see!
BUT THAT PROBABLY WOULDN'T STOP PEOPLE FROM TALKING TO ME...
Oh, no!
Don't talk to me!
YEAH...
That's true...
WHICH MEANS, IT WOULD BE BETTER IF WE SAID WE KNEW EACH OTHER...
HERE'S WHAT OUR STORY WILL BE...
I attended East High, a school with a lot of delinquents...
Whoa...
Though I was intimidated by ruffians around me...
...I slowly befriended them...
There are so many delinquents!
Eventually, I became the school celebrity...
...and I'm still friends with everyone to this day... ☆
I THINK SOMETHING LIKE THAT...
...WOULD SOUND NATURAL.
IS THAT NATURAL?
IT'S INCREDIBLY NATURAL.
BUT IF WE GO WITH THAT...
...IT MEANS THAT I'M THE CURRENT SCHOOL CELEBRITY...
Are you okay with that?
WHY MUST YOU ALWAYS TRY TO FOLLOW IN MY FOOTSTEPS?

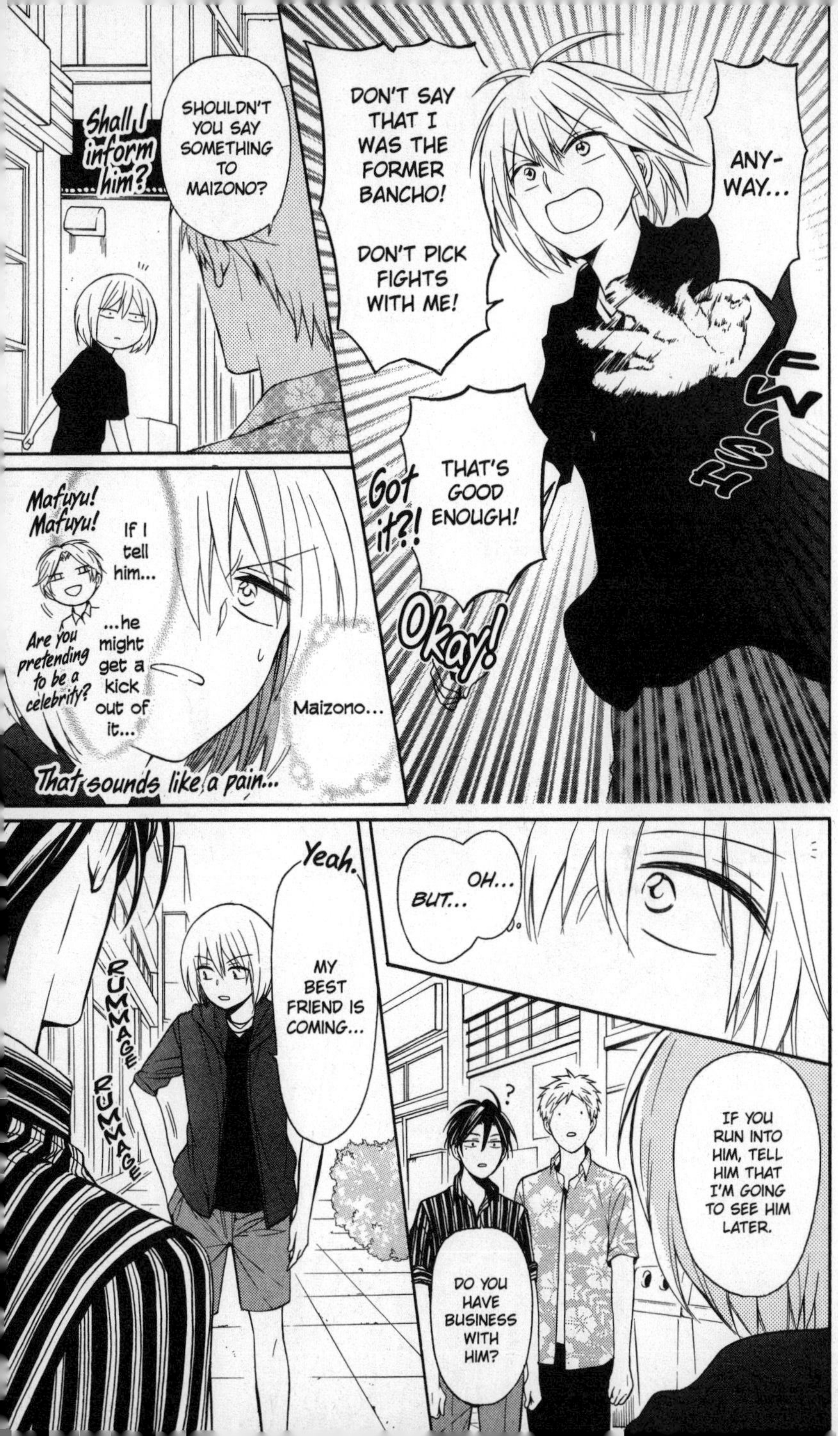
ANY-WAY...
DON'T SAY THAT I WAS THE FORMER BANCHO!
DON'T PICK FIGHTS WITH ME!
FWISH
THAT'S GOOD ENOUGH!
Got it?!
Okay!
Shall I inform him?
SHOULDN'T YOU SAY SOMETHING TO MAIZONO?
Maizono...
If I tell him...
...he might get a kick out of it...
Mafuyu! Mafuyu!
Are you pretending to be a celebrity?
That sounds like a pain...
OH... BUT...
IF YOU RUN INTO HIM, TELL HIM THAT I'M GOING TO SEE HIM LATER.
?
DO YOU HAVE BUSINESS WITH HIM?
Yeah.
MY BEST FRIEND IS COMING...
RUMMAGE
RUMMAGE

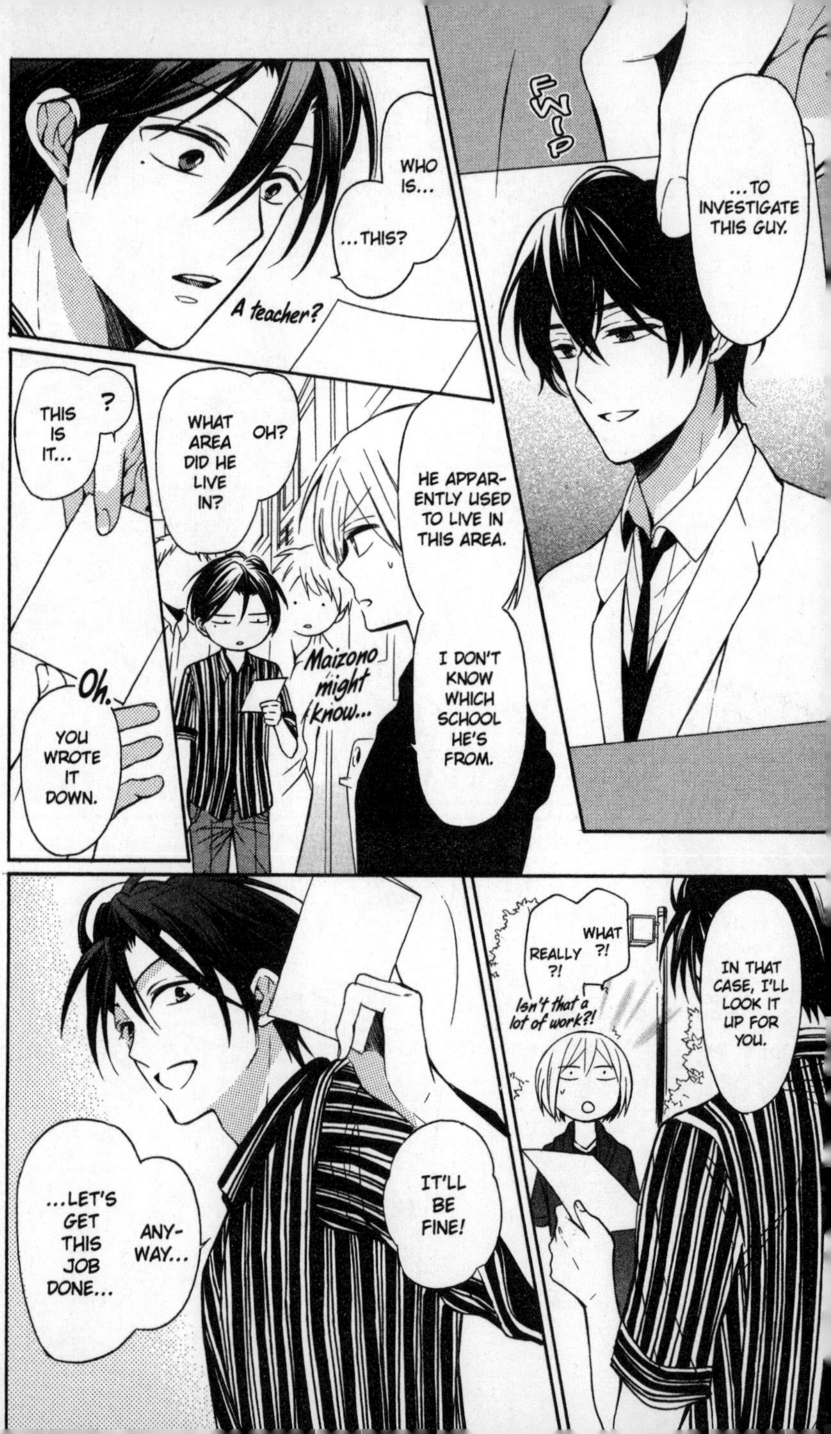
FWIP
...TO INVESTIGATE THIS GUY.
HE APPARENTLY USED TO LIVE IN THIS AREA.
I DON'T KNOW WHICH SCHOOL HE'S FROM.
WHO IS...
...THIS?
A teacher?
OH?
WHAT AREA DID HE LIVE IN?
THIS IS IT... ?
Maizono might know...
Oh.
YOU WROTE IT DOWN.
IN THAT CASE, I'LL LOOK IT UP FOR YOU.
WHAT ?!
REALLY ?!
Isn't that a lot of work?!
IT'LL BE FINE!
ANYWAY...
...LET'S GET THIS JOB DONE...

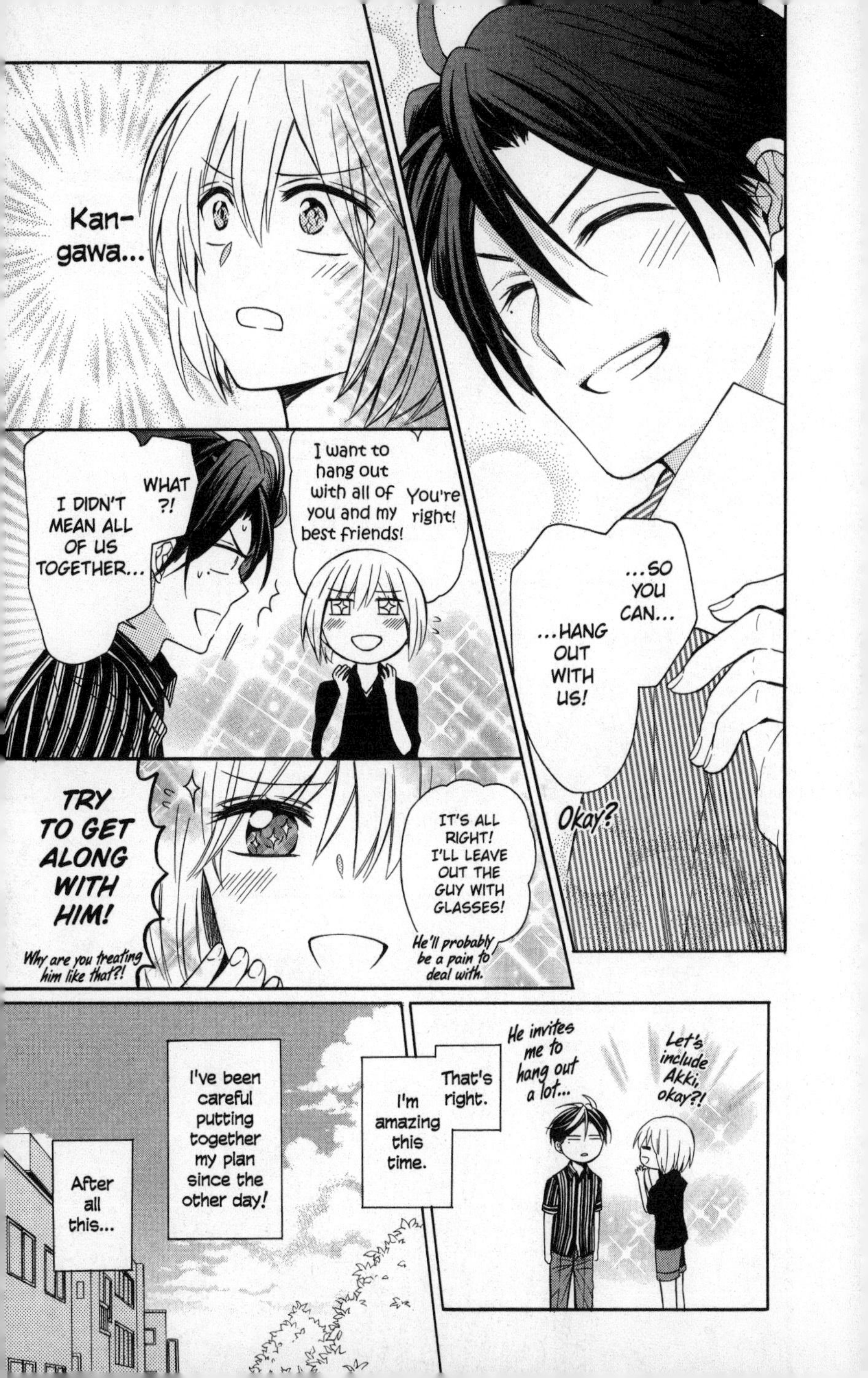
...SO YOU CAN...
...HANG OUT WITH US!
Okay?
Kan-gawa...
You're right!
I want to hang out with all of you and my best friends!
WHAT?!
I DIDN'T MEAN ALL OF US TOGETHER...
IT'S ALL RIGHT! I'LL LEAVE OUT THE GUY WITH GLASSES!
He'll probably be a pain to deal with.
TRY TO GET ALONG WITH HIM!
Why are you treating him like that?!
Let's include Akki, okay?!
He invites me to hang out a lot...
That's right.
I'm amazing this time.
I've been careful putting together my plan since the other day!
After all this...

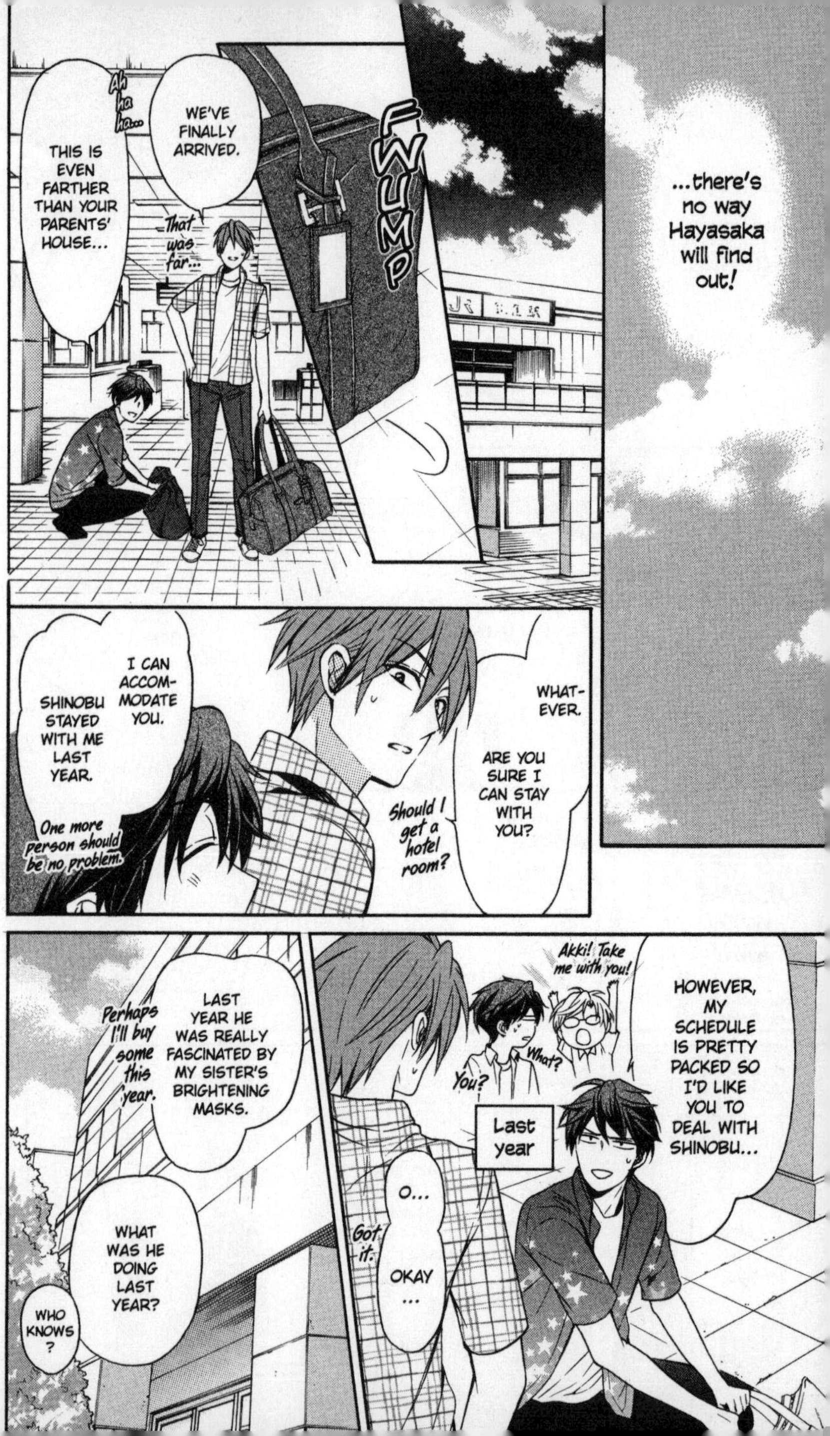
...there's no way Hayasaka will find out!
FWUMP
WE'VE FINALLY ARRIVED.
That was far...
Ah ha ha...
THIS IS EVEN FARTHER THAN YOUR PARENTS' HOUSE...
WHATEVER. ARE YOU SURE I CAN STAY WITH YOU?
Should I get a hotel room?
I CAN ACCOMMODATE YOU. SHINOBU STAYED WITH ME LAST YEAR.
One more person should be no problem.
HOWEVER, MY SCHEDULE IS PRETTY PACKED SO I'D LIKE YOU TO DEAL WITH SHINOBU...
Akki! Take me with you!
What?
You?
Last year
O... OKAY...
Got it.
LAST YEAR HE WAS REALLY FASCINATED BY MY SISTER'S BRIGHTENING MASKS.
Perhaps I'll buy some this year.
WHAT WAS HE DOING LAST YEAR?
WHO KNOWS?

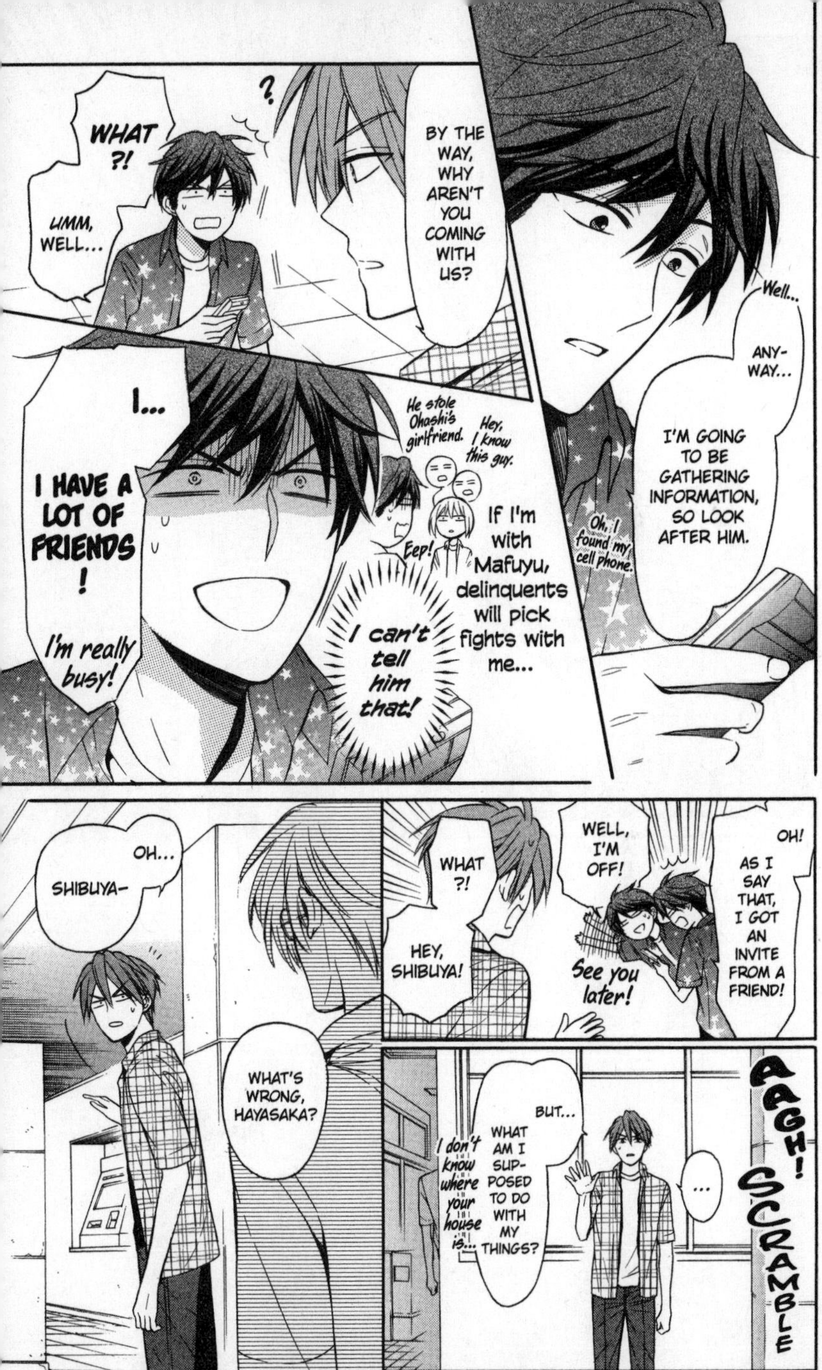

Well...
ANY-WAY...
I'M GOING TO BE GATHERING INFORMATION, SO LOOK AFTER HIM.
Oh, I found my cell phone.
BY THE WAY, WHY AREN'T YOU COMING WITH US?
?
WHAT ?!
UMM, WELL...
He stole Ohashi's girlfriend.
Hey, I know this guy.
Eep!
If I'm with Mafuyu, delinquents will pick fights with me...
I can't tell him that!
I...
I HAVE A LOT OF FRIENDS !
I'm really busy!
OH!
AS I SAY THAT, I GOT AN INVITE FROM A FRIEND!
WELL, I'M OFF!
See you later!
WHAT ?!
HEY, SHIBUYA!
AAGH! SCRAMBLE
...
BUT...
WHAT AM I SUP-POSED TO DO WITH MY THINGS?
I don't know where your house is...
OH...
SHIBUYA-
WHAT'S WRONG, HAYASAKA?

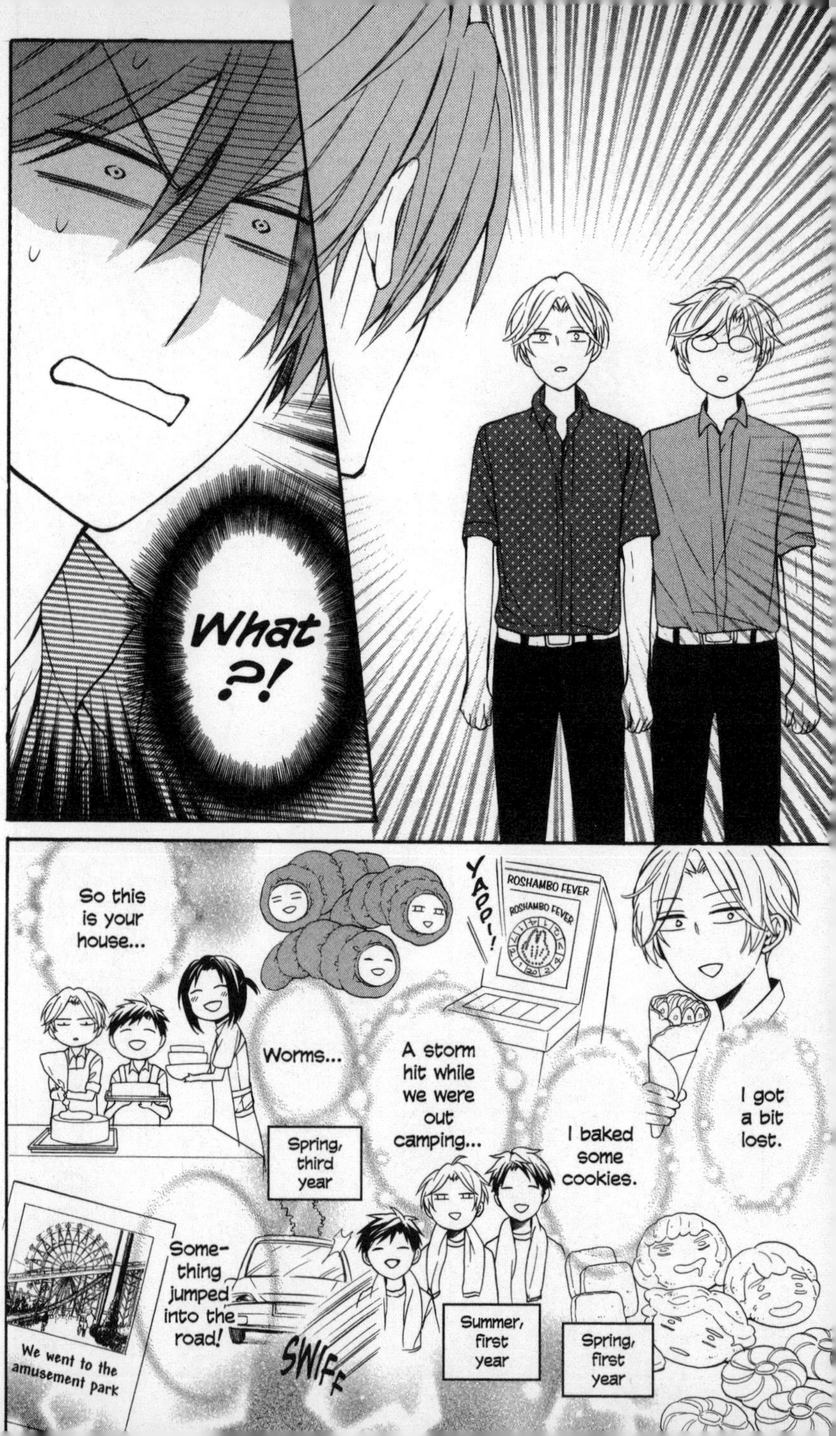
What ?!
I got a bit lost.
ROSHAMBO FEVER
ROSHAMBO FEVER
YAPPI!
I baked some cookies.
Spring, first year
A storm hit while we were out camping...
Summer, first year
Worms...
So this is your house...
Spring, third year
Some-thing jumped into the road!
SWIFF
We went to the amusement park

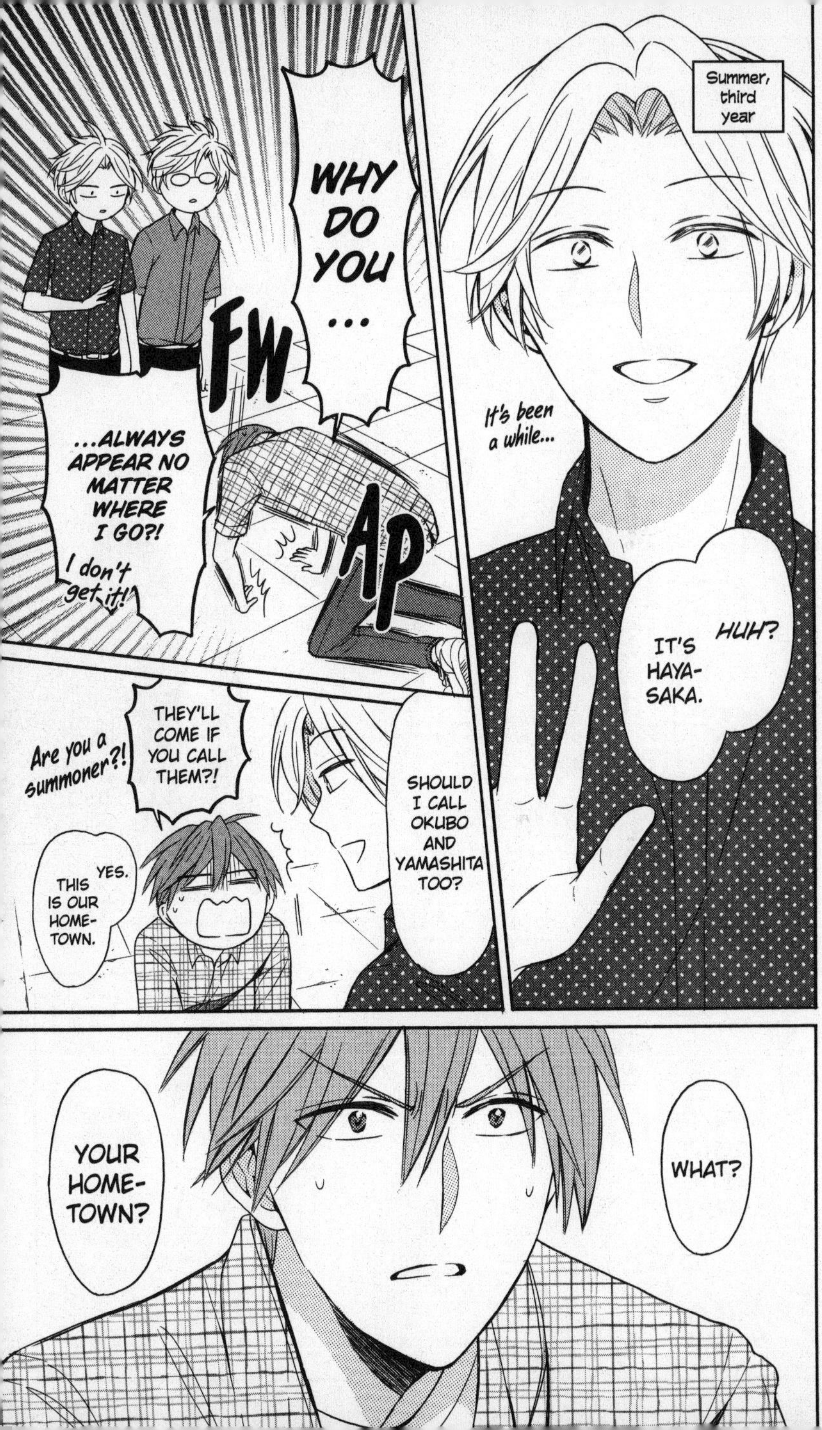
Summer, third year
It's been a while...
HUH?
IT'S HAYA-SAKA.
WHY DO YOU...
FW
AP
...ALWAYS APPEAR NO MATTER WHERE I GO?!
I don't get it!
SHOULD I CALL OKUBO AND YAMASHITA TOO?
THEY'LL COME IF YOU CALL THEM?!
Are you a summoner?!
YES.
THIS IS OUR HOME-TOWN.
WHAT?
YOUR HOME-TOWN?

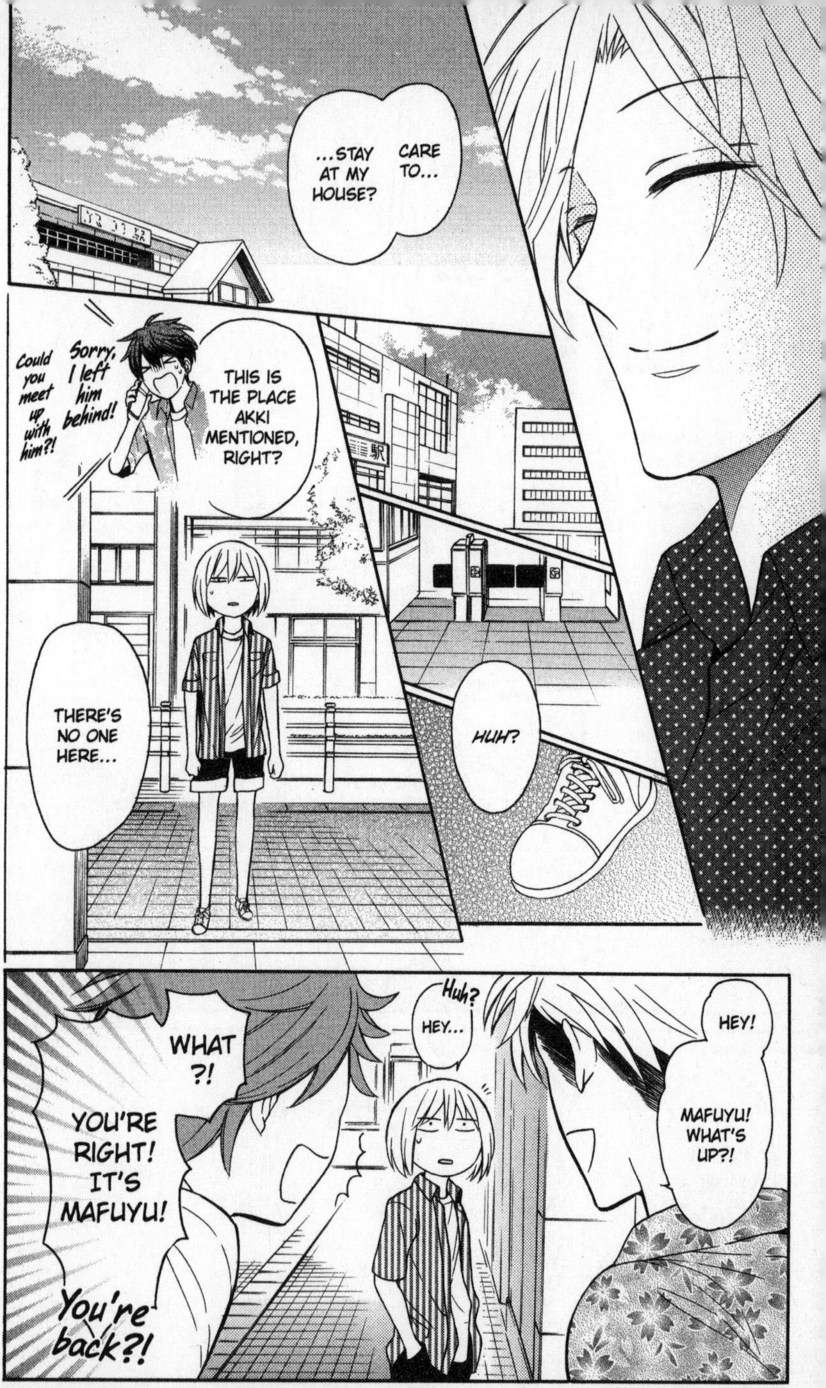
CARE TO...
...STAY AT MY HOUSE?
HUH?
Sorry, I left him behind!
Could you meet up with him?!
THIS IS THE PLACE AKKI MENTIONED, RIGHT?
THERE'S NO ONE HERE...
HEY!
MAFUYU! WHAT'S UP?!
Huh?
HEY...
WHAT?!
YOU'RE RIGHT! IT'S MAFUYU!
You're back?!

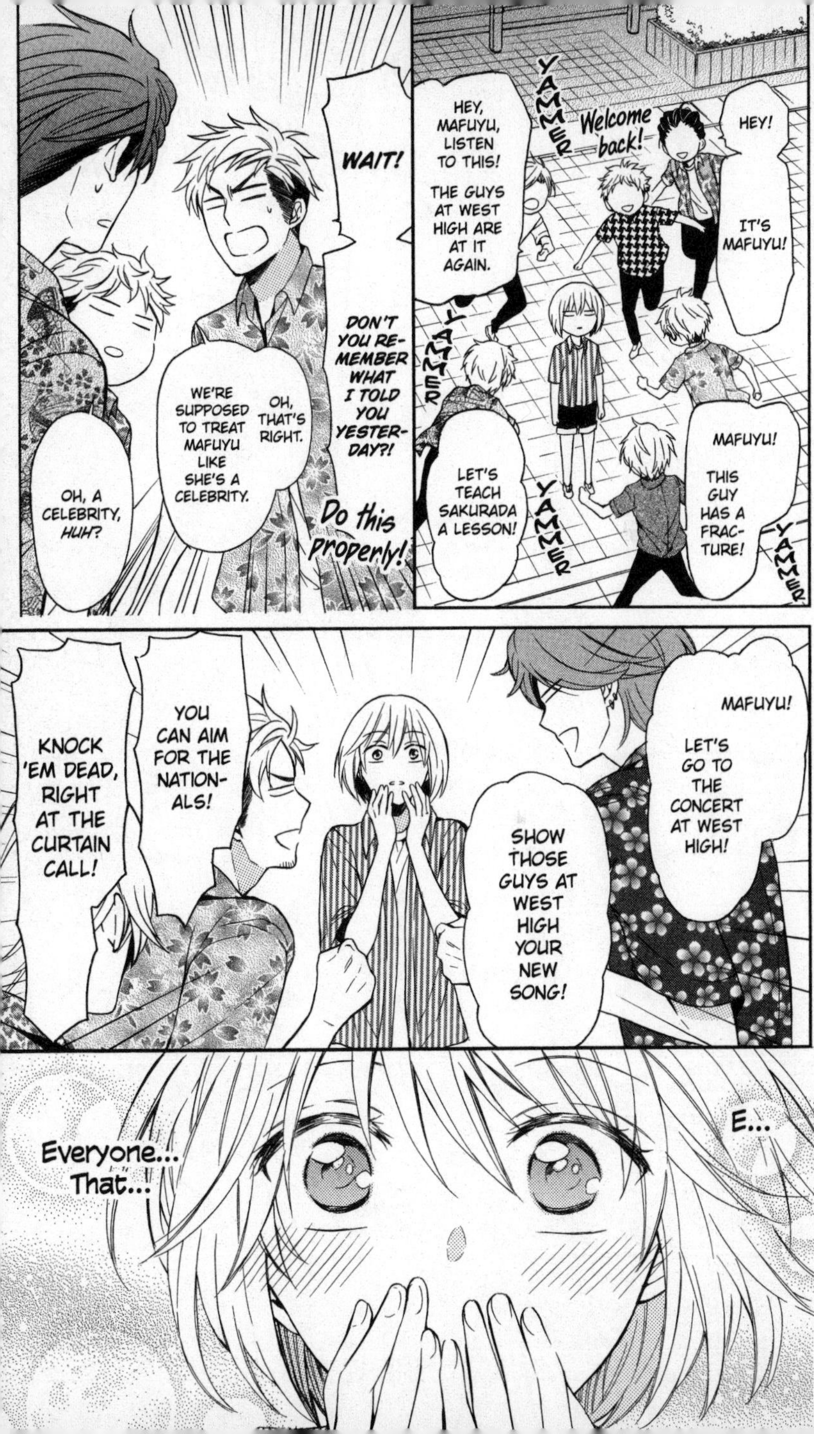
HEY!
IT'S MAFUYU!
Welcome back!
YAMMER
HEY, MAFUYU, LISTEN TO THIS! THE GUYS AT WEST HIGH ARE AT IT AGAIN.
MAFUYU! THIS GUY HAS A FRACTURE!
YAMMER
YAMMER
LET'S TEACH SAKURADA A LESSON!
YAMMER
WAIT!
DON'T YOU REMEMBER WHAT I TOLD YOU YESTERDAY?!
Do this properly!
OH, THAT'S RIGHT.
WE'RE SUPPOSED TO TREAT MAFUYU LIKE SHE'S A CELEBRITY.
OH, A CELEBRITY, HUH?
MAFUYU! LET'S GO TO THE CONCERT AT WEST HIGH!
SHOW THOSE GUYS AT WEST HIGH YOUR NEW SONG!
YOU CAN AIM FOR THE NATIONALS!
KNOCK 'EM DEAD, RIGHT AT THE CURTAIN CALL!
E...
Everyone... That...

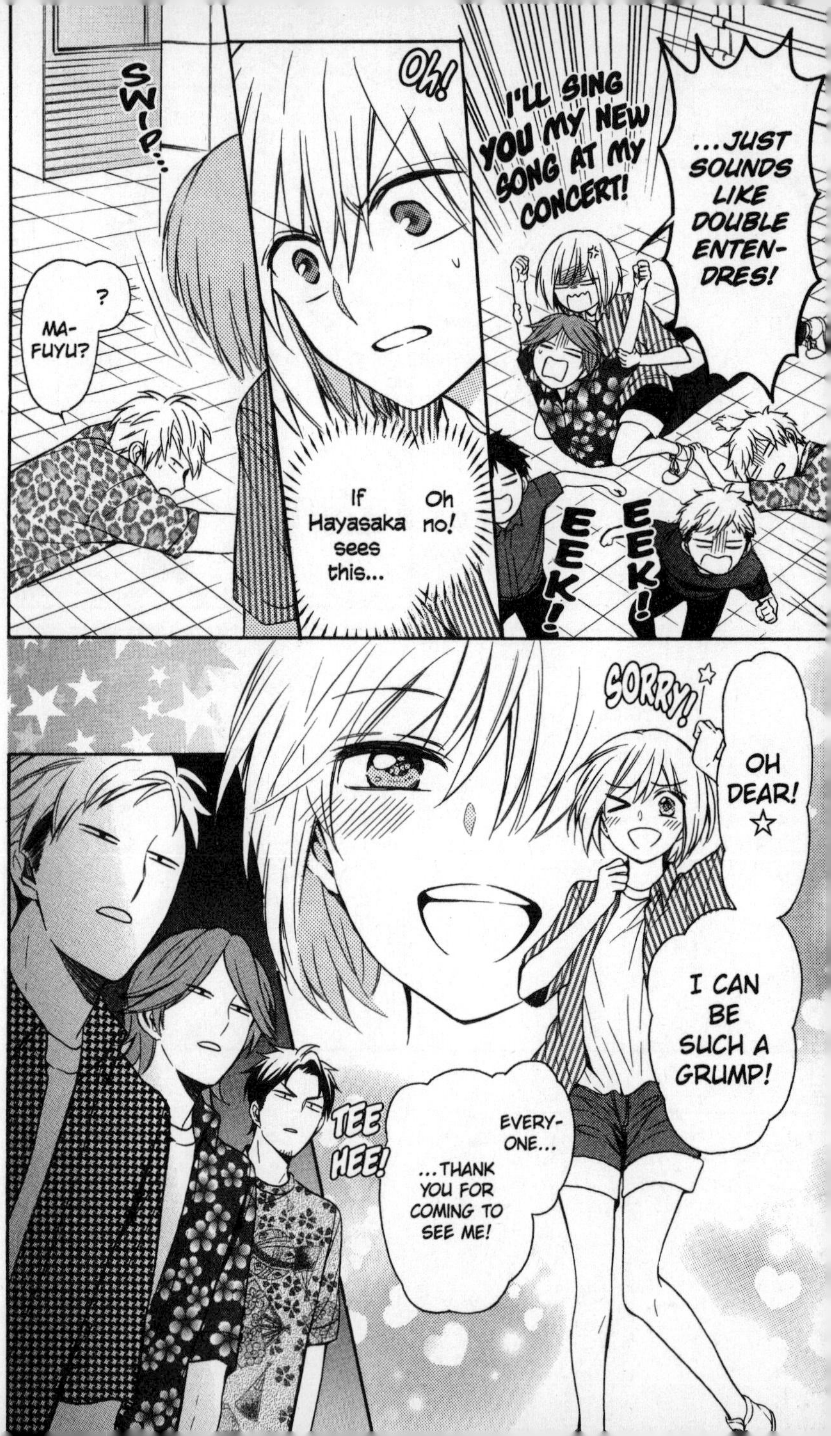
I'LL SING YOU MY NEW SONG AT MY CONCERT!
...JUST SOUNDS LIKE DOUBLE ENTENDRES!
EEK!
EEK!
Oh!
Oh no!
If Hayasaka sees this...
SWIP...
?
MA-FUYU?
SORRY!☆
OH DEAR! ☆
I CAN BE SUCH A GRUMP!
EVERYONE...
...THANK YOU FOR COMING TO SEE ME!
TEE HEE!

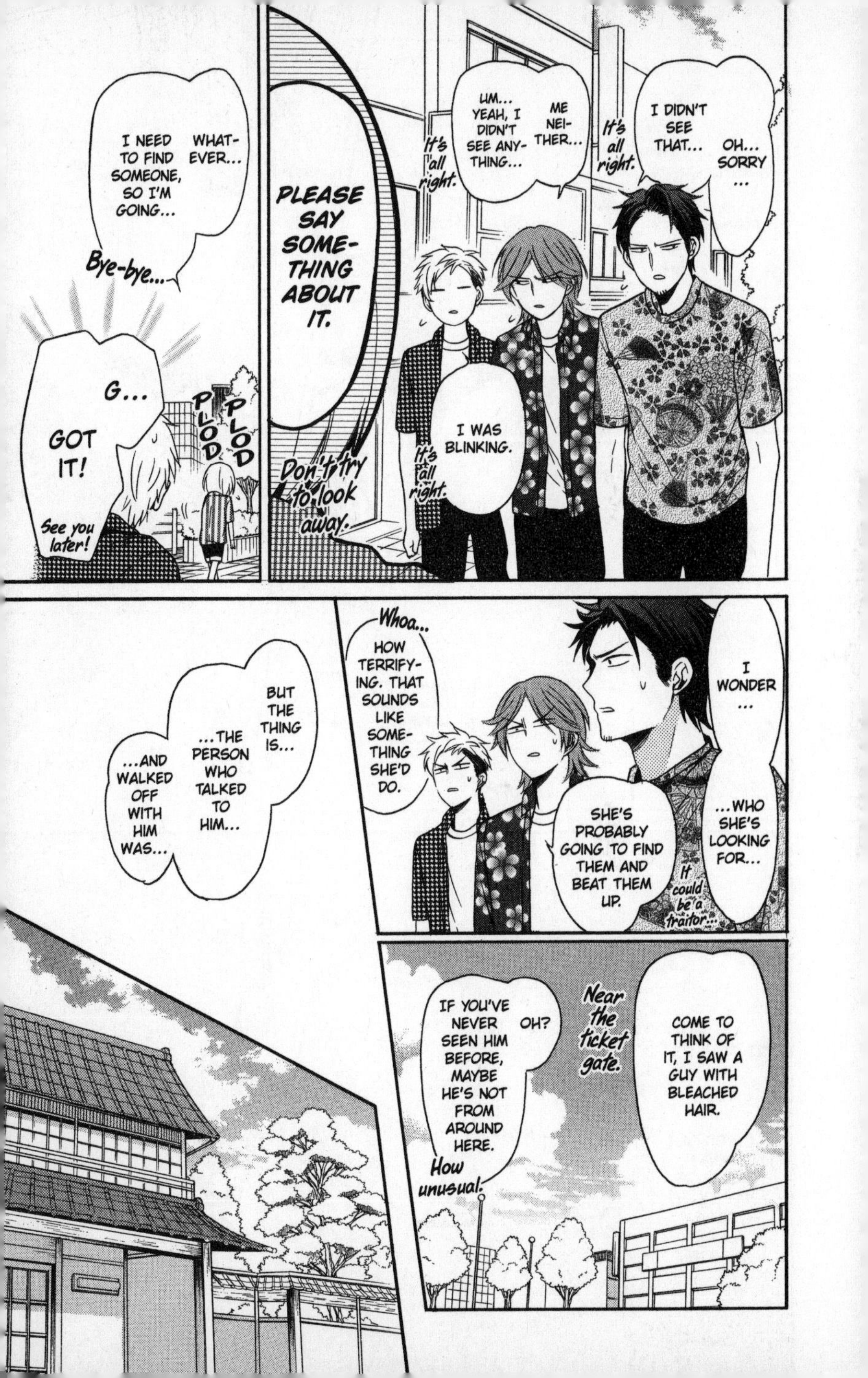
OH... SORRY...
I DIDN'T SEE THAT...
It's all right.
ME NEITHER...
UM... YEAH, I DIDN'T SEE ANYTHING...
It's all right.
PLEASE SAY SOMETHING ABOUT IT.
I WAS BLINKING.
It's all right.
Don't try to look away.
WHATEVER...
I NEED TO FIND SOMEONE, SO I'M GOING...
Bye-bye...
PLOD PLOD
G...
GOT IT!
See you later!
I WONDER...
...WHO SHE'S LOOKING FOR...
It could be a traitor...
SHE'S PROBABLY GOING TO FIND THEM AND BEAT THEM UP.
Whoa...
HOW TERRIFYING. THAT SOUNDS LIKE SOMETHING SHE'D DO.
BUT THE THING IS...
...THE PERSON WHO TALKED TO HIM...
...AND WALKED OFF WITH HIM WAS...
COME TO THINK OF IT, I SAW A GUY WITH BLEACHED HAIR.
Near the ticket gate.
OH?
IF YOU'VE NEVER SEEN HIM BEFORE, MAYBE HE'S NOT FROM AROUND HERE.
How unusual.

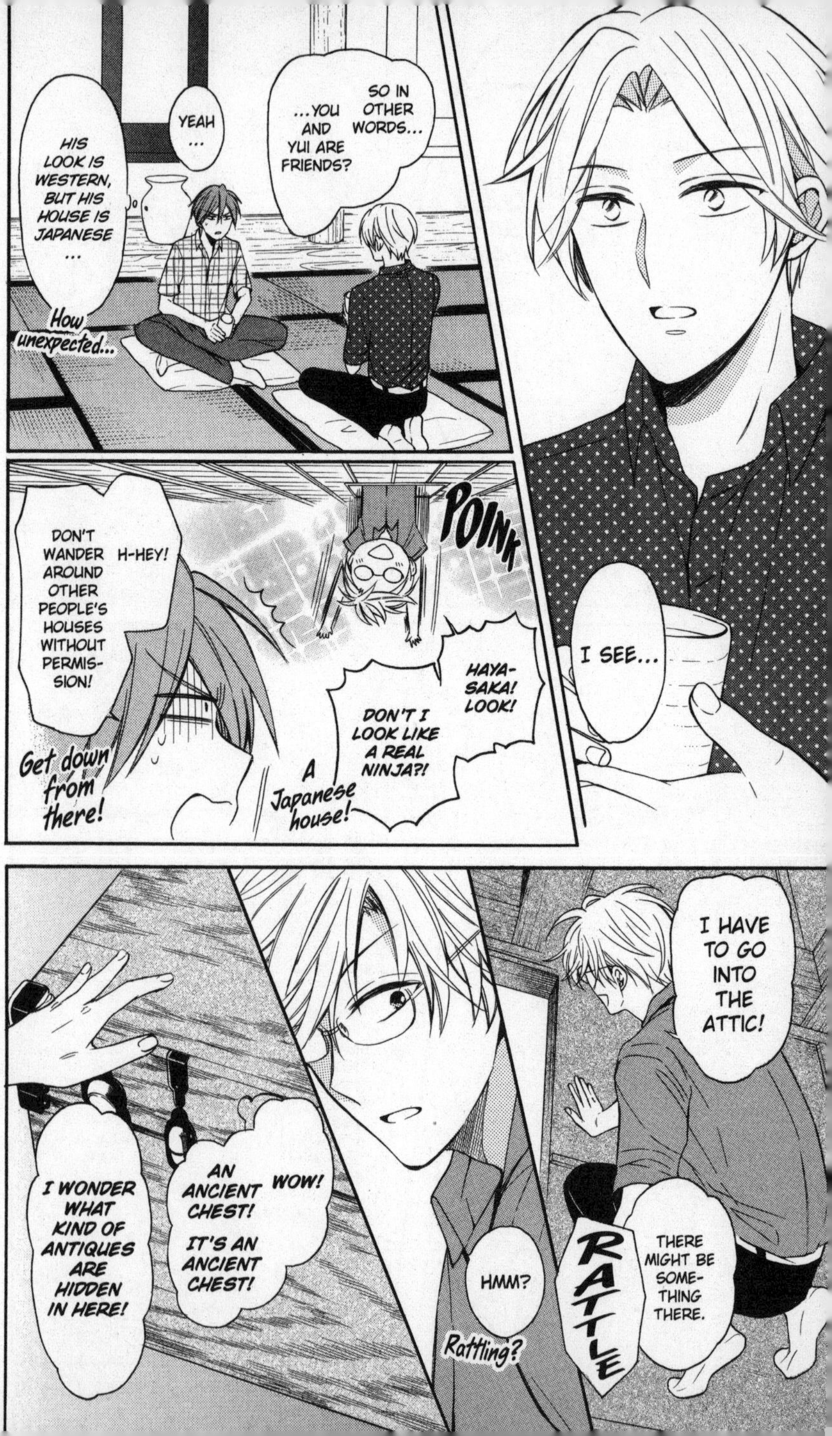
I SEE...
SO IN OTHER WORDS...
...YOU AND YUI ARE FRIENDS?
YEAH...
HIS LOOK IS WESTERN, BUT HIS HOUSE IS JAPANESE...
How unexpected...
POINK
HAYA-SAKA! LOOK!
DON'T I LOOK LIKE A REAL NINJA?!
A Japanese house!
H-HEY!
DON'T WANDER AROUND OTHER PEOPLE'S HOUSES WITHOUT PERMIS-SION!
Get down from there!
I HAVE TO GO INTO THE ATTIC!
THERE MIGHT BE SOME-THING THERE.
RATTLE
HMM?
Rattling?
WOW!
AN ANCIENT CHEST!
IT'S AN ANCIENT CHEST!
I WONDER WHAT KIND OF ANTIQUES ARE HIDDEN IN HERE!

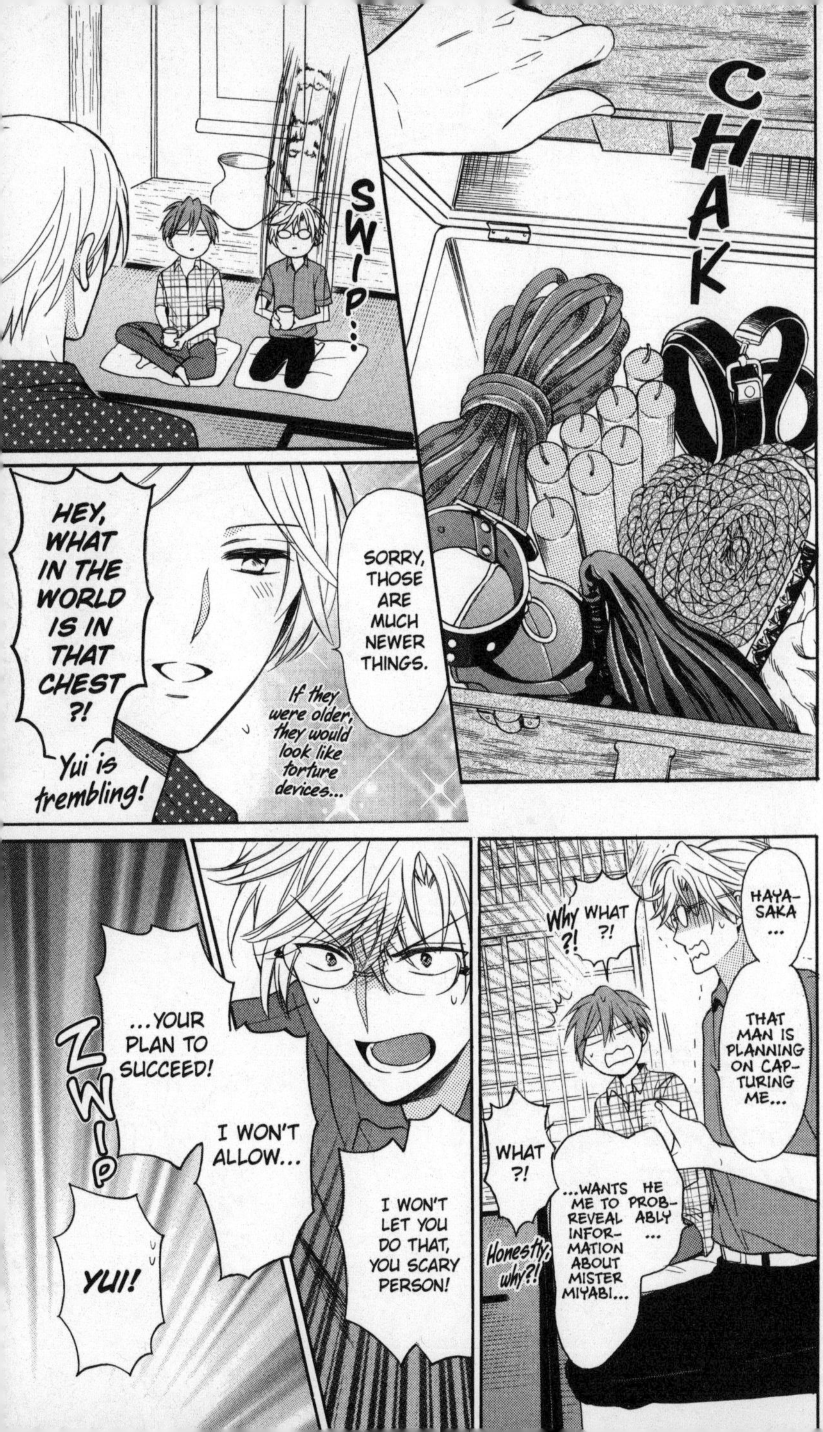
CHAK
SWIP...
SORRY, THOSE ARE MUCH NEWER THINGS.
If they were older, they would look like torture devices...
HEY, WHAT IN THE WORLD IS IN THAT CHEST?!
Yui is trembling!
HAYASAKA...
THAT MAN IS PLANNING ON CAPTURING ME...
WHAT?!
Why?!
HE PROBABLY...
...WANTS ME TO REVEAL INFORMATION ABOUT MISTER MIYABI...
WHAT?!
Honestly, why?!
I WON'T LET YOU DO THAT, YOU SCARY PERSON!
I WON'T ALLOW...
...YOUR PLAN TO SUCCEED!
ZWIP
YUI!

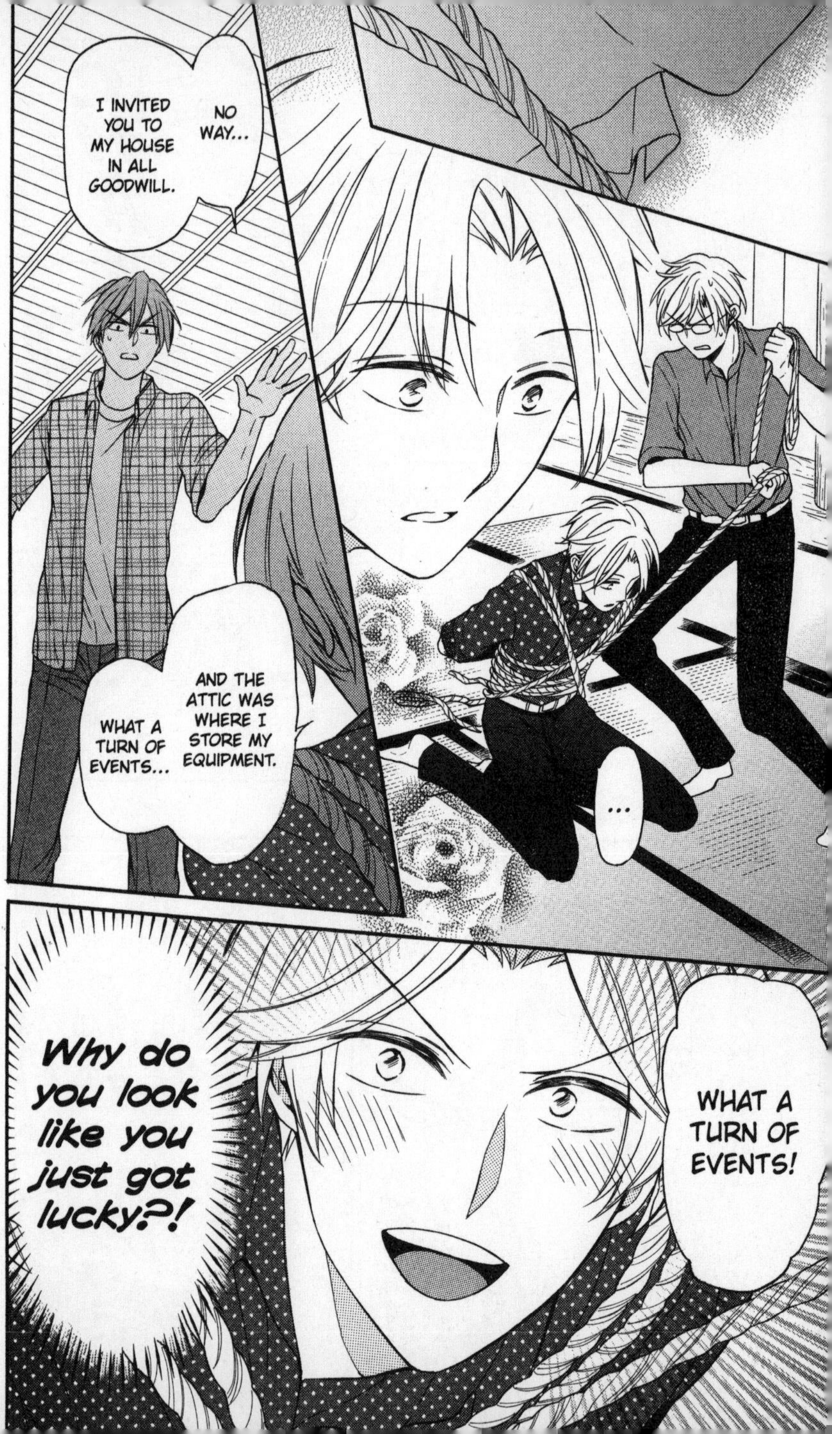
...
NO WAY...
I INVITED YOU TO MY HOUSE IN ALL GOODWILL.
AND THE ATTIC WAS WHERE I STORE MY EQUIPMENT.
WHAT A TURN OF EVENTS...
WHAT A TURN OF EVENTS!
Why do you look like you just got lucky?!

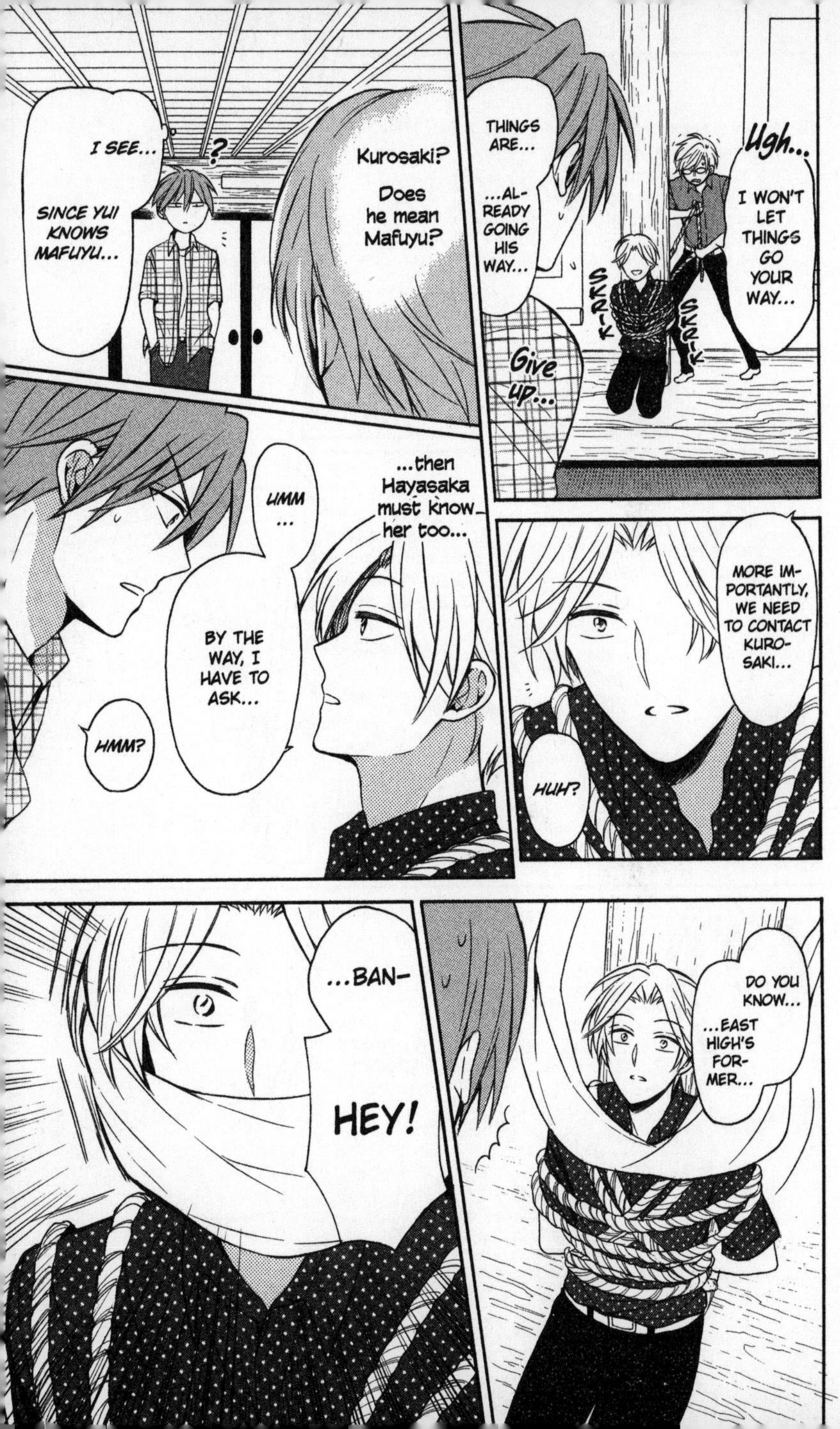

Ugh...
I WON'T LET THINGS GO YOUR WAY...
THINGS ARE...
...ALREADY GOING HIS WAY...
SKRIK
SKRIK
Give up...
Kurosaki?
Does he mean Mafuyu?
I SEE...
?
SINCE YUI KNOWS MAFUYU...
MORE IMPORTANTLY, WE NEED TO CONTACT KUROSAKI...
HUH?
...then Hayasaka must know her too...
UMM...
BY THE WAY, I HAVE TO ASK...
HMM?
DO YOU KNOW...
...EAST HIGH'S FORMER...
...BAN-
HEY!

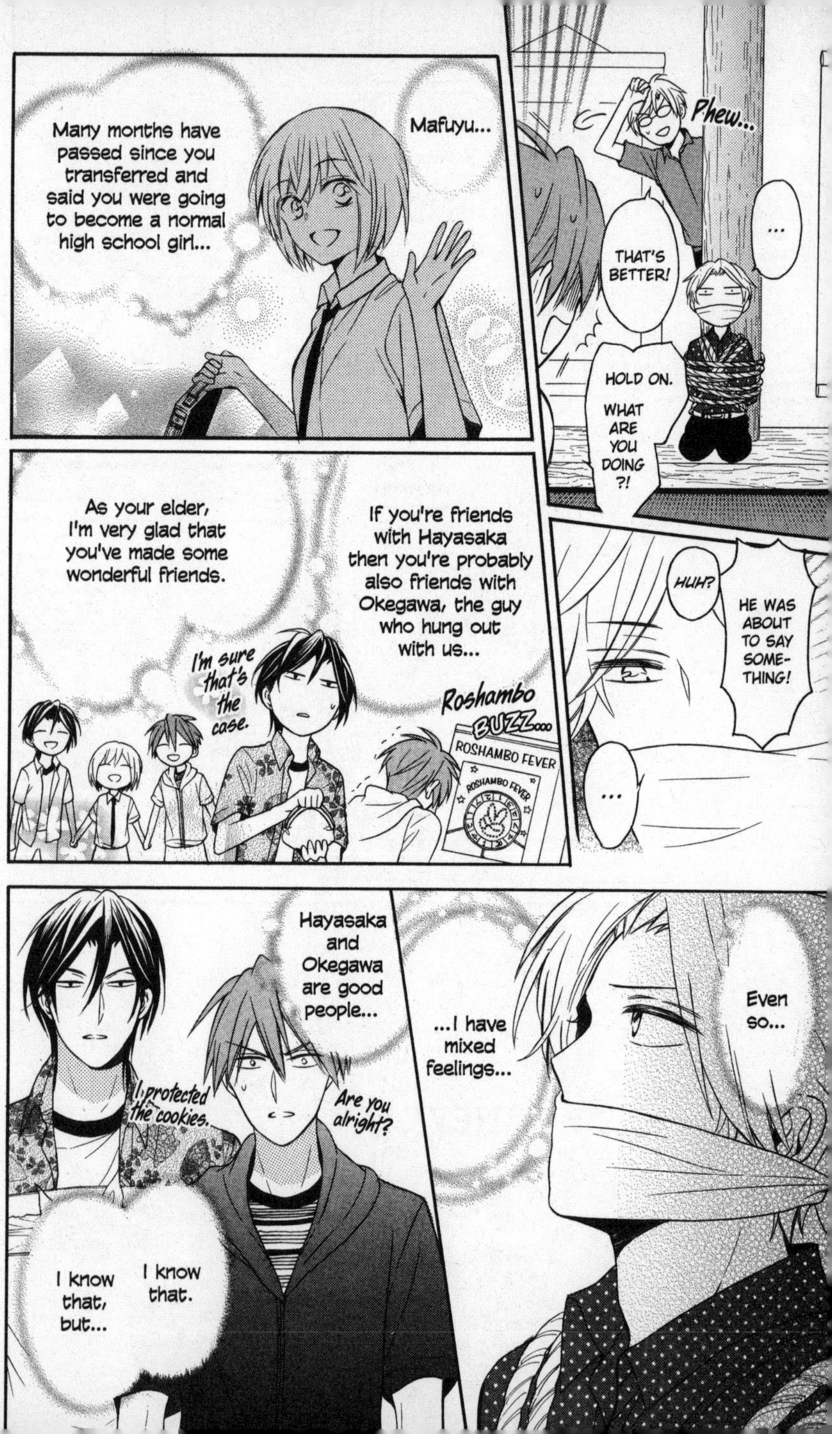
Phew...
...
THAT'S BETTER!
HOLD ON. WHAT ARE YOU DOING?!
Mafuyu...
Many months have passed since you transferred and said you were going to become a normal high school girl...
HE WAS ABOUT TO SAY SOMETHING!
HUH?
...
If you're friends with Hayasaka then you're probably also friends with Okegawa, the guy who hung out with us...
As your elder, I'm very glad that you've made some wonderful friends.
Roshambo
BUZZ...
ROSHAMBO FEVER
ROSHAMBO FEVER
I'm sure that's the case.
Even so...
...I have mixed feelings...
Hayasaka and Okegawa are good people...
Are you alright?
I protected the cookies.
I know that.
I know that, but...

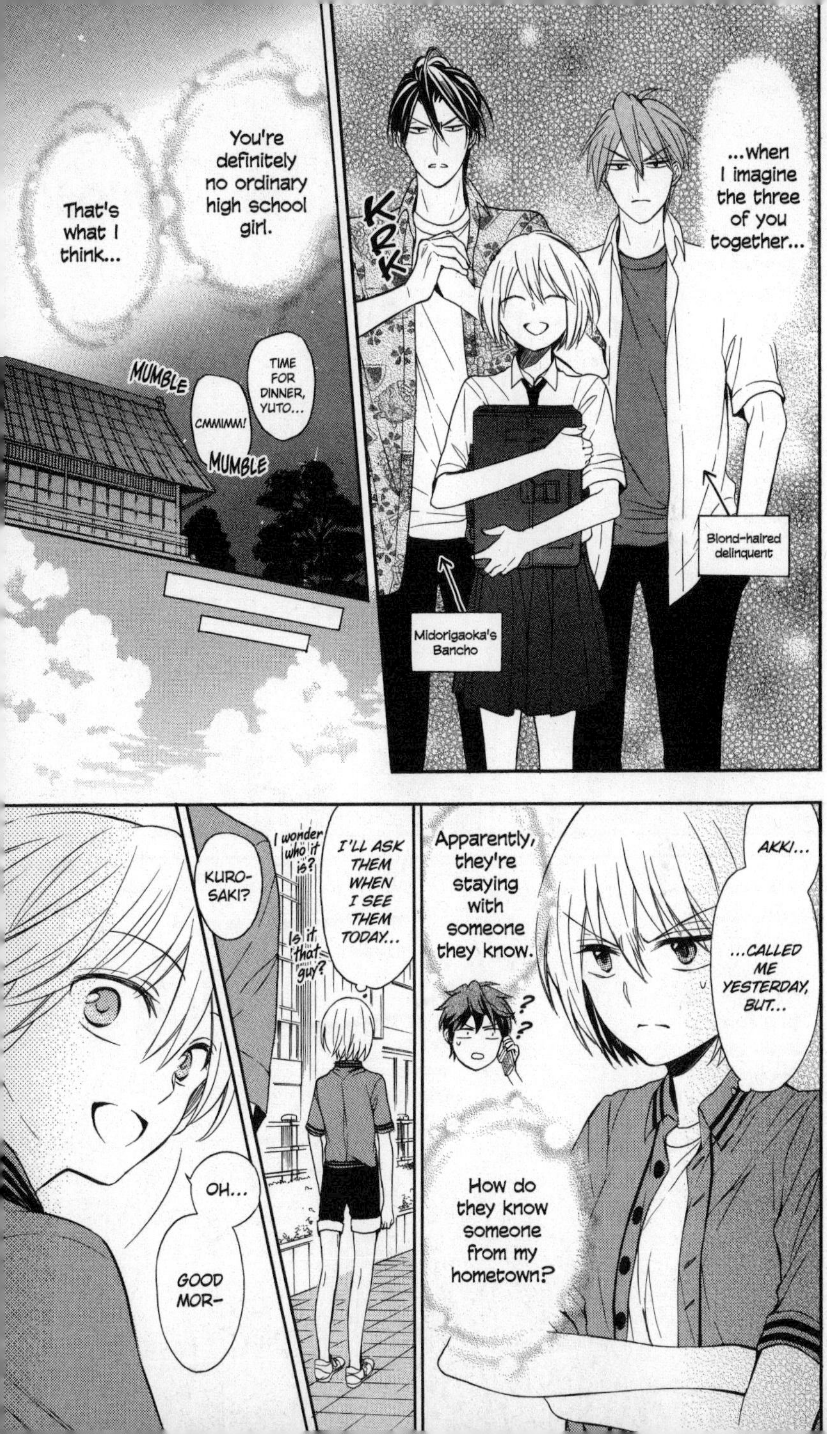
...when I imagine the three of you together...
KRK
Blond-haired delinquent
Midorigaoka's Bancho
You're definitely no ordinary high school girl.
That's what I think...
TIME FOR DINNER, YUTO...
MUMBLE
CMMIMM!
MUMBLE
AKKI...
...CALLED ME YESTERDAY, BUT...
Apparently, they're staying with someone they know.
??
How do they know someone from my hometown?
I'LL ASK THEM WHEN I SEE THEM TODAY...
I wonder who it is?
Is it that guy?
KURO-SAKI?
OH...
GOOD MOR-

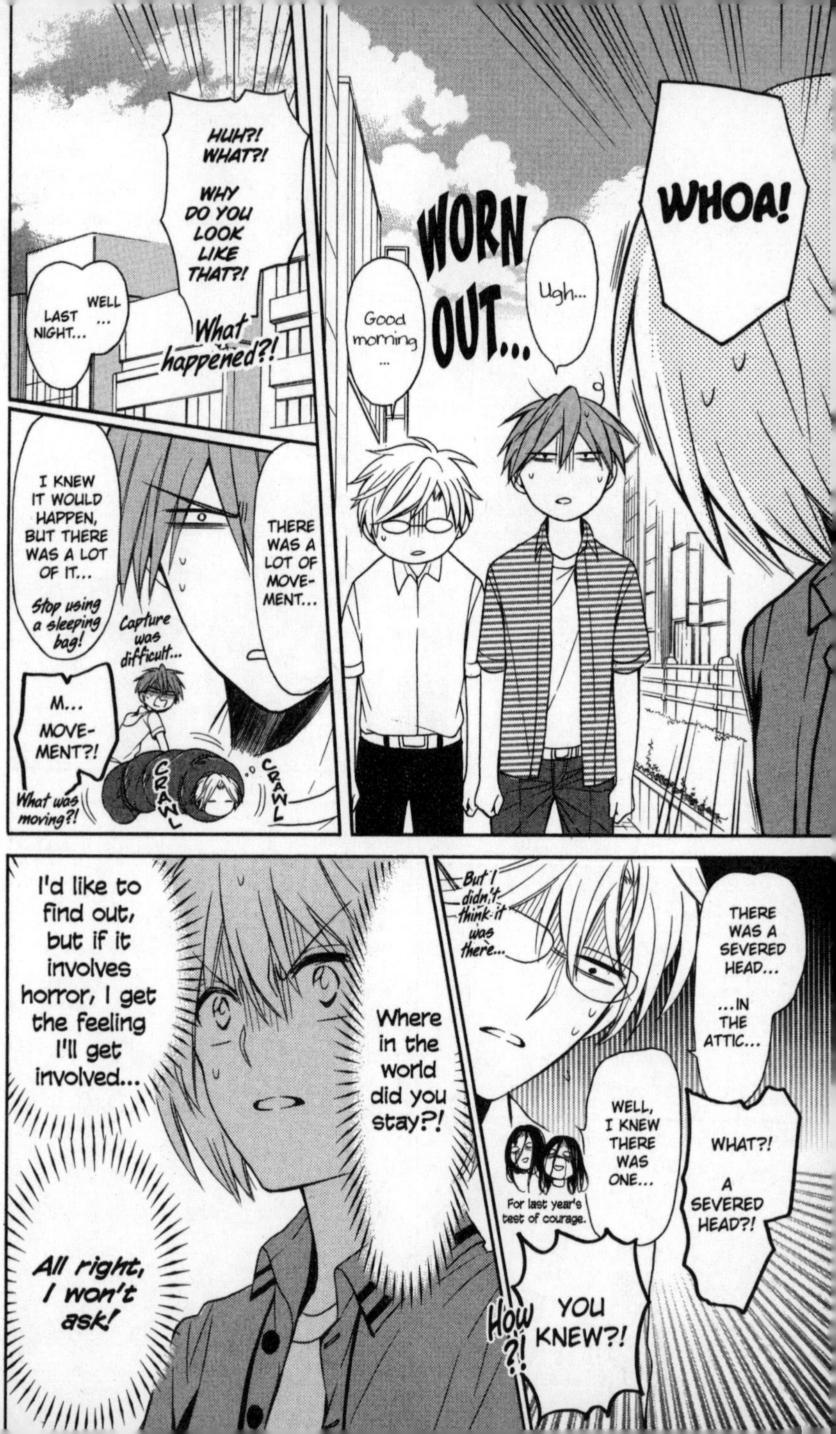
WHOA!
Ugh...
WORN OUT...
Good morning...
HUH?! WHAT?! WHY DO YOU LOOK LIKE THAT?!
What happened?!
WELL... LAST NIGHT...
THERE WAS A LOT OF MOVEMENT...
I KNEW IT WOULD HAPPEN, BUT THERE WAS A LOT OF IT...
Stop using a sleeping bag!
Capture was difficult...
M... MOVEMENT?!
What was moving?!
CRAWL
CRAWL
THERE WAS A SEVERED HEAD...
...IN THE ATTIC...
But I didn't think it was there...
WHAT?! A SEVERED HEAD?!
WELL, I KNEW THERE WAS ONE...
For last year's test of courage.
YOU KNEW?!
How?!
Where in the world did you stay?!
I'd like to find out, but if it involves horror, I get the feeling I'll get involved...
All right, I won't ask!

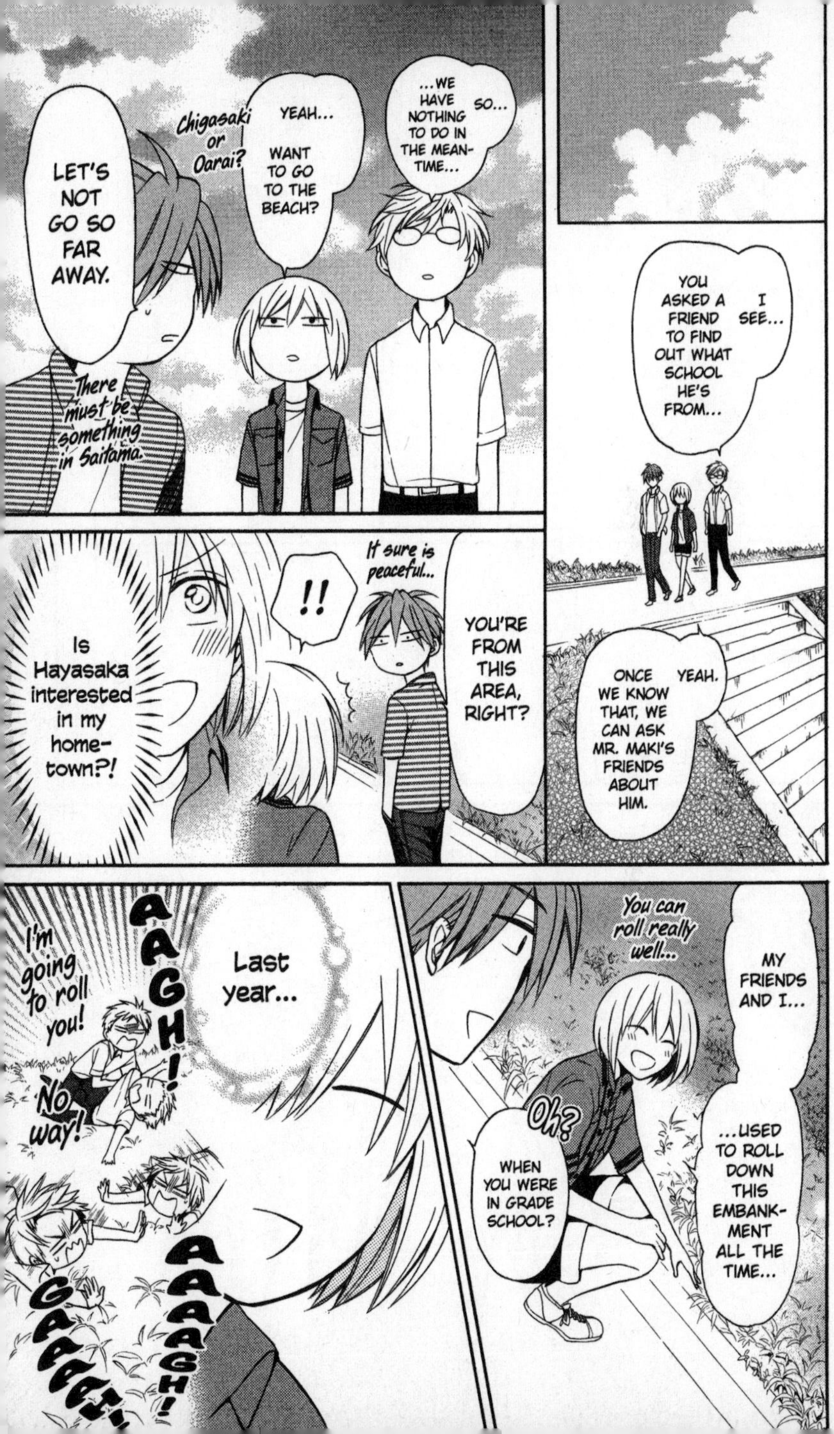
I SEE...
YOU ASKED A FRIEND TO FIND OUT WHAT SCHOOL HE'S FROM...
YEAH.
ONCE WE KNOW THAT, WE CAN ASK MR. MAKI'S FRIENDS ABOUT HIM.
SO...
...WE HAVE NOTHING TO DO IN THE MEAN-TIME...
YEAH...
WANT TO GO TO THE BEACH?
Chigasaki or Oarai?
LET'S NOT GO SO FAR AWAY.
There must be something in Saitama.
It sure is peaceful...
YOU'RE FROM THIS AREA, RIGHT?
!!
Is Hayasaka interested in my home-town?!
MY FRIENDS AND I...
You can roll really well...
...USED TO ROLL DOWN THIS EMBANK-MENT ALL THE TIME...
Oh?
WHEN YOU WERE IN GRADE SCHOOL?
Last year...
AAGH!
I'm going to roll you!
No way!
AAAAGH!
GAAAAH!!

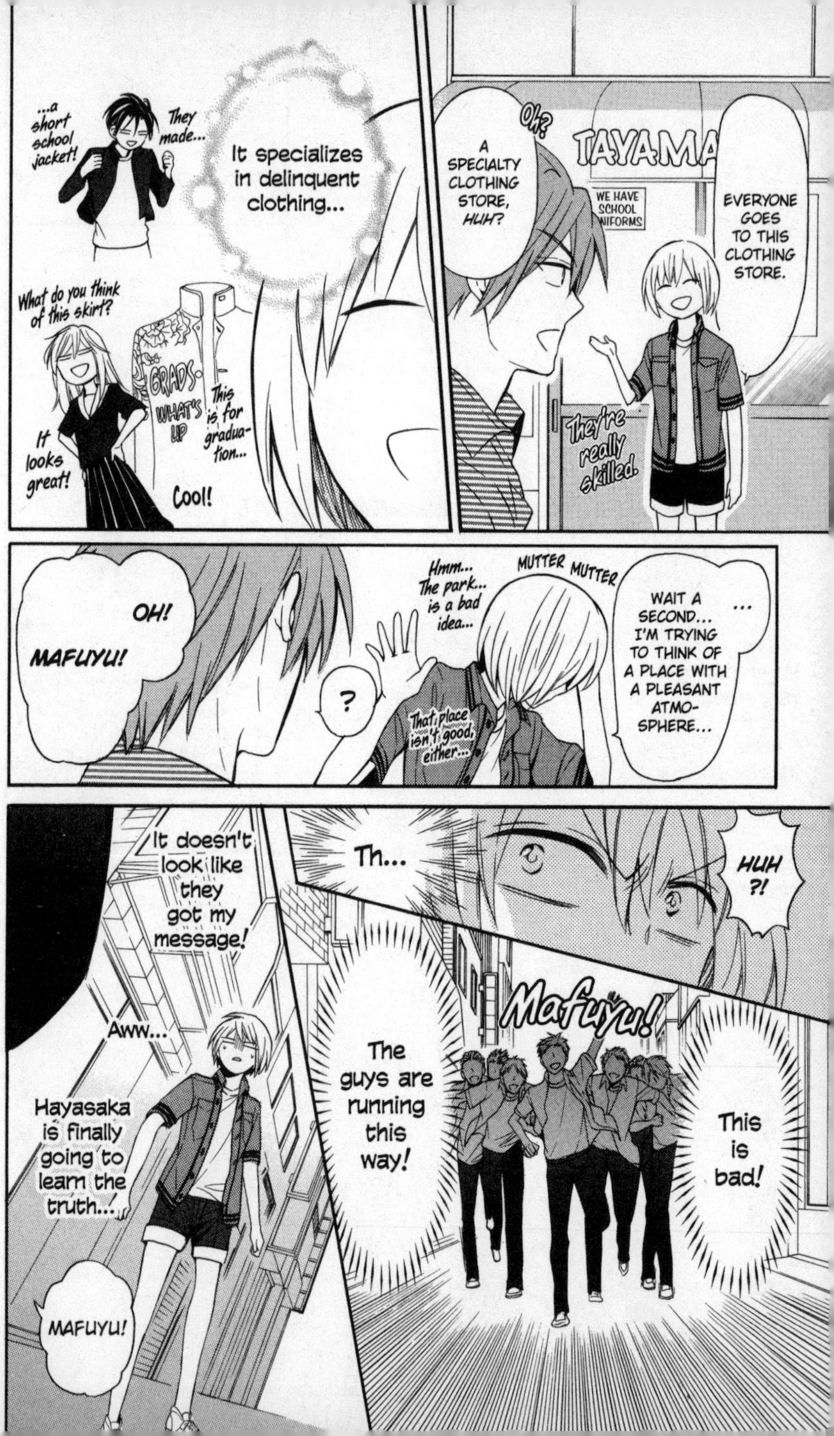
EVERYONE GOES TO THIS CLOTHING STORE.
TAYAMA
WE HAVE SCHOOL UNIFORMS
Oh?
A SPECIALTY CLOTHING STORE, HUH?
They're really skilled.
It specializes in delinquent clothing...
They made...
...a short school jacket!
What do you think of this skirt?
GRADS WHAT'S UP
This is for graduation...
It looks great!
Cool!
WAIT A SECOND... I'M TRYING TO THINK OF A PLACE WITH A PLEASANT ATMOSPHERE...
...
MUTTER MUTTER
Hmm... The park... is a bad idea...
That place isn't good, either...
?
OH! MAFUYU!
HUH ?!
Th...
Mafuyu!
This is bad!
The guys are running this way!
It doesn't look like they got my message!
Aww...
Hayasaka is finally going to learn the truth...
MAFUYU!

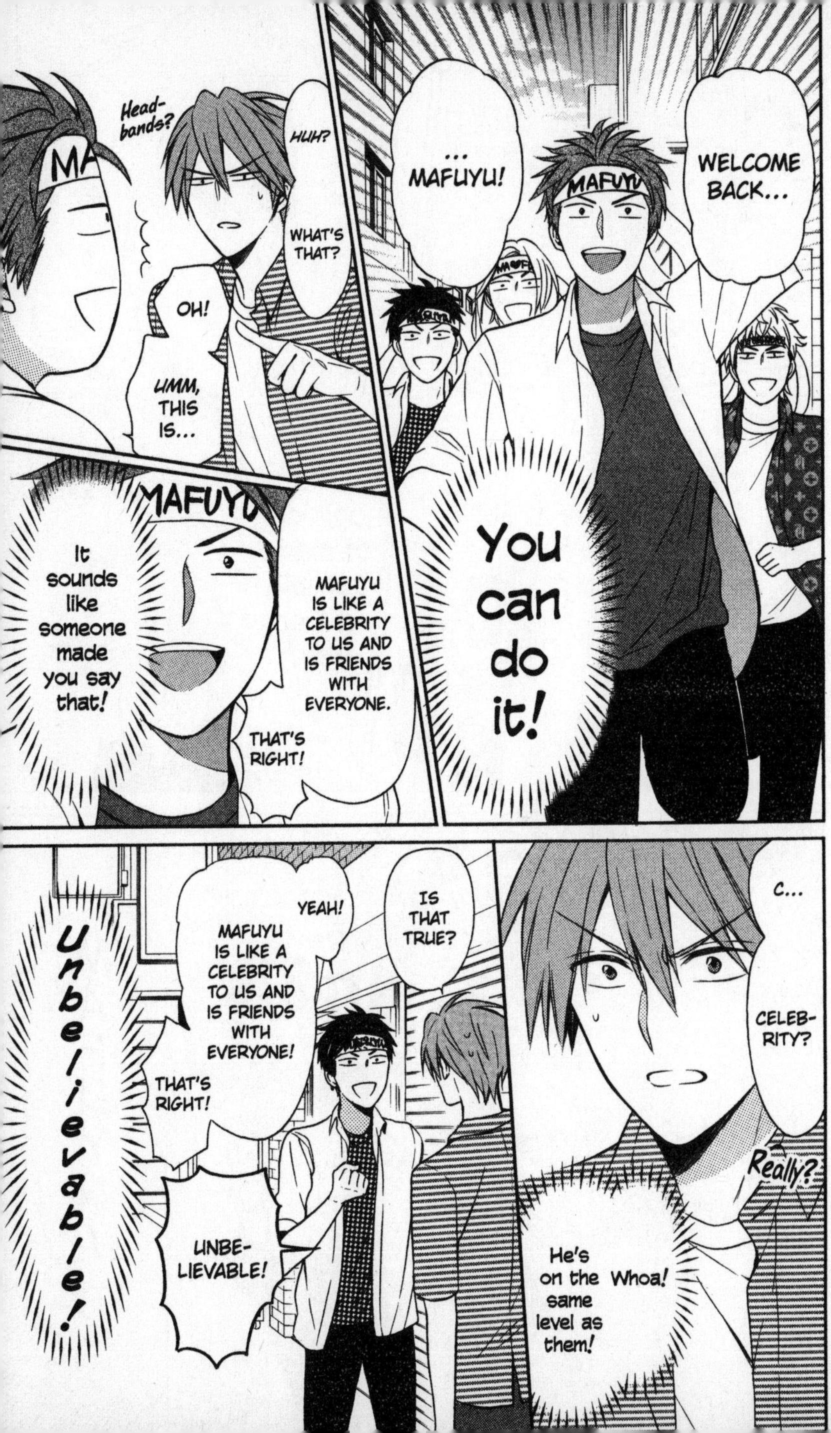
WELCOME BACK...
... MAFUYU!
MAFUYU
You can do it!
HUH?
WHAT'S THAT?
Head-bands?
OH!
UMM, THIS IS...
MAFUYU IS LIKE A CELEBRITY TO US AND IS FRIENDS WITH EVERYONE.
THAT'S RIGHT!
It sounds like someone made you say that!
C...
CELEBRITY?
Really?
Whoa!
He's on the same level as them!
IS THAT TRUE?
YEAH!
MAFUYU IS LIKE A CELEBRITY TO US AND IS FRIENDS WITH EVERYONE!
THAT'S RIGHT!
UNBE-LIEVABLE!
Unbelievable!

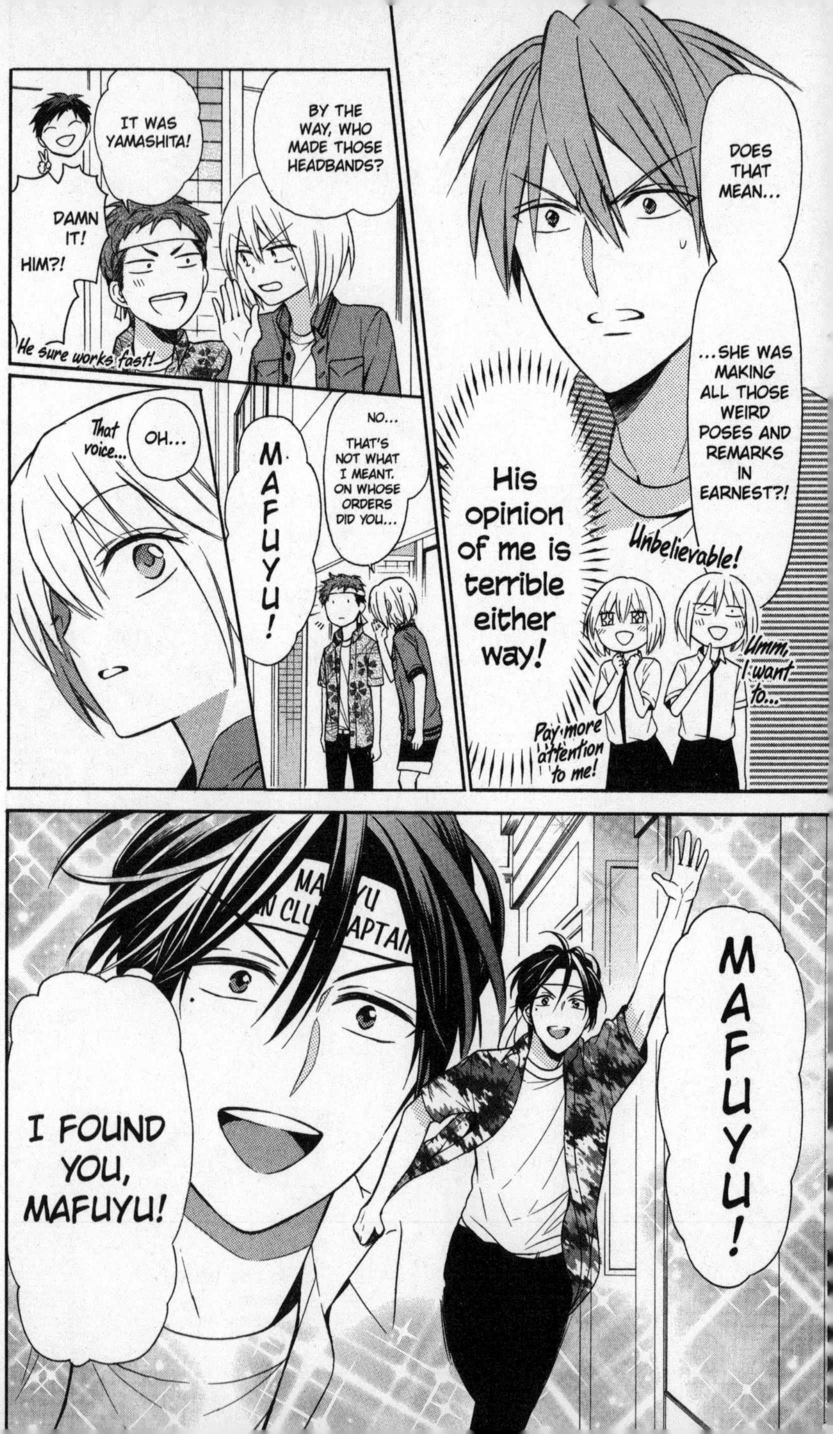
DOES THAT MEAN...
...SHE WAS MAKING ALL THOSE WEIRD POSES AND REMARKS IN EARNEST?!
His opinion of me is terrible either way!
Unbelievable!
Umm, I want to...
Pay more attention to me!
BY THE WAY, WHO MADE THOSE HEADBANDS?
IT WAS YAMASHITA!
DAMN IT!
HIM?!
He sure works fast!
NO... THAT'S NOT WHAT I MEANT. ON WHOSE ORDERS DID YOU...
MAFUYU!
OH...
That voice...
MAFUYU!
I FOUND YOU, MAFUYU!

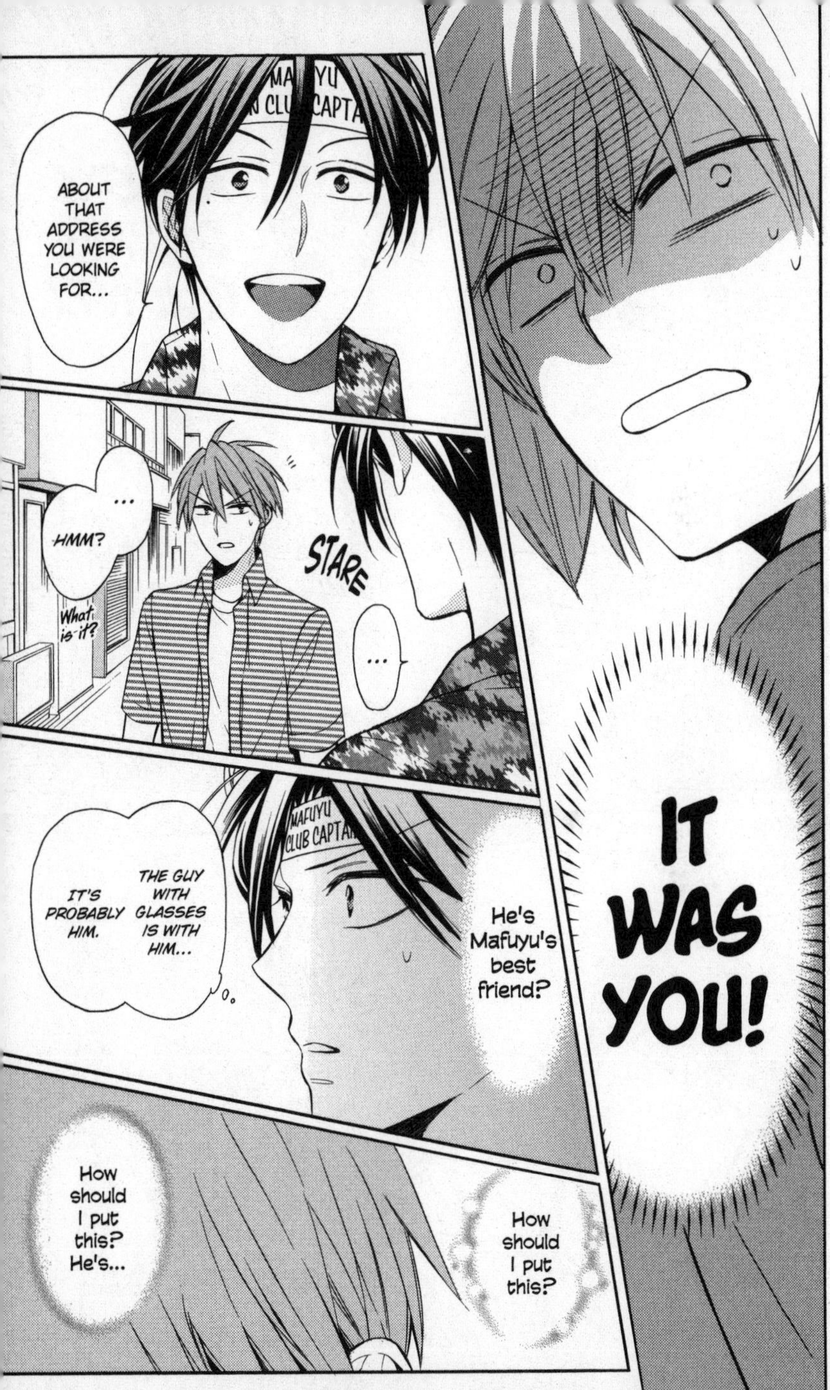
IT WAS YOU!
ABOUT THAT ADDRESS YOU WERE LOOKING FOR...
STARE
...
... HMM?
What is it?
He's Mafuyu's best friend?
THE GUY WITH GLASSES IS WITH HIM...
IT'S PROBABLY HIM.
How should I put this?
How should I put this? He's...

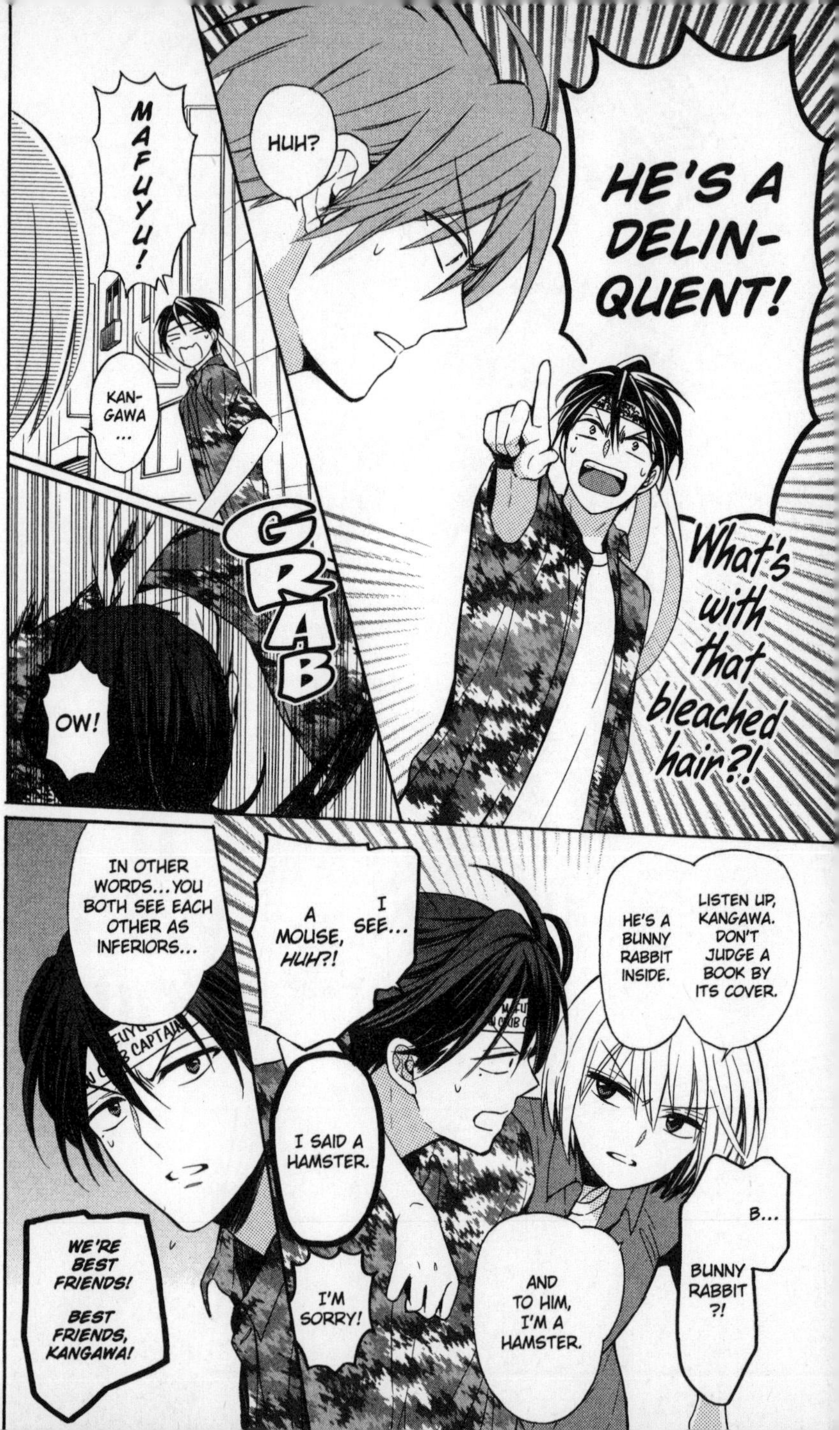
HE'S A DELIN-QUENT!
What's with that bleached hair?!
HUH?
MAFUYU!
KAN-GAWA ...
GRAB
OW!
LISTEN UP, KANGAWA. DON'T JUDGE A BOOK BY ITS COVER.
HE'S A BUNNY RABBIT INSIDE.
B...
BUNNY RABBIT?!
I SEE...
A MOUSE, HUH?!
AND TO HIM, I'M A HAMSTER.
I SAID A HAMSTER.
IN OTHER WORDS...YOU BOTH SEE EACH OTHER AS INFERIORS...
I'M SORRY!
WE'RE BEST FRIENDS!
BEST FRIENDS, KANGAWA!

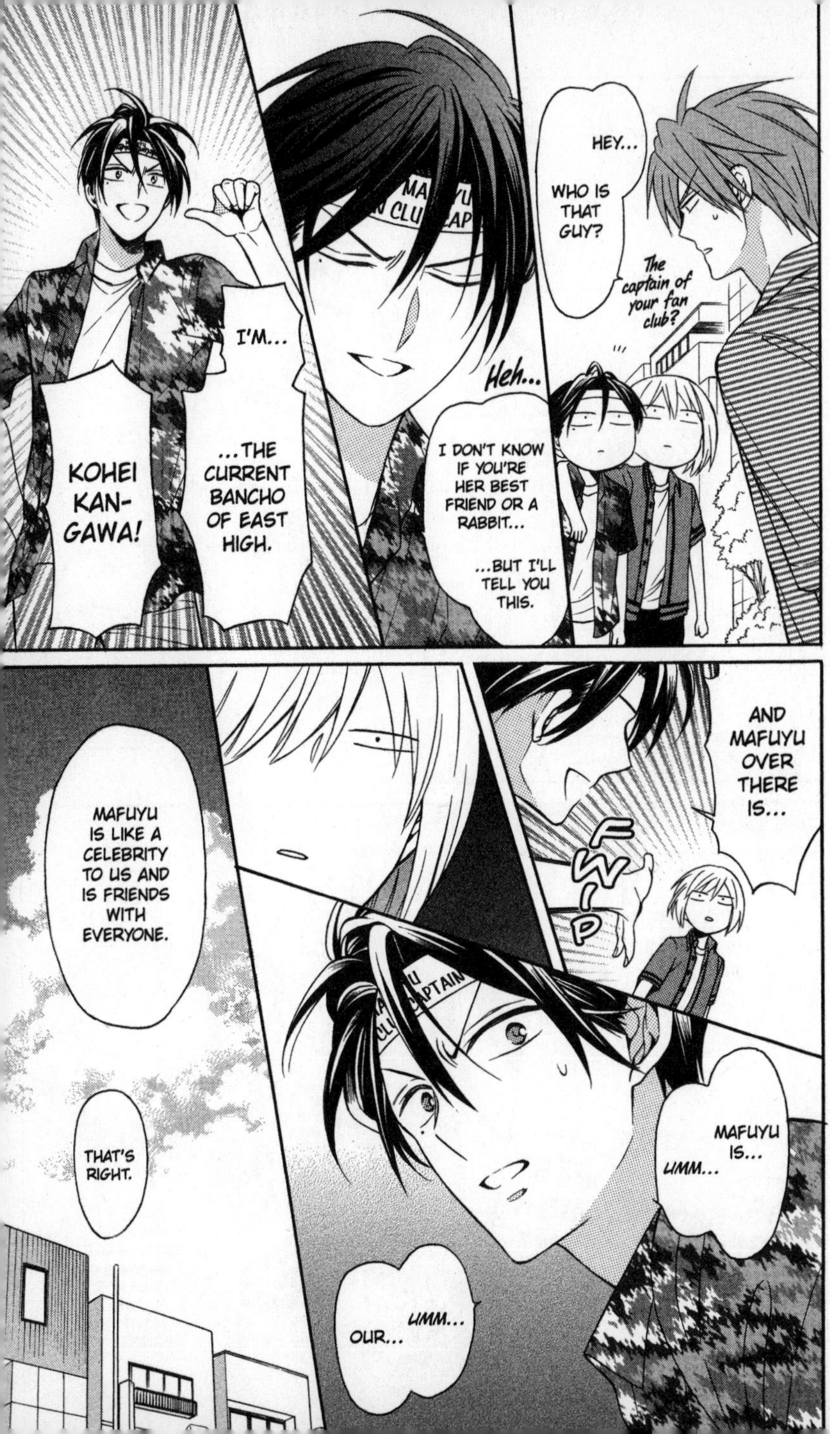
HEY...
WHO IS THAT GUY?
The captain of your fan club?
Heh...
I DON'T KNOW IF YOU'RE HER BEST FRIEND OR A RABBIT...
...BUT I'LL TELL YOU THIS.
I'M...
...THE CURRENT BANCHO OF EAST HIGH.
KOHEI KAN-GAWA!
AND MAFUYU OVER THERE IS...
FWIP
MAFUYU IS...
UMM...
UMM...
OUR...
MAFUYU IS LIKE A CELEBRITY TO US AND IS FRIENDS WITH EVERYONE.
THAT'S RIGHT.

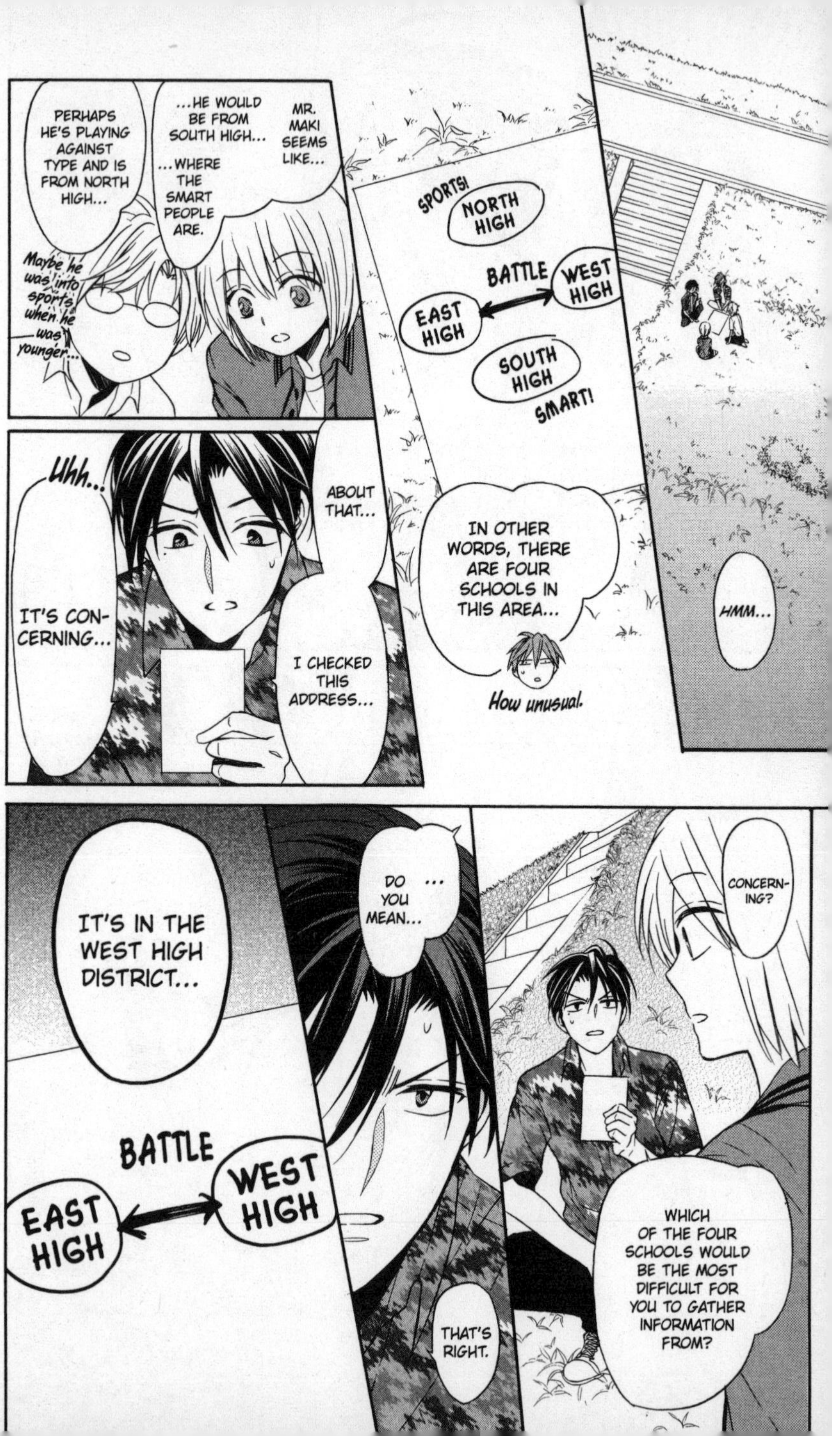
HMM...
SPORTS!
NORTH HIGH
BATTLE
WEST HIGH
EAST HIGH
SOUTH HIGH
SMART!
IN OTHER WORDS, THERE ARE FOUR SCHOOLS IN THIS AREA...
How unusual.
MR. MAKI SEEMS LIKE...
...HE WOULD BE FROM SOUTH HIGH...
...WHERE THE SMART PEOPLE ARE.
PERHAPS HE'S PLAYING AGAINST TYPE AND IS FROM NORTH HIGH...
Maybe he was into sports when he was younger...
ABOUT THAT...
I CHECKED THIS ADDRESS...
Uhh...
IT'S CON-CERNING...
CONCERN-ING?
WHICH OF THE FOUR SCHOOLS WOULD BE THE MOST DIFFICULT FOR YOU TO GATHER INFORMATION FROM?
...DO YOU MEAN...
THAT'S RIGHT.
IT'S IN THE WEST HIGH DISTRICT...
BATTLE
WEST HIGH
EAST HIGH

MAFUYU IS A CELEBRITY ♡

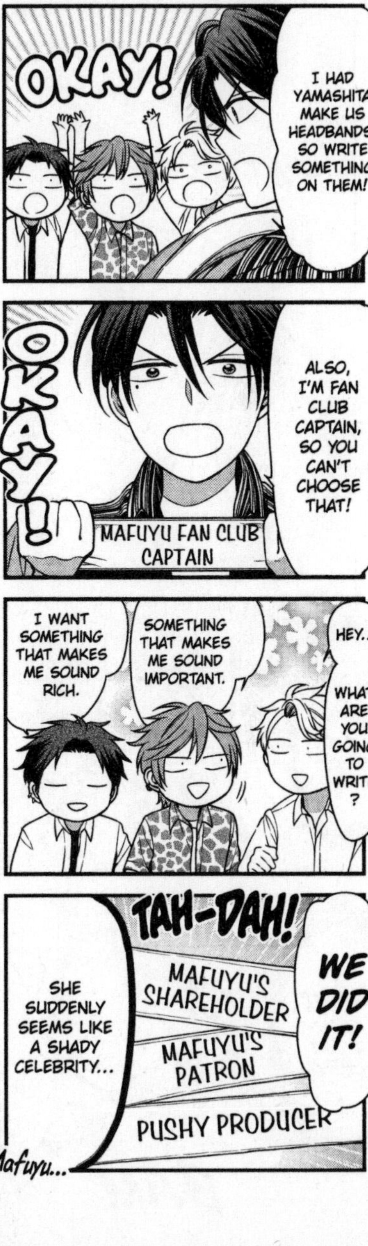
I HAD YAMASHITA MAKE US HEADBANDS, SO WRITE SOMETHING ON THEM!
OKAY!
ALSO, I'M FAN CLUB CAPTAIN, SO YOU CAN'T CHOOSE THAT!
OKAY!
MAFUYU FAN CLUB CAPTAIN
HEY... WHAT ARE YOU GOING TO WRITE?
SOMETHING THAT MAKES ME SOUND IMPORTANT.
I WANT SOMETHING THAT MAKES ME SOUND RICH.
TAH-DAH!
WE DID IT!
MAFUYU'S SHAREHOLDER
MAFUYU'S PATRON
PUSHY PRODUCER
SHE SUDDENLY SEEMS LIKE A SHADY CELEBRITY...
Mafuyu...

QUITE A BIT OMITTED

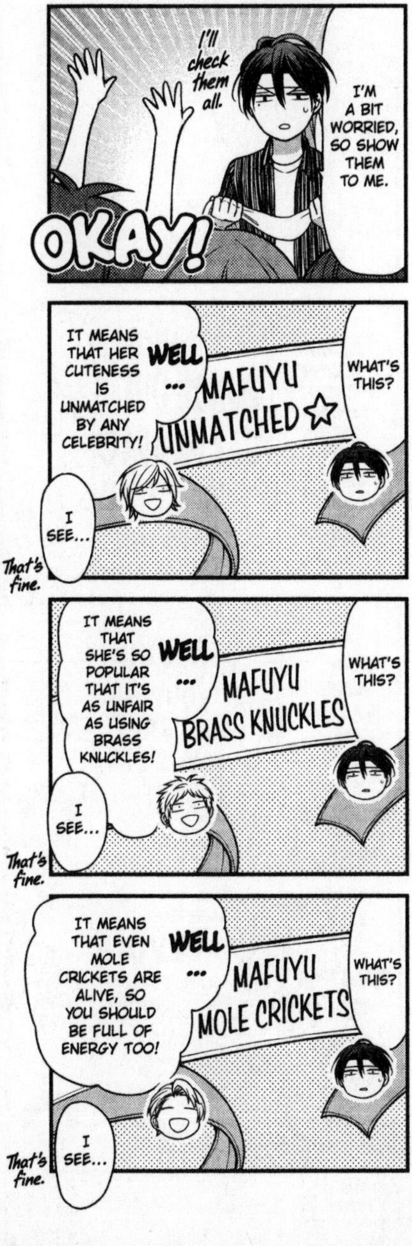
I'M A BIT WORRIED, SO SHOW THEM TO ME.
I'll check them all.
OKAY!
WHAT'S THIS?
MAFUYU UNMATCHED ☆
WELL ...
IT MEANS THAT HER CUTENESS IS UNMATCHED BY ANY CELEBRITY!
I SEE...
That's fine.
WHAT'S THIS?
MAFUYU BRASS KNUCKLES
WELL ...
IT MEANS THAT SHE'S SO POPULAR THAT IT'S AS UNFAIR AS USING BRASS KNUCKLES!
I SEE...
That's fine.
WHAT'S THIS?
MAFUYU MOLE CRICKETS
WELL ...
IT MEANS THAT EVEN MOLE CRICKETS ARE ALIVE, SO YOU SHOULD BE FULL OF ENERGY TOO!
I SEE...
That's fine.

LOOK OVER HERE, MAFUYU!

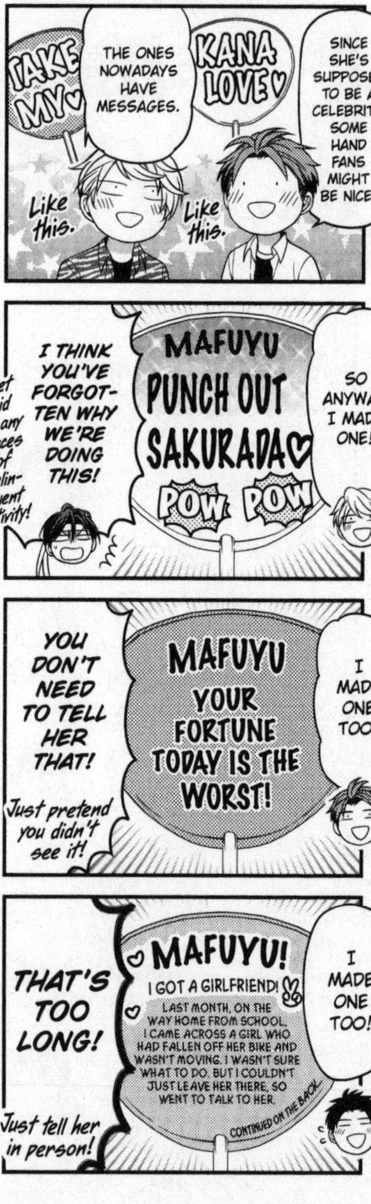
SINCE SHE'S SUPPOSED TO BE A CELEBRITY, SOME HAND FANS MIGHT BE NICE.
KANA LOVE♥
THE ONES NOWADAYS HAVE MESSAGES.
TAKE MY♥
Like this.
Like this.
SO ANYWAY, I MADE ONE!
MAFUYU PUNCH OUT SAKURADA♥
POW POW
I THINK YOU'VE FORGOTTEN WHY WE'RE DOING THIS!
Get rid of any traces of delinquent activity!
I MADE ONE TOO!
MAFUYU YOUR FORTUNE TODAY IS THE WORST!
YOU DON'T NEED TO TELL HER THAT!
Just pretend you didn't see it!
I MADE ONE TOO!
MAFUYU!
I GOT A GIRLFRIEND!
LAST MONTH, ON THE WAY HOME FROM SCHOOL, I CAME ACROSS A GIRL WHO HAD FALLEN OFF HER BIKE AND WASN'T MOVING. I WASN'T SURE WHAT TO DO, BUT I COULDN'T JUST LEAVE HER THERE, SO WENT TO TALK TO HER.
CONTINUED ON THE BACK.
THAT'S TOO LONG!
Just tell her in person!

MY RIVALS

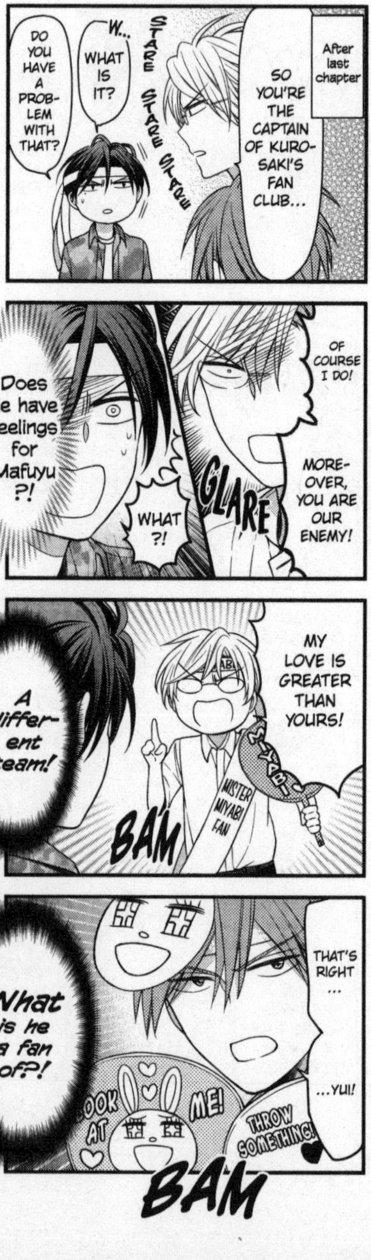
After last chapter
SO YOU'RE THE CAPTAIN OF KUROSAKI'S FAN CLUB...
STARE STARE STARE
W... WHAT IS IT?
DO YOU HAVE A PROBLEM WITH THAT?
OF COURSE I DO!
MOREOVER, YOU ARE OUR ENEMY!
GLARE
WHAT?!
Does he have feelings for Mafuyu?!
MY LOVE IS GREATER THAN YOURS!
MIYABI
MISTER MIYABI FAN
BAM
A different team!
THAT'S RIGHT...
...YUI!
THROW SOMETHING!
LOOK AT ME!
What is he a fan of?!
BAM

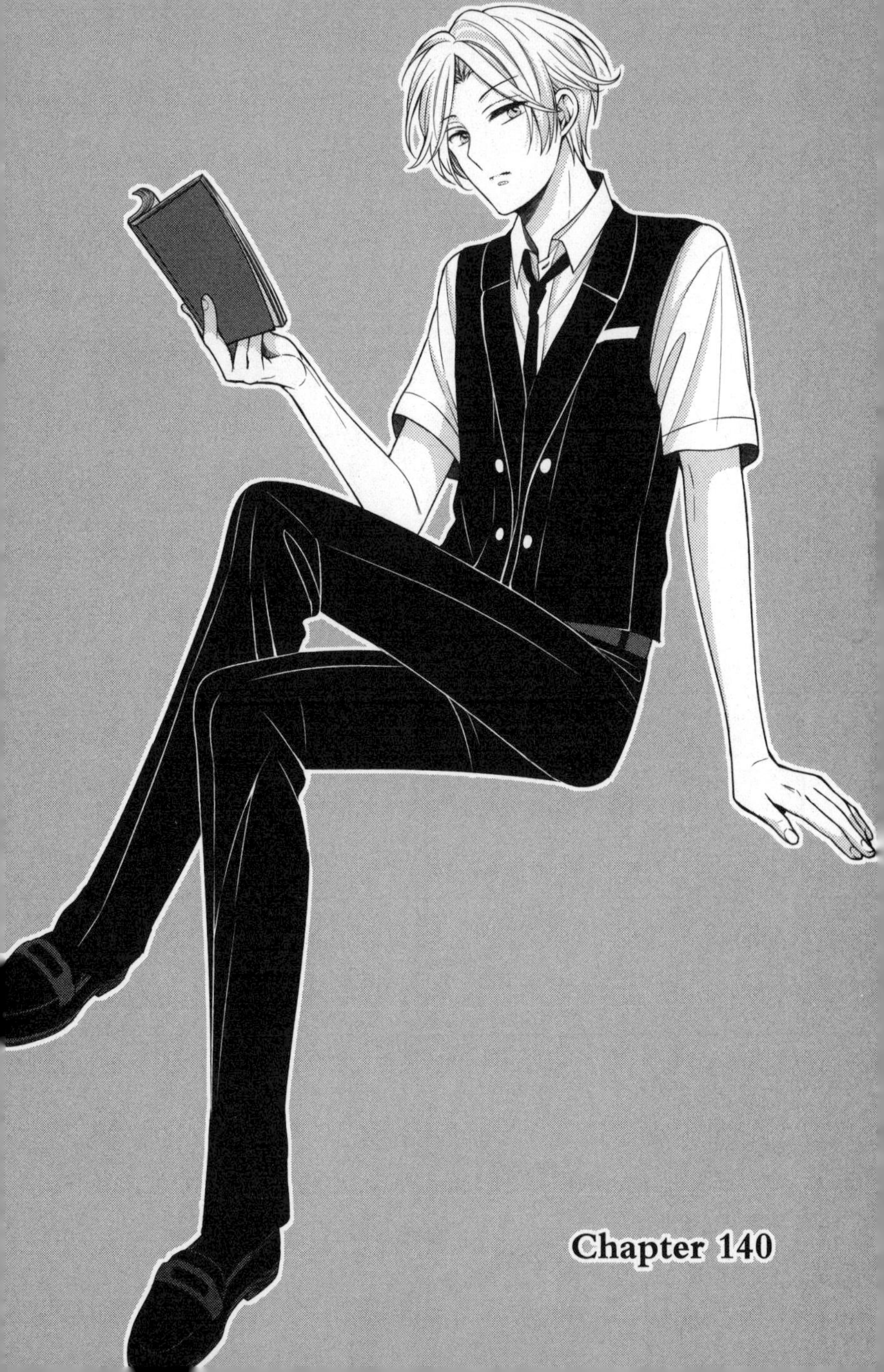

Chapter 140

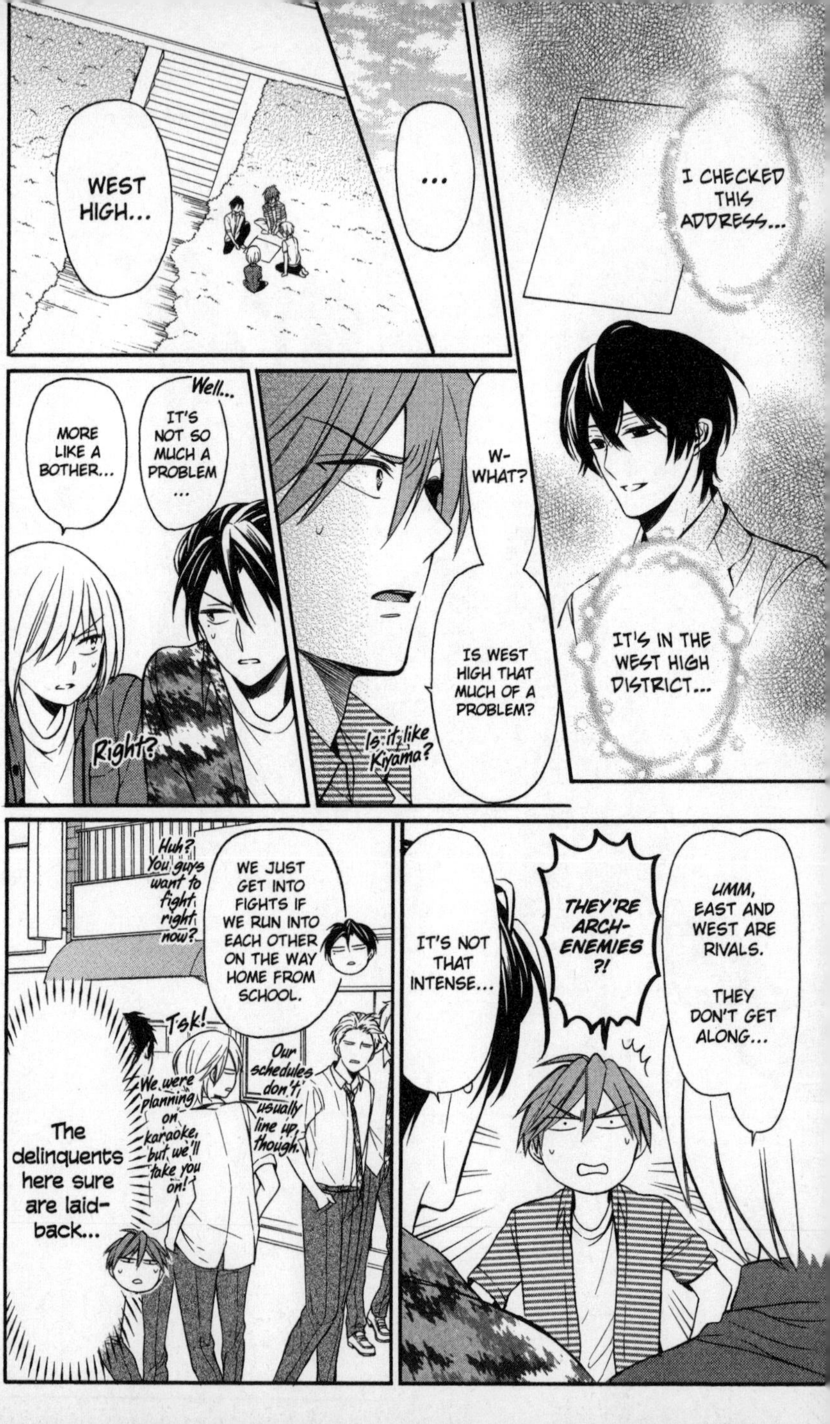
I CHECKED THIS ADDRESS...
IT'S IN THE WEST HIGH DISTRICT...
...
WEST HIGH...
W-WHAT?
IS WEST HIGH THAT MUCH OF A PROBLEM?
Is it like Kiyama?
Well...
IT'S NOT SO MUCH A PROBLEM...
MORE LIKE A BOTHER...
Right?
UMM, EAST AND WEST ARE RIVALS.
THEY DON'T GET ALONG...
THEY'RE ARCH-ENEMIES?!
IT'S NOT THAT INTENSE...
WE JUST GET INTO FIGHTS IF WE RUN INTO EACH OTHER ON THE WAY HOME FROM SCHOOL.
Huh? You guys want to fight right now?
Tsk!
Our schedules don't usually line up, though.
We were planning on karaoke, but we'll take you on!
The delinquents here sure are laid-back...

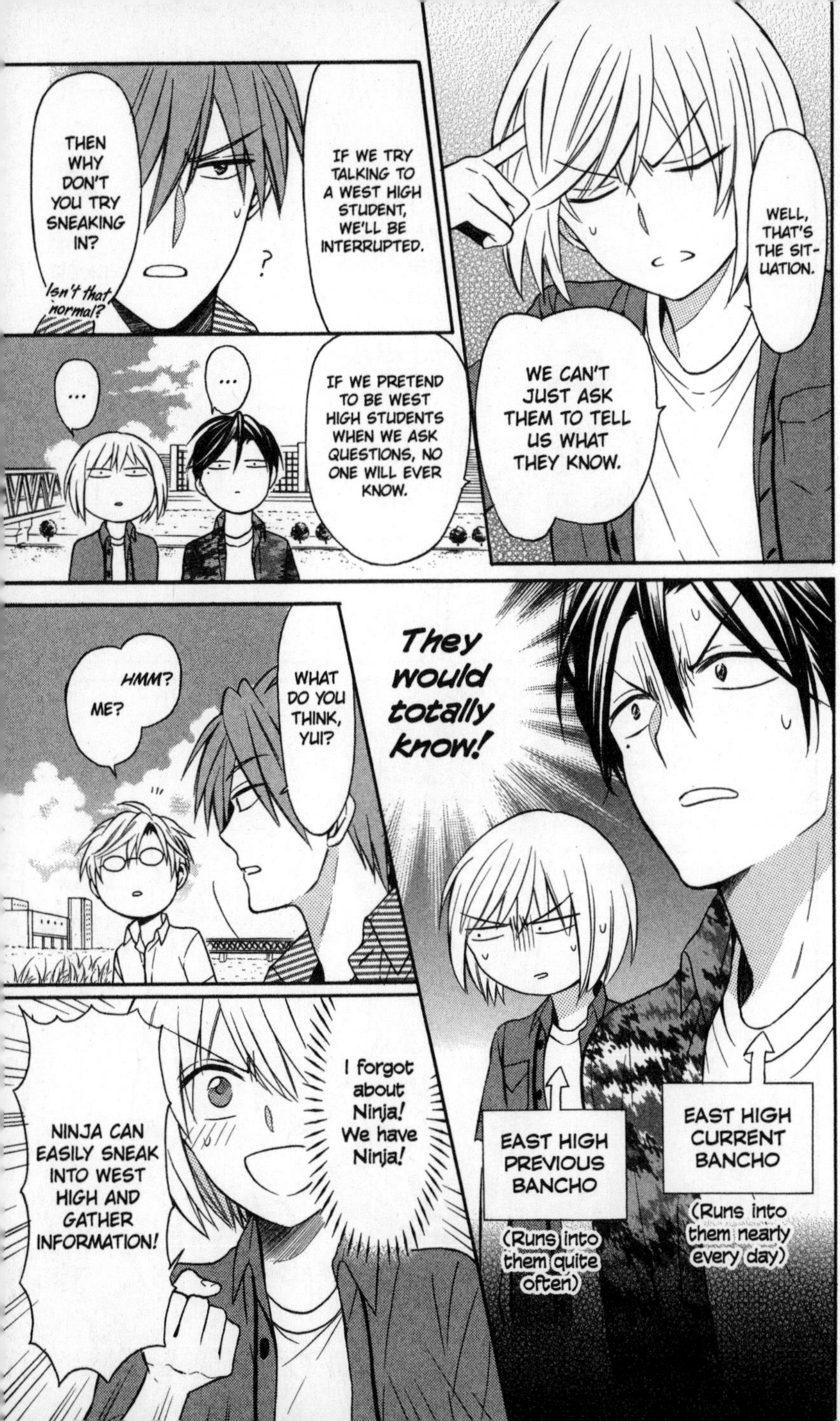
WELL, THAT'S THE SIT-UATION.
WE CAN'T JUST ASK THEM TO TELL US WHAT THEY KNOW.
IF WE TRY TALKING TO A WEST HIGH STUDENT, WE'LL BE INTERRUPTED.
THEN WHY DON'T YOU TRY SNEAKING IN?
?
Isn't that normal?
IF WE PRETEND TO BE WEST HIGH STUDENTS WHEN WE ASK QUESTIONS, NO ONE WILL EVER KNOW.
...
...
They would totally know!
EAST HIGH CURRENT BANCHO
(Runs into them nearly every day)
EAST HIGH PREVIOUS BANCHO
(Runs into them quite often)
WHAT DO YOU THINK, YUI?
HMM? ME?
I forgot about Ninja! We have Ninja!
NINJA CAN EASILY SNEAK INTO WEST HIGH AND GATHER INFORMATION!

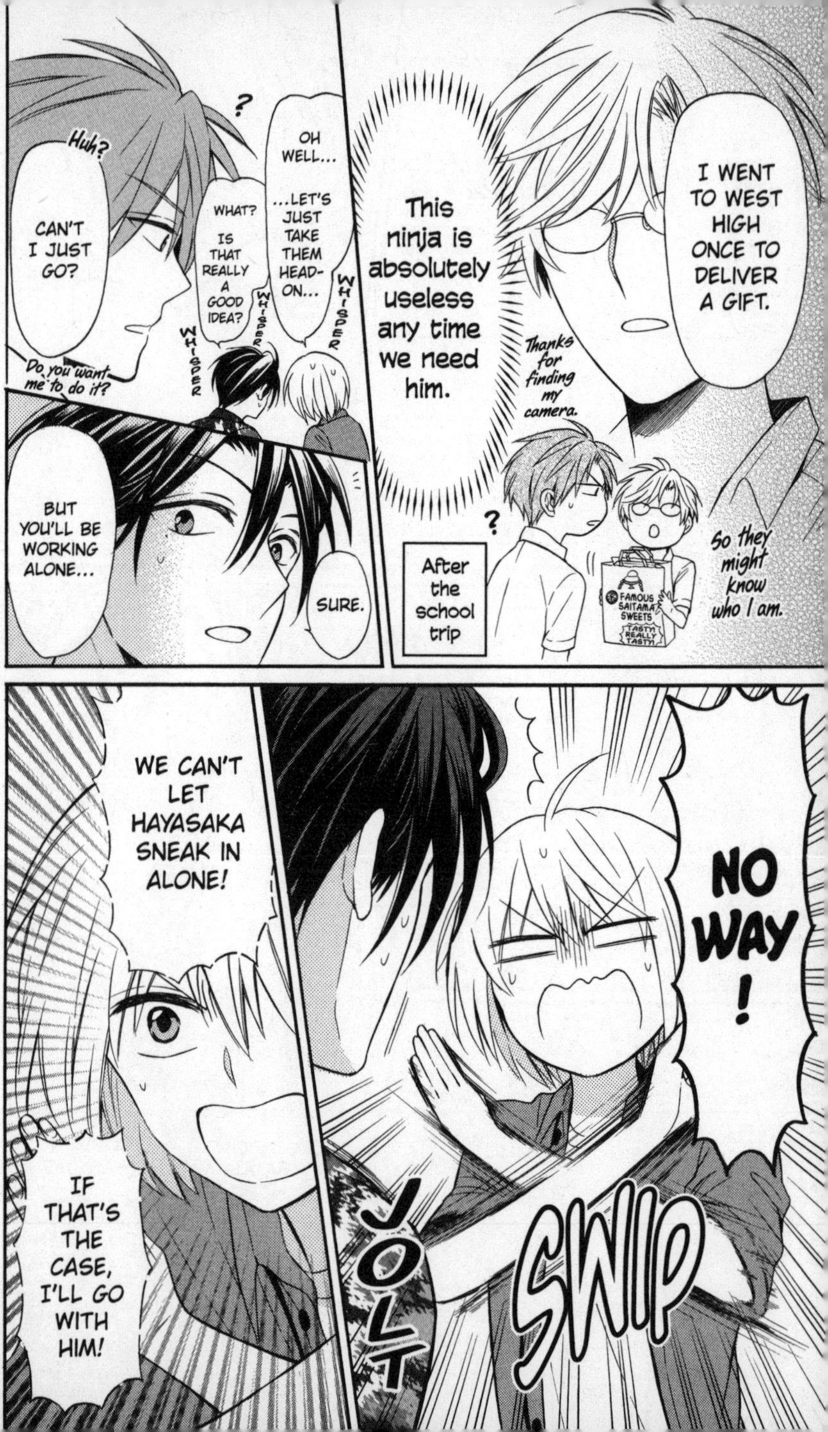
I WENT TO WEST HIGH ONCE TO DELIVER A GIFT.
This ninja is absolutely useless any time we need him.
So they might know who I am.
Thanks for finding my camera.
FAMOUS SAITAMA SWEETS
TASTY! REALLY TASTY!
?
After the school trip
?
OH WELL...
...LET'S JUST TAKE THEM HEAD-ON...
WHISPER
WHAT? IS THAT REALLY A GOOD IDEA?
WHISPER
WHISPER
Huh?
CAN'T I JUST GO?
Do you want me to do it?
SURE.
BUT YOU'LL BE WORKING ALONE...
NO WAY!
WE CAN'T LET HAYASAKA SNEAK IN ALONE!
SWIP
JOLT
IF THAT'S THE CASE, I'LL GO WITH HIM!

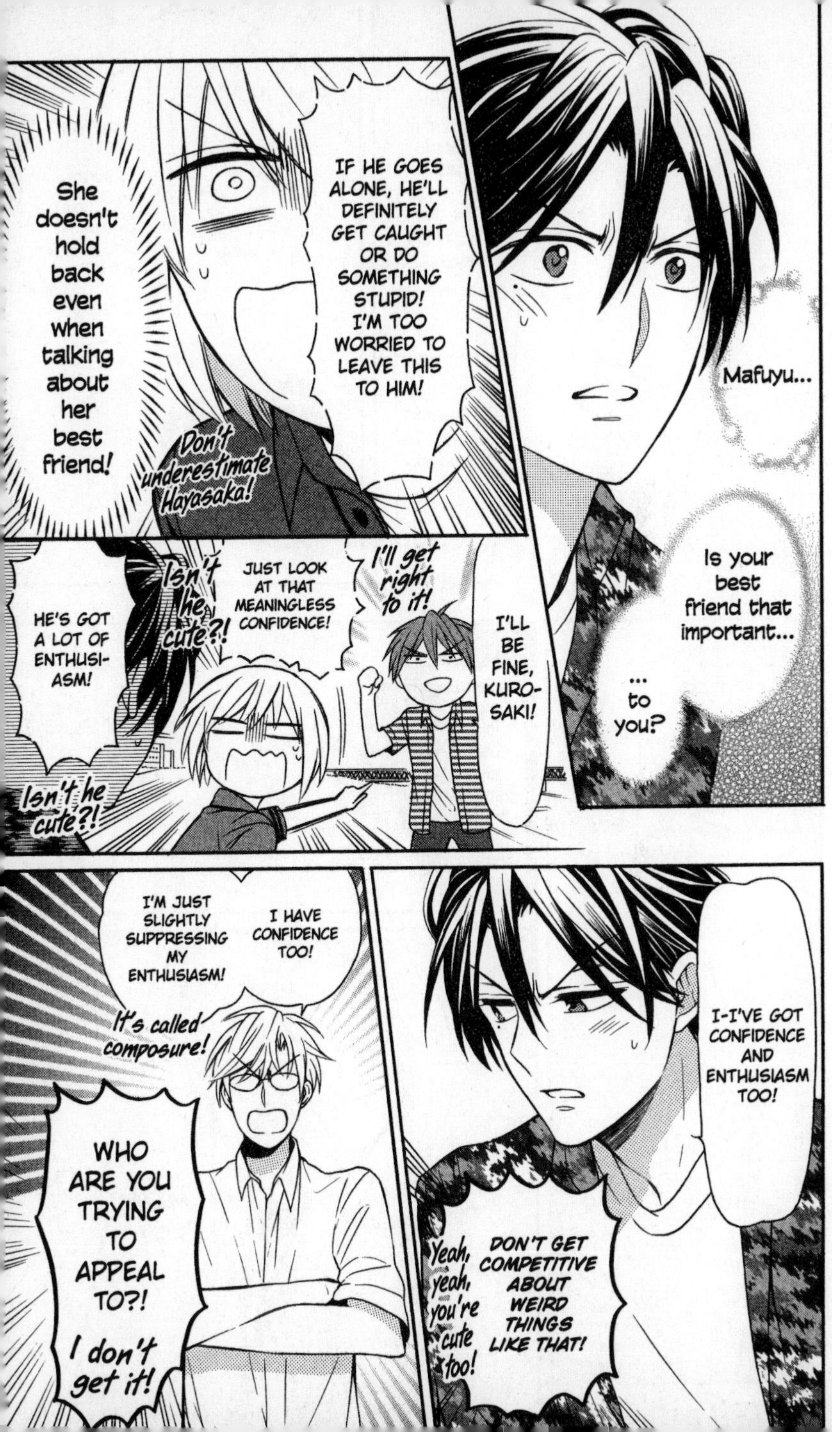
Mafuyu...
Is your best friend that important...
... to you?
IF HE GOES ALONE, HE'LL DEFINITELY GET CAUGHT OR DO SOMETHING STUPID! I'M TOO WORRIED TO LEAVE THIS TO HIM!
She doesn't hold back even when talking about her best friend!
Don't underestimate Hayasaka!
I'LL BE FINE, KURO-SAKI!
I'll get right to it!
JUST LOOK AT THAT MEANINGLESS CONFIDENCE!
Isn't he cute?!
HE'S GOT A LOT OF ENTHUSI-ASM!
Isn't he cute?!
I-I'VE GOT CONFIDENCE AND ENTHUSIASM TOO!
DON'T GET COMPETITIVE ABOUT WEIRD THINGS LIKE THAT!
Yeah, yeah, you're cute too!
I HAVE CONFIDENCE TOO!
I'M JUST SLIGHTLY SUPPRESSING MY ENTHUSIASM!
It's called composure!
WHO ARE YOU TRYING TO APPEAL TO?!
I don't get it!

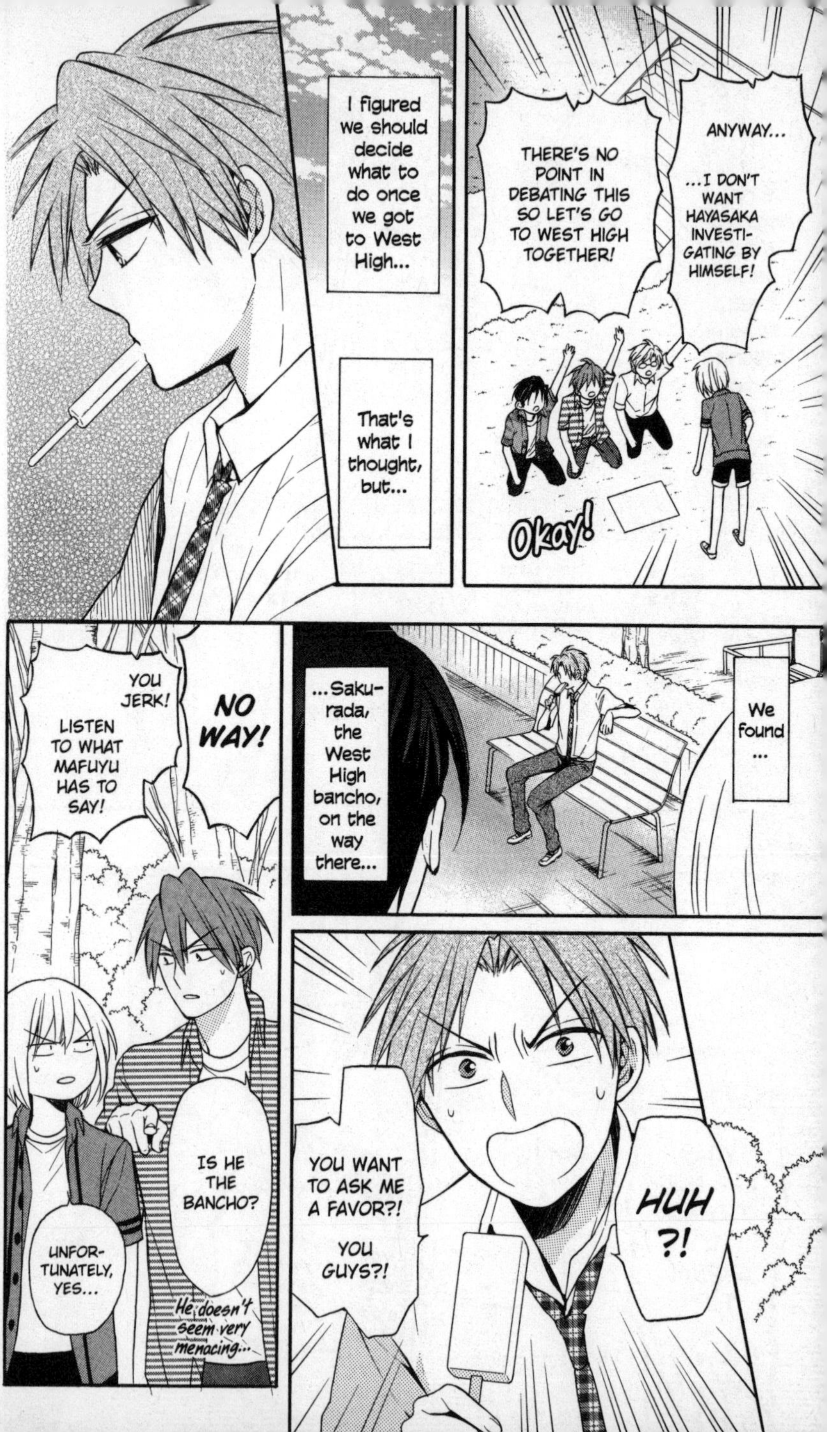
ANYWAY...
...I DON'T WANT HAYASAKA INVESTIGATING BY HIMSELF!
THERE'S NO POINT IN DEBATING THIS SO LET'S GO TO WEST HIGH TOGETHER!
Okay!
I figured we should decide what to do once we got to West High...
That's what I thought, but...
We found...
...Sakurada, the West High bancho, on the way there...
HUH ?!
YOU WANT TO ASK ME A FAVOR?!
YOU GUYS?!
YOU JERK! LISTEN TO WHAT MAFUYU HAS TO SAY!
NO WAY!
IS HE THE BANCHO?
UNFORTUNATELY, YES...
He doesn't seem very menacing...

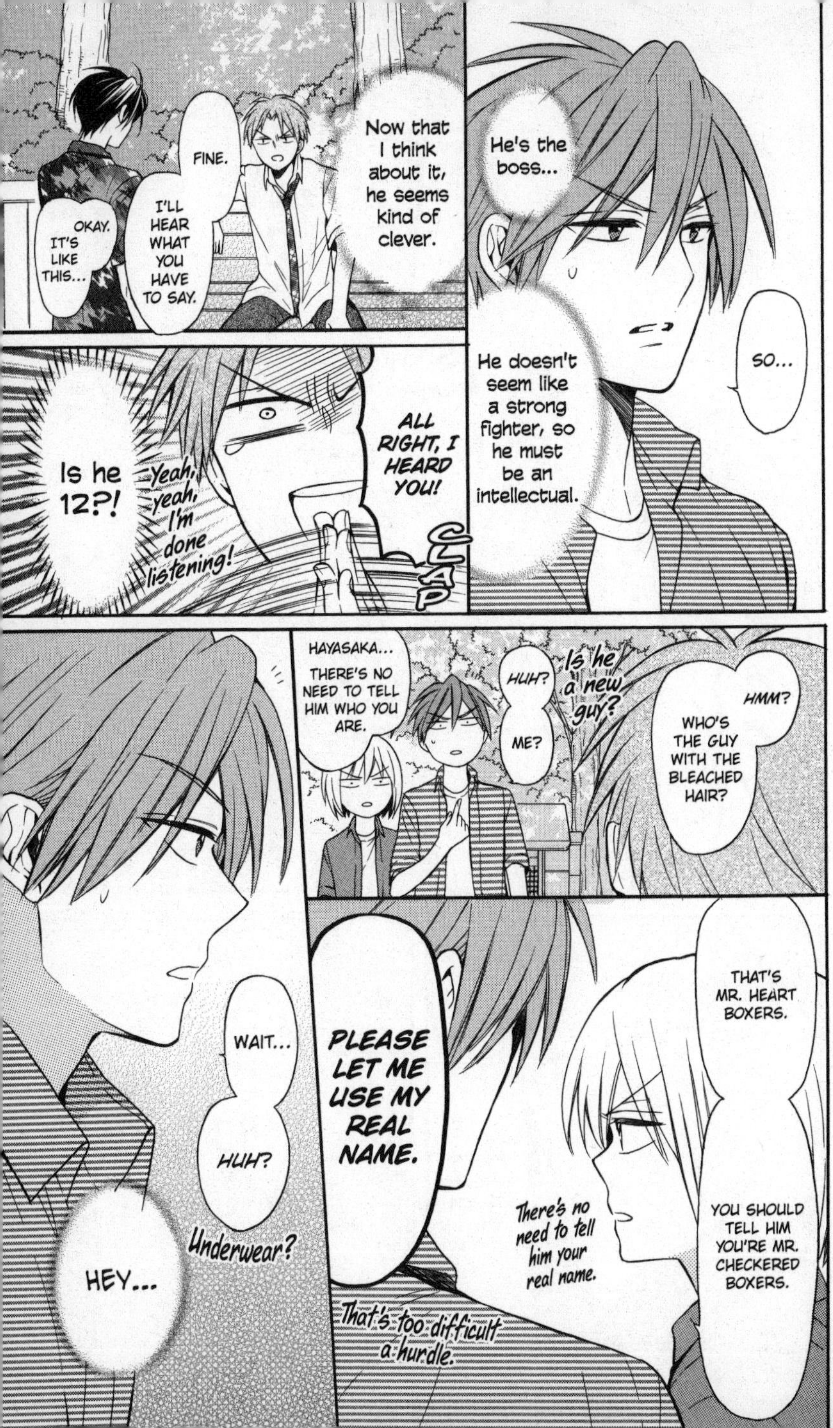
He's the boss...
He doesn't seem like a strong fighter, so he must be an intellectual.
SO...
Now that I think about it, he seems kind of clever.
FINE.
I'LL HEAR WHAT YOU HAVE TO SAY.
OKAY. IT'S LIKE THIS...
ALL RIGHT, I HEARD YOU!
CLAP
Yeah, yeah, I'm done listening!
Is he 12?!
HMM?
WHO'S THE GUY WITH THE BLEACHED HAIR?
Is he a new guy?
HUH?
ME?
HAYASAKA...
THERE'S NO NEED TO TELL HIM WHO YOU ARE.
THAT'S MR. HEART BOXERS.
YOU SHOULD TELL HIM YOU'RE MR. CHECKERED BOXERS.
There's no need to tell him your real name.
PLEASE LET ME USE MY REAL NAME.
That's too difficult a hurdle.
WAIT...
HUH?
Underwear?
HEY...

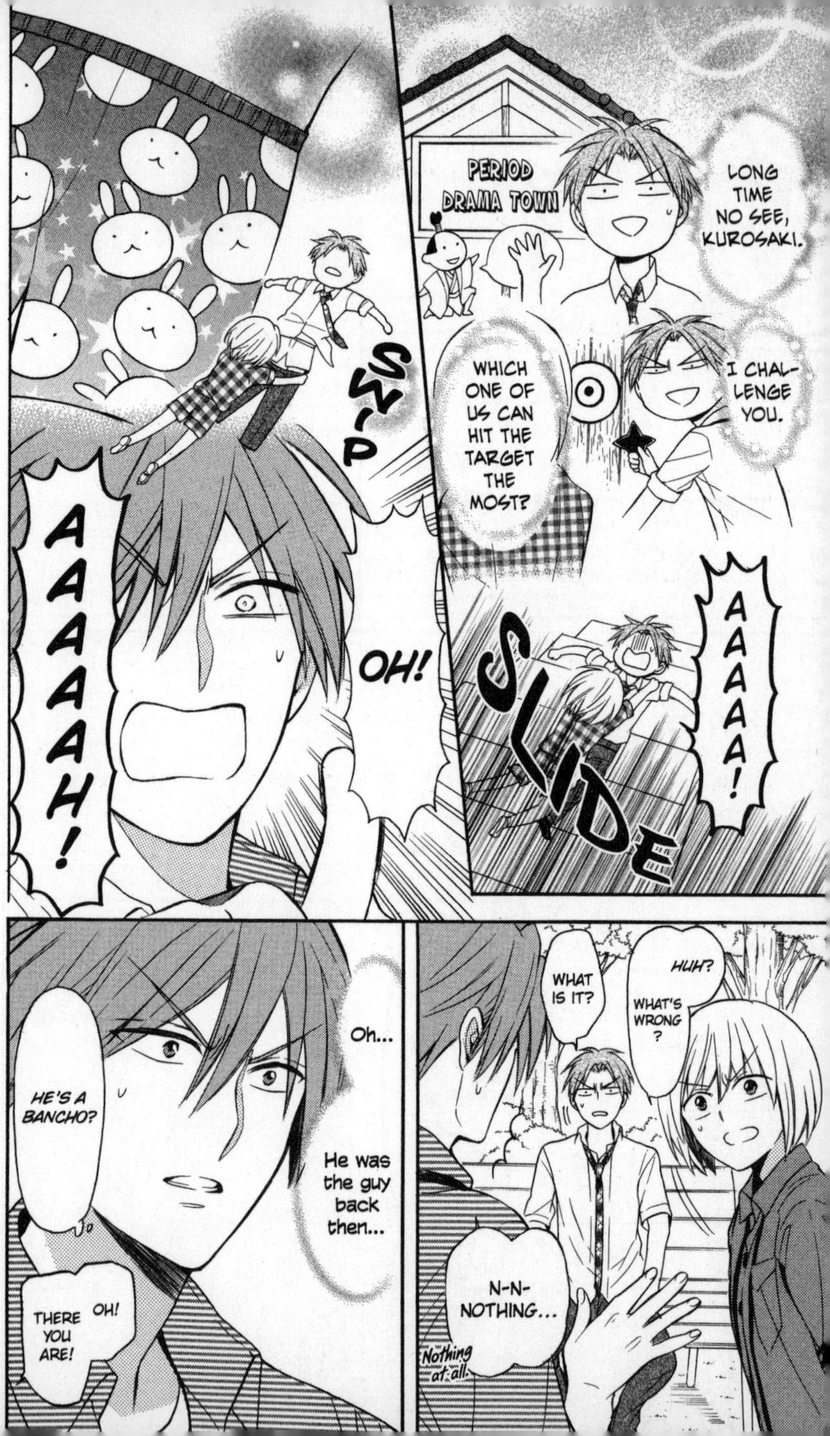
PERIOD DRAMA TOWN
LONG TIME NO SEE, KUROSAKI.
I CHAL-LENGE YOU.
WHICH ONE OF US CAN HIT THE TARGET THE MOST?
AAAAA!
SLIDE
SWIP
OH!
AAAAAH!
HUH?
WHAT'S WRONG?
WHAT IS IT?
N-N-NOTHING...
Nothing at all.
Oh...
HE'S A BANCHO?
He was the guy back then...
OH!
THERE YOU ARE!

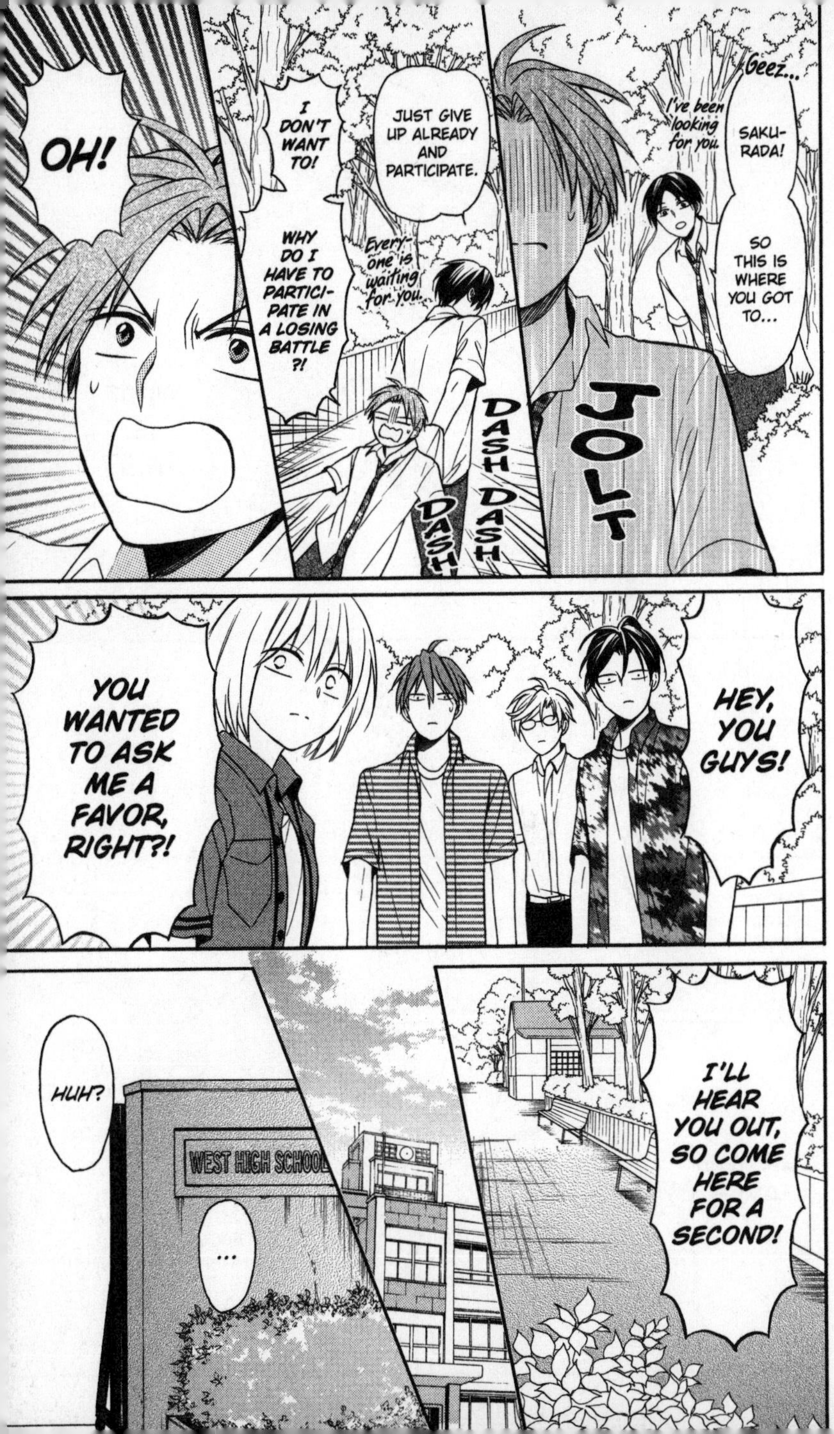
Geez...
I've been looking for you.
SAKURADA!
SO THIS IS WHERE YOU GOT TO...
JOLT
JUST GIVE UP ALREADY AND PARTICIPATE.
Everyone is waiting for you.
I DON'T WANT TO!
WHY DO I HAVE TO PARTICIPATE IN A LOSING BATTLE?!
DASH DASH DASH
OH!
HEY, YOU GUYS!
YOU WANTED TO ASK ME A FAVOR, RIGHT?!
I'LL HEAR YOU OUT, SO COME HERE FOR A SECOND!
WEST HIGH SCHOOL
HUH?
...

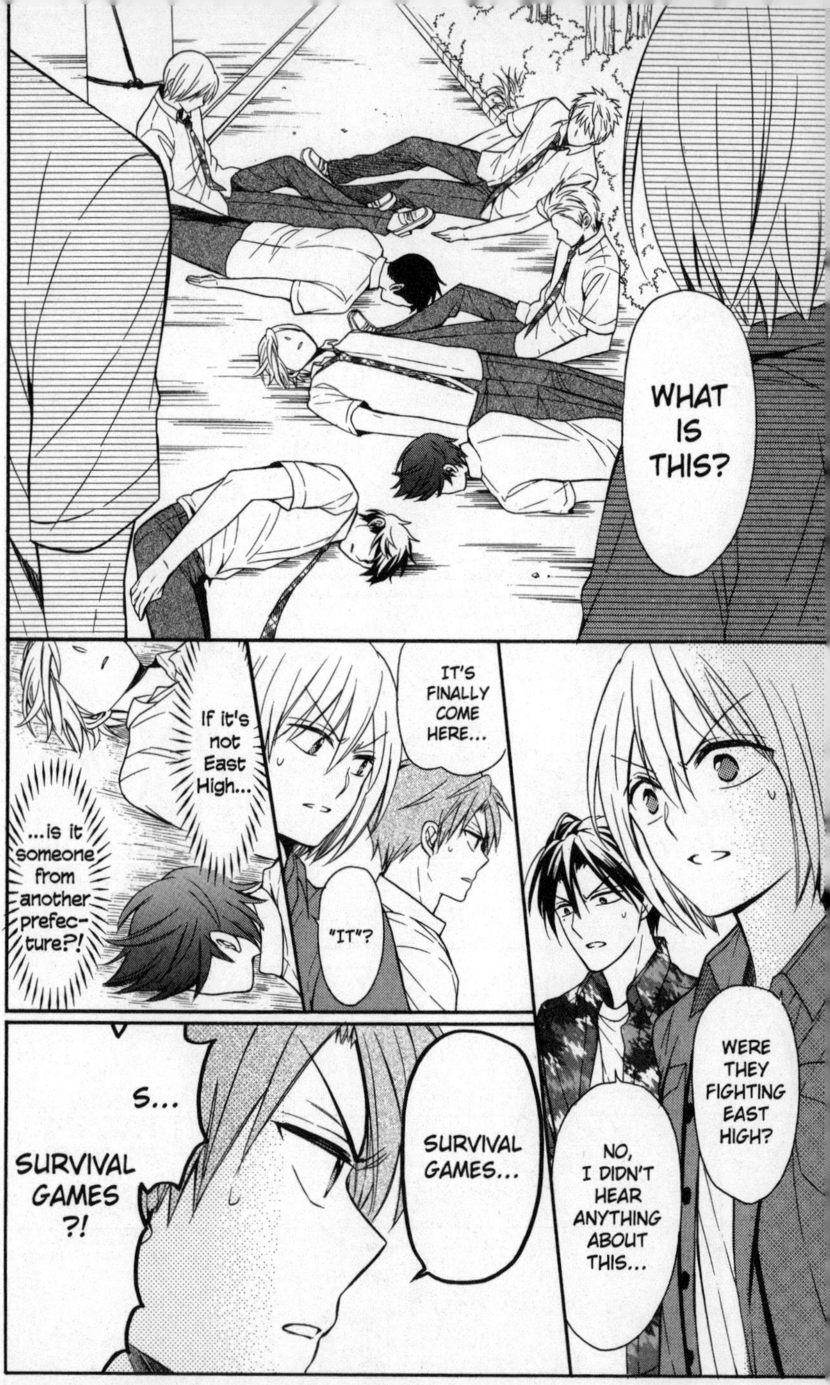
WHAT IS THIS?
WERE THEY FIGHTING EAST HIGH?
NO, I DIDN'T HEAR ANYTHING ABOUT THIS...
IT'S FINALLY COME HERE...
"IT"?
If it's not East High...
...is it someone from another prefecture?!
SURVIVAL GAMES...
S...
SURVIVAL GAMES?!

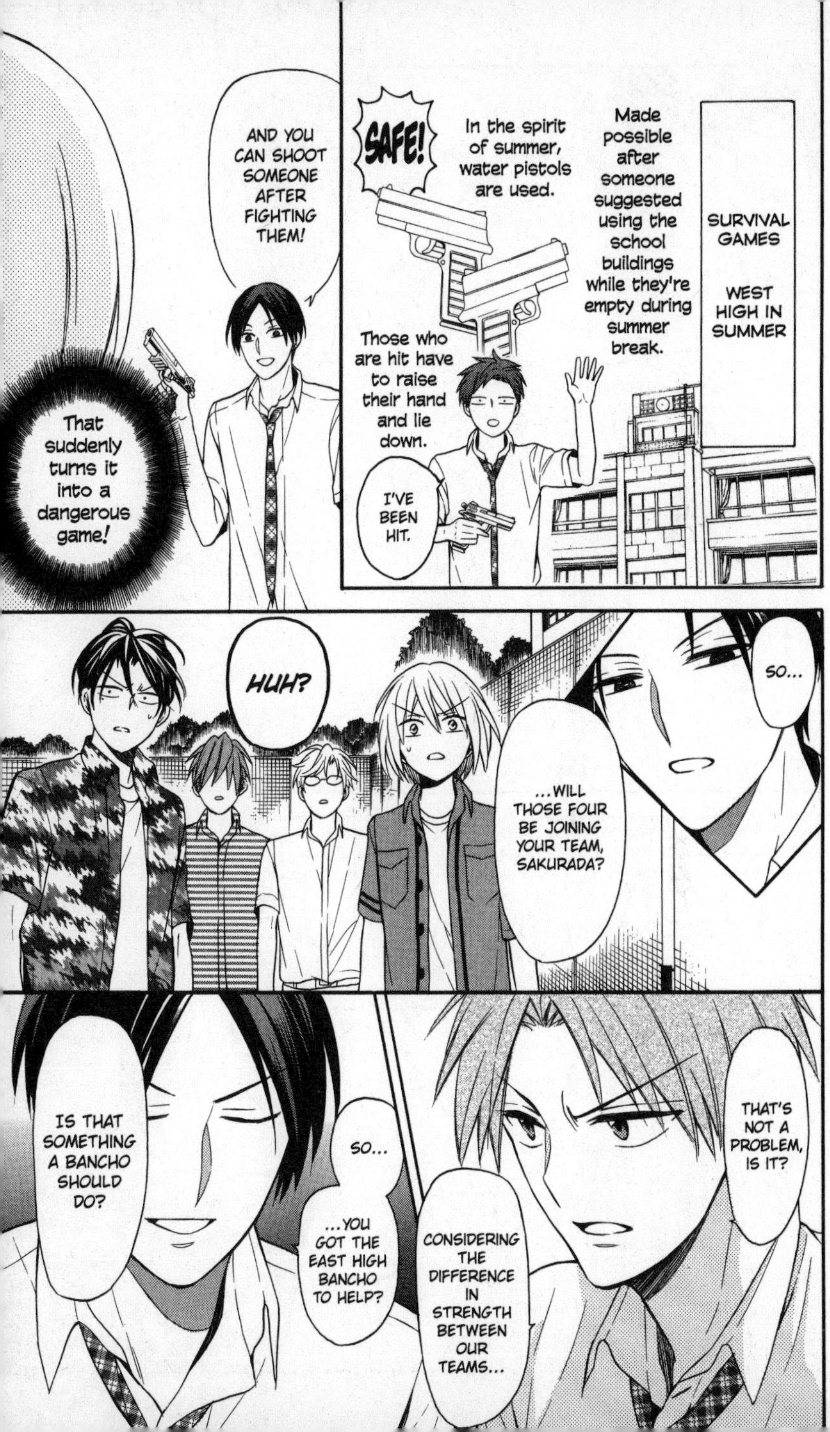
SURVIVAL GAMES
WEST HIGH IN SUMMER
Made possible after someone suggested using the school buildings while they're empty during summer break.
In the spirit of summer, water pistols are used.
SAFE!
Those who are hit have to raise their hand and lie down.
I'VE BEEN HIT.
AND YOU CAN SHOOT SOMEONE AFTER FIGHTING THEM!
That suddenly turns it into a dangerous game!
SO...
...WILL THOSE FOUR BE JOINING YOUR TEAM, SAKURADA?
HUH?
THAT'S NOT A PROBLEM, IS IT?
CONSIDERING THE DIFFERENCE IN STRENGTH BETWEEN OUR TEAMS...
SO...
...YOU GOT THE EAST HIGH BANCHO TO HELP?
IS THAT SOMETHING A BANCHO SHOULD DO?

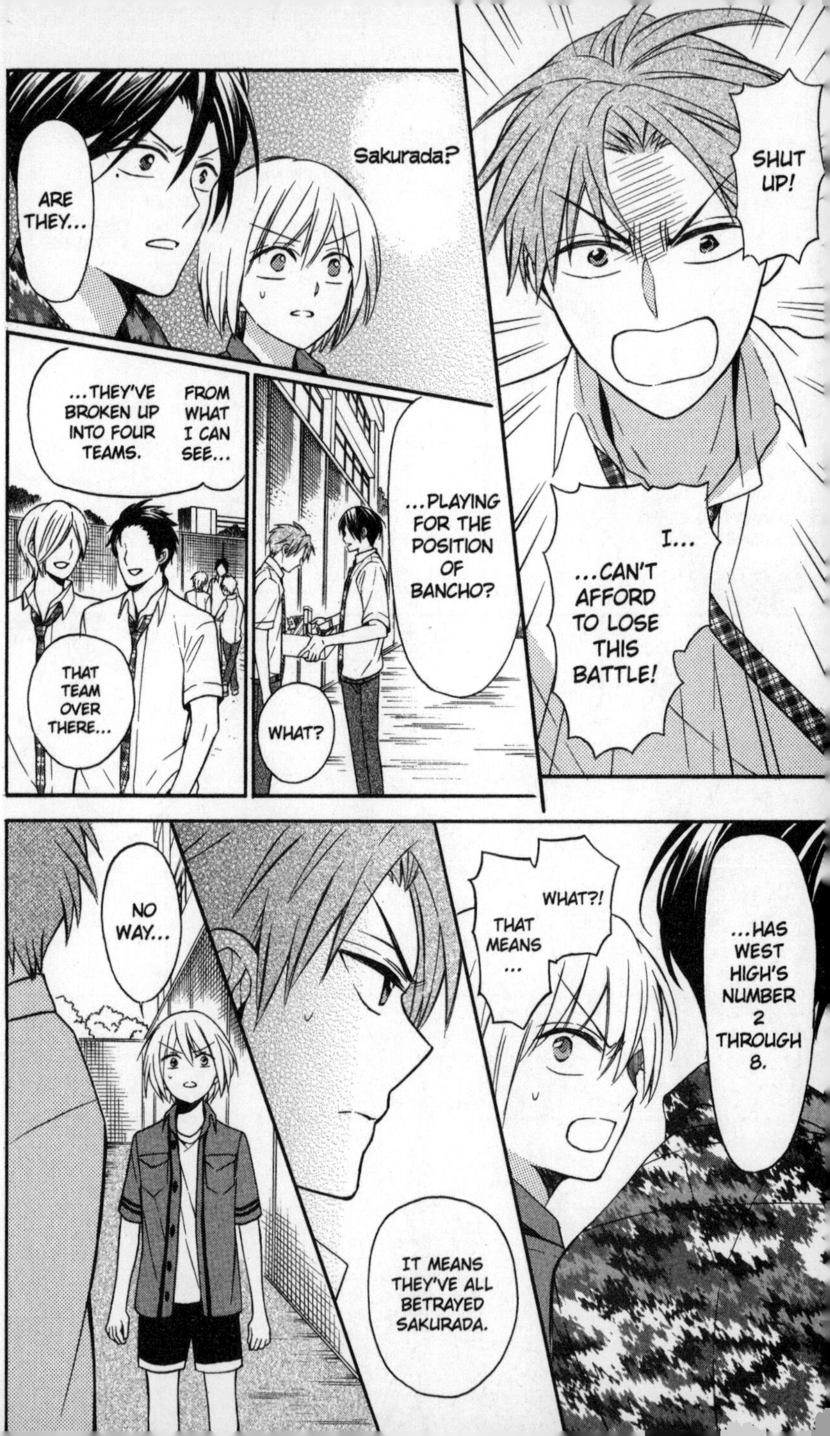
SHUT UP!
I...
...CAN'T AFFORD TO LOSE THIS BATTLE!
Sakurada?
ARE THEY...
...PLAYING FOR THE POSITION OF BANCHO?
WHAT?
FROM WHAT I CAN SEE...
...THEY'VE BROKEN UP INTO FOUR TEAMS.
THAT TEAM OVER THERE...
...HAS WEST HIGH'S NUMBER 2 THROUGH 8.
WHAT?!
THAT MEANS...
IT MEANS THEY'VE ALL BETRAYED SAKURADA.
NO WAY...

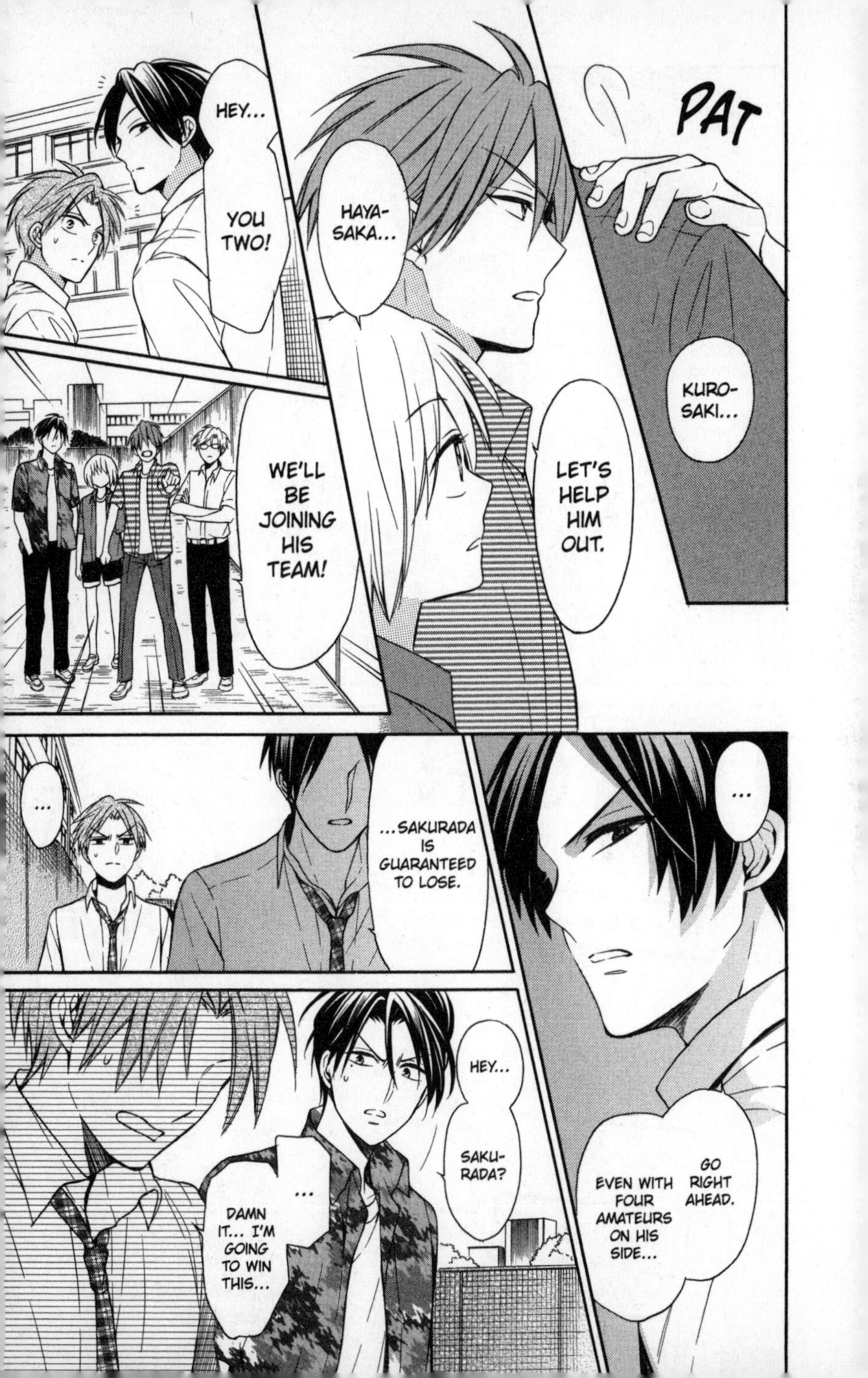
PAT
KURO-SAKI...
HAYA-SAKA...
LET'S HELP HIM OUT.
HEY... YOU TWO!
WE'LL BE JOINING HIS TEAM!
...
GO RIGHT AHEAD.
EVEN WITH FOUR AMATEURS ON HIS SIDE...
...SAKURADA IS GUARANTEED TO LOSE.
...
HEY...
SAKURADA?
...
DAMN IT... I'M GOING TO WIN THIS...

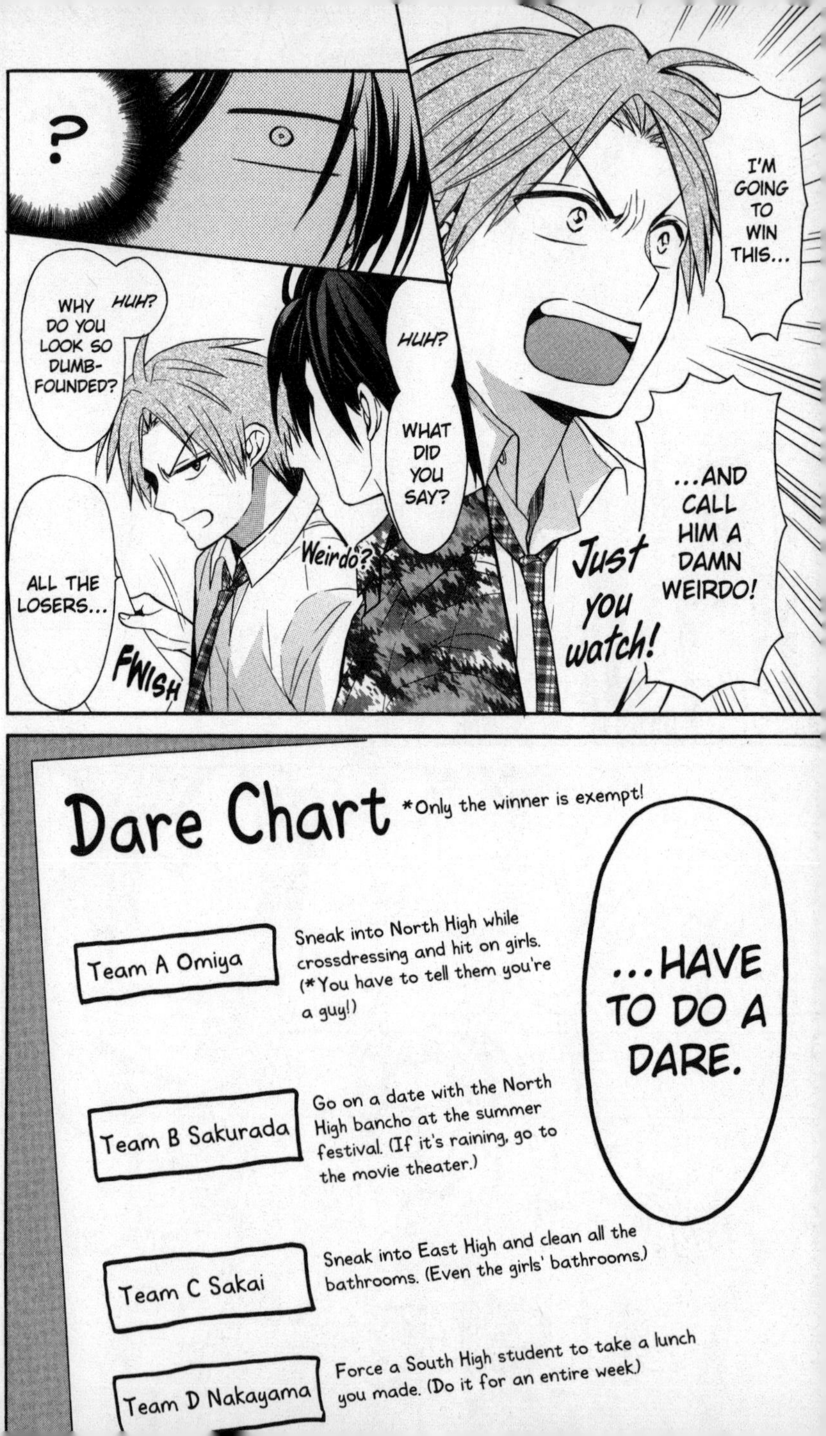
I'M GOING TO WIN THIS...
...AND CALL HIM A DAMN WEIRDO!
Just you watch!
?
HUH?
WHAT DID YOU SAY?
Weirdo?
HUH?
WHY DO YOU LOOK SO DUMB-FOUNDED?
ALL THE LOSERS...
FWISH
...HAVE TO DO A DARE.
Dare Chart
*Only the winner is exempt!
Team A Omiya
Sneak into North High while crossdressing and hit on girls. (*You have to tell them you're a guy!)
Team B Sakurada
Go on a date with the North High bancho at the summer festival. (If it's raining, go to the movie theater.)
Team C Sakai
Sneak into East High and clean all the bathrooms. (Even the girls' bathrooms.)
Team D Nakayama
Force a South High student to take a lunch you made. (Do it for an entire week.)

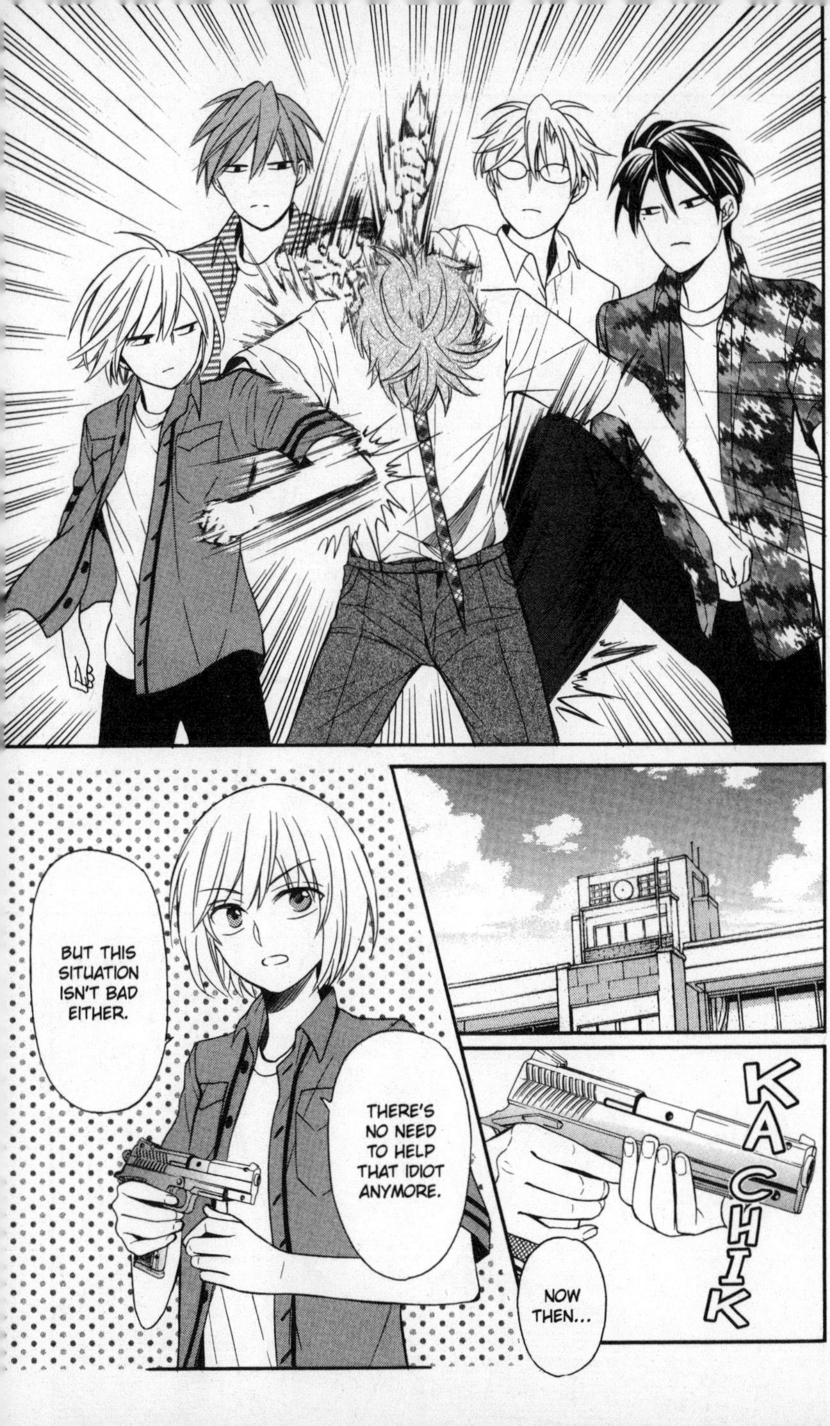
KACHIK
NOW THEN...
THERE'S NO NEED TO HELP THAT IDIOT ANYMORE.
BUT THIS SITUATION ISN'T BAD EITHER.

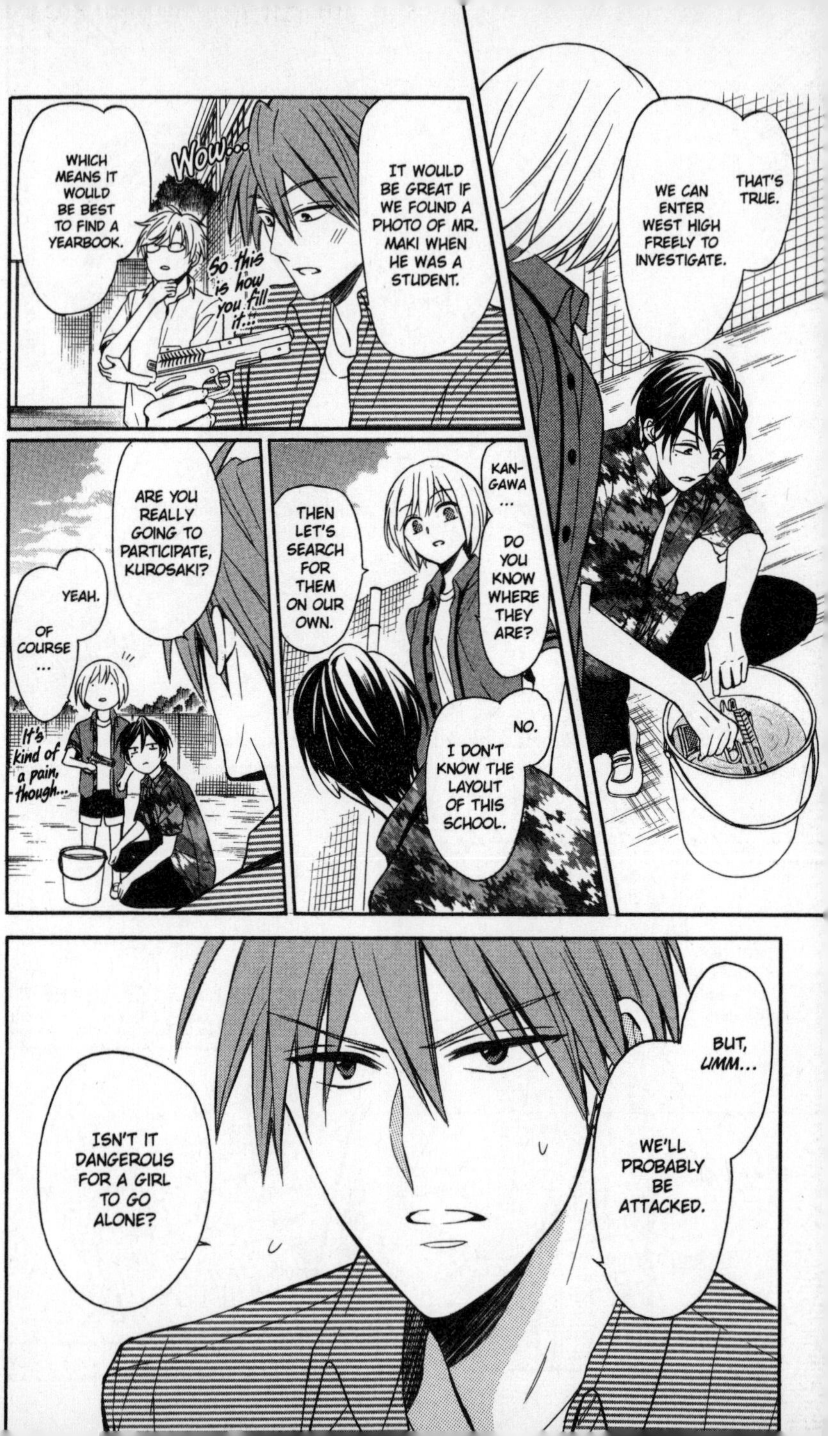
THAT'S TRUE.
WE CAN ENTER WEST HIGH FREELY TO INVESTIGATE.
IT WOULD BE GREAT IF WE FOUND A PHOTO OF MR. MAKI WHEN HE WAS A STUDENT.
Wow...
So this is how you fill it...
WHICH MEANS IT WOULD BE BEST TO FIND A YEARBOOK.
KAN-GAWA...
DO YOU KNOW WHERE THEY ARE?
NO.
I DON'T KNOW THE LAYOUT OF THIS SCHOOL.
THEN LET'S SEARCH FOR THEM ON OUR OWN.
ARE YOU REALLY GOING TO PARTICIPATE, KUROSAKI?
YEAH.
OF COURSE...
It's kind of a pain, though...
BUT, UMM...
WE'LL PROBABLY BE ATTACKED.
ISN'T IT DANGEROUS FOR A GIRL TO GO ALONE?

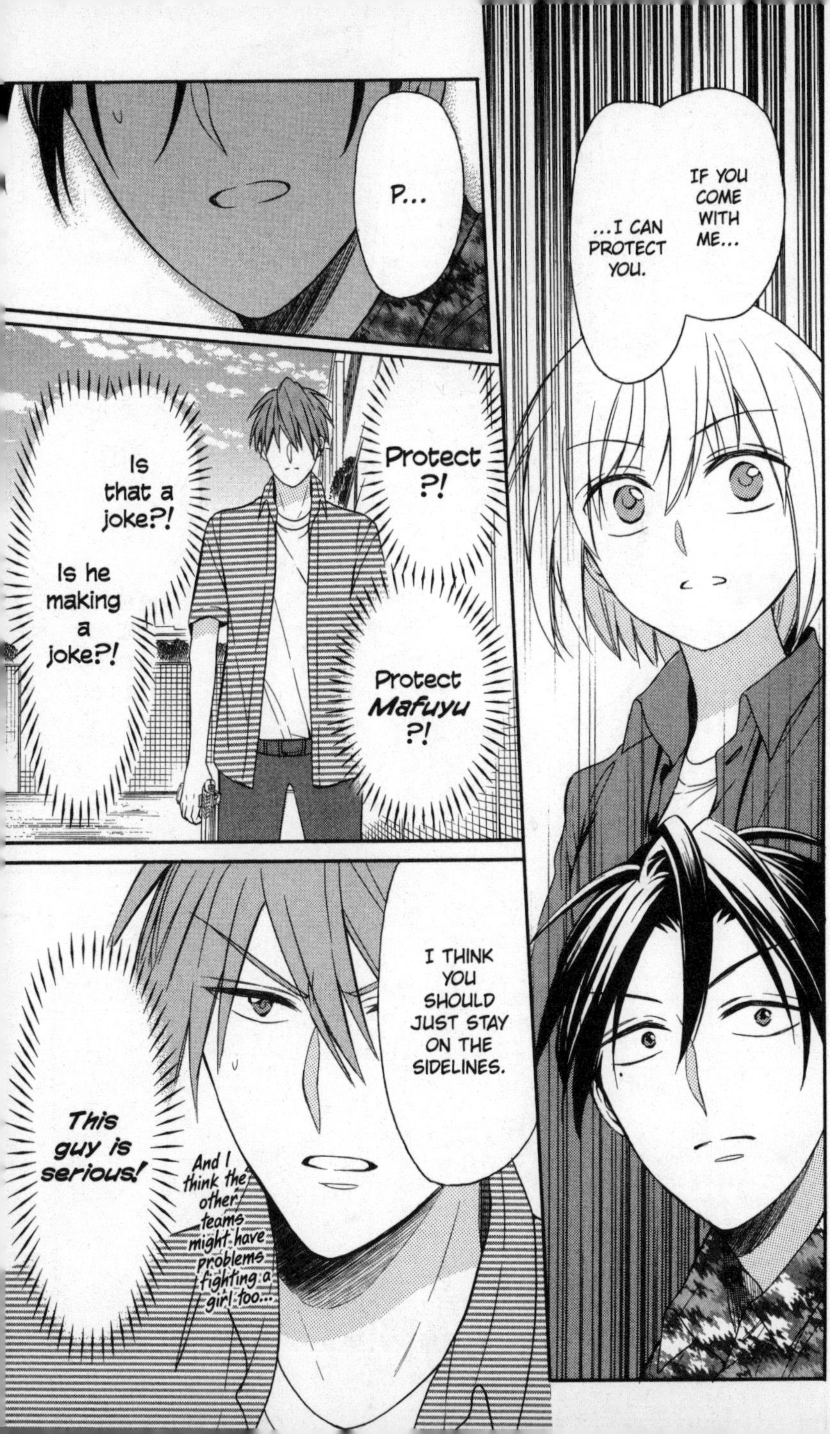
IF YOU COME WITH ME...
...I CAN PROTECT YOU.
P...
Protect ?!
Protect *Mafuyu* ?!
Is that a joke?!
Is he making a joke?!
I THINK YOU SHOULD JUST STAY ON THE SIDELINES.
And I think the other teams might have problems fighting a girl too...
This guy is serious!

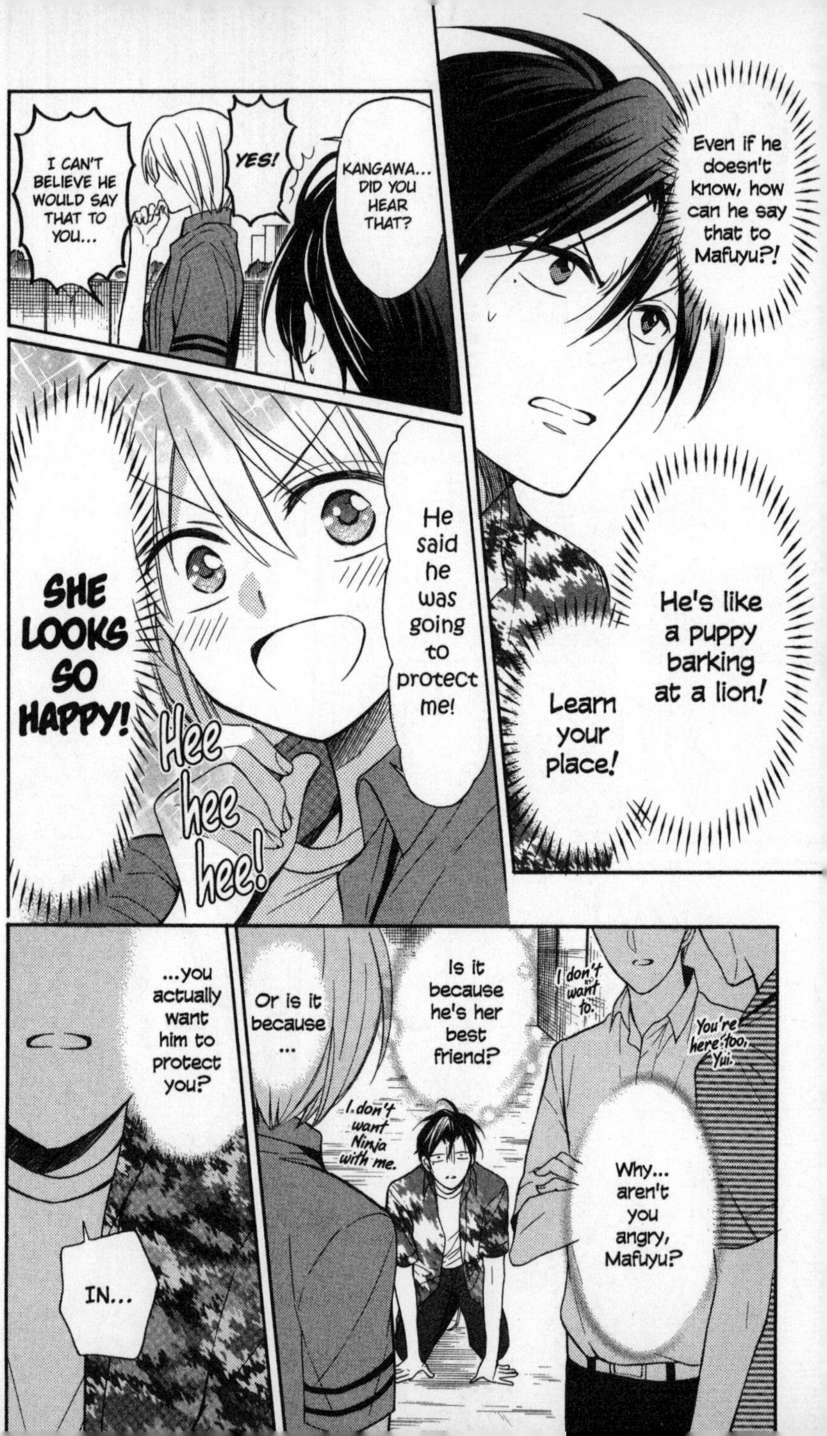
Even if he doesn't know, how can he say that to Mafuyu?!
He's like a puppy barking at a lion!
Learn your place!
KANGAWA... DID YOU HEAR THAT?
YES!
I CAN'T BELIEVE HE WOULD SAY THAT TO YOU...
He said he was going to protect me!
Hee hee hee!
SHE LOOKS SO HAPPY!
You're here too, Yui.
I don't want to.
I don't want Ninja with me.
Why... aren't you angry, Mafuyu?
Is it because he's her best friend?
Or is it because ...
...you actually want him to protect you?
IN...

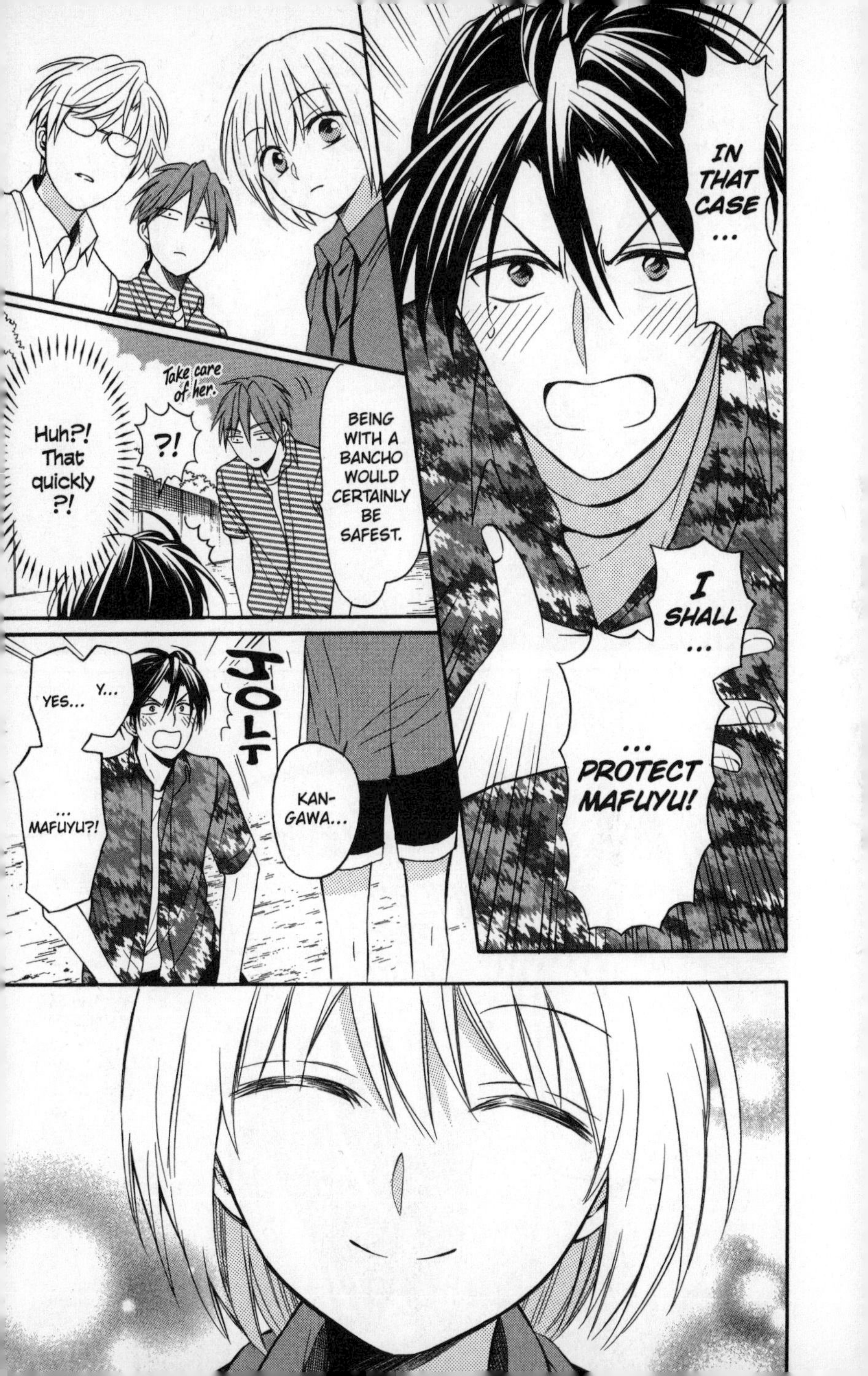
IN THAT CASE ...
I SHALL ...
... PROTECT MAFUYU!
BEING WITH A BANCHO WOULD CERTAINLY BE SAFEST.
Take care of her.
?!
Huh?! That quickly ?!
JOLT
KAN-GAWA...
Y... YES... ... MAFUYU?!

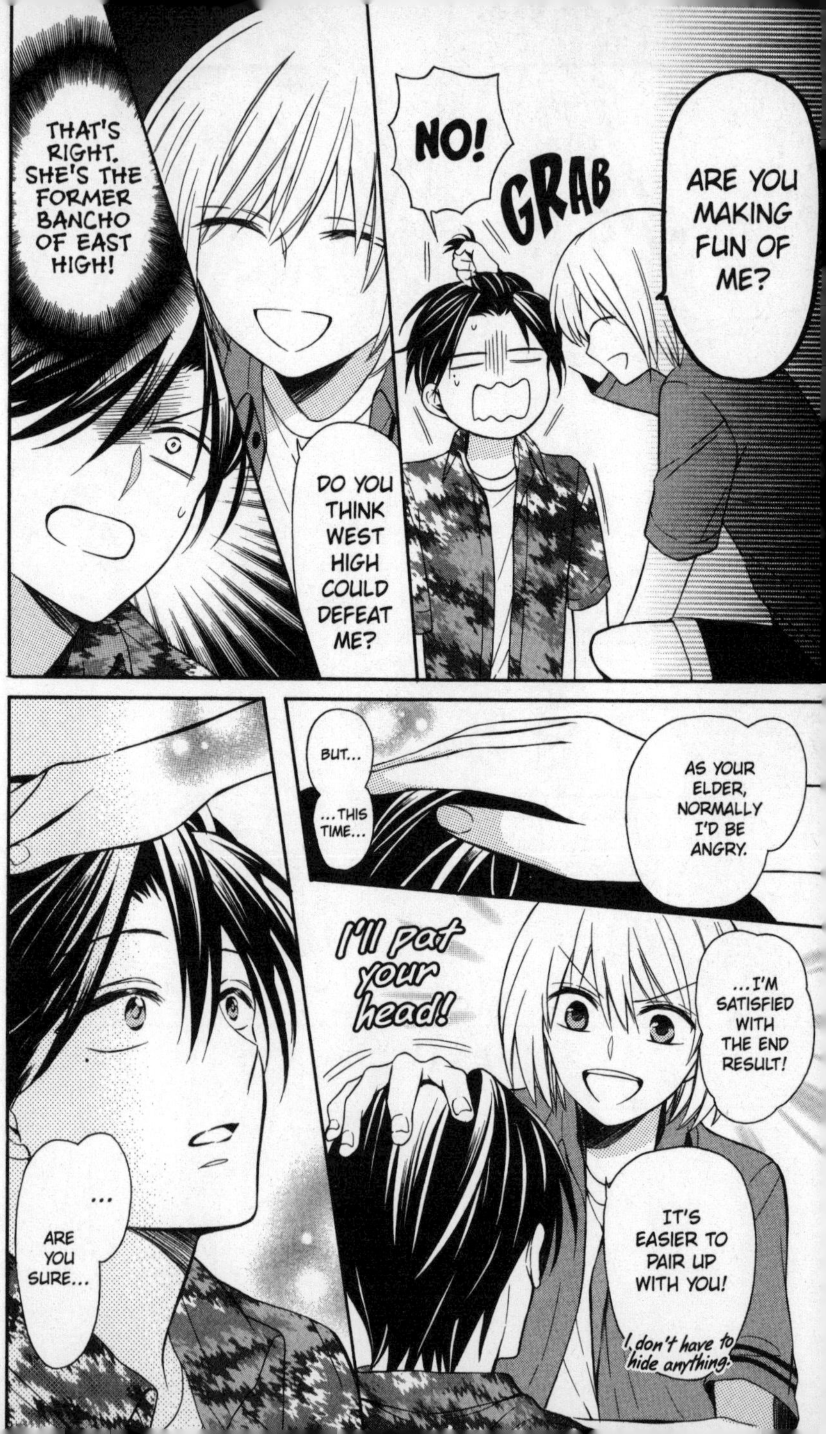

ARE YOU MAKING FUN OF ME?
GRAB
NO!
DO YOU THINK WEST HIGH COULD DEFEAT ME?
THAT'S RIGHT. SHE'S THE FORMER BANCHO OF EAST HIGH!
AS YOUR ELDER, NORMALLY I'D BE ANGRY.
BUT...
...THIS TIME...
...I'M SATISFIED WITH THE END RESULT!
I'll pat your head!
IT'S EASIER TO PAIR UP WITH YOU!
I don't have to hide anything.
...
ARE YOU SURE...

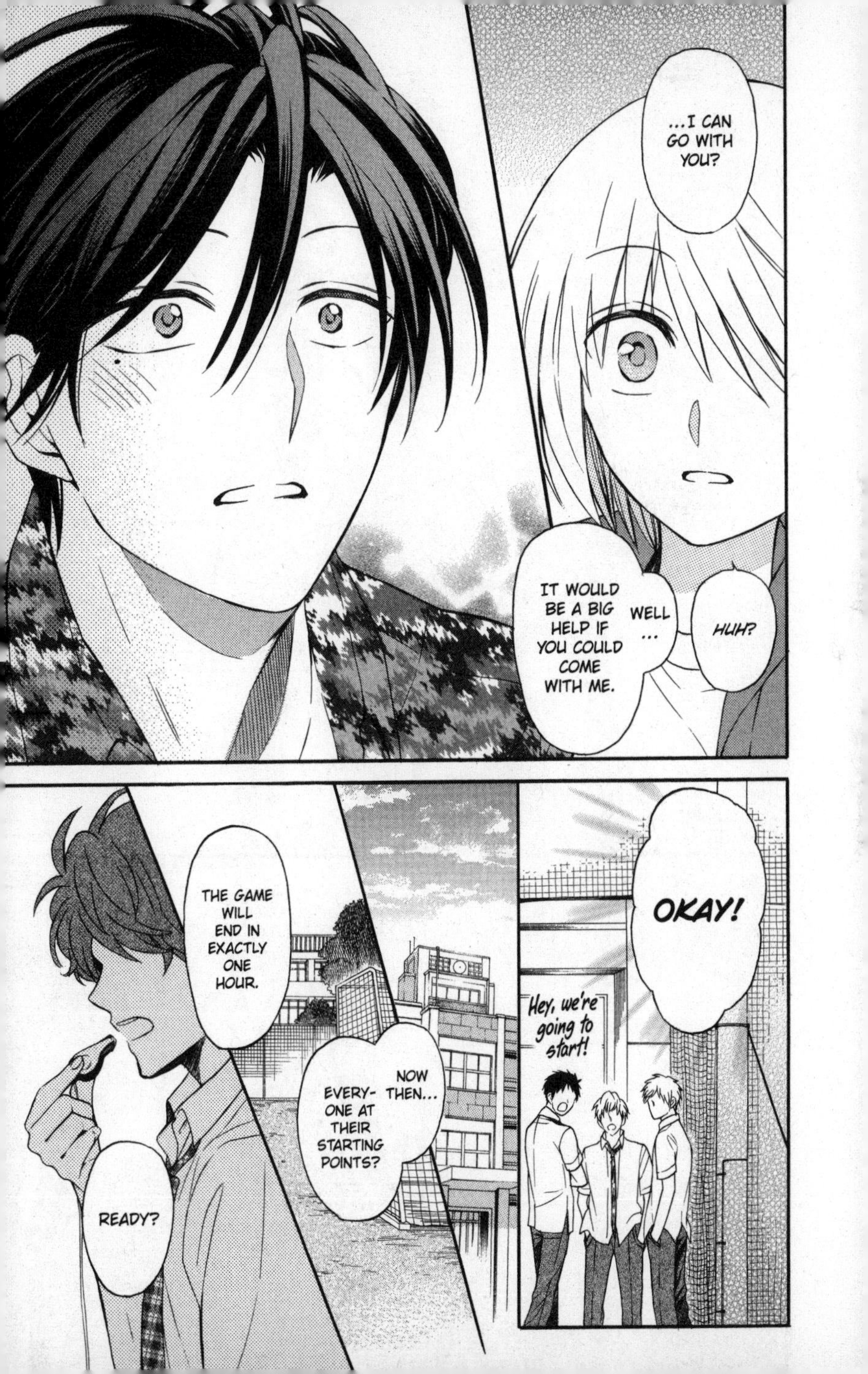
...I CAN GO WITH YOU?
HUH?
WELL...
IT WOULD BE A BIG HELP IF YOU COULD COME WITH ME.
OKAY!
Hey, we're going to start!
NOW THEN...
EVERY-ONE AT THEIR STARTING POINTS?
THE GAME WILL END IN EXACTLY ONE HOUR.
READY?

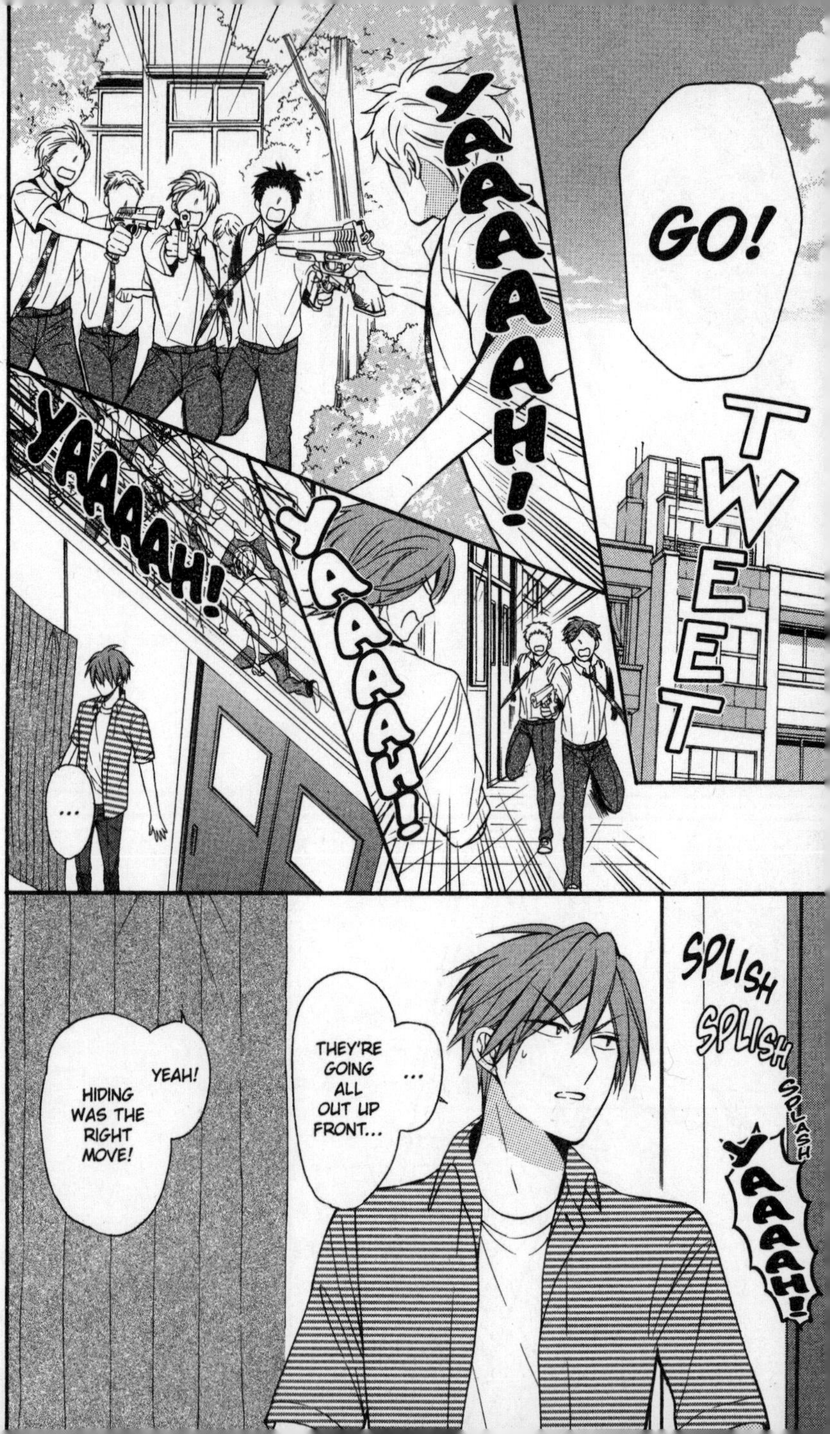
GO!
TWEET
YAAAAAAH!
YAAAAAH!
YAAAAAH!
...
SPLISH
SPLISH
SPLASH
YAAAAH!
THEY'RE GOING ALL OUT UP FRONT... ...
YEAH! HIDING WAS THE RIGHT MOVE!

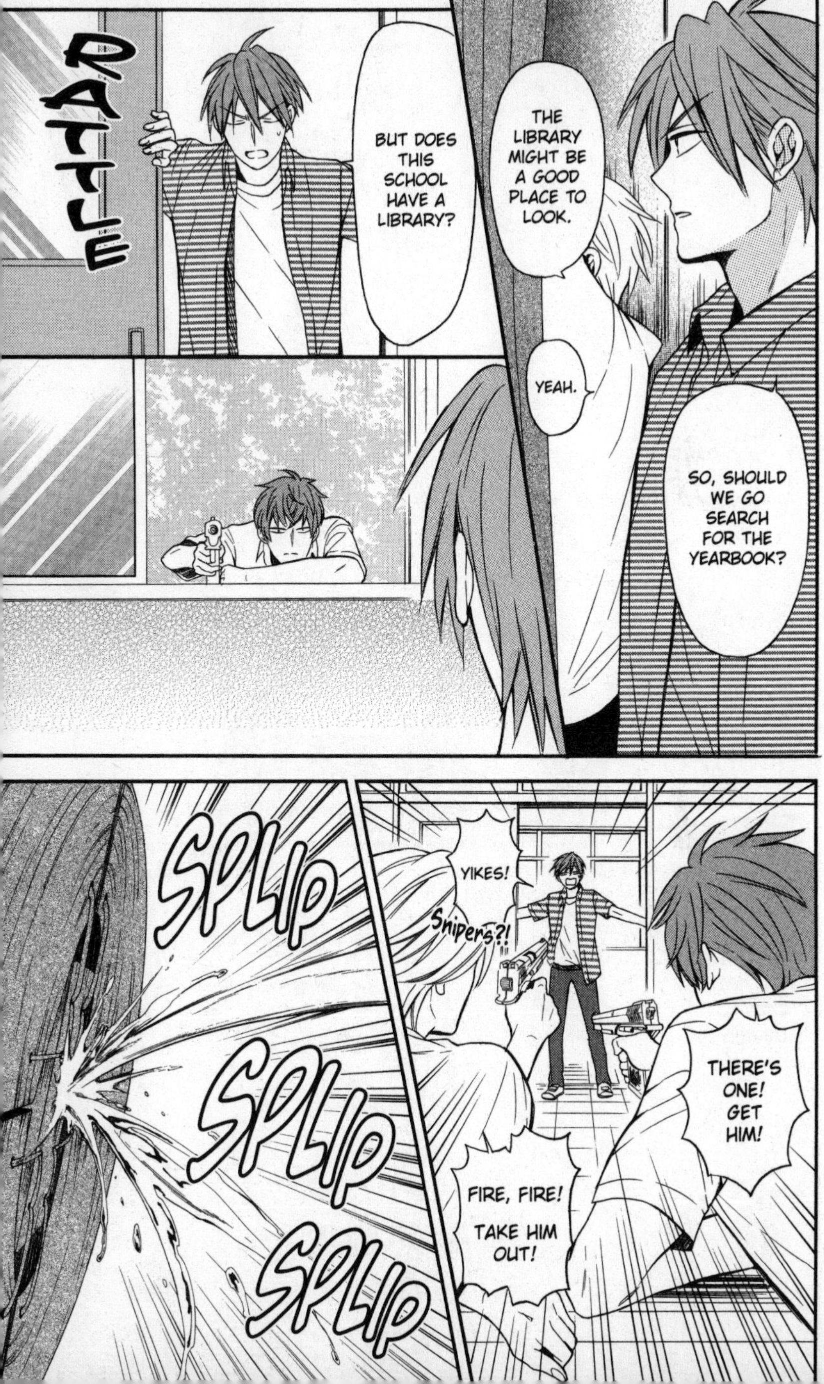
THE LIBRARY MIGHT BE A GOOD PLACE TO LOOK.
YEAH.
SO, SHOULD WE GO SEARCH FOR THE YEARBOOK?
BUT DOES THIS SCHOOL HAVE A LIBRARY?
RATTLE
YIKES!
Snipers?!
THERE'S ONE! GET HIM!
FIRE, FIRE!
TAKE HIM OUT!
SPLIP
SPLIP
SPLIP

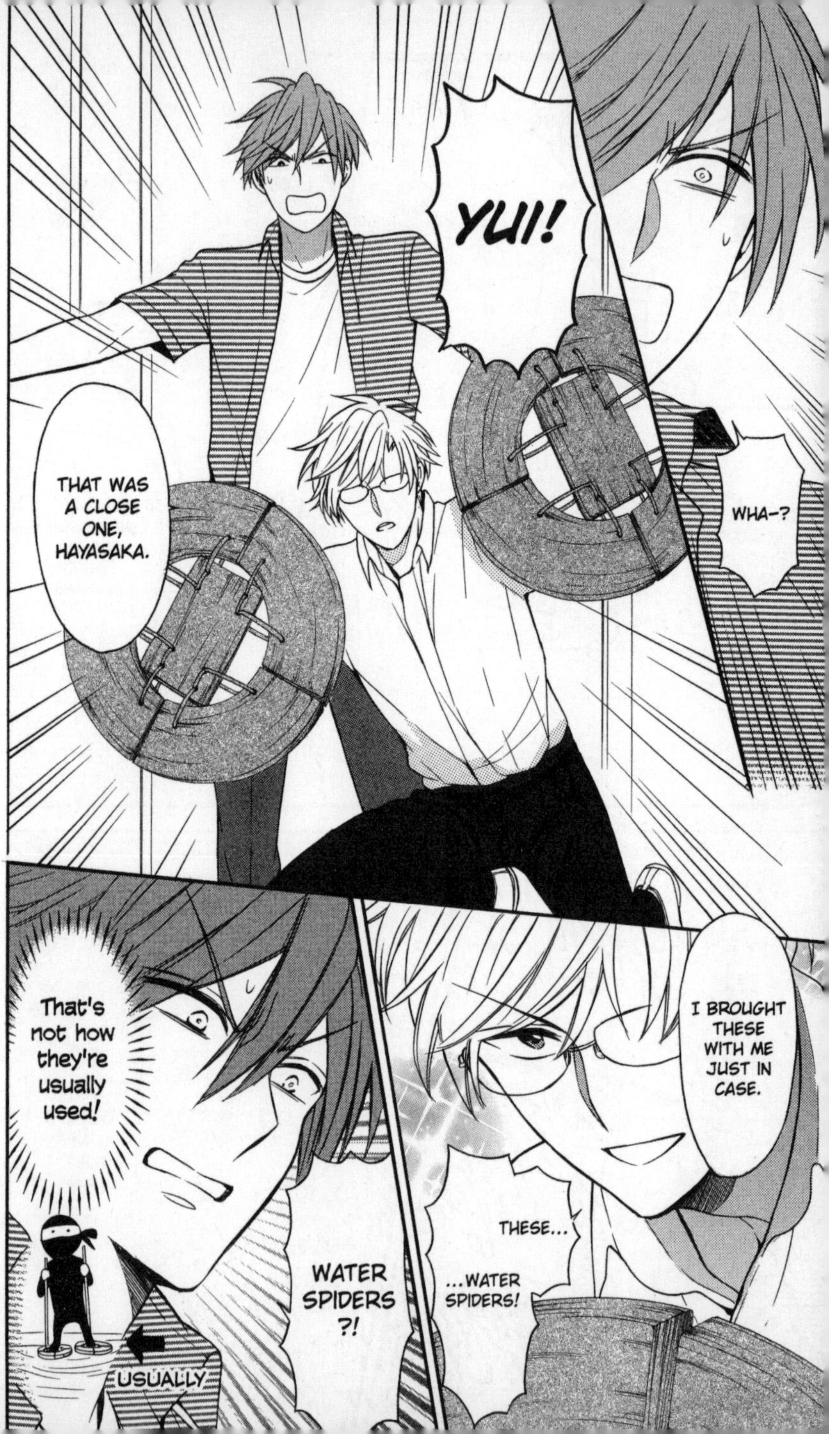
YUI!
WHA-?
THAT WAS A CLOSE ONE, HAYASAKA.
I BROUGHT THESE WITH ME JUST IN CASE.
THESE...
...WATER SPIDERS!
That's not how they're usually used!
WATER SPIDERS ?!
USUALLY

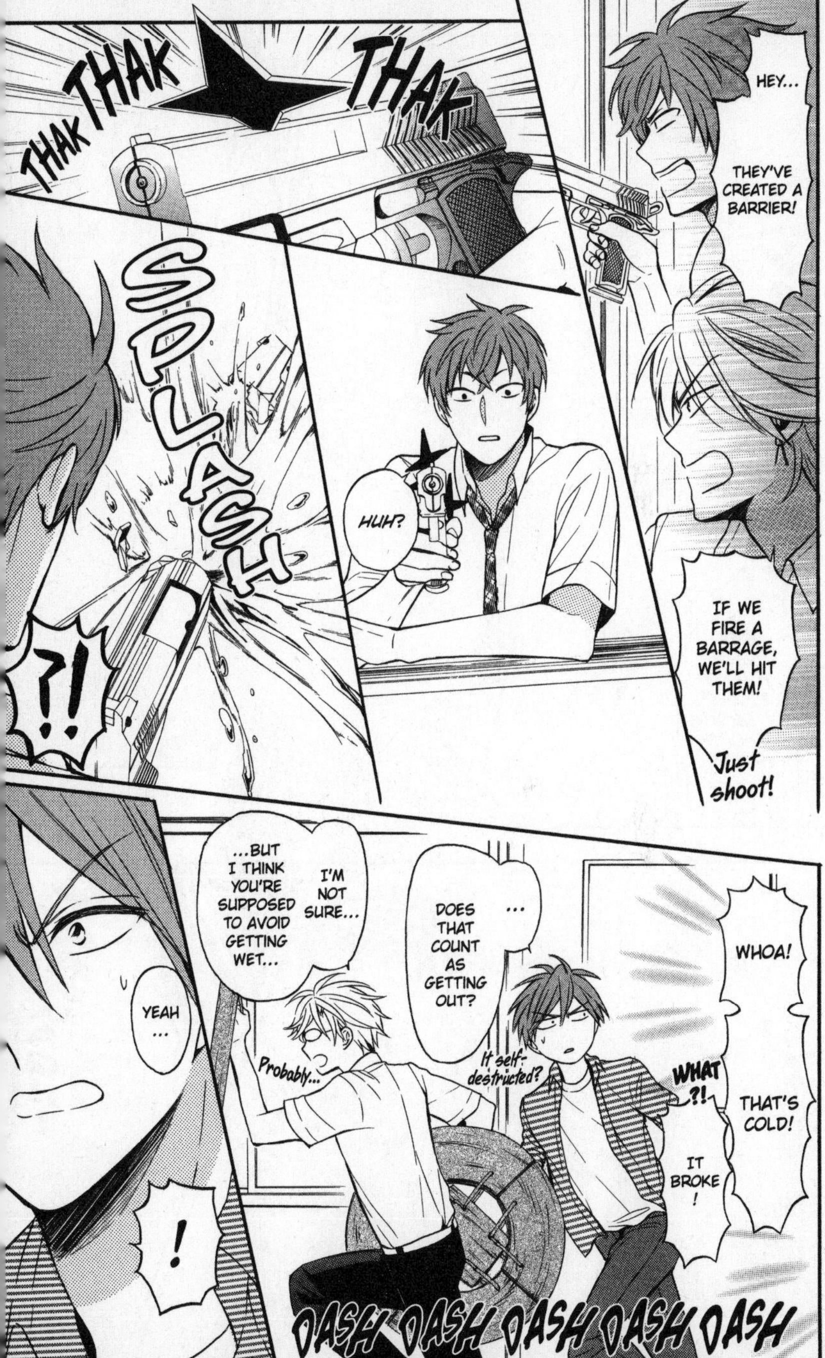
HEY...
THEY'VE CREATED A BARRIER!
IF WE FIRE A BARRAGE, WE'LL HIT THEM!
Just shoot!
THAK THAK THAK
HUH?
SPLASH
?!!
WHOA!
THAT'S COLD!
IT BROKE!
WHAT ?!
It self-destructed?
...
DOES THAT COUNT AS GETTING OUT?
Probably...
I'M NOT SURE...
...BUT I THINK YOU'RE SUPPOSED TO AVOID GETTING WET...
YEAH...
!
DASH DASH DASH DASH DASH

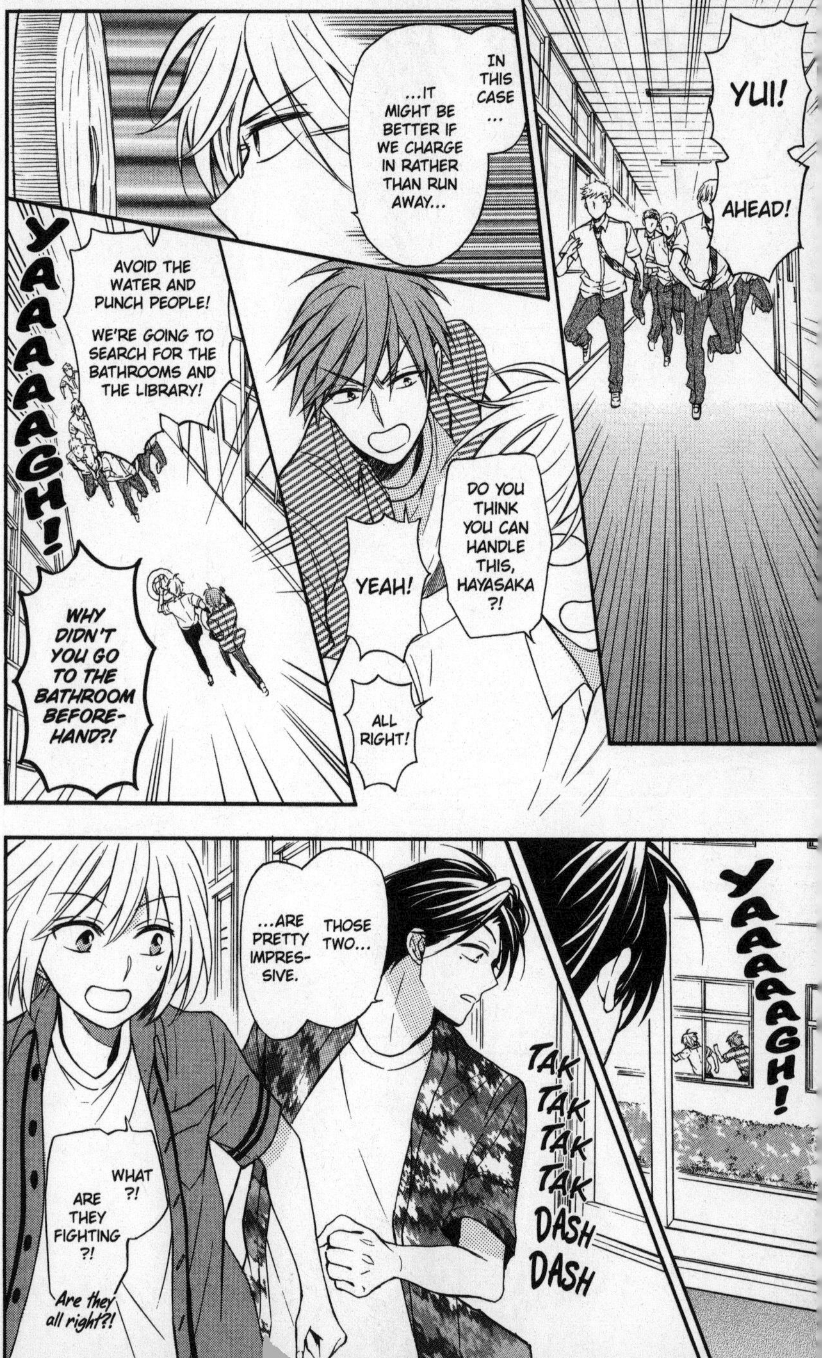
YUI!
AHEAD!
IN THIS CASE...
...IT MIGHT BE BETTER IF WE CHARGE IN RATHER THAN RUN AWAY...
DO YOU THINK YOU CAN HANDLE THIS, HAYASAKA?!
YEAH!
ALL RIGHT!
AVOID THE WATER AND PUNCH PEOPLE!
WE'RE GOING TO SEARCH FOR THE BATHROOMS AND THE LIBRARY!
YAAAAAAGH!
WHY DIDN'T YOU GO TO THE BATHROOM BEFORE-HAND?!
YAAAAAGH!
TAK TAK TAK TAK TAK
DASH DASH
THOSE TWO...
...ARE PRETTY IMPRES-SIVE.
WHAT?!
ARE THEY FIGHTING?!
Are they all right?!

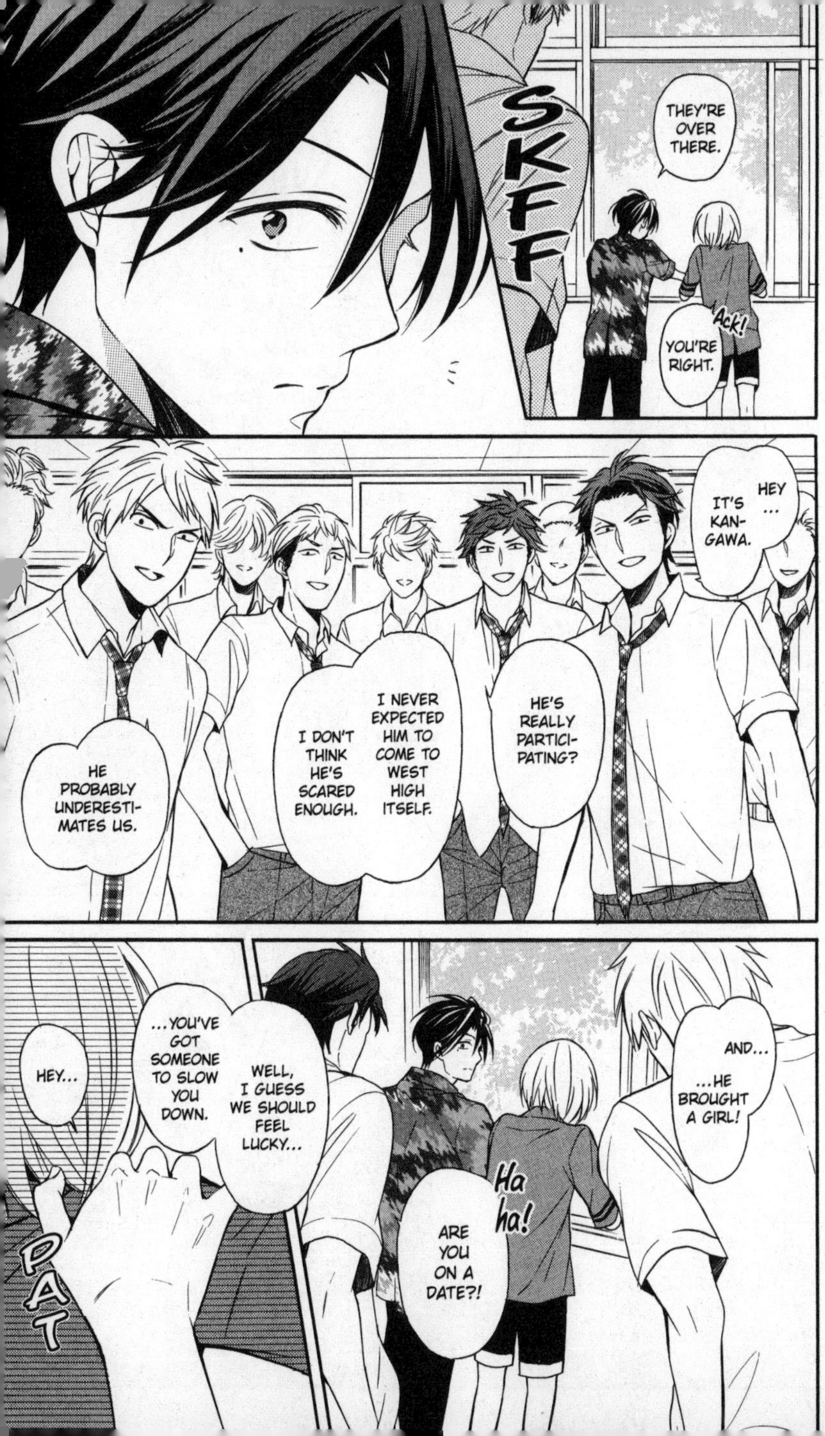
THEY'RE OVER THERE.
Ack!
YOU'RE RIGHT.
SKFF
HEY...
IT'S KANGAWA.
HE'S REALLY PARTICIPATING?
I NEVER EXPECTED HIM TO COME TO WEST HIGH ITSELF.
I DON'T THINK HE'S SCARED ENOUGH.
HE PROBABLY UNDERESTIMATES US.
AND...
...HE BROUGHT A GIRL!
Ha ha!
ARE YOU ON A DATE?!
WELL, I GUESS WE SHOULD FEEL LUCKY...
...YOU'VE GOT SOMEONE TO SLOW YOU DOWN.
HEY...
PAT

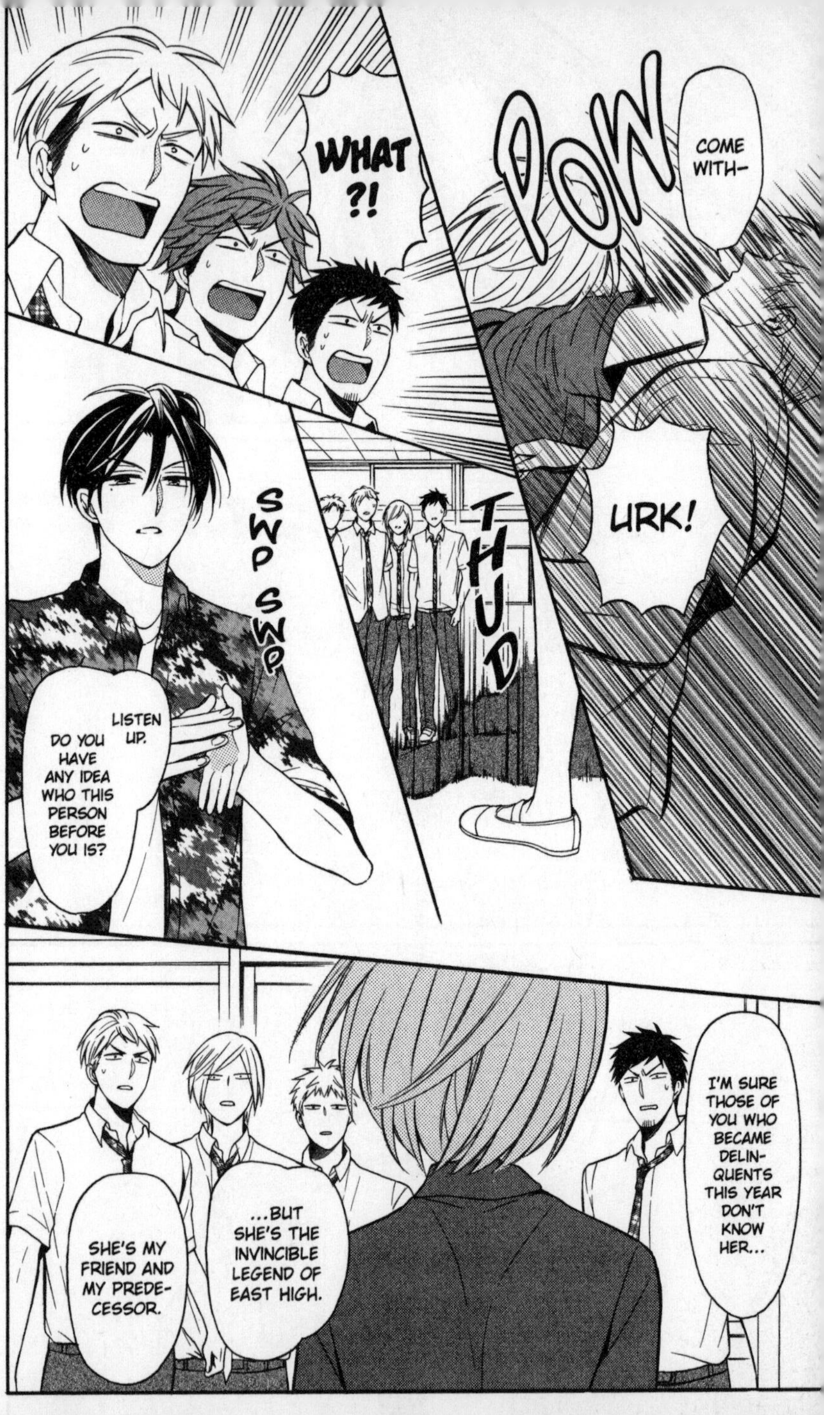
COME WITH-
POW
URK!
WHAT ?!
THUD
SWP SWP SWP
LISTEN UP.
DO YOU HAVE ANY IDEA WHO THIS PERSON BEFORE YOU IS?
I'M SURE THOSE OF YOU WHO BECAME DELIN-QUENTS THIS YEAR DON'T KNOW HER...
...BUT SHE'S THE INVINCIBLE LEGEND OF EAST HIGH.
SHE'S MY FRIEND AND MY PREDE-CESSOR.

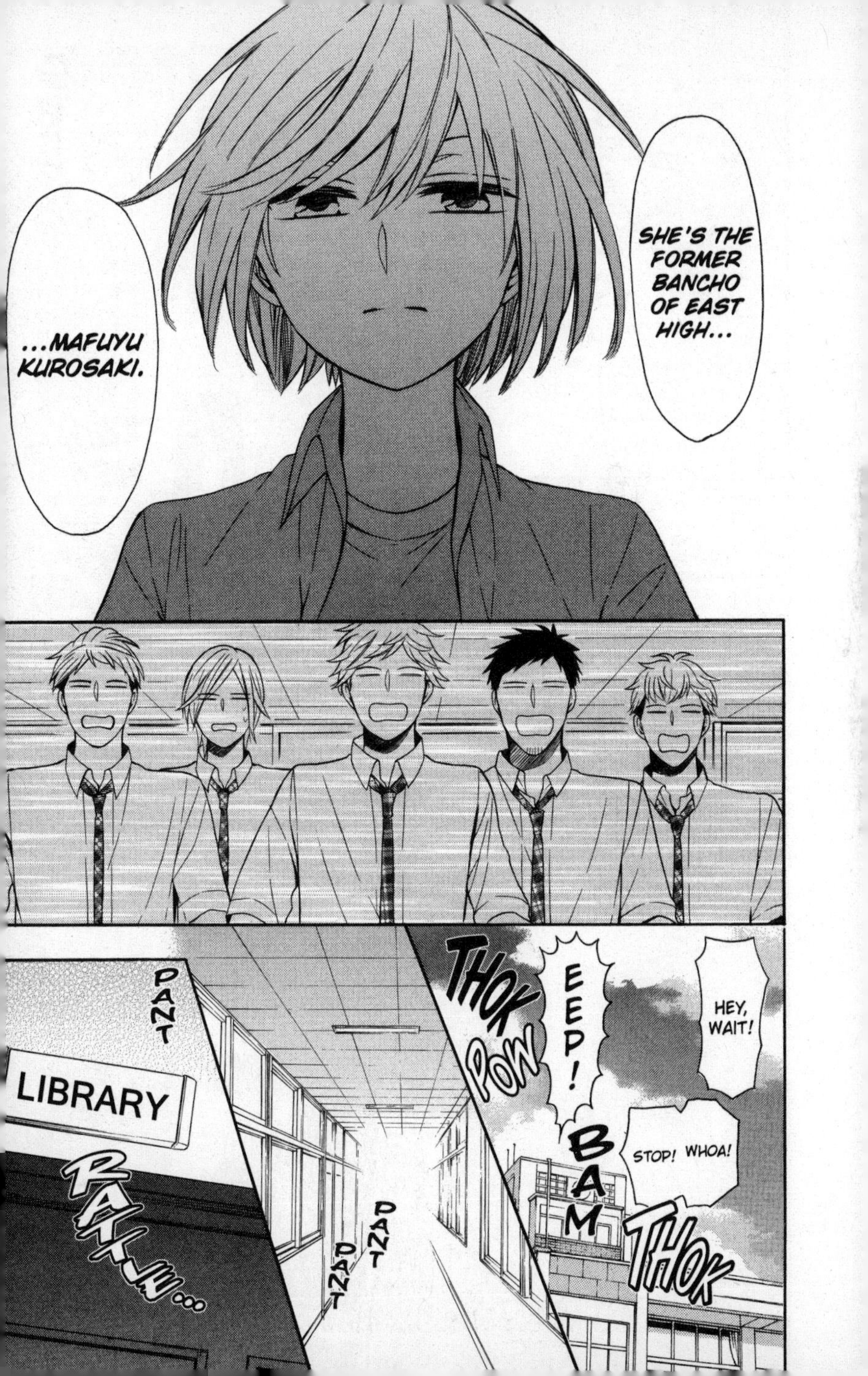
SHE'S THE FORMER BANCHO OF EAST HIGH...
...MAFUYU KUROSAKI.
HEY, WAIT!
THOK
EEP!
POW
STOP! WHOA!
BAM
THOK
PANT
LIBRARY
RATTLE...
PANT
PANT

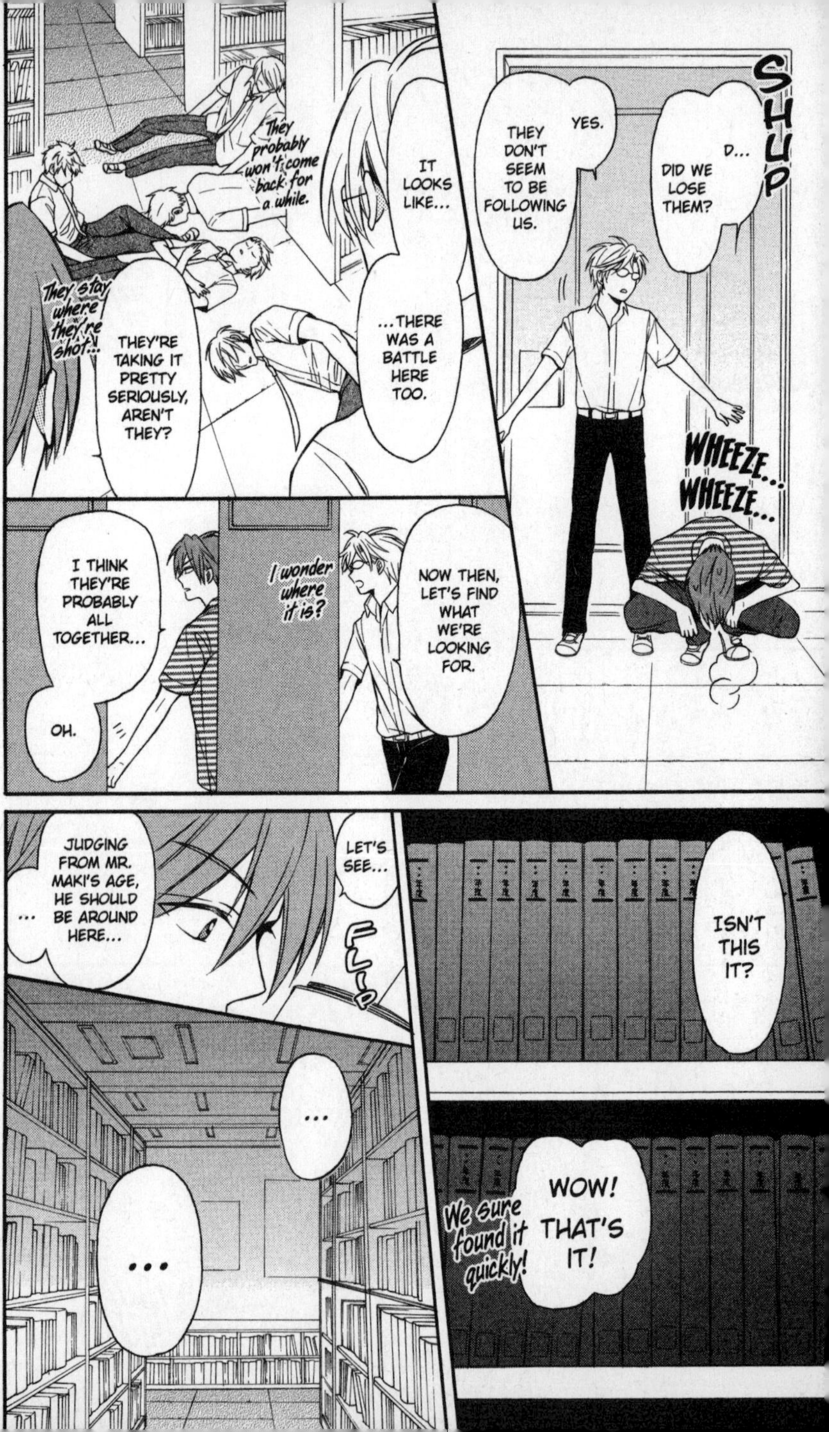
SHUP
D...
DID WE LOSE THEM?
YES.
THEY DON'T SEEM TO BE FOLLOWING US.
WHEEZE... WHEEZE...
IT LOOKS LIKE...
...THERE WAS A BATTLE HERE TOO.
They probably won't come back for a while.
THEY'RE TAKING IT PRETTY SERIOUSLY, AREN'T THEY?
They stay where they're shot...
NOW THEN, LET'S FIND WHAT WE'RE LOOKING FOR.
I wonder where it is?
I THINK THEY'RE PROBABLY ALL TOGETHER...
OH.
ISN'T THIS IT?
WOW! THAT'S IT!
We sure found it quickly!
LET'S SEE...
JUDGING FROM MR. MAKI'S AGE, HE SHOULD BE AROUND HERE...
...
FLIP
...
...

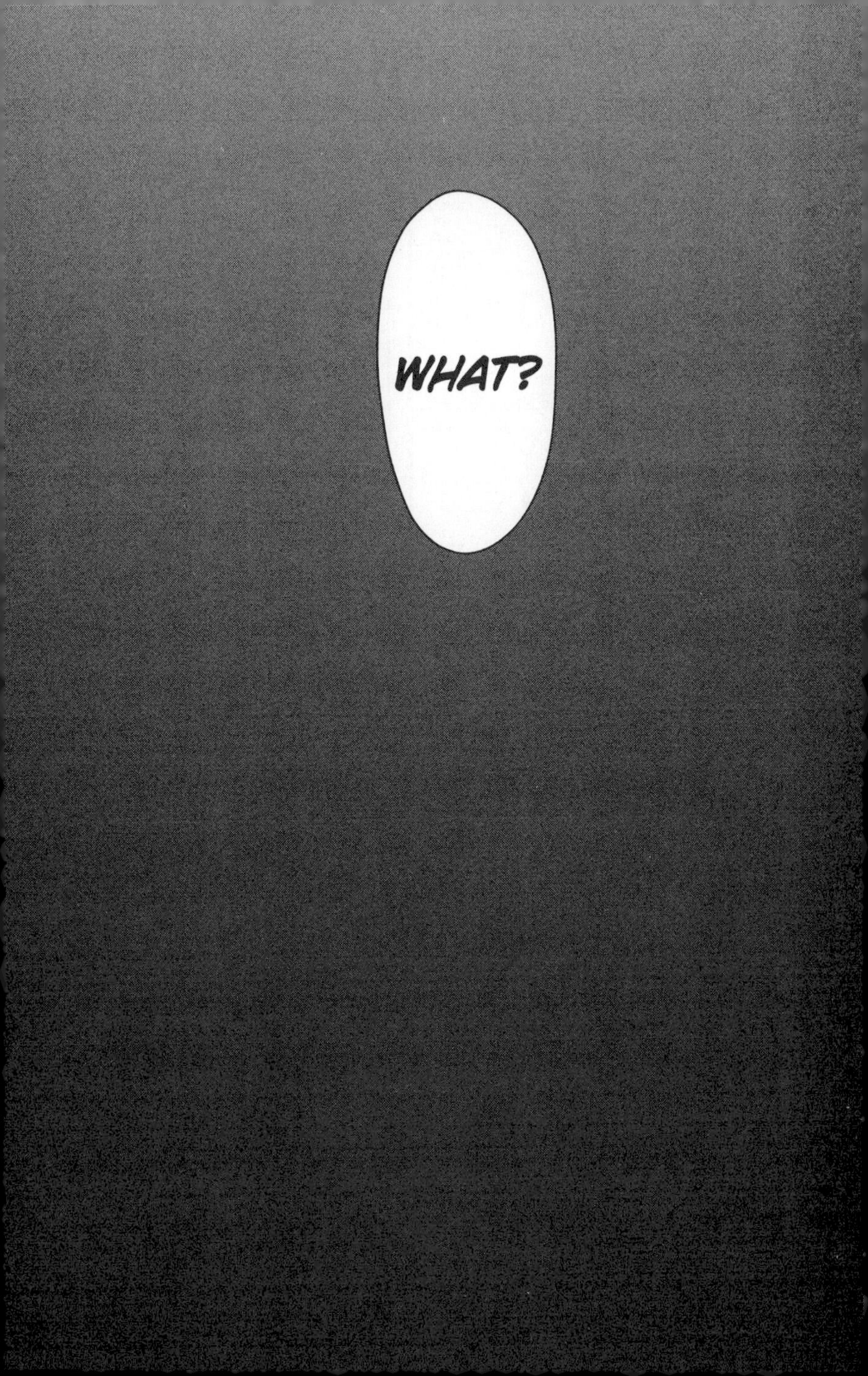
WHAT?

CUSTOM ORDER PUNISHMENT

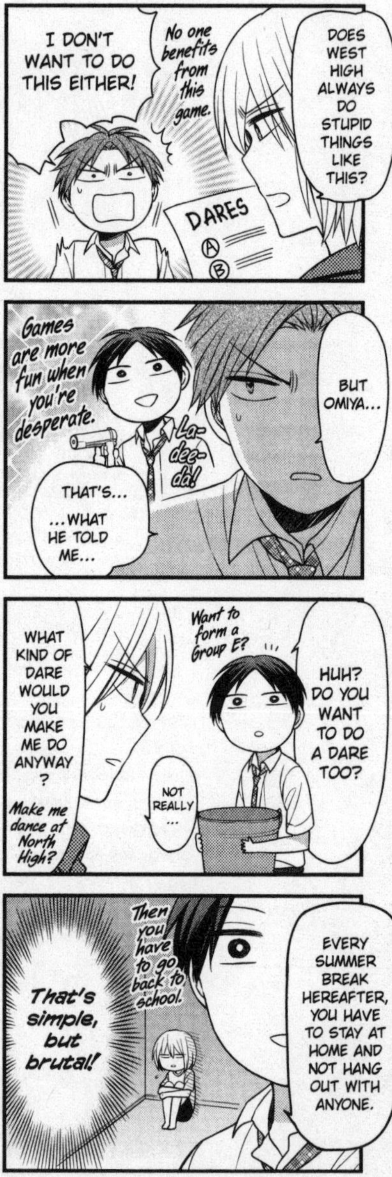
DOES WEST HIGH ALWAYS DO STUPID THINGS LIKE THIS?
No one benefits from this game.
I DON'T WANT TO DO THIS EITHER!
DARES
BUT OMIYA...
La-dee-da!
Games are more fun when you're desperate.
THAT'S... ...WHAT HE TOLD ME...
HUH? DO YOU WANT TO DO A DARE TOO?
Want to form a Group E?
NOT REALLY ...
WHAT KIND OF DARE WOULD YOU MAKE ME DO ANYWAY?
Make me dance at North High?
EVERY SUMMER BREAK HEREAFTER, YOU HAVE TO STAY AT HOME AND NOT HANG OUT WITH ANYONE.
Then you have to go back to school.
That's simple, but brutal!

RUMORS ABOUT MAFUYU

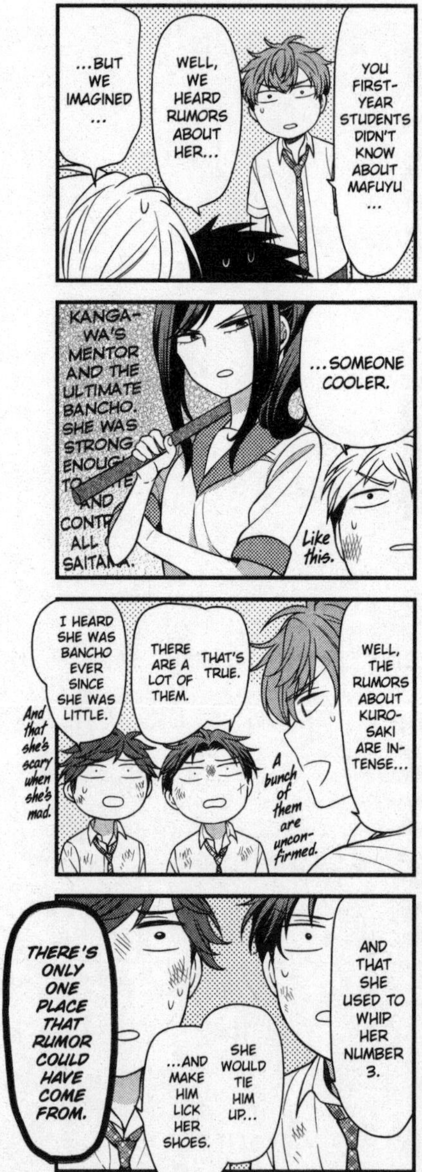
YOU FIRST-YEAR STUDENTS DIDN'T KNOW ABOUT MAFUYU ...
WELL, WE HEARD RUMORS ABOUT HER...
...BUT WE IMAGINED ...
...SOMEONE COOLER.
Like this.
KANGA-WA'S MENTOR AND THE ULTIMATE BANCHO. SHE WAS STRONG
WELL, THE RUMORS ABOUT KURO-SAKI ARE IN-TENSE...
A bunch of them are uncon-firmed.
THAT'S TRUE.
THERE ARE A LOT OF THEM.
I HEARD SHE WAS BANCHO EVER SINCE SHE WAS LITTLE.
And that she's scary when she's mad.
AND THAT SHE USED TO WHIP HER NUMBER 3.
SHE WOULD TIE HIM UP...
...AND MAKE HIM LICK HER SHOES.
THERE'S ONLY ONE PLACE THAT RUMOR COULD HAVE COME FROM.

Izumi Tsubaki began drawing manga in her first year of high school. She was soon selected to be in the top ten of *Hana to Yume's* HMC (*Hana to Yume* Mangaka Course), and subsequently won *Hana to Yume's* Big Challenge contest. Her debut title, *Chijimete Distance* (Shrink the Distance), ran in 2002 in *Hana to Yume* magazine, issue 17. Her other works include *The Magic Touch* (*Oyayubi kara Romance*) and *Oresama Teacher*, which she is currently working on.

ORESAMA TEACHER
Vol. 24
Shojo Beat Edition

STORY AND ART BY
Izumi Tsubaki

English Translation & Adaptation/JN Productions
Touch-up Art & Lettering/Eric Erbes
Design/Yukiko Whitley
Editor/Pancha Diaz

ORESAMA TEACHER by Izumi Tsubaki © Izumi Tsubaki 2017
All rights reserved. First published in Japan in 2017 by HAKUSENSHA, Inc., Tokyo.
English language translation rights arranged with HAKUSENSHA, Inc., Tokyo.

Printed in the U.S.A.

Published by VIZ Media, LLC
P.O. Box 77010
San Francisco, CA 94107

10 9 8 7 6 5 4 3 2 1
First printing, May 2018

www.viz.com
www.shojobeat.com